Detention of Asylum Seeke in Europe: Analy and Perspective

DETENTION OF ASYLUM SEEKERS IN EUROPE: ANALYSIS AND PERSPECTIVES

Edited by
Jane Hughes and Fabrice Liebaut

MARTINUS NIJHOFF PUBLISHERS

Published by Kluwer Law International
P.O. Box 85889
2508 CN The Hague, The Netherlands

Sold and distributed in the USA and Canada by
Kluwer Law International
675 Massachusetts Avenue
Cambridge, MA 02139, USA

Sold and distributed in all other countries by
Kluwer Law International
Distribution Centre
P.O. Box 322
3300 AH Dordrecht, The Netherlands

A C.I.P. Catalogue record for this book is available from the Library of Congress

Printed on acid-free paper

Cover design: Alfred Birnie bNO
Layout: Fabrice Liebaut

ISBN: 90 411 0546 8

© 1998 Kluwer Law International

Kluwer Law International incorporates the publishing programmes of Graham & Trotman Ltd, Kluwer Law and Taxation Publishers and Martinus Nijhoff Publishers

This publication is protected by international copyright law.
All rights reserved. No part of this publication may be reproduced, stored in a retrieval system, or transmitted in any form or by any means, electronic, mechanical, photocopying, recording or otherwise, without the prior permission of the publisher.

Preface

In response to heightened concern among European refugee and human rights organisations about the increasing practice of detaining asylum seekers, the Danish Refugee Council, the Danish Centre for Human Rights and the European Council on Refugees and Exiles (ECRE) held a European Seminar on Detention of Asylum Seekers in November 1995. Two years on, despite some encouraging rulings by international bodies and national courts, there are as yet no signs of a significant change for the better in government policy and practice in this particular area and concern has therefore not diminished. It is for this reason that the organisers of the 1995 seminar have decided to publish a comprehensive book on the subject.

Apart from the chapters on Australia and mental health, the essays are based on the working documents presented at the seminar. Most of the chapters have been extensively revised and updated to the end of 1996, though some contain references from the spring of 1997. The book thus presents a compilation of cross-disciplinary essays written by representatives of non-governmental and inter-governmental organisations, practising lawyers, academics, researchers and a psychiatrist.

Chapters 1 and 2 describe recent trends in western, central and eastern Europe. Chapters 3, 4 and 5 examine detention practice in the United States, Canada and Australia, for the purposes of comparison. Chapter 6 explores UNHCR's approach to detention of refugees and asylum seekers. Chapters 7 and 8 provide an analysis of the relevant European and UN legal instruments, with examples from case law. Chapter 9 addresses the mental health implications of detention from a psycho-medical viewpoint. The book is supplemented by detailed appendices setting out the texts of relevant international legal provisions, together with a number of other reference documents, including UNHCR's 1995 Guidelines on Detention and ECRE's 1996 and 1997 papers on detention and alternatives to detention.

In addition to providing both a description of current practice and a theoretical, legal analysis of this type of administrative detention, this volume is intended to serve as a practical tool and source of reference for individuals and organisations engaged in defending the rights of asylum seekers today. It is hoped that it may stimulate a constructive debate with government decision-makers and immigration authorities so that early signs of a change in climate can be translated into more equitable policies and practices.

Jane Hughes
Danish Refugee Council

Table of Contents

Preface	V
Table of Contents	VII
List of Contributors	XIII
Acknowledgments	XV
Introduction	1

Chapter 1 Recent Trends in the Detention of Asylum Seekers in Western Europe 5
Jane Hughes and Ophelia Field

I	Introduction		5
II	Increase in detention of asylum seekers		7
	II.1	General indications of an increase	7
	II.2	More restrictive legislation in general.........	8
	II.3	Statistical increase	14
	II.4	Increase in the number of detention centres	16
III	The grounds for detention		17
	III.1	Pre-admission detention	17
	III.2	Competence for the initial decision to detain	19
	III.3	Detention in airports	20
	III.4	Detention during the determination procedure	21
	III.5	Pre-deportation detention	23
IV	Rights in detention		26
	IV.1	Information on the grounds for detention ...	26
	IV.2	Access to other information and counselling	27
	IV.2	Review and appeal rights	29
V	Conditions of detention		33
	V.1	Detention facilities	35
	V.2	Duration of detention	38
	V.3	Women and children	41
	V.4	Treatment by staff and staff training measures	43
VI	Final comments		45

Chapter 2 Detention of Asylum Seekers in Central and Eastern Europe **49**
Jane Hughes and Peter Vedel Kessing

I	Asylum background – Developments since 1989		49
II	Central Europe		52
	II.1	Introduction	52
	II.2	Legal basis for detention	53
	II.3	Statistics	55
	II.4	Detention facilities	57
	II.5	Detention and the determination procedure	58
		II.5.1 Pre-admission detention and airport detention ...	58
		II.5.2 Detention and other restrictions on freedom of movement during the determination procedure ..	61
		II.5.3 Pre-deportation detention	62
	II.6	Rights in detention	63
	II.7	Conditions of detention	64
III	Eastern Europe – Russia and the Commonwealth of Independent States		67
	III.1	Transit migration	67
	III.2	Refugee legislation and the legal basis for detention	68
	III.3	Conditions of detention	70
IV	The Baltic States		74
	IV.1	The Baltic States in transition	74
	IV.2	The Baltic States as transit countries	75
	IV.3	Illegal immigrants and asylum seekers	76
	IV.4	Lithuania	77
	IV.5	Latvia	80
	IV.6	Estonia	82
V	Conclusion		83

Chapter 3 Detention of Asylum Seekers: The United States Perspective **85**
Paolo Morante

I	Introduction		85
II	Legal aspects of detention		86
	II.1	Legal provisions	86
	II.2	Previous regime: Exclusion, deportation and the fiction of "entry"	87
	II.3	New laws: Everyone excludable	89

		II.4 Anti-terrorism laws	95
III	Conditions of detention		97
		III.1 Detention facilities	97
		III.2 Service Processing Centers	99
		III.3 State and local prisons	103
		III.4 Private contract facilities	104
IV	Detention by air carriers		108
V	Detention of minors		110
VI	Conclusion		111

Chapter 4 Detention of Asylum Seekers: The Canadian Perspective **113**
Ron Poulton and Barbara Jackman

I	Introduction	113
II	Detention criteria	114
	II.1 Immigration Act, RSC 1985, Section 103	115
	II.2 Immigration Act, RSC 1985, Section 103.1	115
III	Risk to national security	116
	III.1 Immigration Act, RSC 1985, Section 40.1	116
	III.2 Immigration Act, RSC 1985, Section 19	117
IV	Non-rights for non-citizens	118
V	Detention on the grounds of fear of persecution	120
VI	Detention of children	120
VII	Conditions of detention	121
VIII	Conclusion	122

Chapter 5 Detention of Asylum Seekers: The Australian Perspective **125**
Fedor Mediansky

I	Introduction	125
II	The rationale for immigration detention	126
III	Detention and the law	127
IV	Detention centres	132
V	The politics of immigration detention in Australia	135
VI	Current reform initiatives	136
VII	Conclusion – Table	139

**Chapter 6 Comments on the UNHCR Position on Detention of
Refugees and Asylum Seekers** **141**
Karin Landgren

I	Introduction		141
II	UNHCR's role		143
	II.1	Increasing use of detention: The 1995 Survey	143
	II.2	The use of detention: Executive Committee Conclusion No. 44	144
III	The 1951 Convention relating to the Status of Refugees		145
	III.1	Article 31	145
	III.2	Article 26	147
	III.3	Article 8	148
	III.4	Article 9	148
IV	The scope of protection		149
	IV.1	Protected persons	149
	IV.2	Distinguishing refugees and asylum seekers from other aliens	150
	IV.3	The exceptional nature of detention	150
	IV.4	The elements of necessity and proportionality	151
	IV.5	What constitutes detention?	152
	IV.6	Alternatives to detention	154
	IV.7	Procedural safeguards	155
	IV.8	Access to UNHCR	156
	IV.9	Segregation from offenders	157
	IV.10	The detention of minors	157
V	Detention and international solidarity		158

**Chapter 7 Detention of Asylum Seekers in the light of Article 5 of
the European Convention on Human Rights** **161**
Christos Giakoumopoulos

I	Asylum seekers and the European Convention on Human Rights		161
II	Applicability of Article 5 of the European Convention on Human Rights to detained asylum seekers		167
III	Rights guaranteed to detained asylum seekers under the European Convention on Human Rights		173
	III.1	The requirement of lawfulness	174
	III.2	Guarantees as to the duration of the detention	176
	III.3	The right to appeal	177
	III.4	The right to compensation	179

		III.5	Conditions of detention	179
IV			Conclusion: A statement from the *Amuur* judgment	181

Chapter 8 The Relevance of Key UN Instruments for Detained Asylum Seekers 183
Anne-Marie Tootell, Jane Hughes and David Petrasek

I	Introduction	183
II	Substantive criteria	185
	II.1 Beneficiaries	185
	II.2 Definition of deprivation of liberty	186
	II.3 Legality of detention	187
	II.4 Lawfulness and the prohibition of arbitrariness	188
	II.5 Length of detention	190
III	Procedural aspects	191
	III.1 The right to information regarding grounds for detention	191
	III.2 The right to challenge detention	192
	III.3 Impartiality of the reviewing authority	193
	III.4 The right to legal assistance	193
	III.5 Timing and nature of the review	194
IV	Implementing mechanisms	195
V	Conclusion	196

Chapter 9 The Mental Health Implications of the Detention of Asylum Seekers 199
Christina Pourgourides

I	Introduction	199
II	Selected case studies	201
III	Detention and the current reception of asylum seekers in Europe ..	202
IV	Research into the mental health of refugees and detainees	203
V	The 1995–96 research project on the mental health of detained asylum seekers in the United Kingdom: Methodology	205
VI	Findings of the research project	206
	VI.1 Information vacuum	206
	VI.2 Detention conditions	206
	VI.3 Need for external support	206
	VI.4 Effect of detention on the asylum process	207
	VI.5 Medical care	207
	VI.6 General observations	208

VII Concluding comments	208
Appendices	211
Table of Contents	213
Appendix I Universal Instruments	215
Appendix II Universal Standards	225
Appendix III Regional Instruments	255
Appendix IV General Comments by the UN Human Rights Committee	267
Appendix V UNHCR Executive Committee Conclusions	277
Appendix VI UNHCR Guidelines	287
Appendix VII NGO recommendations	297

List of Contributors

Arne Piel Christensen	General Secretary, Danish Refugee Council
Christos Giakoumopoulos	Senior Legal Officer, Directorate for Legal Affairs, Council of Europe
Ophelia Field	Policy Officer, European Council on Refugees and Exiles
Jane Hughes	European coordinator, Asylum Department, Danish Refugee Council
Barbara Jackman	Refugee lawyer, Jackman and Associates, Toronto
Peter Vedel Kessing	Project coordinator, Danish Centre for Human Rights
Morten Kjærum	Director, Danish Centre for Human Rights
Karin Landgren	Chief of General Legal Advice, UNHCR Geneva
Fedor Mediansky	Assistant Professor, School of Political Science, University of New South Wales
Paolo Morante	Graduate of Harvard Law School
David Petrasek	Human rights consultant, formerly refugee coordinator at the International Secretariat of Amnesty International
Ron Poulton	Refugee lawyer, Jackman and Associates, Toronto
Christina Pourgourides	Psychiatrist, North Birmingham Mental Health Trust
Philip Rudge	General Secretary, European Council on Refugees and Exiles
Anne-Marie Tootell	Legal consultant, UNHCR London

Acknowledgements

The authors and editors wish to thank all of the many human rights institutions, refugee agencies, lawyers and other experts who have contributed valuable information and guidance on a number of the chapters in this book.

For Chapter 1, special thanks go to the Austrian, British, French and German Sections of Amnesty International; the International Secretariat of Amnesty International, London; Claus Neumann, Caritas Vienna; Ulrike Brandl, University of Salzburg, Austria; Luc Denys, ELENA Coordinator (European Legal Network on Asylum), Belgium; Sylvie Saroléa, Université Catholique de Louvain, Belgium; Kim Kjær, Danish Centre for Human Rights; Anne la Cour Vågen and Hannah Krog, Danish Refugee Council; Sari Sirva, Finnish Refugee Advice Centre; Anne Castagnos-Sen, France Terre d'Asile, Paris; Herbert Leuninger, Pro Asyl, Germany; Theresia Wolff, Zentrale Dokumentationsstelle der Freien Wohlfahrtspflege für Flüchtlinge (ZDWF), Germany; Greek Council for Refugees; Ursula Fraser, Irish Refugee Council; Maria de Donato, Italian Refugee Council (CIR); Agnès Rausch, Caritas Luxembourg; Frans Lankers, VluchtelingenWerk, Netherlands; Heini Ringel, Norwegian Organization for Asylum Seekers (NOAS); Rita Nogueira Ramos, Portuguese Refugee Council (CPR); Antonio Hernando and Jorge Canarias Fernández-Cavada, Comisión Española de Ayuda al Refugiado (CEAR); Olle Karlsson and Ingemar Strandberg, Swedish Refugee Council; Michael Marugg, Swiss Refugee Council; British Refugee Council, London; Claire Thomas, Refugee Legal Centre, London; Rüdiger Krech, World Health Organisation, Copenhagen; Antonio Cruz, Migration News Sheet, Brussels; Association for the Prevention of Torture in Europe; Trevor Stevens and Patrick Müller, Secretariat of the European Committee for the Prevention of Torture.

For Chapter 2, the authors are grateful for the assistance of Tania Marincheshka, Bulgarian Helsinki Committee; Dorit Hørlyck, Danish Immigration Service; Fergus Kerrigan, Danish Centre for Human Rights; Dr. Judit Juhász, Central Statistical Office, Budapest; Dr. Judit Tóth, Institute of Political Sciences, Budapest; Dr. Judit Székely, Hungarian Interchurch Aid; Dr. Marton Ill, Centre for Defence of Human Rights (MEJOK), Budapest; Alina Branescu, Independent Society for Human Rights, Bucharest; Eugenia Crangariu, Romanian Helsinki Committee; Dr. Barbara Mikolajczyk, University of Katowice, Poland; Mixail Arutiynov, Presidential Commission on Human Rights, Russia; Bill Seary, ECRE; UNHCR branch offices in Kiev, Moscow, Prague, Stockholm and Warsaw.

Stephanie Marks, Eleanor Acer and Sheri Rickert of the US Lawyers' Committee provided assistance with Chapter 3. Chapter 4 was reviewed and updated by Alex Neve, formerly of York University Center for Refugee Studies, Toronto, and now a practising refugee lawyer. Professor Bent Sørensen, Vice-Chairman of the UN Committee against Torture, provided comments and information relating to the Convention against Torture in Chapter 8.

Thanks are also due to Miriam Møller, Danish Centre for Human Rights, for compiling the appendices; to Sarah Hughes for assistance with editing and proof-reading; and, last but not least, to Morten Kjærum, Director of the Danish Centre for Human Rights, and Louise Holck, Head of the Danish Refugee Council's Asylum Department, for their advice and support throughout the preparation of this book.

Introduction

"Under a government which imprisons any unjustly, the true place for a just man is also a prison" (Henry Thoreau)

The United Nations High Commissioner for Refugees has stated that detention of asylum seekers "should normally be avoided". Is this the reality in Europe today? If not, what are the reasons for a derogation from that straightforward principled position? Are the interests of the State and of the individual asylum seeker seriously out of balance, and if so, what measures are necessary to redress the balance? This book sets out to answer these questions by examining the legal and human rights issues involved in the detention of asylum seekers.

The empiricial evidence indicates that there is serious cause for concern and that current practices are often damaging both to the individuals detained and to the reputation of European States. The majority of States claim that detention of asylum seekers is kept to an absolute minimum. However, the reality in most European countries is that the use of detention has spread since the late 1980s. The denial of liberty to any human being is always a serious matter requiring legal and moral justification. The detention of persons who are innocent of any criminal offence and may be fleeing gross violations of their human rights in order to seek asylum is a matter of the utmost concern. In the criminal field in Europe these justifications are clearly laid down, there is judicial scrutiny, and they are the subject of informed public and political debate as to their effectiveness in protecting the public interest on the one hand, and punishing or rehabilitating the detainee on the other. This is not the case for asylum seekers placed in administrative detention.

The diverse arguments advanced in favour of detention are difficult to defend when weighed against the serious infringement of personal liberty involved. It is very rare for asylum seekers in detention to be charged with offences other than illegal entry, which is not a "crime" in itself. Under international refugee law, illegal entry is to be treated with circumspection, with the focus on the nature of the asylum claim rather than the mode of transport or entry to the country. There is an inhuman disproportionality in inflicting detention upon someone who simply falls foul of complex administrative procedures which even a country's own nationals can find confusing. The use of detention in order to verify identity cannot justify a stay of more than a few weeks in these days of high technology databases and international exchange of finger prints. The argument that detention is necessary to prevent absconding has not been justified by reliable studies of the rate of absconding, particularly amongst newly arrived asylum seekers whose claims have not yet been processed. Nor, might one add, have there been any "cost-benefit" studies which could justify detention in terms of costs alone. Finally, the argument that a policy of non-detention would "encourage" arrivals is tantamount to admitting that detention is used to deter arrivals.

Now, in the late 1990s, the concerns of the human rights community focus not only on the legal or civil liberties issues, but also the social and human dimension of detention. Evidence has grown that conditions in certain detention centres are sometimes humiliating and degrading. Even where conditions are satisfactory, the psychological trauma of not knowing the reasons for detention or how long it may last is disturbing. A comfortable prison is still a prison, and any improvement in detention conditions should not obscure the essential fact that detention is not an appropriate response to this category of persons.

In Europe, the practice of detention has to be seen in the context of the increasingly restrictive entry and immigration policies of the Member States of the European Union and the impact of their efforts to harmonise asylum policy on other non-EU countries, including those of central and eastern Europe. Examples of such policies include the restrictive interpretation of the Geneva Convention criteria for granting asylum and the so-called "safe third country" policy, which in effect passes the responsibility for processing asylum claims to other States, often less well-equipped to manage refugee movements.

Non-governmental organisations (NGOs) and human rights experts in Europe have joined with UNHCR in calling for the development of a refugee policy that maintains the institution of asylum in Europe while pursuing all possible avenues to guarantee the protection of refugees and internally displaced persons worldwide. They argue that fair and efficient procedures are fundamental to refugee status determination and, given the necessary resources and legal aid, that asylum claims can be handled expeditiously and detention can normally be avoided.

The current approach to refugee policy is undermined by a continued failure on the part of States to develop differentiated policies to deal with asylum seekers in need of international protection and other aliens seeking entry. It is important, both with regard to the subject matter of the present volume but also in view of the need for better analysis of public policy in this area in general, to provide a clear definition of the terms and scope of the refugee question. There has inevitably been a blurring of the categories of asylum seekers and other migrants, due to the fact that since the early 1970s access to European territory has effectively been closed except for business, tourism and family reunification. Asylum is thus the only other viable channel of entry, with the result that asylum seekers and illegal entrants are too often "lumped together" in the public mind and in official policy responses.

The practice of detention of asylum seekers has a significance beyond the incarceration of individuals. It is symptomatic of the wider European problem of addressing the full significance of refugee movements at the end of the 20th century:

INTRODUCTION

how to generate the appropriate kinds of policy responses which comply with legal and moral obligations, guarantee protection for those who are in need of it and, at the same time, how to respond to public concern? In so far as European States play a leading part in international efforts to assist and protect refugees, their example receives close attention elsewhere in the world. During the 20th century, European countries have been key actors in defining standards and norms for international refugee protection based on a firm conviction of national, regional and global solidarity. Any measures which undermine these standards in Europe consequently have widespread ramifications, not least of which is that they lend support to other regimes elsewhere in the world whose commitment to these norms is less strong.

We are starting to see positive indications that European States are alert to the danger that the failure to assert human rights values for any one category of person is a failure of the whole system of mutual respect and obligations through which decent, pluralistic, democratic life is conducted. After many ugly attacks, both verbal and physical, on asylum seekers amongst others, European States are now taking joint initiatives to combat the alarming levels of racism, intolerance and xenophobia in our societies. A similar hopeful sign is the action, led by the European Union, to tackle the manifestations of social exclusion in many sectors of European society – the poor, the homeless, the unemployed and other socially marginal groups – which in turn inhibit the successful settlement and integration of refugees in their receiving societies. However, the effects of "compassion fatigue" on a more global level, together with a trend away from internationalism noticeable in many European countries, pose a threat to the engagement of all States to confront the widespread human rights violations leading to refugee movements in the first place.

The future management of refugee flows is a complex and challenging human rights concern for all European States. As the initiators of this detention project, from seminar to book, we are committed to the notion that a dialogue between NGOs, governments, the relevant international agencies and refugees themselves should be promoted by studies of this kind, where problems can be analysed and positive solutions proposed which are in conformity with long-standing European traditions of respect for human rights and the institution of asylum.

Philip Rudge	Arne Piel Christensen	Morten Kjærum
General Secretary	General Secretary	Director
ECRE	Danish Refugee Council	Danish Centre for Human Rights

Chapter 1 Recent Trends in the Detention of Asylum Seekers in Western Europe

By Jane Hughes and Ophelia Field

Contents

Part I   Introduction
Part II Increase in detention of asylum seekers: II.1 General indications of an increase – II.2 More restrictive legislation in general – II.3 Statistical increase – II.4 Increase in the number of detention centres
Part III The grounds for detention: III.1 Pre-admission detention – III.2 Competence for the initial decision to detain – III.3 Detention in airports – III.4 Detention during the determination procedure – III.5 Pre-deportation detention
Part IV Rights in detention: IV.1 Information on the grounds for detention – IV.2 Access to other information and counselling – IV.2 Review and appeal rights
Part V   Conditions of detention: V.1 Detention facilities – V.2 Duration of detention – V.3 Women and children – V.4 Treatment by staff and staff training measures
Part VI Final comments

I   Introduction

Detention of asylum seekers has been the subject of controversial debate between governments and refugee assisting non-governmental organisations (NGOs) in western Europe since the late 1980s. Despite government assertions that detention is used as a last resort in a minute proportion of cases, the 1995 UNHCR survey on detention of asylum seekers in Europe[1] confirmed findings by local UNHCR branch offices that in recent years there has been an increase in the number of asylum seekers who are being detained. Whilst many NGOs acknowledge that a limited

---

1   *Detention of Asylum-Seekers in Europe*, European Series, Volume 1 No. 4, October 1995, reprinted in January 1996, UNHCR Geneva. The survey provides comprehensive information on international standards and national legislation and practice, in addition to presenting new guidelines to governments (reproduced in Appendix VI.1 to this book).

period of detention may be necessary in some specific instances, they oppose the almost routine use of detention in many countries.

The use of detention in western Europe must be placed in the context of more restrictive entry and immigration policies in EU Member States, in particular "safe third country" policies, visa requirements for nationals of refugee producing countries, airline carrier fines for transporting undocumented passengers, accelerated asylum procedures, and in general the failure to distinguish adequately between asylum seekers in need of international protection and other aliens seeking entry.[2, 3] The current climate of xenophobia also plays a role: asylum seekers have been "contaminated" by long association with "terrorists", "illegals" and other "undesirable aliens", to the extent that the very act of seeking asylum is at risk of becoming criminalised in the public imagination. However, it would be simplistic to characterise detention solely as the consequence of restrictive policies: current trends would justify describing detention as an instrument of deterrence in its own right.

This chapter outlines the main areas of concern to refugee and human rights organisations which are active in defending the rights of detained asylum seekers in western Europe today. For a detailed, factual description of immigration-related

---

2   With reference in particular to rejected asylum seekers, it was observed by a UNHCR speaker at the European Seminar on Detention of Asylum Seekers in 1995 that there was "vast confusion regarding the concepts of refugee, rejectee, de facto refugee and deportee on formal or substantive grounds. Rejected cases cover a lot of categories, which was why UNHCR spoke in terms of 'persons not in need of international protection' rather than 'rejectees'. To illustrate the difference in government practices and the problem of definitions, the recognition rate in Canada was 70%, whereas in Norway it was 5%. Persons in need of international protection should not be detained, but that did not mean that UNHCR found it justifiable to detain others. More actors needed to be involved in taking a hard look at whether it was really necessary to detain a lot of 'illegal' aliens, such as those whose governments would not take them back, or those who had lost their citizenship. Although a distinction between those in need of protection and those not in need was relevant for the work of UNHCR, such a distinction should not leave illegal aliens without support. Like everybody else, illegal aliens were human beings and had human rights." *Final Report of the European Seminar on Detention of Asylum Seekers*, Copenhagen 17 November 1995, published by the Danish Refugee Council in January 1996, pp. 51–52.

3   By way of example, following intervention by the Austrian Asylum Commission (comprising 11 humanitarian organisations including UNHCR and Amnesty International), it is reported that "[t]here have been five cases in 1996 when UNHCR had to issue a 'letter of protection' in favour of asylum seekers who had been rejected by the Austrian authorities even though there were no doubts that they were covered by the provisions of the Geneva Convention. A UNHCR spokesperson pointed out that this 'letter of protection', which, strictly speaking, has no legal relevance for the Austrian authorities, was issued as an emergency measure, 'unique' in western Europe, in order to try and give at least a minimum form of protection against deportation to the asylum seekers concerned"; see *Migration News Sheet*, August 1996, p. 7.

CHAPTER 1   WESTERN EUROPE

detention practices in all the countries of western Europe, the reader is referred to the above-mentioned UNHCR survey on detention of asylum seekers. The aim here is to present a critical analysis of current trends in the region, with emphasis on those areas where the need for reform is most urgent.

In addition to drawing on existing NGO reports and academic papers, the chapter is based extensively on information provided directly by western Europe's leading refugee NGOs and lawyers. It should be pointed out that in some countries the issue of detained asylum seekers has been in the spotlight: Austria, Belgium, Denmark, Germany, Switzerland and the United Kingdom are examples. In others, detention for immigration purposes is either less common or there is little public awareness of the problem, as is the case with Greece, Italy, Luxembourg, Portugal and Spain. It should be added that the network of NGOs may be more developed in some of the above countries than in others.

This chapter starts by examining the indicators of an increase in the use of detention by European immigration authorities. It gives an overview of the grounds (both official and unofficial) for detaining asylum seekers at the various stages of the refugee determination procedure. The chapter goes on to discuss the rights and conditions of detained asylum seekers, drawing particular attention to areas where their rights are inferior to those of nationals detained on criminal charges. Reference is made throughout to the relevant international standards set out in the UN Body of Principles for the Protection of All Persons under Any Form of Detention or Imprisonment, endorsed by western European governments at the time of its adoption in 1988.[4] The chapter finally assesses the effects and effectiveness of detention, and concludes by arguing that far greater use should be made of existing, non-custodial alternatives.

II   Increase in detention of asylum seekers

II.1   General indications of an increase

A general increase in the use of detention of asylum seekers was reported in 1995 by both refugee NGOs and UNHCR branch offices in western Europe, notably Austria, Belgium, Germany and the United Kingdom. Norway alone among western

---

[4]   The *Body of Principles for the Protection of All Persons under Any Form of Detention or Imprisonment* (reproduced in full in Appendix II.3 to this book) was adopted by the UN General Assembly on 9 December 1988 (Resolution 43/173). Although not legally binding on States, it was adopted with their consensus and is the most recent and comprehensive international instrument setting out safeguards for persons in detention. Importantly for detained asylum seekers, it makes a clear distinction between a "detained person" (any person deprived of personal liberty except as a result of conviction for an offence) and an "imprisoned person" (any person deprived of personal liberty as a result of conviction for an offence).

7

European countries recorded a decrease in the use of detention, but even there NGOs observed several cases where asylum seekers have been held "on special grounds" beyond the prescribed maximum period of 12 weeks. The overall increase in detention in western Europe should be seen against a background of what might be described as a "culture of incarceration", a general rise in the prison population – the problem of overcrowding is common to many European countries, with a growing proportion of foreigners in European prisons.[5] This trend has been accompanied by a parallel increase in deportation proceedings, with pre-deportation detention becoming increasingly used as a means of ensuring the enforcement of deportation orders. Nevertheless, recent amendments in national legislation and available statistics also point to a clear increase in the detention of asylum seekers as a specific category.

II.2   More restrictive legislation in general

The principal indicator of a general increase in the practice of detaining asylum seekers is the enactment of new, more restrictive legislation. Several countries have recently amended, or are in the process of amending, their legislation so as to increase their powers to detain asylum seekers and to authorise longer periods of detention.

For example, as a result of amendments to the German Aliens Act in 1993 (Section 57(2)), certain categories of rejected asylum seeker may now be detained for a three-month period. This may be renewed for up to a total of 18 months, though in principle not when the reasons for detention are beyond the individual's control.

In the United Kingdom, since the introduction of the 1971 Immigration Act and the 1993 Asylum and Immigration Appeals Act, giving immigration officers broad discretionary powers to detain with no recourse to the courts, it has been estimated by various sources, including Amnesty International, that the number of detained asylum seekers has doubled in recent years.

In Switzerland, a new law was introduced in February 1995 (Federal Law on Security Measures to be taken in Relation to Foreigners) authorising imprisonment of foreign nationals above the age of 15 without temporary or permanent residence permits. Whereas under previous legislation asylum seekers could be detained in certain cases for a maximum of 30 days, they may now be detained for three months while the decision on the right of temporary residence is being prepared, and for a further six months, or even one year with the agreement of the judicial authority, pending expulsion. Asylum seekers awaiting the outcome of an appeal may

---

5   For a more detailed discussion of this aspect of detention, see *Foreigners in Prison* by Katarina Tomasevski, European Institute for Crime Prevention and Control, Publication Series No. 24, May 1994.

CHAPTER 1   WESTERN EUROPE

therefore now be detained if there are "concrete indications" that they will not comply with an expulsion order.[6]

France also introduced an amendment to its legislation in December 1994,[7] creating new international "waiting zones" in railway stations. In practice, this means that asylum seekers who were previously not detained at all may now be detained for up to 20 days. Detainees may also be transferred from one waiting zone to another (for example, from Dunquerque, a port, to Roissy, an airport).

In June 1995, the Danish Parliament amended the Aliens Act to allow for the detention of certain categories of asylum seekers dealt with under the manifestly unfounded procedure. The administrative practice had previously been criticised by human rights organisations and was suspended after being declared unlawful by the courts in January 1995.[8]

In Belgium, amendments to Section 51 of the Aliens Act in application of the Schengen Agreement were published in the laws of 10 and 15 July 1996. These allow for the detention of an asylum seeker while deciding the country responsible for determining the claim and arranging the transfer to that country. The maximum permissible length of detention of asylum seekers was previously two months, but once the new legislation enters into effect on 1 January 1998, it will be possible to renew detention orders for a total of up to eight months, with some exceptions such as Schengen transfer cases, where the legal maximum is still two months. In practice there is at the present time no clear maximum limit – a situation which will continue until the end of 1997.

The removal or cutting of welfare benefits and other forms of social assistance to asylum seekers is another deterrent policy which, in several countries, is employed in conjunction with detention, or which provides grounds for detention. In

---

6   Public opposition to the proposed law (critics included the former director of the Federal Department of Justice, also a member of the Swiss delegation to the European Court of Human Rights) was such that a national referendum was held. The new law was, however, supported by a large majority (72.9% in favour). The law was one of the principal subjects of concern of the UN Human Rights Committee in its November 1996 concluding observations regarding the initial report of Switzerland under Section 40 of the *International Covenant on Civil and Political Rights* (CCPR/C/79/Add.70, para. 15). For a detailed analysis of the new law, see *Zwangsmassnahmen im Ausländerrecht: Situationsbericht* by Patrizia De Cecco *et al.*, published by the Swiss Organisation for Aid to Refugees (Schweizerische Flüchtlingshilfe), September 1995.

7   Law No. 94–1136, 27 December 1994, Art. 2.I.

8   The practice of detaining was introduced in response to a "crime-wave" in the vicinity of the refugee reception centre north of Copenhagen, for which some young asylum seekers from the Baltic republics and some eastern European countries were found to be largely responsible. Whereas previously it was only possible to detain asylum seekers on arrival if they were unidentified or prior to deportation if they refused to cooperate after being rejected in the procedure, under the new amendment it is now possible to detain certain categories of asylum seekers during the processing of their case in the manifestly unfounded procedure.

the United Kingdom, under the 1996 Asylum and Immigration Act, asylum seekers must apply for asylum at the point of entry (port/airport) in order to be eligible for national welfare benefits; yet, as further described below, detention is much more likely to occur at a port or airport than if the asylum seeker waits a few days and applies in-country. The stark choice for the well-informed asylum seeker would therefore be between detention or destitution. On 1 April 1995 the *Land* of Salzburg, along with several other *Länder* in Austria, changed its Social Security Law to exclude asylum seekers without a residence permit from receiving welfare benefits. They now have to prove that they are being cared for privately, otherwise they face the penalty of detention pending possible deportation.

Many European NGOs predict that, due to the increased responsibility of governments for transit migration under the Schengen Agreement, and with the Dublin Convention due to enter into force on 1 September 1997, the number of detentions is very likely to increase. The implementation of the "safe third country" concept has already provided governments with an additional incentive to detain asylum seekers.[9] A few case histories will suffice to illustrate the detention implications of "safe third country" removals, in conjunction with regimes providing for accelerated procedures, carrier sanctions and other penalties for the use of false documents:

Case History No. 1: An Iraqi asylum seeker arriving at Copenhagen airport on 29 September 1995 via Jordan and Athens was denied entry at the border on "safe third country" grounds (paragraph 48.2 of the Danish Aliens Act) and returned to Athens, where he had been in transit for eight hours. However, the Greek authorities refused to accept his asylum application precisely on the grounds that he was only in transit and had therefore not technically entered Greek territory according to Section 8(1) of the Greek Aliens Act.[10] An unsuccessful attempt was made to deport him to Jordan, but he was immediately returned to Greece, where he was placed in detention at the airport. Repeated attempts to submit an asylum application failed, but he was

---

9   For a detailed analysis, see *Safe Third Countries: Myths and Realities*, ECRE, February 1995 and the *Report on "Safe Third Country" Policies in Europe* by the Danish Refugee Council (to be published in 1997).

10 On 12 December 1996 the Greek Parliament adopted amendments to Sections 24 and 25 of the Aliens Act concerning the admissibility procedure at the borders. According to the new Section 25, all applications submitted by aliens upon arrival at a point of entry in a port or airport must be examined in a "prioritised and accelerated procedure". Applicants are to remain in the "waiting zone" during examination of their asylum application, but for no longer than 15 days. Suitable facilities for accommodating asylum seekers are to be specified in an inter-ministerial decree. Although the new provisions were expected to come into force in early 1997, Section 8(1) of the Aliens Act regarding airport transit had not yet been abolished and refugee organisations expected a conflict in both law and practice with the amended Section 25.

allegedly told that if he could pay for the ticket he could return to Denmark. A fellow detainee lent him a telephone card enabling him to call family members in Denmark (two brothers, both recognised refugees) requesting that they send him a ticket to Copenhagen. During his detention at Athens airport, meals were only provided for detainees who could pay, and the asylum seeker was forced to rely on the generosity of fellow detainees. He also reported that he was visited by two Arab-speaking men who tried to persuade him to return to Iraq. He believed they had been sent by the Iraqi Embassy in Athens. Despite receiving a ticket to Copenhagen from his family and despite assurances given by the airport authorities to a lawyer from the Greek Council for Refugees, the asylum seeker was again returned to Jordan, where in the presence of the Iraqi Consul in Amman he was forced to sign an application for a *laissez-passer* to Iraq and reveal information regarding his remaining family members in the country. He was placed in detention pending deportation to Iraq, and it was only through the combined efforts of his family, the Danish Refugee Council, the Danish Immigration Service, UNHCR and the Danish Consulate in Amman that he was finally released from detention and returned to Denmark on 10 October 1995, where he was admitted to the determination procedure.[11]

Case History No. 2: On 1 January 1996, three Iranian asylum seekers arrived at Madrid airport on a flight from Teheran via Zurich. They applied for asylum and were detained for seven days under the provisions of the Spanish Asylum Law pursuant to the processing of asylum applications at border points (introduced by Law 9/1994 of 19 May 1994). After one week of detention, the asylum applications were declared to be manifestly unfounded and the Spanish authorities arranged for them to be removed to the country of transit, Switzerland. This proved impossible, however, and the continued detention of the asylum seekers became illegal.[12] The Spanish authorities instead decided to send the asylum seekers to Italy on "safe third country" grounds. The reasons for this decision are not known, but it is believed to be based on incorrect information given by Swiss Air. The asylum seekers arrived in Rome on 15 January 1996, but were refused entry by the Italian authorities because there was no evidence to suggest that they had travelled via Italy en route to Spain. Following intervention by the Italian Refugee Council, the asylum seekers were sent back to Spain, but were again placed in detention on arrival. Through the further intervention of the Spanish Refugee Council, more

---

11 Case documented by the Danish Refugee Council, UNHCR Stockholm and the Greek Council for Refugees.
12 Under Spanish legislation (Asylum Regulation approved by Royal Decree 2203/1995, Section 22.3), once the time limit for asylum proceedings expires (seven days), the asylum seeker must be granted provisional entry into Spain if deportation is not possible.

information about the asylum applications emerged, a *habeas corpus* claim was filed and the asylum seekers were released from detention and allowed to enter Spanish territory on 22 January 1996.[13]

Case History No. 3: In the notorious *Iqbal* case,[14] a Pakistani asylum seeker was detained from the moment of his arrival in the UK on 3 March 1996 until the date of his return to France on 10 April 1996 after an unsuccessful appeal against removal on "safe third country" grounds. He was detained on the grounds that he lacked travel or identity documents. A family friend in the UK was subsequently able to arrange for Mr Iqbal's Pakistani identity card to be sent to the UK, but it arrived after his removal to France. On arrival in France, despite the fact that he presented the authorities with a standard letter in English and French, supplied by the Refugee Legal Centre stating that he wished to apply for asylum and that his case had not been considered on its merits in the UK, he was immediately placed in detention as an illegal immigrant (Section 35*bis* of the 2 November 1945 Ordinance providing for detention pending expulsion). The police ignored his asylum claim, treating his presence in France as a resumption of his previous illegal stay there. A French refugee lawyer (offering his services free of charge) successfully argued for the release of the asylum seeker, *inter alia* on the grounds that the case had been dealt with under the wrong procedure. Even after the asylum seeker's release, the police argument that it was correct to treat him as an illegal immigrant was upheld in the appeal to the Administrative Tribunal.[15] Indeed, the asylum seeker was subsequently re-arrested at the Paris *Préfecture* when he presented himself in order to obtain the requisite asylum application forms, and an attempt was made to force him onto a plane bound for Karachi. The pilot

---

13 Case documented by the Spanish Refugee Council (CEAR) and the Italian Refugee Council (CIR).
14 The asylum seeker's "Kafkaesque" attempts to submit an asylum application and the French authorities' abortive attempt to forcibly deport him have been documented in detail by the Refugee Legal Centre (London) in *Ali Iqbal: Case Summary*, the Danish Refugee Council (*supra* note 9), France Terre D'Asile (Paris) and the Institute for Human Rights and the Association for the Prevention of Torture in *De la prévention des traitements inhumains et dégradants en France*, Cahier No. 2, October 1996, Université Catholique de Lyon, pp. 119–120.
15 The reasoned explanation of the Administrative Tribunal, published some months later in July 1996, states in its rejection of the asylum seeker's appeal against the deportation order that "[i]t emerges from the documents in the case that the petitioner had already stayed in France for about a fortnight before going to Great Britain, the country in which he wished to have his petition for asylum investigated; that thus in the circumstances of the case in point it is obvious that the sole purpose of his alleged intention to apply for asylum is to frustrate an order of escort to the frontier, with the aim of gaining time." (Translation by the Refugee Legal Centre).

CHAPTER 1   WESTERN EUROPE

refused to board him because of the strength of his protests and the distress caused to other passengers. Following media attention and the intervention of France Terre D'Asile, he was finally admitted to the full refugee determination procedure, which is in effect an admission that he should never have been detained and threatened with return.[16]

Notwithstanding this bleak picture of detention legislation and practice in western Europe, there have been a few improvements in some national laws. Luxembourg revised its aliens legislation in 1994, reducing the maximum length of each detention order from six months to one month. A detention order may, however, be extended twice, bringing the total maximum length of detention to three months. The Swedish Aliens Act has been amended so that, as of 1 January 1997, young persons under the age of 18 (previously 16) may not be detained. There continue to be certain exceptions to this general rule, however, allowing for the detention of minors under the age of 18 for up to 72 hours, which may in exceptional cases be extended by a further 72 hours if the Immigration Board believes that the minor is likely to abscond. As a result of the 1996 *Amuur* judgment by the European Court of Human Rights on airport detention,[17] Belgium is in the process of amending domestic legislation to grant asylum seekers detained in airports the same appeal rights as other detainees. Belgium was previously among those countries that argued that airport detention was not "detention" as such, in that asylum seekers held in airport transit (or "waiting") zones were technically at liberty to leave the country. The 1996 Irish Refugee Act (to enter into force in 1997) includes a provision for prioritising (as opposed to accelerating) the asylum application of anyone held in detention.

There have also been some encouraging rulings by national courts, which could ultimately lead to legislative changes and to the improvement of the situation of detained asylum seekers. In August 1995, for example, the Swiss Federal Court ruled for the first time in a case concerning conditions of detention of asylum seekers, noting that if conditions were inadequate, detainees should be released (see Section V.1 below on detention facilities). On 2 May 1996, the Federal Court ruled

---

16 By way of an epilogue, a British Special Adjudicator ruled in a later "safe third country" case (Appeal No. HX/66443/96) that the *Iqbal* case was not "an isolated example of bureaucratic incompetence" but provided "detailed and incontrovertible evidence" that the French authorities did not appear to be carrying out their obligations under French law and the Anglo-French Protocol (of 20 April 1995 relating to the return of non-admitted passengers), and that France could not therefore be considered a "safe" third country. In August 1996, however, the UK amended its Immigration Rules, abolishing appeal rights in cases where asylum seekers are to be returned to other EU Member States on "safe third country" grounds.

17 Judgment No. 17/1995/523/609 of 25 June 1996; see *infra* note 35; see also the section on airport detention below and Chapter 7 of this book for a detailed analysis of this case.

that persons detained while awaiting expulsion should benefit from conditions more liberal than those imposed on convicted persons.

On 12 August 1996, a group of eight hunger-striking Afghan asylum seekers was allowed to enter Germany by the Administrative Court of Frankfurt despite earlier being refused entry by the Federal Ministry of the Interior. The Administrative Court described their detention as an "inadmissible deprivation of liberty" and referred to the *Amuur* judgment, which considers that a distinction cannot be made between "retention" and "detention" in airports. The asylum seekers had spent 50 days in the transit zone of Frankfurt airport, but could not be returned to Moldavia, the last country of transit, because there was no readmission agreement between Germany and Moldavia. The Federal Border Police appealed against the ruling.[18]

Also of general relevance to detained asylum seekers, in November 1996, the Spanish Constitutional Court ordered that a Moroccan detainee awaiting repatriation should be released pending a ruling on his appeal. The authorities had ordered his detention "for the period of time necessary to carry out his expulsion". The Constitutional Court pointed out that the authorities had not taken into account the man's personal situation, and stressed that the judiciary must avoid "arbitrary detention" and that the deprivation of liberty "must abide by the principle of exceptional circumstances". The Court ruled that the reasons given by the authorities for detaining the man did not justify his detention, lacked grounds and violated constitutional rights such as the fundamental right to freedom and effective judicial control.[19]

II.3 Statistical increase

Obtaining figures for detained asylum seekers is problematic for a number of reasons.[20] The very definition of what constitutes "detention" varies, both between countries and among the different interest groups involved, particularly with regard to the situation in airports. Under "safe third country" procedures, turn-around may be so rapid that many people are never registered as having been detained. In some countries, statistics are either not accessible or are simply not compiled at all. In others, such as France, competence for detention may be shared between different ministries. In federal countries (such as Austria, Germany, Spain and Switzerland),

---

18 Case ref. AZ.:5G 50448/96.A(2), reported in Migration News Sheet, September 1996, p. 10.
19 Reported in Migration News Sheet, December 1996, p. 7.
20 Rule 7 of the *UN Standard Minimum Rules for the Treatment of Prisoners* (reproduced in full in Appendix II.2) specifies that a registration book be kept "in every place where persons are imprisoned" in order to record a) identity, b) the reasons for detention and the authority therefor, c) the day and hour of admission and release.

CHAPTER 1   WESTERN EUROPE

statistics may be compiled at regional level depending on the practice of the individual federal state, but not necessarily at national level.

In a report by the German Federal Ministry of the Interior of 25 February 1994 on the effects of the 1993 amendments, it was stated that "there is no evidence of an increase in detention as a result of the new Section 57(2)". However, according to figures released by the Ministry of the Interior of the *Land* of North Rhine-Westphalia on 9 September 1994, there were 1,500 such detainees at that time, double the figure for the previous year and ten times the number in 1992. According to the statistical tables published in a more recent report by the Federal Ministry of the Interior in October 1996, the total number of detained rejected asylum seekers in the German *Länder* increased from 10,798 in 1992 to 36,165 in 1993.[21]

In many countries, no distinction is made in detention statistics between asylum seekers and other aliens. According to figures released by the Austrian Federal Ministry of the Interior in May 1995, for example, there were 1,330 aliens in detention prior to expulsion, divided into 16 categories. There was no reference, however, to whether these people had applied for, or been refused, asylum. In 1995, a total of 15,070 illegal or "undesirable" aliens – including children between the ages of 14 and 18 – were detained in Austria prior to expulsion (the figure for the whole of 1994 was 14,675).[22]

In Switzerland, there were numerous arrests of foreign nationals (no distinction is made between illegal aliens and asylum seekers) following the entry into force of tougher legislation in February 1995. According to the Federal Office for Refugees, 2,271 individuals were in detention on 1 July 1995, and according to NGOs, the figure was 4,300 at the end of October.

In Finland, there is a national detention register, but again this does not clearly or uniformly state the reasons for detention and it is therefore not possible to obtain accurate data on the number of detainees who are asylum seekers. The Finnish Refugee Advice Centre estimates that, based on the unofficial register kept by the Helsinki Police Aliens Unit, approximately 70 to 80 asylum seekers were detained out of the total of 849 asylum seekers entering the country in 1995.

According to the Danish Section of Amnesty International,[23] over 16,000 foreign nationals were detained between 1991 and 1996 under the provisions of the Danish Aliens Act. Of the 5,896 asylum seekers who arrived spontaneously in Denmark in 1996, approximately 2,000 were detained, some for only a few days, but others for several months. There are no statistics available on the number of asylum seekers detained under the provisions of the 1995 amendment to the Aliens

---

21   *Bericht zur Situationen im Bereich der Abschiebungshaft*, 8 October 1996 (BMI-A5-936047/4(10)), quoted by Hubert Heinhold in *Abschiebungshaft in Deutschland – Eine Situationsbeschreibung*, Asyl Praxis Bibliothek von Löper Literaturverlag, 1997, p. 106.
22   International Helsinki Federation *1996 Annual Report*, p. 28.
23   *Amnesty*, Monthly magazine of the Danish Section, No. 2, April 1997, p. 16.

Act allowing for the detention of certain categories of asylum seekers in the accelerated procedure who are believed to be from "safe countries of origin".

According to figures released by the French Ministry of the Interior, a total of 5,386 aliens were held in French "waiting zones" in 1994, as compared with 3,938 in 1993. Of the aliens held in 1994, 536 were asylum seekers. This figure relates only to those who applied at ports or airports, and excludes arrivals from the United Kingdom at the Gare du Nord in Paris, arrivals from Schengen States and all arrivals of accompanied children. Of the aliens held in 1995, 516 were asylum seekers, a slight decrease on the 1994 figure, although this should be seen against a 22.5% fall in applications in 1995 (20,170) compared with 1994 (27,044). The figure for the first half of 1996 was 254.

In the United Kingdom, statistics may be given in response to parliamentary questions in the House of Commons. Figures released in this way would indicate that approximately 10,000 persons are detained annually under the provisions of the 1971 Immigration Act, of whom some 3,500 are asylum seekers. Whereas the British government estimates that approximately 1.5% of asylum seekers may be detained at any one time, this is disputed by NGOs such as the Detention Advice Service, which estimates that up to 12.5% of asylum seekers may be detained each year (this was the case in 1996, for example, when arrivals totalled 27,900). British NGOs estimate that due to the rise in the number of applicants claiming asylum at ports of entry, the number of asylum seekers in detention has doubled or even tripled between 1993–1996.[24]

Figures on detainees at the detention centre at Zaventem airport in Belgium show that a total of 951 persons were detained in the last six months of 1996, with monthly averages ranging from 145 in July to 179 in December.

Although some idea of the numbers involved can be obtained from estimates by non-governmental organisations, they are frequently hampered by restricted access to detained asylum seekers, particularly in airports. Most of the figures currently available give only a "snapshot" of the situation (i.e. numbers detained on a particular date). Where year-on-year figures can be obtained, they tend to corroborate unofficial estimates of a significant overall rise in the number of detained asylum seekers.

II.4   Increase in the number of detention centres

Another indication of the trend in detaining can be seen from plans in a number of countries, including Belgium, France, Germany, Switzerland and the United Kingdom, to open new detention centres or extend existing ones.

---

24   See *Prisoners without a Voice*, Amnesty International, expanded edition of May 1995, p. 2, and *Legal and Social Conditions for Asylum Seekers and Refugees in Western European Countries*, Danish Refugee Council, January 1997, p. 232.

The authorities in the *Land* of North Rhine-Westphalia in Germany foresaw that it would be necessary to increase the number of available places in detention centres, and requested that the capacity for accommodating pre-deportation deportees be doubled: from 1,200 places in 1994 to 2,500 in 1995. According to the German organisation Pro Asyl, a new detention centre was due to be opened in Bremen at the end of 1997.

In the UK, Amnesty International notes that since the opening of a new, purpose-built detention centre at Gatwick airport (Tinsley House) in May 1996, the number of asylum seekers detained at any one time has risen to more than 850. The organisation observes that the number of detainees has steadily increased with the opening of new facilities, from some 250 in 1993, to 600 by March 1995 and 750 by June 1996.[25]

In Italy, on the other hand, there are no facilities designed specifically for the detention of asylum seekers, nor are there any plans on the part of the Italian government to establish any such centres. In Finland, in the amendments to the 1993 Aliens Act (639/93) it was stated that due to current economic difficulties it would not be possible to build separate facilities for persons detained under the provisions of the Aliens Act. This in itself can lead to unsatisfactory conditions, as described later in this chapter.

III   The grounds for detention

III.1   Pre-admission detention

With the introduction of accelerated procedures for "manifestly unfounded" and "safe third country" cases, there has been a rise in the number of asylum seekers who are detained while awaiting a decision on their admissibility to the determination procedures and/or to the territory of the host country concerned. Detention is not usually a measure applied to in-country applicants (except when applications are made at the time of arrest on grounds of illegal presence, as will be discussed below), but is predominantly reserved for border applicants in countries such as Austria, Belgium, Germany and the United Kingdom.

Between 1 July and 30 September 1996, the UK government reported that 642 asylum seekers who applied at ports/airports were detained.

In Austria and Germany, approximately 90% of asylum seekers enter by land from neighbouring States, all of which are designated "safe countries". In Austria, in fact, "safe third country" and "manifestly unfounded" rules are applied so strictly, enforced by a human chain of border guards, that it is virtually impossible to enter the country legally. In Germany, it is reported by NGOs that the threat of detention

---

25   *Prisoners without a Voice*, supra note 24, p. 4.

is used to deter would-be entrants, including asylum seekers, at the land borders. In Austria, detention at the point of entry is particularly common in Burgenland where asylum seekers arrive from Hungary, but detention also occurs if they manage to reach Vienna or Traiskirchen.

For most countries, the range of grounds for pre-admission detention focuses on the need, due to a lack of documentation, to establish the asylum seeker's identity or travel route, though the national origin of the individual is likely to contribute unofficially towards this early decision to detain. Human rights advocates in Denmark believe that the practice of singling out young male asylum seekers in the accelerated procedure from certain supposedly "safe" countries (mainly the Baltic republics, some eastern European countries and some African States) and detaining them on the grounds that they may attempt to evade removal if subsequently rejected in the procedure is discriminatory in the sense of Article 14 of the European Convention on Human Rights.[26]

Continued insistence on the validity of false documentation or evidence of previous applications under another identity may also contribute towards the decision to detain prior to admission. But in a large number of countries (including Austria, Belgium, France, Germany, Switzerland and the United Kingdom) it is increasingly the case that arrival without documentation is accepted as sufficient evidence that the asylum seeker will fail to comply with the procedure. This practice is a clear departure from UNHCR recommendations (Conclusion No. 44 of the Executive Committee) agreed by all the above countries.[27] In the UK, Amnesty International reports a growing number of convictions and prison sentences (ranging from 14 days to three months) for the offence of "possession of a false document".[28]

Portugal, in contrast, does not consider illegal entry as grounds for penal proceedings provided the asylum seeker submits his claim "immediately", defined as a maximum period of 48 hours by Section 84.1 of the 1993 Aliens Act (Law of 3 March 1993), and the charges are dropped in those cases where the refugee is recognised. In Italy, there are no legal provisions for the detention of asylum seekers as a specific category, so their detention at the borders is therefore covered by the penal law and they are treated in the same way as Italian nationals held on remand.[29]

---

26 See Working Document No. 7 by Pia Justesen (researcher at the Danish Centre for Human Rights), *Detention practice in the light of Article 14 of the ECHR*. Copies of the Working Documents for the 1995 European Seminar on Detention of Asylum Seekers may be obtained from the Danish Refugee Council.

27 See Chapter 6 for a detailed analysis of ExCom Conclusion No. 44 and UNHCR's position on detention.

28 *Cell Culture*, Amnesty International 1996, p. 26 *et seq*. According to figures provided by the Home Office, criminal convictions for possession of false documents at Heathrow airport increased from 53 in 1993–94, to 126 in 1994–95 and 376 in 1995–96.

29 According to Section 7(2) of Law 39/90, "[a]liens who violate the regulations regarding entry and residence will also be expelled from Italian territory". Thus irregular asylum

The increasing use of illegal entry as a ground for detention at European borders is a direct product of measures agreed on by EU Member States, such as visa restrictions and carrier sanctions, restricting legal access to the territory.[30] As a result, the percentage of asylum seekers arriving in western European countries without documents or with forged documents is estimated to have risen from 50–60% in the late 1980s to approximately 70% in 1994.[31]

Denmark, the United Kingdom, Ireland and Italy, for example, all practise supposedly short-term detention for what is said to be investigative purposes, though in reality such pre-admission detention can sometimes last for weeks, even months.

III.2 Competence for the initial decision to detain[32]

In Austria, local police authorities without training in asylum law are empowered to take the initial decision to detain asylum seekers, which is then forwarded for confirmation to the national authority dealing with all aliens, rather than to the Federal Asylum Office. In Finland and France, the police officer or border official who takes the initial decision to detain must be of a senior rank.

In the United Kingdom, the decision to detain upon arrival is taken by an immigration official. It is a discretionary administrative power, which the British Home Office claims is only used as a "last resort", although both the statistical scale of detention and the arbitrary elements which have been proved to affect such decisions – the number of places which happen to be available in detention centres, for example – clearly refute this claim. In Italy, where an immigration authority has yet to be established, the Italian border police are responsible for dealing with asylum applicants.[33]

---

seekers who have not submitted an asylum application to the border police may be expelled without having the possibility of making a claim.

30   These are provisions developed within the process of inter-governmental cooperation, as asylum matters have not (at the time of writing) been "communitarised". Thus they have not been referred to the Commission, European Parliament or national parliaments, are therefore not adopted democratically, and do not fall within the competence of the European Court of Justice; see ECRE's *Position on the Treaty of the European Union in relation to Asylum Policy*, updated version, March 1997.

31   *The key to Europe – a comparative analysis of entry and asylum policies in Western countries*, International Centre for Migration Policy Development, Stockholm, 1994, p. 64.

32   Principle 4 of the BOP (*supra* note 4) states that: "Any form of detention or imprisonment and all the measures affecting the human rights of a person under any form of detention or imprisonment shall be ordered by, or be subject to the effective control of, a judicial or other authority." This is defined as a body "under the law whose status and tenure should afford the strongest possible guarantees of competence, impartiality and independence".

33   According to the Association for the Prevention of Torture, cooperation with the Italian border police is relatively good, but the police are often unfamiliar with procedures and the relevant conventions, they lack training and do not have the resources to employ

III.3   Detention in airports[34]

Throughout Europe, pre-admission detention and pre-deportation detention have become increasingly indistinguishable, and nowhere more so than in airports, where current debate focuses both on the legal status of so-called "international zones" or "waiting zones" in airports and the definition of detention itself, i.e. whether confinement to these areas constitutes detention.

The French and Belgian authorities, for example, have maintained – irrespective of the asylum seekers' claim to need international protection – that detention in airports is not really "detention" because asylum seekers are supposedly free to leave the country whenever they wish, i.e. to return to the country from which they came (although, as mentioned above, Belgium is in the process of amending its legislation in the light of the *Amuur* ruling). Airport detention was ruled illegal by the *Hoge Raad der Nederlanden* (Dutch High Court) on 9 December 1987 (the year in which Dutch authorities began to detain asylum seekers at the airport), but the government passed an emergency act two weeks later to legalise this type of detention. This pattern was repeated again in 1991 when legislation was modified in order to give detention in transit areas a legal basis, prior to an anticipated High Court ruling (8 July 1992) finding it to be illegal.

In Spain, on the other hand, where there is a strict legal doctrine allowing no intermediate stage between detention and liberty, the authorities have defined the seven days in which an asylum seeker may be confined at Madrid airport in the accelerated procedure as detention in the fullest sense. However, if it is then decided that it is a "manifestly unfounded" or "safe third country" case, the individual may continue to be held under exactly the same conditions and in the same location, though in principle he or she is no longer detained. Asylum seekers in this situation are technically deemed free to return to the country from which they came or through which they transited.

In Portugal, the 1993 Asylum Law (Law No. 70/93 of 29 September 1993) is used to justify an unknown number of detentions at airports. In theory the same law allows for detention in-country without a judicial order. However facilities have not yet been built to implement this measure.

In a case involving four Somalis held at Paris Orly airport in 1992 (the so-called *Amuur* case) the European Human Rights Commission considered that the conditions of their confinement in an airport hotel would have constituted detention, but the circumstances of their case meant that they were not in detention because they had a "safe country" (Syria) to which they could return. The case was

---

interpreters. *Rapport sur les conditions de détention et les mauvais traitements en Italie*, August 1995, p. 57. The organisation also criticised the decision of 7 May 1995 to allow the army to intercept refugees from Albania.

34   See ECRE's 1993 *Working Paper on Airport Procedures in Europe*, p. 4 in particular.

subsequently referred to the European Court of Human Rights, which in June 1996 issued a judgment supporting the views of the dissenting members of the Commission and finding that the situation did indeed amount to detention.[35]

At Frankfurt airport, a special airport procedure (*Flughafenverfahren*) has operated since 1993, where the asylum applications of those arriving directly from "safe countries of origin" are processed while in detention (see Section V.1 below on conditions of detention in the detention centre (*Hafthaus*) at Frankfurt airport, and Section V.2 on duration of detention in Frankfurt airport).

III.4   Detention during the determination procedure

During determination procedures, asylum seekers in western Europe are in general permitted to be detained only when there are serious reasons to believe that they will not cooperate with the procedure, either by failing to appear for interviews, by disappearing completely or by resisting deportation if rejected. States may also detain asylum seekers during the determination procedure under exceptional circumstances, for example on the grounds of a threat to public order or national security, or to another person's life. They may also be detained for causing a disturbance at a port of entry, or of course in relation to criminal activities. It is important to point out here that the incidence of asylum seekers who commit crimes is extremely low: in Italy, for example, only five asylum seekers were detained on criminal charges in 1995. In Finland, one asylum seeker was detained during the procedure in the spring of 1996 in connection with police investigations into human trafficking from Russia to Finland.

In practice, asylum seekers in accelerated procedures for "manifestly unfounded" claims are at a greater risk of being detained, as are those awaiting the outcome of an appeal after an initial rejection and those who have been in the country illegally for some time prior to applying for asylum.[36]

Of all the grounds for detention, "likelihood of absconding" is the least clearly defined and thus the most open to abuse under discretionary powers.[37] There are

---

35 Case of *Amuur* v. *France*, application No. 19776/92, report of the Commission of 10 January 1995, judgment of the European Court of Human Rights No. 17/1995/523/609 of 25 June 1996, to be published in Reports of Judgments and Decisions for 1996, Carl Heymans Verlag, Köln; see Chapter 7 for a detailed discussion of this case.

36 In the United Kingdom, a High Court judge ruled in January 1995 (in the case of *Ex parte Khan and others*) that it was unlawful to detain asylum seekers who had entered the country illegally and claimed asylum prior to detention. This ruling, which could have led to the release of hundreds of detained asylum seekers, was overturned by the Appeals Court in February 1995.

37 There are virtually no statistics at all on rates of absconding in European countries. The UK Home Office minister acknowledged in a radio interview in October 1994 that the number of absconders was low, and in February 1995 he informed Parliament that of the 37,120 persons who were refused asylum in the three-year period 1992–94, only 220

internal guidelines in existence in several countries, but these are not prescribed by law, not applied in a predictable manner, and not cited in the explanations issued to lawyers and their clients concerning the grounds for detention in individual cases. In Belgium, the definition of "likely to resist deportation if rejected" is based on the following elements: evidence of having made multiple claims; belonging to a national group likely to be rejected; coming from a country which produces many economic migrants; ease of deportation. In Switzerland, the suggested criteria are similar but slightly more concrete: evidence of multiple claims; refusal to reveal identity; repeated and unjustified failure to attend official appointments; failure to comply with restrictions placed upon the asylum seeker's freedom of movement after having been deemed a threat to public order; being subject to prosecution for having threatened public order.

It is common in the United Kingdom for asylum seekers detained on pre-admission grounds to continue to be detained even after their application has been declared admissible, without any recourse to the courts. Those most likely to be detained are those who are also considered most likely to be rejected and deported. Existing sets of internal Home Office guidelines indicate that the following elements are used to assess the prospects of compliance with immigration requirements: previous record of absconding; a history of general non-compliance with immigration law; illegal entry or use of false documentation; likelihood of removal, and if so, after what period of time; the authorities' expectations regarding the outcome of the claim; existence of incentives for the person to remain in contact with the authorities; family ties to the United Kingdom; and, finally, any other compassionate circumstances. The speed with which false documentation is admitted to be false is also considered, as is the arbitrary factor of the availability of alternative accommodation at the time of the initial decision.

Lawyers in the United Kingdom argue that the authorities should not always refer back to the initial decision taken on the credibility of the claim, but should rather take into account the accumulating evidence related to the substance of the claim. Persons whose cases are developing positively may be said to have an incentive to stay in touch with the authorities and not abscond, and this factor should be taken into account whenever the necessity of prolonging detention is reviewed. In other words, expectations with regard to the outcome of an asylum claim are not static and should therefore be continually re-examined after someone has been detained.

In Scotland (unlike England and Wales) the legal requirement is to prove a higher than average risk of absconding based on individual grounds. It is this element, a presumption in favour of release, which is generally lacking in European

---

were known to have absconded (the equivalent of 0.59%). Information supplied by Amnesty International in *Prisoners without a Voice, supra* note 24, p. 20.

practice and which sets asylum seekers apart from persons detained on criminal grounds, who are considered "innocent until proven guilty".

As previously mentioned, the June 1995 amendment to Section 36 of the Danish Aliens Act allows for the detention of certain categories of asylum seekers with manifestly unfounded claims (the manifestly unfounded procedure is post-admission in Denmark). The revised law states that detention for the purpose of ensuring the asylum seeker's presence during the asylum procedure must be based on a "concrete, individual assessment" in each case. In practice, however, detention is often based on general criteria, such as age, gender and country of origin, and human rights organisations have denounced detention orders as being issued on a routine basis, "conveyor-belt" style.[38]

In Norway, detention is supposed to be used only when there are no alternatives, generally in a case of unverified identity when an obligation to report regularly to the authorities "is not complied with or is deemed to be clearly insufficient". In Germany, the only power to detain an asylum seeker once he or she has been given leave to enter the territory is through the criminal justice system; however, this apparently liberal view should be seen in the context of massive pre-deportation detention, as described in the section below.

The general conclusion is that detention during the full determination procedure (after a claim has been determined to have some foundation and prior to the first rejection) is rare in western European countries apart from the United Kingdom, although Austria too has been criticised by NGOs for "the widely-used practice of placing asylum seekers in detention pending their asylum procedure".[39] According to one recent report, "[t]he lack of secure legal status for most asylum seekers has meant that on average at least 11% of applicants were detained while their applications were decided in 1996. This figure was reported to be considerably higher, however, in the *Land* of Burgenland that borders on Hungary. There, the majority of applicants were reported to have spent the determination procedure in detention pending deportation."[40]

III.5   Pre-deportation detention

In many countries, deportation orders are issued concurrently with the initial rejection of the asylum claim. Some individuals may therefore be placed in detention for the purpose of enforcing a deportation order while still in the process of appeal. In general, legislation providing for such detention rarely differentiates between rejected asylum seekers and other migrants awaiting expulsion. NGOs believe that, quite apart from the question of rights which apply to all migrants,

---

38 *Amnesty,* Danish Section, *supra* note 23, p. 16.
39 *Migration News Sheet*, August 1996, p. 7.
40 United States Committee for Refugees, *1997 World Refugee Survey*, p. 168.

many of the asylum seekers detained prior to deportation would actually be at risk of serious human rights violations if returned to their country of origin.[41]

The trend in several western European countries (in particular Austria, Belgium, Germany and Switzerland) can be summarised as one of extending the duration of pre-deportation detention, and using broader criteria for judging that persons subject to deportation orders may attempt to abscond.[42] In Austria, any unauthorised entrant who seeks asylum must present him or herself to the authorities (rather than claim at the time of arrest) in order to avoid detention.

Unofficially, the majority of those detained pre-deportation will come from countries that are expected to readily accept back their nationals and are near or easy to deport to, while the groups held for the longest period of time will be those from non-cooperative countries of origin. To some extent this explains why certain national groups are over-represented among pre-deportation detainees,[43] though of course it does not explain why these individuals should be penalised for their government's position or the unsettled situation in their country of origin which makes return impossible.

A distinction may be made between western European countries which detain at the pre-deportation stage on the suspicion that the rejected asylum seeker will abscond (so-called "preventive detention"), and those that issue a compulsory exit order or pre-deportation reporting requirements in order to limit their freedom of movement, and then detain if these controls are disregarded. In France, for example, failure to comply with a deportation order can lead to arrest for three months – but

---

41 A further, serious cause for concern is that the procedure for expulsion or deportation often follows that for extradition, i.e. embassies in the host country will be asked to issue travel documents, and the authorities in the country of origin may even be informed of the rejected asylum seeker's date of arrival. This can lead to reprisals, including further imprisonment on the assumption that a person who has been in detention is *per se* a criminal. It is known that rejected Algerian asylum seekers are particularly at risk of being detained upon return to Algeria, and that rejected Iraqi asylum seekers face execution if the authorities discover that they have asked for asylum abroad.

42 In Switzerland in August 1995, the Federal Court annulled the detention order against a Syrian asylum seeker who had been rejected in the procedure. He had no identity papers and had not left Switzerland by the required date. The Federal Court declared that this could not be taken as a concrete indication that the person concerned would attempt to evade expulsion, particularly in view of the fact that he had always remained in the registration centre (CERA) to which he had been assigned and had always attended scheduled interviews. Case reported in *La détention et le traitement des demandeurs d'asile – Belgique, Hongrie, Suisse*, Observatoire international des prisons, December 1995, p. 11.

43 According to Ragnhild Witherow, in an article published in *Immigration & Nationality Law & Practice* (Volume 9 No. 2, 1995), in the United Kingdom "an Indian asylum seeker appears to be 30 times more likely to be detained than somebody from former Yugoslavia; a Zaïrean 12 times more likely than a Somali; and a Ghanaian 13 times more likely than an Iranian".

at least this proven failure to comply with an order is a more justifiable ground for detaining a person than the mere suspicion that a person may not comply.[44] In Portugal, prior to the 1993 Aliens Act, there were no legal provisions for detention of rejected asylum seekers: they were given 30 days to leave after rejection in the full procedure and 15 days to leave under the accelerated procedure. Under the new 1993 Act, however, a Portuguese judge may issue a detention order either because the reporting restrictions have been violated, or for the purposes of enforcing a deportation order. This form of "preventive detention" must be ordered by a judge and, according to Section 84.2, "cannot last for more time than is necessary for the execution of the expulsion decision, and never more than 40 days". Similarly, the Spanish authorities may detain rejected asylum seekers for up to 40 days if they do not comply with an expulsion order.

In Italy, people are not detained prior to deportation unless they have failed to comply with restrictions deriving from special surveillance measures, in which case they may be sentenced to a prison term of up to two years. If they have deliberately destroyed their documents in order to avoid expulsion or have failed to cooperate with consular authorities, they may be sentenced to imprisonment for between six months and three years. In practice, this is very rare, and such persons are accompanied to the border by the police. According to the Italian Refugee Council, expulsions of rejected asylum seekers are rarely carried out. The effective deportation of illegal aliens is currently the subject of national debate, and it is understood that amendments are due to be presented before the Italian Parliament.

In Denmark, as a result of long-standing difficulties experienced by the police in carrying out forcible deportations of rejected asylum seekers, the Aliens Act was amended on 7 May 1996. Aliens, including asylum seekers who have received a final negative decision, and who refuse to cooperate in obtaining the necessary travel documents, may now be forcibly presented to the diplomatic representation of their country in order to facilitate deportation proceedings. Such action must be based on a court decision, and it is a prerequisite that the police must already have attempted unsuccessfully to enlist the alien's cooperation in obtaining the travel documents or visas necessary in order to remove him from the country. Refusal to cooperate can result in a fine or prison sentence.

---

44 An additional problem, however, is that these persons are often released *sans papiers* (without identity documentation) and are therefore liable to be re-arrested if stopped in a spot-check.

IV Rights in detention

IV.1 Information on the grounds for detention

The right to information on the grounds for their detention is crucial for all detained asylum seekers, who are unfamiliar with the language, procedures and their rights in the country detaining them and who may be in an anxious and confused state of mind due to experiences suffered in their own country.

It is a legal requirement in all western European countries that detained aliens, including asylum seekers, be informed of the reasons for their detention.[45] In the majority of countries this information is given in writing (usually in the language of the detaining country) and translated orally. In Denmark and Sweden the information is given in the asylum seeker's language, both in writing and orally. In Belgium and Portugal the information may be given either in writing or orally. Portugal also requires that it be in a language understood by the person concerned. In the United Kingdom this information is given only orally.[46] In the *Iqbal* case mentioned above, failure by the French authorities to make an interpreter available was one of the grounds argued successfully in court for obtaining the asylum seeker's release: under French law, an administrative decision cannot be executed until it has been communicated to the person concerned and his appeal rights have been explained. It was noted throughout the documentation of the case, including by the French police, that Mr Iqbal could neither speak nor understand French.

Despite the many ways in which the grounds for detention are in theory explained, it is clear from surveys of asylum seekers themselves, and from the agencies and lawyers assisting them, that many do not understand why they are detained.[47] It must be emphasised that this is rarely the case with other detainees in remand on criminal charges. Although language is a major barrier, unhelpful attitudes on the part of the detaining officials and the uninformative nature of the reasons given (in some cases no reasons are given at all) have also been cited as contributory factors.

---

45 See Article 5(2) of the ECHR. Principle 14 of the BOP further specifies that: "A person who does not adequately understand or speak the language used by the authorities responsible for his arrest, detention or imprisonment is entitled to receive promptly in a language which he understands the information referred to in Principle 10 ... and to have the assistance, free of charge, if necessary, of an interpreter in connection with legal proceedings subsequent to his arrest."

46 In a letter to Amnesty International (15 November 1994), the Home Office minister states in response to concern expressed by the organisation that "if a written statement were to be provided as a matter of routine it would only be effective if it were translated into a language fully understood by the detainee, which would be time-consuming and cause delays".

47 In a February 1994 report by the UK Asylum Rights Campaign, 52 detainees out of a group of 125 interviewed were unaware of the reason for their detention.

CHAPTER 1   WESTERN EUROPE

IV.2   Access to other information and counselling

Given the isolation (geographic, linguistic, social and mental) of detained asylum seekers, access to information concerning their rights in detention and how to exercise them is essential both to their case and their welfare.[48]

Once again, the situation in western Europe varies widely from country to country, both in theory and in practice. And once again, the problems are compounded by certain factors, such as language, location of the detention centre, availability of public transport and transfers with little or no advance notification, which place administrative detainees at a disadvantage compared with people detained on criminal charges.

A number of countries provide detained asylum seekers with written information on their rights, though not necessarily in their own language, and this is sometimes supplemented by an oral briefing. In Belgium, an official leaflet in English, Dutch and French is supposed to be distributed to asylum seekers explaining their right to contact UNHCR, a social counsellor and a chaplain and to receive visits. A more detailed leaflet was produced by a Belgian NGO in the ten languages most commonly spoken by asylum seekers, but it does not appear to have been distributed.

In the United Kingdom, posters giving details of how to contact the Refugee Legal Centre (an NGO providing free legal counselling to asylum seekers and refugees) are displayed in detention centres, but apparently not in prisons, where up to 350 asylum seekers may also be detained. The Detention Advice Service points out that unlike the criminal system, where people are informed of their right to contact a solicitor, there is no such provision for asylum seekers at ports of entry.

Free legal assistance is available in a few countries, such as Denmark and Finland, where detained asylum seekers are automatically assigned a lawyer by the State.[49] These countries are definitely in the minority, however. In Switzerland and the United Kingdom (under the "Green Card" scheme), lawyers are not informed by the authorities of individual cases until they can prove that they have been authorised beforehand by the asylum seekers themselves, or in the case of

---

48   Principle 13 of the BOP states that: "Any person shall, at the moment of arrest and at the commencement of detention or imprisonment, or promptly thereafter, be provided by the authority responsible for his arrest, detention or imprisonment, respectively with information on and an explanation of his rights and how to avail himself of such rights." The provisions contained in Principle 14 (*supra* note 45) regarding language also apply here.

49   In Belgium, incompetence and lack of motivation have been reported to be a problem amongst the state-appointed lawyers affiliated to Centre 127*bis*, and there have even been reports of large fees being demanded in cases where a negative outcome in the procedure is inevitable; see *La détention et le traitement des demandeurs d'asile – Belgique, Hongrie, Suisse, supra* note 42, p. 5.

Switzerland, if the detention is expected to be extended for longer than three months. Quite apart from making legal representation of detained asylum seekers time-consuming and costly, a system of this kind will inevitably mean that some detainees never see a lawyer.[50]

In most countries, detained asylum seekers have access to a telephone, though some may only receive in-coming calls and others may only be allowed to make a telephone call under the supervision of staff. Free telephones were installed in detention centres in Belgium in response to complaints, including by the European Committee for the Prevention of Torture,[51] that asylum seekers were not allowed to contact their lawyers.

In Frankfurt airport there is a list of lawyers whom asylum seekers can telephone, as is required by the law. However, the list does not differentiate between immigration lawyers and other lawyers, so that an asylum seeker using a pay telephone might randomly pick the number of a divorce lawyer who only speaks German. In a ruling on 22 August 1996, the Administrative Court of Düsseldorf criticised the authorities of Düsseldorf airport for not adequately providing the minimum required legal advice to asylum seekers. It referred to the ongoing practice of failing to bring to the attention of asylum seekers rejected under the accelerated procedure in airports the possibility of obtaining temporary legal protection by lodging an appeal. The judges recalled the case law of the Federal Constitutional Court which, in its ruling of 14 May 1996, stated that it was prohibited and inadmissible to render difficult or jeopardise access to legal protection in the accelerated airport procedure.[52]

In Italy, asylum seekers detained at the border have no access to telephones, little contact with lawyers and no free legal assistance. It is reported that they are generally not informed about the progress of their applications.

In Switzerland, the four registration centres (CERA) for asylum centres are closed and are reported to be run like prisons, with no external intervention even by a chaplain provided for in three of them (Kreuzlingen, Basel and Chiasso), and a total lack of information on the asylum procedure in Kreuzlingen.[53]

---

50 Principle 18 of the BOP lays down detailed standards for communication between a detained person and his legal counsel.
51 The Committee was set up by the Council of Europe in order to monitor the implementation of the *European Convention on the Prevention of Torture*. The Committee visits prisons and detention centres throughout Europe, and its subsequent reports to governments concerned are proving instrumental in bringing about improvements in conditions of detention.
52 Case reference AZ.: 19 L 2975/96.A, reported in Migration News Sheet, September 1996, p. 10.
53 *La détention et le traitement des demandeurs d'asile – Belgique, Hongrie, Suisse*, supra note 42, p. 12.

CHAPTER 1   WESTERN EUROPE

UNHCR and specialised NGOs have been campaigning throughout western Europe for the right to have direct access to detained asylum seekers, both in detention centres and in airports.[54] Although this is clearly still a major problem, there have been some recent break-throughs: in May 1995, UNHCR and NGOs were granted limited access to waiting zones in French airports, though humanitarian agencies have challenged the restrictions before the Higher Administrative Court (*Conseil d'Etat*) where a decision is still pending. French agencies are already allowed access to immigration detainees, including asylum seekers, in other detention centres around the country (with the exception of the infamous dépôt des étrangers in Paris, mentioned below).

Another positive development is the provision in the 1996 Irish Refugee Act that every detained asylum seeker has the right to contact UNHCR.

In June 1995, following an amendment to the Danish Aliens Act after several years of negotiations, asylum seekers who are denied entry on "safe third country" grounds are entitled, if they wish, to personal counselling by the Danish Refugee Council (DRC) in the airport. They are informed of this right by the airport police. The DRC already has access to detained asylum seekers in the closed section of the Red Cross reception centre at Sandholm (35 km north of Copenhagen) to provide legal counselling.

In Austria, some local groups of Amnesty International are allowed to visit detained asylum seekers, and Caritas has access to the transit area at Vienna airport. UNHCR, together with Caritas, organises legal aid to detained asylum seekers. They can also assist detainees in bringing their cases before the European Court of Human Rights.

In the UK, a nation-wide network of visitors to immigration detainees, launched in March 1995, has done much to improve the situation regarding provision of information and social support to detainees; their contribution has been acknowledged not only by ex-detainees themselves, but also by the Home Office.[55]

IV.3   Review and appeal rights

It is not only a lack of proper information that prevents detained asylum seekers from exercising their rights in detention: review and appeal procedures are in practice deficient in a number of western European countries.[56] In most, the initial

---

54   According to Principle 16(2) of the BOP, "[i]f a detained person is a foreigner, he shall also be promptly informed of his right to communicate by appropriate means with ... the representative of the competent international organisation, if he is a refugee or is otherwise under the protection of an intergovernmental organisation".
55   Statement made by a representative of the Home Office at the Day-School on Detaining Immigrants and Asylum Seekers, held at Oxford University on 11 March 1995.
56   Principle 11 of the BOP states in paragraph 1 that: "A person shall not be kept in detention without being given an effective opportunity to be heard promptly by a judicial

review of detention is automatic, but subsequent reviews are frequently not. In most countries, the reviewing authority is independent, but elsewhere, (notably the United Kingdom) it is not.

If an asylum seeker is to effectively lodge an appeal against the detention decision, the services of a lawyer will be needed; however, not all countries which provide free legal assistance at the outset continue to do so at the appeal stage.[57, 58]

Judicial review of detention is almost always limited to the legality of detention on procedural grounds: length of detention is very rarely taken into consideration, and the asylum-related aspects of the case practically never. In some countries, local courts and judges have special training in asylum-related matters, but most do not. There have also been complaints that the courts are over-inclined to bow to the arguments of the detaining authorities.[59]

One of the main problems in federal countries, such as Switzerland, is that lack of clarity in the wording of certain provisions leaves room for differing interpretations of the law by the individual regions or cantons. The application of the law is particularly severe in Zurich, and the Swiss Federal Court (*Tribunal Fédéral*) has intervened on at least 40 occasions, in particular regarding the requirement that there must be "concrete indications" that an asylum seeker may attempt to evade expulsion and on the question of conditions of detention.[60]

---

or other authority. A detained person shall have the right to defend himself or to be assisted by counsel as prescribed by law." Paragraph 3 states that: "A judicial or other authority shall be empowered to review as appropriate the continuance of detention." The BOP defines "judicial or other authority" as a body whose status and tenure should afford the strongest possible guarantees of competence, impartiality and independence.

57　Principle 17 of the BOP states that: "1. A detained person shall be entitled to have the assistance of a legal counsel. He shall be informed of his right by the competent authority shortly after arrest and shall be provided with reasonable facilities for exercising it. 2. If a detained person does not have a legal counsel of his own choice, he shall be entitled to have a legal counsel assigned to him by a judicial or other authority in all cases where the interests of justice so require and without payment by him if he does not have sufficient means to pay."

58　In the case of the UK, the UN Human Rights Committee has voiced its concern in this respect: "The Committee notes with concern that adequate legal representation is not available for asylum seekers effectively to challenge administrative decisions." *Concluding observations/comments on the fourth periodic report of the United Kingdom of Great Britain and Northern Ireland* (CCPR/C/95/Add.3), July 1995.

59　In Finland, for example, the courts – especially in Helsinki – are reported to be very unsympathetic to the arguments of defence lawyers, and in 99% of cases, according to the Refugee Advice Centre, the courts authorise extensions of detention until the police release the detainee (normally after several weeks). In a very few cases, courts have expressed dissatisfaction with the work of the police and have released asylum seekers detained for more than two or three months.

60　*La détention et le traitement des demandeurs d'asile – Belgique, Hongrie, Suisse, supra* note 42, p. 11.

CHAPTER 1   WESTERN EUROPE

In some countries, asylum seekers detained at borders and in airports have fewer review or appeal rights than those detained in-country. In Germany, for example, there is no right of appeal against detention in an airport. There is provision for an administrative appeal against detention in waiting zones at French airports, but this is rarely used.[61] In Belgium, there is still no right of appeal against detention at borders, including airports, but, as mentioned above, legislation is to be amended in the wake of the *Amuur* ruling, allowing for appeals against detention.[62]

The timing of the initial review of detention varies from country to country, but mostly occurs within a few days of detention, in accordance with international standards (two days in Portugal, for example, three days in Denmark, three days in Spain but seven for airport applicants, four days in Switzerland, and four days for border applicants in France). In both Denmark and Switzerland, human rights advocates have drawn attention to the fact that detention orders are reviewed more promptly (within 24 hours in Denmark and 24 or 48 hours in Switzerland) in the case of individuals arrested on criminal charges.[63, 64]

In Finland and the Netherlands, subsequent reviews of detention are automatic. In Finland, the court will review the case on its own initiative every two weeks until the individual is released. The police, who take the decision to detain, also contact lawyers (paid for by the State) to act on behalf of detained asylum seekers. In the Netherlands, a detained asylum seeker may make a written application against

---

61   According to the Institute of Human Rights and the Association for the Prevention of Torture (*supra* note 14, p. 111), asylum seekers in French waiting zones do not have a real possibility of appealing against their detention. This is firstly because the information they receive regarding their rights and how to exercise them is either poor or totally lacking: they have one full day within which to exercise their right to appeal, but in practice this is virtually impossible for foreigners who do not speak French, are not familiar with French procedures and do not have a pre-arranged contact with a legal adviser. Secondly, as appeals do not have suspensive effect, as many as 90% of foreigners refused entry are removed before their appeals have been heard.

62   There is however a right of appeal to the Commissioner General for Aliens against a decision of non-admissibility of an asylum claim for persons detained at borders. Where the appeal is successful, the detention order will immediately be lifted.

63   The Danish Constitution (Section 71 para. 6) contains a specific reservation to the 24-hour rule in the case of foreign nationals detained under the Aliens Act. Kim Kjær also observes that a further consequence of this reservation is that court reviews are more superficial in the case of aliens: whereas a review of detention on criminal grounds is both obligatory and automatic, in the case of administratively detained foreign asylum seekers, the review is not automatic. The legality of detention is only reviewed by a court if the asylum seeker requests it; see K. Kjær in *Grundloven og menneskerettigheder i et dansk og europæisk perspektiv*, Jurist- og Økonomforbundets Forlag, 1997, p. 254 *et seq*.

64   The 96-hour time limit for judicial review of detention has also been criticised by the UN Human Rights Committee (*supra* note 6, p. 3, paragraph 15), which finds the length excessive and discriminatory, particularly in the light of the fact that in penal matters this review is guaranteed after 24 or 48 hours depending on the canton concerned.

detention to the district court, which must hear the case within two weeks and render a decision two weeks after that. If a person has been in detention for over four weeks without lodging an appeal, the court is automatically notified. In deportation cases, if deportation is still not feasible, the judge is likely to consider detention measures unfounded and order the release of the individual.

In Austria, review of detention is not automatic. The initial decision to detain is taken by the aliens police. Complaints can be submitted to the Independent Administrative Senate (an independent, quasi-judicial body) from the moment of detention until six weeks after detention, but they must be written in German, otherwise they will be dismissed for failing to conform to the required procedure. Detained asylum seekers are at a disadvantage compared with persons detained on criminal charges, as the latter will be released after 14 days if a court hearing has not taken place. Appeals against detention are rarely successful in Austria because detention orders may only be appealed on grounds of illegality, and this is rarely the case with asylum seekers.

In Germany, the legality of detention post-asylum determination is reviewed after three months. Prior to this, complaints may be lodged after 14 days, but inadequate provision of information regarding this right, coupled with language problems, means that detained asylum seekers rarely make use of this mechanism. The judge is required to examine the reasons for detention, but with up to 50 cases to be heard per day, it is commonplace for judges simply to confirm the reasons given by the detaining authorities (no fixed address, no means of support, no indication that the person concerned will depart voluntarily). In principle, the detainee has the right to respond at the hearing, with the assistance of an interpreter and a lawyer. But even where a lawyer is hired or provided, there are frequent complaints that short notice of the hearing and the brevity of the hearing itself (often no longer than three minutes) prevent the lawyer from being present.

In the UK, review mechanisms have been strongly criticised by human rights NGOs, immigration lawyers and the UN Human Rights Committee[65] on the grounds that these reviews are purely internal, with no recourse to the courts or any other impartial body. Furthermore, not only are lawyers hampered by the scant reasons officially given for detaining in the first place, but lawyers and their clients are not even present at the hearing, nor are they allowed to present their case in writing.[66]

In practice, the only real opportunity for obtaining a review of detention in the United Kingdom is to apply for bail.[67] The procedural rules in the UK have changed

---

65 *Concluding observations/comments on the fourth periodic report of the United Kingdom of Great Britain and Northern Ireland, supra* note 58.
66 *Ibid.*
67 The term "bail" is used in the UK to denote a financial deposit placed with the authorities in order to obtain conditional release and guarantee the asylum seeker's future attendance for interviews during the processing of his case.

following the introduction of the new 1996 Asylum and Immigration Act, and there are new administrative forms to be completed by all bail applicants. These forms are more complex than the previous ones, and include the requirement that a rejected bail applicant must state what has changed in his case if he re-applies. Eligibility for bail is restricted in the sense that the asylum application must be under consideration, or an appeal against a first negative decision lodged, before the person is eligible to apply. In other words, it is not possible for persons classed simply as "illegal entrants" to apply for bail. Large sums are required for bail guarantees (the average is estimated to be at around GBP 4,000, though there have been cases where bail has been refused even up to GBP 10,000), and obtaining such large sums effectively excludes the persons concerned from being entitled to welfare benefits upon release. In a recent survey conducted by Amnesty International (British Section), only 14% of asylum seekers in a sample of 150 had had a bail application heard or granted.[68] It is therefore clearly not an effective legal remedy.

V Conditions of detention[69, 70]

Although conditions in detention centres in many western European countries are described as inhuman and degrading by a number of human rights organisations, there have been important improvements in the conditions under which asylum seekers are detained in Europe over the last few years. For example, the centre at Walem in Belgium was closed down in April 1994 after conditions had been described by the European Committee for the Prevention of Torture (CPT) as "totally unacceptable" during its visit in 1993.

Sometimes, tragedy strikes before governments act. On 26 February 1995, Mr Abijou Tilaye, a 39-year old Ethiopian asylum seeker, committed suicide in a detention centre in Würzburg, Germany. He and his wife, also in detention, belonged to the Amhara ethnic group which, according to human rights organisations, is subject to persecution in Ethiopia. He had been detained for exactly six months when he died.[71]

---

68 *Cell Culture, supra* note 28, pp. 17–22.
69 Principle 6 of the BOP states that: "No person under any form of detention or imprisonment shall be subjected to torture or to cruel, inhuman or degrading treatment. No circumstance whatever may be invoked as a justification for torture or other cruel, inhuman or degrading treatment or punishment."
70 See also Chapter 9 on the mental health implications of detention.
71 According to Amnesty International, Mr Tilaye had been arrested and tortured in Ethiopia on account of his political activities. Mr Tilaye's claim in Germany was dismissed as "manifestly unfounded" on procedural grounds (failure to attend an interview and lodge an appeal), and he and his wife were placed in pre-deportation detention (the short notice given for hearings in Germany is mentioned above). Mr Tilaye refused to sign the requisite papers and was taken to the Ethiopian Embassy (the confusion between deportation and extradition proceedings has been mentioned *supra,* note 41). The

Conditions of detention and fear of deportation have resulted in suicides and attempted suicides, even by juveniles, in a number of other countries, including Austria, the Netherlands, Switzerland and the United Kingdom. In Norway, an Algerian asylum seeker died on 22 January 1996 after setting his prison cell on fire. He had been detained for ten months, although under Norwegian law an asylum seeker should not normally be held in prison for longer than 12 weeks. His detention was on the grounds of disputed identity. The Norwegian Organisation for Asylum Seekers subsequently criticised the quality of the police investigation into his identity, observing that "it took a member of the local Islamic Cultural Centre only two weeks after Mr Cheref's death to establish his true identity".

After the suicide of a young North African in the Paris *dépôt des étrangers* (a detention centre for aliens, including asylum seekers) on 14 March 1995 and an appeal by unions of lawyers, judges and human rights associations, a judge finally inspected the centre and ordered its closure (the centre was temporarily closed in May 1995 "for renovation") and the release of all the foreigners detained there. Conditions at the centre had been severely criticised by the Committee for the Prevention of Torture, which had visited it in both 1991 and 1994, between which dates none of the recommended improvements were made. The 1994 report states that "the large majority of detainees alleged never having seen a doctor, even after having explicitly requested one" and "some of them have complained of the breaking off of treatment for serious infections, notably AIDS and tuberculosis". Lack of medical screening, both for physical illnesses and for signs of trauma or suicidal intent, is universally inadequate in western Europe given the standards of care available for those at liberty.

Any improvements as a result of criticism by the Committee for the Prevention of Torture or pressure brought to bear by the media and NGOs should be acknowledged as important achievements. Continuing reports of poor conditions can only fuel speculation that the conditions themselves are used as a deliberate deterrent, encouraging detained asylum seekers to abandon their claims, and discouraging others from seeking asylum in the first place. Caritas Austria believes that "the everyday fear of detention drives people out of the country or causes psychological breakdown". Once detained, many asylum seekers in Austria resort to hunger-strike because they can be released on health grounds after 15–25 days (of the 15,070 aliens detained prior to expulsion in 1995, a total of 1,787 persons were reported to have resorted to hunger-strikes).

Improvements must also be seen against the background of the more restrictive detention legislation being introduced: in other words, the amelioration of physical

---

Ethiopian Embassy refused to issue travel documents, however, and the couple remained in detention thereafter. Although social workers informed the prison authorities that Mr Tilaye's mental state of health was very poor, he was never seen by a psychologist or psychiatrist.

CHAPTER 1   WESTERN EUROPE

conditions should not deflect attention from the essential fact that asylum seekers are incarcerated although not charged with any criminal offences, and the great majority should not be detained at all. There is inevitably a risk that efforts to promote the development of specific standards of detention for asylum seekers implicitly legitimise their detention.[72]

V.1   Detention facilities

A central question surrounding conditions of detention is whether asylum seekers are held in prisons along with other remand prisoners or whether they are held in separate facilities.[73] Unfortunately, even where they are held separately, this does not necessarily mean that conditions in the detention centres are any better than in ordinary prisons.

In the United Kingdom, the practice of holding asylum seekers in prisons is particularly prevalent, although the Home Office's own rules make it clear that detention centres are a more appropriate response than prisons. In October 1996, the UK government reported that 343 asylum seekers were at being held in prisons, unsegregated from other remand prisoners. This is officially partly due to lack of space in special detention centres, but detainees may also be transferred from centres to prisons if they are seen as "trouble-makers". Detention in prisons has thus been described as a form of "double deterrent" in that it is not only used as a threat to potential arrivals overseas, but also as a warning to other immigration detainees in centres not to disrupt routines, by going on hunger-strike, for example. Most recently, a series of hunger-strikes in Rochester prison in the United Kingdom in January 1997 attracted widespread media attention and raised the question of why the 17 hunger-strikers (and nearly 200 other asylum seekers) were held in a prison in the first place.[74] In January 1997, the Prison Service considered moving immigration and asylum detainees from prisons to a prison hulk in Portsmouth

---

72   See Working Document No. 8 by Katarina Tomasevski (senior researcher at the Danish Centre for Human Rights) for the European Seminar on Detention of Asylum Seekers in Western Europe, *International Standards of Treatment of Detained Asylum Seekers*, p. 13. Available from the Danish Refugee Council.

73   Principle 8 of the BOP states that: "Persons in detention shall be subject to treatment appropriate to their unconvicted status. Accordingly, they shall, whenever possible, be kept separate from imprisoned persons."

74   "The practice is so alien to British justice that it requires more specific justification than the Home Office's broad assertion that detention is necessary in these cases ... The law meets a need, which is to prevent those with threadbare claims to asylum from melting into the community and to counter illegal immigration rings. For the same reason, many other European countries require asylum seekers to live in supervised hostel accommodation or camps. But prison is a different matter." Editorial in The Times, *Laws of asylum – prison is not the answer for Britain's queues of asylum seekers*, 31 January 1997.

35

Harbour – a practice which has not been repeated since the dramatic experience of October 1987, when a converted car ferry holding over 100 immigration detainees broke loose from its moorings in a violent storm and began to sink.

In Finland,[75] Ireland, Italy and Portugal, there are no special facilities – prisons are always used for the small numbers of asylum seekers detained. In most regions of Austria and Switzerland, asylum seekers are detained in the same penitentiary institutions as convicted persons, but are internally segregated from them.

In Sweden, there are five detention centres where rejected asylum seekers are kept pending their deportation but, as the authorities have been increasingly faced with financial difficulties, such persons have at times been kept in ordinary prisons. One Nigerian detainee spent a total of nine months in prison, and in December 1995 there was a case of a 16-year old Somali girl detained in a prison cell. The chief warden at Kronoberg prison in Stockholm has called such cases "humiliating and degrading", pointing out that asylum seekers were neither aggressive nor had they committed a crime, and that his staff were not trained to care for this category of persons.[76] Criticism of this practice also came from the Human Rights Commissioner of the Council of Baltic Sea States. Under the new Aliens Act, which entered into force on 1 January 1997, responsibility for persons detained under aliens legislation has been transferred from the police authorities to the Swedish Immigration Board. This means that all immigration detainees should now be accommodated in special premises run by the Immigration Board.

In Germany, practice varies from one *Land* to another – some, such as Bavaria, do hold asylum seekers in prisons, whereas others, such as North Rhine-Westphalia have opened a number of special detention centres.[77] Ironically, one of these was in fact a former prison, converted in such a way as to enable it to accommodate a greater number of detainees.

---

75 Section 47 of the Finnish Aliens Act (1991) specifies that "[w[here applicable, the provisions for the treatment of prisoners on remand are to apply to aliens held in detention". The *travaux préparatoires* of the 1991 Aliens Act also state that individuals detained under the Aliens Act should be held in separate facilities and that they should not be kept in police custody or common prisons unless there are exceptional reasons. However, the 1993 amendments to the Aliens Act (639/93) stated that due to current economic difficulties it would not be possible to build separate facilities for individuals detained under the Aliens Act. All detainees are therefore being held in common remand prisons. This practice was criticised by the Parliamentary Ombudsman in a decision of 31 December 1996, in which he explicitly stated that holding such detainees in common prisons may in some cases amount to a violation of Article 5 of the *European Convention on Human Rights*. He called for the original wording of Section 47 of the Aliens Act to be restored, obliging the Finnish authorities to build separate facilities.

76 Svenska Dagbladet, 12 December 1995, reported also in Migration News Sheet, January 1996, p. 10.

77 For a detailed comparative description of Germany's individual detention centres (*Hafthaüser*), see Heinhold in *Abschiebungshaft in Deutschland – Eine Situationsbeschreibung, supra* note 21.

CHAPTER 1   WESTERN EUROPE

Meanwhile, in the Netherlands, a court (*Rechtseenheidskamer*) ruled on 2 November 1995 that asylum seekers may not be detained with criminals, and that no asylum seeker awaiting deportation may be held in a police cell for more than ten days.[78]

In France, according to the Association for the Prevention of Torture, no official list of detention centres in "waiting zones" in stations has been published, and "unofficial" detention centres may be in use.[79] In France, stowaways have been prevented from disembarking in order to submit asylum applications, and have only been able to do so through the intervention of lawyers, NGOs and as a result of media attention. The practice of confining asylum seekers on board ship is illegal, according to recent French jurisprudence. In one case involving three asylum seekers, one of whom was a minor, the judge ruled that the authorities had failed to have the detention confirmed by a court within the prescribed 96-hour time limit, counting the period of detention from the date of arrival of the ship and not from the date of transfer to the waiting zone.[80]

There are many ways in which conditions for detained asylum seekers may be counted as worse than those of criminals:[81] accommodation may be more cramped, opportunities for leisure, sports or educational activities are minimal (no-one knows how long they will stay, and there is no intrinsic purpose for their detention, such as social rehabilitation), and in practice it is difficult to enjoy visiting rights. The largest detention centre in Germany, Büren (currently accommodating an estimated 1,500 people), is situated eight km from the nearest village and there is no public transport, making it difficult for detainees to receive visitors.[82] A method known as "long distance" operates in Germany, whereby detainees may be transferred without any prior notice to centres far away from where they have friends and relatives.[83]

---

78   AWB 95/6472 and AWB 95/6282.
79   *De la prévention des traitements inhumains et dégradants en France*, supra note 14, p. 118.
80   *Ibid.*, pp. 116–118.
81   On 2 May 1996, the Swiss Federal Court ruled, *inter alia*, that persons detained while awaiting their expulsion from Switzerland must benefit from conditions more liberal than those imposed on persons with a criminal conviction.
82   Principle 15 of the BOP states that "... communication of the detained or imprisoned person with the outside world, and in particular his family or counsel, shall not be denied for more than a matter of days".
83   Principle 19 of the BOP states that: "A detained or imprisoned person shall have the right to be visited by and to correspond with, in particular, members of his family and shall be given adequate opportunity to communicate with the outside world, subject to reasonable conditions and restrictions as specified by law or lawful regulations."
    Principle 20 states that: "If a detained or imprisoned person so requests, he shall if possible be kept in a place of detention or imprisonment reasonably near his usual place of residence."
    Principle 16 states that: "Promptly after arrest and after each transfer from one place of detention or imprisonment to another, a detained or imprisoned person shall be entitled to

Conditions in the detention centre at Frankfurt airport illustrate why it is vitally important to categorise airport detention as formal detention: the centre accommodates up to 200 people at any one time, yet nobody takes responsibility for maintaining it (neither the federal authorities, the authorities of the *Land*, nor the airport authorities). Therefore it has become very dilapidated, with broken furniture, a dirty piece of carpet with a few toys on it called "the children's area", windows facing walls and poorly controlled room temperatures, insufficient staff to guarantee that detainees have supervised time in the fresh air every day, virtually no recreational facilities (a few books and one television that is often broken). After 8 p.m. everyone is locked into their rooms and a single guard is left on duty. Tensions inside the detention centre can run high, with many people falling into severe depression and attempting suicide after spending several months there.[84]

Detention conditions have been criticised by NGOs in Switzerland on a number of grounds, including failure to separate immigration and asylum detainees from other persons under arrest, overcrowding, inadequate diet and lack of contact with refugee assisting organisations. In August 1995, the Swiss Federal Court ruled for the first time in a case relating to conditions of detention. A complaint was lodged by an asylum seeker held in the wing of Luzern prison reserved for persons awaiting expulsion, where there were no proper facilities for outdoor exercise. During the five months of his detention, he had only been allowed out three times, and on each occasion he had been handcuffed. The federal judges ruled that this practice was inadmissible and that, despite the "silence of the law" on this point, a one-hour period of outdoor exercise was a minimum right. They also noted that if conditions of detention were inadequate, detainees should be released.[85]

V.2   Duration of detention

Length of detention varies considerably from one country to another, and there are differences between the maximum length of pre-admission detention and pre-deportation detention. In some cases there is no absolute maximum length of detention at all (Denmark, Finland, Greece and the UK). Generally speaking, there appears to be a trend towards increasingly long periods in detention, particularly prior to expulsion. Length of detention – and the fact that the total period to be spent in detention is unknown – is a serious cause for concern, as described above.

---

notify or to require the competent authority to notify members of his family or other appropriate persons of his choice of his arrest, detention or imprisonment and of the place where he is kept in custody."

84   Heinhold (*supra* note 21, pp. 145–146) records 26 cases of suicides in German detention centres between October 1993 and November 1996; see also C. Niekrawitz, *Erfahrungen des Flughafen-Sozialdienstes Frankfurt am Main mit dem "Flughafenverfahren" nach paragraph 18a AsylVerfahrungsGesetz*, Flughafen-Sozialdienst 1996.
85   *La détention et le traitement des demandeurs d'asile*, supra note 42, p. 11.

CHAPTER 1   WESTERN EUROPE

In France, the maximum period of "administrative retention" is 24 hours, whereas the normal length of "judicial retention" is three months (this can be extended by a judge). Under Swiss legislation introduced in December 1994, the maximum length of pre-deportation detention is three months, but if expulsion is impossible, the judge may extend detention for a further six months. This has been a cause of concern *inter alia* to the UN Human Rights Committee, which has noted that "these time limits are considerably in excess of what is necessary, particularly in the case of detention pending expulsion".[86]

In Germany, the maximum length of pre-deportation detention is three months, but this may be extended for up to 18 months. However, there is no limit to the detention of rejected asylum seekers under the airport procedure. In a significant ruling concerning the detention of an asylum seeker in the transit area of an airport, the regional Higher Court (*Oberlandesgericht*) of the *Land* of Hessen ruled on 5 November 1996 that a rejected asylum seeker who cannot be sent back to his home country may not be detained for months at the airport. In the case in question, an Indian asylum seeker rejected under the accelerated asylum procedure on 6 March 1996 was detained for eight months at Frankfurt airport after two attempts to repatriate him (on 7 and 19 March 1996) failed because of inadequate travel documents.[87]

In its ruling, the *Oberlandesgericht* observed that a foreigner may only be kept in an airport during the time when his asylum application is being processed. The law provides for a maximum of 19 days of "administrative detention" at the airport, a period which may be extended only if an appeal is pending before the Federal Constitutional Court (*Bundesverfassungsgericht*). If an appeal is not pending, the detention may only be extended by a court order.

In practice, repatriation can take many months, but the law is silent on the question of how long rejected asylum seekers awaiting repatriation may be kept in the transit area. Only if repatriation is deemed impossible will the authorities allow entry into Germany with "tolerated" status (*Duldung*), but such decisions are discretionary. The longest known detention in the transit zone of Frankfurt airport is that of a rejected Algerian asylum seeker who was held for 258 days.

In Austria, the maximum length of pre-deportation detention was increased from three to six months in 1992. Amnesty International is aware of a number of

---

86   *Concluding Observation/Comments on the initial report of Switzerland* (CCPR/C/81/Add.70), adopted in November 1996, para. 15.

87   Case reference AZ.: 20 W 352/96, reported in Migration News Sheet, December 1996, p. 12. According to the editor, "one highly significant aspect of the present case is the kind of court that has handed down the ruling ... Such courts (OLG) [*Oberlandesgericht*] deal with penal matters as opposed to administrative ones. The fact that these courts have ruled on the question of keeping asylum seekers in the transit area of an airport implies an implicit recognition that they were held under 'detention' as opposed to 'administrative retention'".

cases where, if an asylum seeker cannot be deported and must be released from detention after six months, he runs the danger of being re-arrested in another *Land* of Austria and placed in detention again – for a further six months.[88] In December 1994, the Constitutional Court ruled for the first time that six months was the total amount of detention allowed, but Amnesty has not yet seen significant improvements in practice in response to this decision. Now a new proposal unfortunately could mean that it would be permitted to re-detain an alien for further six months after a period of two years. According to lawyers and NGOs, the average length of such a detention in Austria was estimated to be four–five months in 1994, the same as the figure for 1993, but an increase in respect of 1992, when the average length of detention was three months (this was also the maximum length of detention under the former Aliens Police Law).

In the United Kingdom the 1971 Immigration Act gives power to the authorities to detain for an indefinite period. The Home Office admitted in July 1995 that there were at that time 14 asylum seekers who had been detained in excess of one year. According to figures given by the British Refugee Council (BRC),[89] the number of asylum applicants detained for one month or longer steadily increased from 120 persons in April 1991 to 486 in October 1994.

The case of Mr Karamjit Singh Chahal, a Sikh asylum seeker in the United Kingdom, was widely reported in the British press, drawing attention to the long detention endured by many asylum seekers. The UK government suspected him of being associated with a terrorist organisation in India. He subsequently lodged an application accusing the UK government of violations of a number of articles of the European Convention on Human Rights. The Human Rights Commission found *inter alia* a violation of Article 5(1) (right to liberty and security of person) and Article 8 (right to family life), and a decision by the European Court of Human Rights was rendered on 15 November 1996.[90] In its ruling, the Court found no violation of Article 5(1). The Court did not consider the period of six years and three months that Mr Chahal was in fact detained, but only the three and a half year period until the government refrained from deportation in compliance with a request from the Commission, and found that "none of the periods taken by the courts or the executive ... could be regarded as excessive". However, the Court did find a violation of Article 5(4) (requiring that the deprivation of liberty be subject to effective judicial control) because the domestic courts had no access to the evidence of the alleged threat to national security, the stated reason for detention.

---

88   *Innocently Illegal*, Amnesty International, December 1994.
89   British Refugee Council, Factsheet No. 4, February 1995.
90   Case of *Chahal* v. *United Kingdom*, application No. 22414/93, report of the Commission of 27 June 1995, judgment of the European Court of Human Rights No. 70/1995/576/662 of 15 November 1996, to be published in Reports of Judgments and Decisions for 1996, Carl Heymans Verlag, Köln.

CHAPTER 1   WESTERN EUROPE

The dissenting opinions of some of the judges reveal widely diverging views on the complaints under Article 5. One judge acknowledged that the initial decision to detain was lawful, but nevertheless criticised it as being "clearly excessive". Two others found it "difficult to understand" how the Court could rule unanimously that Article 5(4) and Article 13 had been violated, whilst concluding by a majority of 13 to 6 that Article 5(1) had not, in other words, that the detention of Mr Chahal for more than six years did not constitute arbitrary deprivation of liberty. In the view of another judge, Mr Chahal was treated "more severely than a criminal sentenced to a term of imprisonment". The judge underlined that "the principle contained in Article 5 of immediately bringing a detained person before a court is intended to protect liberty and not to serve as a 'cover' for detention".[91]

V.3   Women and children[92]

Where the detention of women and children is unavoidable, they must be given special facilities. In Austria, women are held separately from men and their cells are supposed to be kept private from male staff, though in two centres no female staff are employed. The situation is different in each province and in each detention facility; some minor improvements have been reported, in the Salzburg area for example. In Belgium, similarly, there is separate accommodation in detention for women and children. In November 1993, a Brussels court ruled that detention of a woman asylum seeker and her new-born baby in the Walem detention centre (a converted 19th century fort) in a windowless room measuring 1m60 by 2m20 with no door or curtain was a violation of Article 3 of the European Convention on Human Rights (inhuman and degrading treatment).[93]

In the Sandholm detention facility in Denmark, there is a separate wing for women and couples, and in the case of families with children, it is only the head of the family who is detained, whilst the others are accommodated in the adjacent Red Cross reception centre and are allowed to visit for several hours every day.

A further issue which is central to any assessment of conditions and to many NGO campaigns for reform is that of the minimum age of detainees. Again comparisons should be made with the rights of citizens in the host population. Under 16s who are non-nationals, including asylum seekers, may be detained according to the Austrian Aliens Act, whereas the national penal code otherwise prohibits the detention of any Austrian child under 16. The Austrian authorities have given as grounds for detention the risk that these minors could form street gangs if left at liberty.

---

91   Reported *inter alia* in Migration News Sheet, December 1996, p. 9.
92   See ECRE's *Position Paper on Refugee Children*, November 1996.
93   Tribunal civil de Bruxelles (référés), 25 November 1993, Jurisprudence de Liège, Mons et Bruxelles, 93/1305.

In the United Kingdom, an Inspector must authorise the detention in a regular prison of women or under 18s; in Denmark, under 18s are rarely detained.

In Germany, the minimum age for detention is 14, and children under 16 are meant to be detained only in exceptional circumstances, in separate juvenile centres. NGOs dispute that this is in fact the practice, however, and the UNHCR survey on detention of asylum seekers in Europe mentions 52 minors found detained in one location in September 1993. Until mid-1994, unaccompanied refugee children arriving at Frankfurt airport were taken into care by welfare agencies in Frankfurt and assigned a guardian. They were then placed in a children's home pending a decision on the case. However, since a new law came into effect, unaccompanied minors have been subject to the same detention as adults, though at they are now accommodated separately. At a news conference on 15 August 1995, the Green Party strongly denounced such detention of children. One member of the Green Party said that children as young as two years old had been detained by armed officials.[94]

In Sweden, since a law amendment which took effect on 1 January 1997, the minimum age for any detention is now 18. According to a representative of the Swedish government delegation responding to questions put by members of the Human Rights Committee in its consideration of the fourth periodic report of Sweden, out of a total of 4,177 detainees, 79 had been children under the age of 16 (the legal age limit at that time) and virtually all these cases of detention were in connection with the enforcement of an expulsion order. "Of the 79 children, 41 had been held for less than 24 hours, 27 had been held for one to three days, and ten had been held for longer periods."[95] In 1995, Sweden placed 57 teenagers aged 16–17 in detention.[96] One case which was of concern to the Swedish Red Cross was that of an unaccompanied Afghan minor, who arrived in Sweden, where he had an uncle, on 10 March 1995. Despite displaying symptoms of strong anxiety, hysteria and a fear of death, he was held in a detention centre until 8 April 1995, when he was removed to Kenya (where he had no relatives) on "safe third country" grounds. He was denied entry into Kenya and detained in the airport for three months before being transferred to a centre for unaccompanied minors. Following intervention by UNHCR, he was finally readmitted to Sweden in November 1996 under the Swedish resettlement programme.[97]

---

[94] Reported in Migration News Sheet, September 1995, p. 5.
[95] Human Rights Committee, summary record of the 1456th meeting, CCPR/C/SR 1456, p. 16.
[96] *Swedish Refugee Policy in Global Perspective*, Refugee Policy Commission, Ministry of Labour, August 1996, English summary of report (SOU 1996:75), p. 221.
[97] Case documented by UNHCR Stockholm in connection with the *Report on "Safe Third Country" Policies in Europe* by the Danish Refugee Council, *supra* note 9.

CHAPTER 1   WESTERN EUROPE

In the United Kingdom, the British Refugee Council reported at least 18 cases of asylum seeking minors under the age of 17 being detained for periods of up to six months in 1994. The BRC was informed of 28 cases of minors held in detention in 1995, and 22 in 1996. The Home Office would dispute these figures on the grounds that they would not accept the BRC's assessment of age in all cases. According to the BRC, however, there were only two or three cases out of the total 48 where the organisation was in any doubt. The government argues that such detention was only resorted to as a form of emergency accommodation. The frequency with which this explanation has been produced is questioned by the BRC's Children's Division.

In France, where the minimum age for detention is 15, France Terre d'Asile has reported the case of a 12-year-old unaccompanied Somali boy who had been detained in the "waiting zone" at Roissy airport and was subsequently deported to Kenya, where he "disappeared" until finally reappearing in Italy some months later.[98]

Disagreements between governments and NGOs have also arisen with regard to the issue of age assessment and medical testing for the purpose of detention. This is a more general problem affecting the rights of asylum seekers whose documents may have been falsified to present them as an adult for the purpose of travelling, but it is particularly important when the age assessment will make the difference between detention and liberty. What should be, but is not, beyond dispute is that the rights contained in the UN Convention on the Rights of the Child should apply to any person below the age of 18 on the territory of a signatory State, without discrimination as to the child's legal status.

V.4   Treatment by staff and staff training measures

There have been disturbing reports of violence and racist abuse towards detained asylum seekers in several European countries. Allegations concerning mistreatment by staff are of course very difficult to verify. It is clear, however, from the inquest findings that Mr Omasese Lumumba died in a British prison at the hands of staff using disproportionate force. Amnesty International has called in vain for a full, impartial inquiry into his death.[99] The UN Human Rights Committee is also "gravely concerned at incidences of the use of excessive force in the execution of deportation orders", and has recommended that "all those who are involved in the detention of prisoners be made fully aware of the international obligations of the

---

98   Case documented by France Terre d'Asile for the Danish Refugee Council's *Report on "Safe Third Country" Policies in Europe, supra* note 9.
99   See Amnesty's report of November 1993 (EUR 45/13/93).

State Party concerning the treatment of detainees, including the 1955 United Nations Standard Minimum Rules for the Treatment of Prisoners".[100]

In Belgium, a number of organisations have denounced brutal deportation methods, strip searching and other degrading practices, and the unnecessary use of isolation cells. In 1994, the Belgian Health Minister also criticised the lack of regulations concerning the use of isolation cells and the conditions for detainees, some of whom had been held for over ten days in windowless cells measuring 1m50 by 3m, equipped only with a bed and without any sanitation.[101] The European Committee for the Prevention of Torture (CPT) has highlighted the maltreatment of Albanians awaiting deportation from Greece. In Denmark, allegations of racist abuse by prison staff led to reforms after the intervention of the Ombudsman in 1990.

The 1994 CPT report on the conditions of detention of foreigners in police buildings in Paris expressed concerns over police brutality: "the persistence of a certain number of allegations of bad treatment (slaps, punches, beatings with truncheons) indicates that the vigilance of the French authorities in this matter must remain constant." The Observatoire international des prisons[102] and the Association for the Prevention of Torture (APT)[103] have documented numerous cases of brutal treatment in Switzerland, including in airports, and human rights organisations believe that there have also been cases of sexual abuse.

The CPT has more generally commented that problems arise from the lack of special staff training on the issue of asylum, from cultural differences, and from the inability to understand the anger and depression which such persons, detained without criminal grounds or adequate appeal rights, inevitably express. While UNHCR and the International Institute of Humanitarian Law in San Remo have organised training courses for border officials, which should improve the treatment of those detained at the border, less attention has so far been given to the training of staff in detention centres and prisons. In Italy, the border police have the task of dealing with asylum seekers and are at present not given training to deal with vulnerable groups, such as children and torture victims.

---

100 See the *Concluding Observations/Comments on the fourth periodic report, supra* note 58. The 1955 UN Standard Minimum Rules for the Treatment of Prisoners are reproduced in full in Appendix II.2 to this book.
101 According to the Observatoire international des prisons (*supra* note 42, p. 4), detainees placed in isolation cells included not only persons who were violent or posed a threat to other detainees, but also people who had refused to board a plane at the moment of expulsion, or who had an administrative problem (lack of papers, refusal by the authorities in the country of origin to readmit them etc.) in connection with their expulsion. The organisation believes that practice has changed, partly as a result of media attention.
102 *Ibid.*, pp. 12–14.
103 *Suisse: violences inadmissibles et renvois illégaux à l'aéroport de Genève*, APT, May 1995.

CHAPTER 1   WESTERN EUROPE

Both in some German *Länder* and in the United Kingdom private security firms with no special training in refugee or immigration matters are being used to staff detention centres for asylum seekers. This practice raises serious questions of accountability and has been criticised by the UN Human Rights Committee in the above-mentioned comments of July 1995 on the report submitted by the United Kingdom: "The Committee is concerned that the practice of the State Party in contracting out to the commercial sector core State activities which involve the use of force and the detention of persons weakens the protection of rights under the Covenant [on Civil and Political Rights]."

Some countries are nevertheless aware that caring for detained asylum seekers requires special skills and knowledge. In Denmark, for example, staff at the special centre for detained asylum seekers at Sandholm now follow special training courses to heighten their awareness of potential cultural and communications problems, and the regime has been changed to involve staff in advisory, educational and leisure activities in order to establish better contact with detainees.

VI   Final comments

Despite the many exhortations contained in national and international rules, allowing for detention of asylum seekers only "under exceptional circumstances", "where there are serious grounds", "giving individually motivated reasons", "as a last resort" or "where it is necessary to achieve the purpose", human rights organisations have good reason to believe that the great majority of detained asylum seekers in western Europe today are being deprived of their liberty on the basis of arbitrary decisions and unclear legal procedures and practices.

The cost of detaining in human terms cannot be over-stated (see Chapter 9 of this book). The detained asylum seeker is prey to a sense of insecurity, of being an object in an uncertain process. The feelings of powerlessness, passivity, humiliation, fear of the unknown and the possibility of being returned to the country where he or she may be at risk of persecution, result in depression, aggression, even self-harm or suicide. One detainee described his experience in detention as follows:

"During my stay ... I found the situation like being jailed for life. Nobody informed me about the progress of my case; no court recommended me to be detained; I was only told I was not entitled to bail rights. All I could do was sit and wait. Some of us chose hunger strike as a means to draw attention to our plight; others saw suicide as a way out of their predicament ... The ordeal of my detention has not been easy to recover from ... Some detainees continue to fight after release to regain their normal state. One thing I know for sure: nervousness never leaves you."[104]

The economic cost would also appear to be high, but again, exact figures are not readily available. For example, in Germany the cost has been estimated at DM 116 per asylum seeker per day by the Federal Ministry of the Interior, which on the basis of available figures would amount to a yearly total of over DM 50 million. In 1996 a warden reported the cost at his centre to be DM 160 per person without including any capital outlay.[105] In 1996, the high cost of detaining asylum seekers at Frankfurt airport became the subject of some dispute between the regional and federal authorities. In July, the regional government of the *Land* of Hessen sent Bonn a bill for DM 8.1 million for costs incurred for holding asylum seekers at its international airport since 1986. The Regional Ministry for the Family argued that these asylum seekers had not yet entered the country and were therefore not within the territory of Hessen. The Federal Chancellor rejected this argument. As Frankfurt airport is the largest in Germany, the *Land* of Hessen decided to draw up a burden-sharing proposal aimed at distributing these costs amongst all the German *Länder*.[106]

In the United Kingdom, according to figures released by the Home Office, the total cost of detention rose from GBP 1.2 million to GBP 7.8 million between 1984 and 1993, and by early January 1997 official estimates put the cost at GBP 20 million annually.[107] In 1996, the Home Office estimated that the average weekly cost of detaining an asylum seeker in an immigration service detention centre was GBP 600. The cost of detention in police or prison cells ranges from GBP 298 to GBP 874 per night.[108] One prison's own Visitors' Board stated in its Annual Report for 1994 that holding asylum seekers in prisons "constitutes an improper use of Prison Service resources and taxpayers' money".[109]

---

[104] Quoted in *Detained without trial: a survey of Immigration Act detention* by Mark Ashford, Joint Council for the Welfare of Immigrants, 1993, pp. 60–61.
[105] Money and valuables are confiscated from detained asylum seekers in Germany to meet the cost of detention.
[106] Reported in Migration News Sheet, August 1996, p. 10.
[107] Part of the cost may have been offset by income generated from carrier sanctions: in a written answer to the House of Commons of 30 October 1996, it was revealed that fines totalling GBP 97.6 million had been imposed on over 440 airlines and shipping companies since the introduction of the Immigration (Carriers' Liability) Act in March 1987. The UK government has been accused of sending the bill for detention costs directly to the airline companies which originally brought the asylum seeker to the country. Where the airline is state-owned, this is tantamount to charging the asylum seeker's country of origin. See *Cell Culture, supra* note 28, pp. 29 and 41.
[108] *The Guardian*, 25 July 1995.
[109] HMPrison Wandsworth: Board of Visitors Annual Report for 1994, quoted in *Prisoners without a Voice, supra* note 24, p. 59.

CHAPTER 1   WESTERN EUROPE

In the light of these human and financial costs, it seems reasonable to ask whether detention can be described as effective in fulfilling its stated purpose, which, apart from verifying identity, is primarily to prevent asylum seekers from absconding. It is a cause for consternation that no clear criteria for identifying those individuals most likely to abscond are prescribed by law anywhere in western Europe, and that there are virtually no government statistics to indicate that the scale of non-compliance and disappearance by asylum seekers warrants such a drastic policy.[110] In Germany, practitioners claim that up to 40% of persons detained for the purpose of deportation are subsequently released without being removed from the country.[111]

Alternative measures to detention,[112] such as surrender of identity and travel documents, bail, reporting to the police or compulsory residence, do exist and are used by a number of western European countries (although penalties for failing to comply with the terms of release may be high in certain countries: detention, a fine or even dismissal of the asylum application). Furthermore, the use of less restrictive measures than detention as a first option is a legal requirement in most European countries. A number of countries have reported, through UNHCR, that reporting restrictions have proved as effective as detention. In 1994, out of 3,950 asylum seekers temporarily admitted to the UK and whose appeal against a negative decision was pending, or who were awaiting removal after a final negative, only 280 were reported to have absconded.[113]

Moreover, although NGOs acknowledge that States have the right to control the entry of aliens into their territory, it cannot be argued that an increase in the numbers of detained asylum seekers is simply a reflection of increasing arrivals of asylum seekers – in fact, the number of arrivals has been either stable or falling in most western European countries since 1993.[114]

---

110   In February 1995, in reply to a request in Parliament for statistics on absconders, the UK Home Office Minister stated that between 1992 and 1994, only 220 asylum seekers were known to have absconded or were classified as missing, a percentage of 0.59%.
111   *Abschiebungshaft in Deutschland – Eine Situationsbeschreibung*, supra note 21, p.148.
112   See ECRE's *Research Paper on Alternatives to Detention* in Appendix VII.2 to this book.
113   Source: Home Office Minister, Nicholas Baker, in a written reply to the House of Commons, 22 March 1995.
114   It would be difficult to prove any correlation between national asylum application figures and detention policy. For example, the Netherlands and the United Kingdom both recorded increases of 48.5% and 47% respectively in the number of applications in 1994 despite having very divergent detention policies: in the Netherlands the Aliens Act was revised in January 1994, reducing the maximum period of detention to four weeks and making detention a rare occurrence, whereas in the United Kingdom there is at present no limit to the length of detention, and hundreds of asylum seekers are detained. Yet the Netherlands recorded a decrease from 52,600 asylum seekers to only 29,260 in 1995, whereas the UK continued to record an increase during the same period.

Detention may seem to be expedient as a means of securing the presence of asylum seekers at all stages of the determination procedure – it may in some cases be a cheaper option than providing alternative accommodation and using other, less restrictive methods. But in the words of the Nordic scholar on refugee questions, Atle Grahl-Madsen:

> "Detention may not be resorted to just for the convenience of the authorities. Such a measure must, in order to be legal, really be deemed necessary. It does not suffice that detention is considered convenient for the police or immigration authorities. Under the terms of Article 31(2) [of the Geneva Convention], the authorities have to accept inconvenience."[115]

Continued failure by governments to use less restrictive alternatives to detention and to countenance implementation of the many other recommendations advanced by UNHCR and human rights organisations inevitably leads critics in the NGO community to the conclusion that detention is indeed being used by western European States alongside stringent entry policies in an effort to deter asylum seekers from seeking protection in Europe.

---

115 Atle Grahl-Madsen, *The Status of Refugees in International Law*, Sijthoff, Leiden, 1972, p. 418.

Chapter 2 Detention of Asylum Seekers in Central and Eastern Europe

By Jane Hughes and Peter Vedel Kessing

Contents

Part I Asylum background – Developments since 1989
Part II Central Europe: II.1 Introduction – II.2 Legal basis for detention – II.3 Statistics – II.4 Detention facilities – II.5 Detention and the determination procedure – II.5.1 Pre-admission detention and airport detention – II.5.2 Detention and other restrictions on freedom of movement during the determination procedure – II.5.3 Pre-deportation detention – II.6 Rights in detention – II.7 Conditions of detention
Part III Eastern Europe – Russia and the Commonwealth of Independent States: III.1 Transit migration – III.2 Refugee legislation and the legal basis for detention – III.3 Conditions of detention
Part IV The Baltic States: IV.1 The Baltic States in transition – IV.2 The Baltic States as transit countries – IV.3 Illegal immigrants and asylum seekers – IV.4 Lithuania – IV.5 Latvia – IV.6 Estonia
Part V Conclusion

I Asylum background – Developments since 1989

The gradual transformation of the central and eastern European countries (CEECs) from refugee producing to refugee receiving countries over the past decade has called for the introduction of new legislation and a complete overhaul of existing institutions and structures. This has been taking place against the background of unprecedented political and economic reforms with far-reaching social effects, including increased unemployment, the rapid impoverishment of large sections of society and a widespread sense of insecurity and uncertainty about the future. Emerging legislation and practice regarding asylum seekers in general still varies greatly among the 20 or more CEECs, and only recently has attention begun to be focused on detention as an issue of concern in some of these countries.[1]

---

1 Detention of asylum seekers was cited as a particular protection problem by the majority

Although it is assumed (certainly in the west) that the CEECs will come to emulate the detention policies and practices of their neighbours to the west – for good or for bad – one must be wary of drawing hasty parallels between the situation in the two "halves" of Europe. There are a number of distinctive elements common to the CEECs which set them apart from the countries of western Europe and which need to be borne in mind in order for the issue of detention to be seen in context.

First and foremost among these is, as already mentioned, the status of refugee legislation itself. The development of refugee policies and procedures is very recent in central and eastern Europe. Although the majority of countries have acceded to the 1951 Geneva Convention and its 1967 Protocol,[2] national refugee laws – where they have been adopted – are only fully operational in a few countries.[3]

To some extent, the differing rates of development of refugee legislation reflect the sheer scale and pressure of the internal economic and social problems experienced by the countries concerned during the transition to democracy – according to some analysts, demographic changes of the magnitude experienced since 1989 can only be compared with situations of famine and war.[4] There are vast numbers of people seeking protection within the region, including internally displaced and "stateless" persons, although it is impossible to estimate the full scale of the problem.[5] In addition, local ethnic tensions that had been suppressed by totalitarian regimes have exploded into open conflict, in some cases (notably the civil war in the former Yugoslavia) with wider European and international reverberations.

Differences in human rights history and traditions also play their part. Public attitudes to refugees are broadly similar right across Europe, western and eastern:

---

of the speakers at the *International Symposium on Protection of Refugees in Central and Eastern Europe*, in Sofia in 1994; see the Report and Proceedings of the Symposium, UNHCR, European Series, Volume 1 No. 1, April 1995.

2   Exceptions are Belarus and Ukraine.
3   Notably the Czech Republic, which as a consequence saw a 52% increase in asylum applications between 1995 and 1996, and Poland, which recorded an increase in applications from 843 in 1995 to 3,295 in 1996; see the *1997 World Refugee Survey*, US Committee for Refugees, pp. 179 and 201.
4   See G.A. Cornia and R. Paniccià in *The Demographic Impact of Sudden Impoverishment: Eastern Europe During the 1989–94 Transition*, Innocenti Occasional Papers Economic Policy Series No. 49, UNICEF International Child Development Centre, July 1995, p. 2.
5   In Ukraine, for example, refugees constitute only a small part of the major migration phenomenon affecting the country since its independence in 1991: more than 1.4 million people have arrived in Ukraine following the break-up of the Soviet Union (approximately 1.1 million persons returning from former Soviet republics and 300,000 ethnic Germans and Jews returning from countries outside the Commonwealth of Independent Sates (CIS)), and there are more than 150,000 internally displaced people as a result of the Chernobyl nuclear disaster. Information based on the Danish Refugee Council's *Report on "Safe Third Country" Policies in Europe*, to be published in 1997.

CHAPTER 2   CENTRAL AND EASTERN EUROPE

famine and civil war in other countries produce an immediate humanitarian response everywhere, yet throughout Europe this is offset by active or passive resistance to the arrival of people from other parts of the world. However, there are some significant ways in which attitudes in central and eastern Europe differ from those in western Europe. In particular, xenophobia (including "hate speech") is expressed more openly than in the west in public and on the media. It should, however, be remembered that in the immediate period after the political changes of 1989, positive attitudes towards refugees were often expressed by former dissidents, reflecting gratitude towards the world community for the reception of refugees from central and eastern Europe in the previous decades.

The most fundamental difference between the CEECs and western European countries is the phenomenon of transit migration: asylum tends to be requested only when all opportunities for proceeding to western Europe have been cut off.[6] Thus where asylum seekers' freedom of movement is restricted, this is not so much to prevent them establishing themselves illegally in the country as to prevent them from moving on to western Europe. As a result of readmission agreements (none of which make special provisions for persons in need of protection) and in the absence of genuine burden-sharing arrangements, the countries of central and eastern Europe are bearing the brunt of western Europe's restrictive asylum policies, "safe third country" policies in particular.

Finally, it must be remembered that NGO activity in the region still faces considerable challenges.[7] In particular, public acceptance of NGOs is low in some countries and a working relationship with the government can be difficult to establish and maintain. These difficulties, and the consequent financial and staffing restraints, mean that NGOs in the region are even less able than their western counterparts to collect reliable data on all aspects of a refugee situation which is in constant change and to draw attention to specific issues such as detention.

This chapter is based largely on information provided, in the form of either written reports or telephone interviews, by local NGOs and refugee experts or, where NGO activities are limited, local UNHCR branch offices. The section on the Baltic States is also based on the first-hand work experience of one of the authors in those countries. The aim is to give a general overview of detention practice in the region, rather than a detailed country-by-country description – for this, readers are referred to the 1995 UNHCR survey on detention of asylum seekers in Europe,[8]

---

6   The causes of this are discussed in *Promotion of Refugee Protection in Central and Eastern Europe: Report on Activities October 1992–June 1993*, European Council on Refugees and Exiles (ECRE), August 1993.
7   For a fuller discussion of this see *Promotion of Refugee Protection in Central and Eastern Europe: Report on Activities August 1993–July 1995*, ECRE, October 1995, section 3.5.
8   *Detention of Asylum-Seekers in Europe*, European Series, Volume 1 No. 4, October 1995, UNHCR Geneva.

with the caveat that the situation is fluid, as legislation is slowly evolving and practice is changing accordingly. It should also be pointed out that information on the region is patchy, with a considerable amount of data available on some countries and virtually none on others.

For the purposes of the present chapter, the information is presented by placing the CEECs into three broad groups based on geographical proximity and cultural and legal similarities:

i) central Europe (Poland, the Czech Republic, the Slovak Republic, Hungary, Slovenia, Romania and Bulgaria), where refugee legislation is relatively well-developed and where practices are increasingly modelled on those of western Europe;[9]

ii) Russia and the other countries of the Commonwealth of Independent States (CIS) where, despite major variations, there are common elements, including the legal system and social factors;

iii) the Baltic Republics, whose geographical location has turned them into buffer States between east and west, warranting special consideration.

The countries of the former Yugoslavia and Albania are not included in this chapter because of the exceptional internal conditions prevailing there.

II Central Europe

II.1 Introduction

Detention of asylum seekers has recently become an issue in several central European countries. At the beginning of the nineties, the countries of the region were anxious to take on the full range of international obligations in the humanitarian and human rights fields. In part they displayed this by adopting relaxed policies on refugee questions. In addition, many countries of the region were unable for financial reasons to accommodate asylum seekers or to deport people whose applications for status had been turned down. More recently, however, partly as a response to developments in the European Union, they have been taking a firmer line on refugee questions in general and in some cases this is reflected in an increased use of detention. It is common for people to be detained for short periods by border guards before being returned to the country they have just left. Longer term restrictions on the freedom of movement of people who have attempted to

---

9   In terms of economic and political development, including parliamentary democracy, some commentators would draw a further dividing line to the south-east, placing Bulgaria and Romania in the same category as their Balkan neighbours in the former Yugoslavia or with the successors of the Soviet Union to the east.

CHAPTER 2   CENTRAL AND EASTERN EUROPE

cross a border illegally are widespread. Most noticeably, the region has seen a considerable growth in the phenomenon of people being stranded in airport transit zones or held in hostels which are considered to be an extension of the transit zone. It should be added that conditions in some camps or centres for asylum seekers are so restrictive that in practice they may be considered as a form of detention.

II.2   Legal basis for detention

Most asylum seekers would appear to be detained under provisions contained in the aliens legislation of the countries of central Europe, usually in connection with illegal entry or residence. In Hungary, the 1994 Aliens Act contains provisions restricting the freedom of movement of foreigners and introduces two forms of detention or "detention-like" measures: compulsory residence in a designated place and alien regulatory custody ("ARC").[10] Hungarian human rights organisations have stated that certain provisions of the 1994 Aliens Act conflict with the government decree for its execution (promulgated on 30 April 1994). Other organisations have also criticised the legislation for being ambiguous and arbitrarily applied.[11] In particular, the border guards enjoy considerable powers of discretion in the interpretation and application of rules. Since the issuing of another decree on 6 January 1995, "regulatory" detention can take place in prisons, whereas previously it was only possible to hold foreigners in police cells. Foreigners who have attempted to evade expulsion or have failed to respect residence requirements may be detained for five days. Detention may be prolonged by a local court and must be automatically reviewed if it exceeds 30 days. There is no maximum length of detention, which is a cause for concern among human rights organisations.

In Poland, aliens found guilty by a competent court of the offence of illegal border crossing may be imprisoned under the provisions of Section 288 of the Polish Penal Code. Asylum seekers who are prosecuted are usually repeat offenders who have made several attempts to cross the border illegally or who have engaged in other more serious offences, such as human trafficking. UNHCR reports that such cases are not numerous. In a March 1995 amendment to the Polish Aliens Act of 1963, the police and border guards were granted the right to detain foreigners

---

10   It should be noted that due to the geographical reservation made by Hungary to the 1951 Geneva Convention (which at the time of writing had not been lifted by the Hungarian Parliament), non-European aliens seeking asylum in Hungary are placed in a determination procedure conducted by the UNHCR branch office in Budapest. Most non-Europeans, however, only submit their applications for asylum when deportation proceedings are initiated against them on the grounds of illegal entry or stay, and many therefore find themselves detained as illegal entrants; see *Detention of Asylum-Seekers in Europe*, supra note 8, p. 138.
11   *La détention et le traitement des demandeurs d'asile – Belgique, Hongrie, Suisse*, Observatoire international des prisons, December 1995, p. 7.

entering the country illegally and to hold them for up to 48 hours. The Aliens Act of 1963 (as subsequently amended) also incorporates the legal concept of detention pending deportation. This provides for two forms of deprivation of liberty: detention and temporary arrest.[12] When the *Voivod* (Provincial Authority) decides to expel an alien, the Public Prosecutor may issue a 90-day detention order. Detention in the administrative context is resorted to on grounds prescribed by law to verify the identity of asylum seekers or to determine the elements on which the asylum claim is based.

In Romania, the Law concerning the Status and the Regime of Foreigners was adopted in April 1996 and entered into force in May 1996, but is still not fully implemented. It contains no reference to universal principles regarding fair and efficient asylum procedures, nor to the 1951 Geneva Convention or the 1967 Protocol, but it does provide for detention prior to "removal" upon the order of the Minister of the Interior of foreigners who fail to observe legal provisions regarding aliens. This would appear to conflict with Section 19 of the 1991 Romanian Constitution, which states that "expulsion" or "extradition" must be decided by a court, which must give precedence to international human rights provisions when taking such a decision.

In the Czech Republic, apart from an initial 24-hour period of confinement in order for the Aliens Police to prepare the asylum application and a period of quarantine (normally about 21 days), there are no legal provisions concerning detention of asylum seekers for the purpose of the refugee determination procedure, and detention is only referred to in the context of criminal law (Criminal Procedure Law of 1961, as amended).

In Slovenia, a new Asylum Act is being prepared, but at present there are no specific legislative or administrative provisions allowing for the detention of asylum seekers. Foreigners who entered the country illegally and cannot be expelled under a readmission agreement may find themselves detained under the 1991 Law on Foreigners (which does not define the term "asylum seeker").

In Bulgaria, the border police are not issued with specific instructions on how to deal with asylum seekers and are not trained in refugee law. They therefore continue to apply the Law on the Stay of Foreigners rather than the Refugee Ordinance from 1994 – which does not provide for detention of asylum seekers – and thus do not make a distinction between illegal immigrants and asylum seekers. As a consequence, foreigners (including asylum seekers) who are undocumented, have false documents or have no visa are subject to routine detention, sometimes for longer periods (see Section II.5.1 on pre-admission detention and airport detention below). Detention is often followed by summary deportation without consideration of asylum claims on their merits.

---

12   UNHCR, *Detention of Asylum-Seekers in Europe*, supra note 8, pp. 158–159.

CHAPTER 2   CENTRAL AND EASTERN EUROPE

In Slovakia, the Refugee Act of November 1995 is not yet implemented, and asylum seekers may in practice be detained under the provisions of the 1995 Act (No. 73/1995) on the Stay of Foreigners. Detention normally occurs at the borders with either the Czech Republic or Ukraine. As in some western European countries, restrictions on freedom of movement may also be regarded in some instances as measures akin to detention, however: under the 1992 Aliens Law, asylum seekers are encouraged, but not forced, to remain in reception centres provided by the Ministry of the Interior. If they leave the centres (and in some cases they require authorisation to do so), access to state benefits will be withdrawn and they may be subject to deportation according to internal regulations of the Ministry of the Interior.

The practice of detaining asylum seekers in the transit zones of airports is widespread in the region, although this may not be recognised as detention as such by the authorities. This is the case in both Romania and Bulgaria (see Section II.5 on detention and the determination procedure below). Human rights organisations maintain that airport detention prior to removal is illegal.[13]

In practice, detention may in some instances be based on internal regulations of the authorities which are often not published. In Bulgaria, the Refugee Ordinance of 1994 makes no explicit provision for the detention of asylum seekers, and it is assumed by UNHCR that, in practice, the specific basis for detention of asylum seekers is set out in unpublished internal regulations of the Ministry of the Interior.[14] In Romania, where the drafting of refugee legislation proved to be a slow process, interdepartmental guidelines were used prior to the adoption of legislation in 1996. These were drafted in 1992 and were not adopted as legal instruments. They proved to be inadequate, resulting in frequent violations of asylum seekers' rights. According to the International Helsinki Federation, the governmental Romanian Committee for Migration Issues (CRPM) admitted that the guidelines were not legally binding, although the CRPM had partially adopted them and used them in daily practice.[15]

II.3   Statistics

Accurate (or indeed any) statistics on detained asylum seekers are extremely difficult to obtain, not least because in most cases no distinction is made between asylum seekers and other aliens and because detention is often not acknowledged as such.

---

13   International Helsinki Federation for Human Rights, *1996 Annual Report*, p. 153; see also Association for the Prevention of Torture, *Rapport sur les mauvais traitements et les conditions de détention en Roumanie*, April 1996, p. 30.
14   UNHCR, *Detention of Asylum-Seekers in Europe*, supra note 8, p. 93.
15   IHF, *1996 Annual Report*, supra note 13, p. 153.

In Poland several hundred people a year are detained for illegal border crossing (out of the 14,300 people apprehended at or near the border in 1994, for example), with little or no consideration being given to whether or not the people concerned are in need of protection, making it difficult to estimate the proportion of aliens who are asylum seekers.

In Bulgaria, according to official figures given by the Ministry of the Interior, the number of foreign nationals detained at the Bulgarian border or returned to Bulgaria from neighbouring States was 3,262 in 1991, 2,242 in 1992 and 2,164 in 1993. Over 90% of these persons were reported to have entered the country legally. It was estimated in 1994 that there were between 12,500 and 15,000 foreigners staying illegally in Bulgaria, though approximately 40,000 aliens have reportedly entered Bulgaria with transit entry clearance but have not officially left the country. In 1992 and 1993, over 8 million foreign nationals passed through Bulgaria, an estimated 60–70% of whom were in transit. The main national groups were Syrians, Lebanese, Iranians and Nigerians.[16]

In the Czech Republic, according to some sources, as many as 43,300 foreign nationals were detained or returned at the Czech-German border in 1993, an increase of 35% on the previous year. The majority were citizens of the former Yugoslavia (60%), Bulgaria (11%) and Romania.[17] All asylum seekers (1,143 in 1995, 2,156 in 1996) are detained in quarantine for a two or three week period. After that in most cases they are subject to restrictions on their movements throughout the procedure.

In Hungary no figures for the numbers of detained asylum seekers are available, although it is estimated that approximately half of the aliens expelled from Hungary (some of whom may well be asylum seekers) spend some time in prison or detention prior to expulsion. The number of expulsions rose from 2,311 in 1992 to 17,999 in 1995. 4,568 aliens were forcibly deported in the first half of 1996. 160 cases of detention were recorded by the Aliens Police in 1995 – the figure for the first half of 1996 was 188 – but the grounds for detention are not specified. However, of the 5,454 cases of criminal proceedings initiated against aliens in 1994, it is known that 100 were on the grounds of "serious forms of illegal border crossing". The figures were 156 such cases out of a total of 5,939 in 1995, and 70 out of 2,154 for the first six months of 1996. Under the minor offences procedure against aliens, of the 2,647 cases reported in 1994, 35 were for illegal border crossing and 44 for other infringements of the Aliens Law. The figures for 1995 were 3 and 44 respectively, out of a total of 1,949 offences committed. In 1994, 11,190 aliens were subject to residence requirements in shelters run by the Aliens

---

16 *International Symposium on Protection of Refugees in Central and Eastern Europe, supra* note 1, pp. 34 and 46.
17 *Ibid.*, p. 52.

CHAPTER 2   CENTRAL AND EASTERN EUROPE

Police. The figure for 1995 was 10,373, and for the first six months of 1996, 4,042.[18]

II.4   Detention facilities

There are few purpose-built or specially adapted detention centres in the region. In Poland, there are two guarded centres in the Warsaw area, the first of which was opened in Lesznowola Radomska in 1996, and has a capacity of 100 detainees. In addition, there are 24 "deportation arrests" located in various Polish cities.

Hungary has ten centres which house illegal migrants, including some asylum seekers. Most of the centres have a capacity of 20–25 persons, though the largest, at Gyor, houses 120 persons. Apart from the centre at Budapest's Ferihegy airport, most are situated near the borders, approximately 200 km from Budapest (making access by NGOs and UNHCR difficult), and are under the surveillance of the border guards. One other centre – a camp built by the Nazis in the Second World War at Kistarcsa (Kerepestarcsa) – was closed down in 1995 following severe criticism by human rights organisations (see again Section II.7 below). There are also two prisons run by the Immigration Service, one for men in Nagyfa and one for women in Palhalma.

In Romania, asylum seekers and illegal immigrants are detained in the transit zone in Bucharest's Otopeni airport (see conditions of detention below), in some cases for over one month. There are at present no special facilities for detained asylum seekers in Romania – in addition to the airport, asylum seekers are detained in prisons or police cells, unsegregated from convicted persons, or in the state-run Gociu hostel, which consists of a block of flats for workers without families, of which two floors are reserved for refugees. There have also been reports of foreigners (mostly Sri Lankans and Bangladeshis) arrested on grounds of illegal entry or presence being detained in military barracks north of Giurgiu prior to repatriation.[19] The Romanian authorities are reportedly planning to open a new detention centre to replace the detention facility at Otopeni airport.[20]

In Bulgaria, adult aliens detained under the aliens' legislation may be held at the airport and at the Drouzhba-2 centre, situated mid-way between Sofia and the airport. During its visit in 1995, the delegation from the Council of Europe's Committee for the Prevention of Torture (CPT) welcomed the fact that a special establishment had been set up for this category of detainees, rather than holding them in ordinary police stations or prisons.

---

18   Figures supplied by the Hungarian Institute of Political Sciences.
19   APT, *Rapport sur les mauvais traitements et les conditions de détention en Roumanie*, supra note 13, p. 30.
20   UNHCR, *Detention of Asylum-Seekers in Europe*, supra note 8, p. 174.

In Slovakia, foreigners have been detained, sometimes for several weeks, in detention cells at Bratislava Municipal Police Headquarters, which was built in 1953 and was described by the CPT as "quite inappropriate for prolonged periods of detention".[21] The organisation recommended that the Slovak authorities create special centres for persons detained under aliens legislation, and received assurances that in April 1997 the Ministry of the Interior would open a refugee centre for foreigners staying illegally in the Slovak Republic which would meet the criteria demanded by the CPT. Asylum seekers may also be placed in quarantine in the holding centre for asylum seekers in Adamov-Gbely, a former motel converted in 1992 to provide temporary accommodation for asylum seekers. Quarantine normally lasts between four and seven weeks, during which time it is strictly forbidden to leave the premises.

II.5   Detention and the determination procedure

II.5.1 Pre-admission detention and airport detention

Most of the major airports of the region now appear to hold asylum seekers in the transit zone before deciding whether to admit them into the country. Normally this detention is limited to a few hours or at most one or two days, though there have been significant exceptions, notably in Bulgaria and Romania. In general, it seems that asylum applications which are explicitly made during this period are referred to the appropriate authorities and dealt with by them. In Poland this is the case at Warsaw airport, but the procedure used is extremely brief and the person concerned is deported immediately after receiving a first negative decision. It is believed that very few people apply for asylum upon arrival at Warsaw airport and there have been allegations by asylum seekers who managed to contact UNHCR from the airport that their asylum requests have been ignored by the authorities. In the Czech Republic also, the majority of asylum seekers (over 80%, according to the Czech Directorate of Aliens and Border Police) apply for asylum once they are inside the country.

UNHCR does have access to the transit zone in Budapest's Ferihegy airport, but on the other hand there is no maximum limit to detention in the airport when asylum seekers arrive without the necessary papers, and they can be held for several months. At some airports the authorities may not admit that their practice amounts to detention. The International Helsinki Federation states in respect of Bucharest's Otopeni airport that: "The inhuman conditions to which aliens are subjected ... are mostly due to the refusal of the Ministry of the Interior and its subordinate bodies to

---

21 Report by the CPT on its visit to Slovakia in 1995.

acknowledge that these people are detained."[22] In both Romania and Bulgaria, persons detained in the airport are considered to be the responsibility of the national airlines.

A number of individual cases of lengthy airport detention in Sofia have been reported in recent years, including one person who was detained for as long as 12 weeks in 1994. Most of these cases came to light by chance, although UNHCR has recently reported improved conditions of access to the airport. It must be presumed that they represent only a proportion of the total number of similar cases. In 1995, an Iraqi couple and their two-year-old daughter were finally allowed into Bulgaria (though they were not admitted to the asylum procedure) after being held in the airport for a month. In February 1995, two separate groups of Somali women and children were held in the airport, in each case for about a fortnight. It is believed that UNHCR was actively prevented from interviewing either of them. An Iraqi man and his daughter were also detained in the airport in April 1995 and held for about seven weeks. Airport officials refused to allow them to apply for asylum in Bulgaria. They were eventually provided, against their will, with an Iraqi *laissez-passer*, and were only saved from *refoulement* by the intervention of a sympathetic airport official in Amman.

UNHCR reported several more cases of airport detention in July 1996, though the length of detention was shorter than in previously reported cases. Most of the individuals concerned had been returned to Bulgaria from other European countries, presumably on "safe third country" grounds and were detained for a few days before being removed without consideration of their asylum claims, mostly to unknown destinations, but there was at least one case of direct *refoulement*. In one case, the Somali asylum seeker was believed to have been returned from Germany. He was accompanied by three minor children, and was deported to Kenya after 14 days in detention. Three asylum seekers, including two with minor children, were released from detention and admitted to the determination procedure following intervention by UNHCR. One was a pregnant Iraqi woman with one child, who had been removed from Sweden (where she had numerous relatives) via Austria on "safe third country" grounds despite the fact that she claimed never to have been in Bulgaria before (she told UNHCR that she had not been in an airport where the Cyrillic alphabet was used, as in Sofia). The Bulgarian authorities intended to deport her to Iraq, but UNHCR intervened to prevent *refoulement* and she was admitted to the procedure. Another, a Rwandan asylum seeker arriving via Poland, would have been deported because he was unable to support himself financially during the procedure, had it not been for the intervention of UNHCR.[23]

---

22 IHF, *1996 Annual Report, supra* note 13, p. 153.
23 Cases reported by UNHCR Sofia in connection with the Danish Refugee Council's *Report on "Safe Third Country" Policies in Europe, supra* note 5.

The position at land borders in central European countries is not always clear, and little information is available, primarily because of the practical problem of access by UNHCR and humanitarian NGOs. It seems certain that most countries detain illegal or refused migrants in the border area before returning them to the country from which they came. This detention is believed to be of short duration in nearly all cases and is deemed necessary to ensure that the people do not disappear while their return transport is being arranged. In some cases detention can be extended by a prosecutor or by the courts and people can be formally imprisoned for attempting to cross a border illegally – in Romania, for example, a prison sentence of between three months and two years may be imposed.

In Poland, the authorities do not usually impose penalties relating to the first illegal border crossing or presence in Poland – first-time offenders may be detained for a short period (usually a few hours). Upon their release, they will be allowed to travel to Warsaw in order to file an asylum application with the Department for Migration and Refugee Affairs of the Ministry of the Interior. In Poland, as already mentioned, repeated attempts to cross the border illegally may lead to formal imprisonment in a temporary arrest under the Penal Procedure Code.

It is less clear that implicit asylum applications (for example, explanations of the danger that the person faces in their country of origin) are dealt with effectively in central European countries. There have been cases where, contrary to the evidence of the refugees or their families, the authorities denied that asylum applications had been made.[24] The problem is exacerbated in situations where relatively untrained border guards, who often speak only their own mother tongue and have no interpreters available, are empowered to take the initial decision on whether foreigners have the requisite documentation to enter the country – this is the case for example in Romania and Hungary (as mentioned above).

In Bulgaria, there have been reports of cases where asylum seekers lacking valid travel documents have been detained and deported even after formal acknowledgement of the request for asylum.[25] As mentioned above, there have also been instances where asylum seekers, including some arriving with valid travel and identity documents, have been refused access to the procedure because they did not have sufficient financial means to support themselves during the procedure, and have instead been detained and deported. UNHCR has noted that the Bulgarian authorities do not follow many of the provisions of the Refugee Ordinance, and that border guards do not consider asylum seekers as *bona fide* applicants if they

---

24　One of these is described in *Safe Third Country: myths and realities*, ECRE, February 1995. A Somali family stranded at Bratislava airport came to the attention of UNHCR. In spite of intervention by the local branch office at various levels, the Slovak authorities deported them to Ukraine, giving as part of the grounds that they had not applied for asylum.

25　IHF, *1996 Annual Report, supra* note 13, p. 61.

CHAPTER 2   CENTRAL AND EASTERN EUROPE

previously travelled through Bulgaria and did not request asylum before travelling on to a third country.[26]

II.5.2   Detention and other restrictions on freedom of movement during the determination procedure

Practice in this area varies across central Europe, but by and large there is little detention of asylum seekers once they have been admitted to the procedure. In some instances, registered asylum seekers are given some basic documentation and then left to find their own resources for living (in some cases with UNHCR funded assistance). At the other extreme, as in the Czech Republic for example, asylum seekers are put into "quarantine" for up to four weeks and are thereafter normally required to reside in a government-run centre. In yet other countries, assistance may only be available to people in camps which involve restrictions on the freedom of movement. In Slovakia, asylum seekers are not required to register in a reception centre, but they only receive food and housing support if they do. Once registered at the centre, they can only leave with the permission of the Director. Failure to respect this requirement can lead to termination of the procedure and possibly to deportation, as mentioned earlier.

It is common for authorities to restrict the freedom of movement of asylum seekers who have been returned to the country under a readmission agreement or who have entered the country illegally, particularly if they are apprehended in the border area. In the Czech Republic the authorities may adopt a tougher attitude towards granting permission to leave the camp.

In Hungary, non-European asylum seekers are not subject to restrictions on freedom of movement during the procedure, but as many only submit a request for asylum after they have been arrested for illegal entry or presence, in practice they may be detained as illegal immigrants. Between October 1990 and July 1995, non-Europeans who entered Hungary illegally (or attempted to exit illegally), or whose claims were rejected by UNHCR, were held at the Kerepestarcsa camp on the outskirts of Budapest.[27] There was no provision for detention at that time, but a legal basis was created by the Aliens Act which came into force on 1 May 1994 and provides that foreigners who are residing illegally in the country, who cannot find accommodation of their own, and who cannot be removed from the country because they lack the necessary documents may be subject to compulsory residence requirements. Although compulsory residence may constitute a restriction on their freedom of movement, it may not by law be the equivalent of custody. European asylum seekers are placed in reception centres until a decision on their status has

---

26   See also *1997 World Refugee Survey, supra* note 3, p. 176.
27   See the *Report on the Aliens' Police Shelter in Kistarcsa*, Hungarian Helsinki Committee, the Centre for the Defence of Human Rights and the Veritas Foundation, June 1995.

been taken. Technically they are not detained, but a number have reported problems in obtaining permits to leave the camps. In the Gyor camp, for example, asylum seekers are allowed to leave the camp between 2 p.m. and 8 p.m., but require a permit to do so. Permits may be withdrawn for up to a week as a form of punishment, for example, for returning to the camp after 8 p.m. It has been reported that in some cases asylum seekers have been refused permits on the grounds that they could not offer sufficient financial guarantees.[28]

II.5.3   Pre-deportation detention

Deportation is not widely practised in the region, largely because of the costs involved – governments often issue an expulsion order but, for financial reasons, refrain from physically expelling people. It should however be pointed out that pre-admission detention, particularly in airports but also at a number of land borders (for example between the Czech and Slovak Republics) can quickly merge into pre-deportation detention.

With the exception of Poland, detention prior to deportation is almost entirely limited to people whose freedom of movement was restricted pending a decision on their asylum application.

Since March 1995 Polish police have had the power to detain foreigners who have no right to remain in Poland and who do not comply with an expulsion order. Where there are reasonable grounds for suspecting that a person will not comply with a deportation order, a request may be made to the Public Prosecutor to authorise detention pending deportation. The question of deportation of foreigners is a politically sensitive one in Poland. There has been criticism over the handling of appeals from a number of people in pre-deportation custody as one single case, although the Code of Administrative Procedure requires that all appeals be handled individually.[29] Furthermore, the lack of involvement by a court in these cases is exceptional in the Polish legal system, in that it is only in the cases of aliens that a court order is not required to authorise detention. This system will be changed once the new draft Aliens Act comes into force, however, and Public Prosecutors will lose their competence to detain, with detention both in the criminal and administrative context becoming the exclusive competence of the courts.[30]

---

28 OIP, *La détention et le traitement des demandeurs d'asile – Belgique, Hongrie, Suisse*, supra note 11, p. 8.
29 IHF, *1996 Annual Report*, supra note 13, p. 142.
30 The draft Aliens Act regulates the situation as follows: "The decision on placing the alien in a guarded centre or in arrest with a view to temporary expulsion shall be issued by the regional court appropriate with regard to the seat of the voivod appropriate to issue the decision on expulsion, upon his or her motion or upon the motion of the Police or Border Guard."

CHAPTER 2   CENTRAL AND EASTERN EUROPE

The Polish Refugee Office will accept applications for asylum from foreigners placed in pre-deportation detention, but this does not result in an exemption from the 90-day detention period and does not automatically prevent deportation. However, very frequently, the period permitted for detention expires prior to a decision on refugee status being reached, and in such cases detained asylum seekers are released. UNHCR is aware of only a very few cases of positive decisions reached with regard to asylum seekers held in detention pending deportation.

An alien staying in a guarded centre or in detention must be immediately released if the reasons justifying the imposition of these measures have ceased, or if within 90 days from the moment of detention the decision on deportation has not been executed. No extension of this period is allowed. An alien may not be expelled to a country where he or she could be the subject of persecution on Convention-related grounds or torture, as Poland is a party to the 1951 Geneva Convention and the European Convention on Human Rights.

In Romania, the detention facility at Otopeni airport was initially intended for foreigners who were not allowed entry into Romania. Nowadays, however, the majority of detainees are foreigners who have been arrested for living illegally in the country and are brought to the airport detention centre, usually after having been detained in police stations, to await repatriation. Detention here can be lengthy, depending on how long it takes to obtain the necessary travel documents (it can take up to four months in the case of India, for example).

In Hungary, where in 1995 only 130 asylum seekers were granted refugee status out of several thousand applications,[31] those who receive a negative decision but who cannot be returned to their country of origin because of risks to their safety are left in a very insecure position: without travel documents, or the right to work or claim social benefits, many attempt to travel illegally to the west. If intercepted, however, they are placed in the custody of the aliens police, where they can be held indefinitely.

II.6   Rights in detention

It is clear that language and communications problems are widespread in the region, with officials and asylum seekers alike often being unable to understand one of the international languages. Many countries are required to provide free interpretation, but are unable to meet this requirement in practice. Lack of information on rights and procedures, coupled with inadequate access to UNHCR and NGOs or lawyers

---

31   There was a significant decline in applications after the Hungarian government discontinued its policy of granting temporary protection to asylum seekers arriving from the former Yugoslavia, except for cases of family reunification – there were only 65 new arrivals recorded in 1996, as opposed to 4,425 in 1995. US Committee for Refugees, *1997 World Refugee Survey, supra* note 3, p. 193.

for counselling purposes, means that the great majority of asylum seekers are unable to exercise any rights they may have and rarely, if ever, challenge their detention in a court.

In the Gyor camp in Hungary, for example, legal counselling is quite inadequate, and the Centre for Human Rights (MEJOK) reported after its visit in October 1995 that some detainees had been without information concerning their rights and the progress of their case for over one month.

In Poland, decisions to detain must be authorised in writing, stating the reasons for the decision. There is a right of appeal to the district court within seven days. However, given the lack of interpreting services and general legal advice, detainees are normally unaware of this right of appeal which, as a result, is almost never exercised.

State practice regarding access to UNHCR and/or NGOs varies widely. At Sofia airport, access to asylum seekers has been limited to humanitarian visits with even UNHCR being excluded, although the situation is understood to have improved in the course of 1996. Elsewhere access is usually possible, though sometimes it is restricted to cases where the potential counsellors can name the person they will visit. NGOs in the Czech Republic cannot see the asylum seekers while they are in the quarantine period, which means that the formal interview has taken place before NGOs can offer advice. In Hungary, the authorities seem to encourage access by UNHCR and certain NGOs. In Poland, the Public Prosecutor's Office instructed all prosecutors that they were not responsible for issuing authorisation for leave to visit detainees in deportation arrests and guarded centres. Responsibility for such authorisation lies instead with the Police. UNHCR and NGOs do not report any problems with access. UNHCR is also aware of cases where relatives and representatives of foreign NGOs have been allowed to visit detention facilities (a formal request is required in advance).

II.7 Conditions of detention

Where formal detention centres exist, conditions appear to be reasonable. The detention centre at Ljubljana in Slovenia was inspected by the Council of Europe's Committee for the Prevention of Torture (CPT) which found no serious violations. Complaints about the conditions in Czech camps are understood to be rare. Where complaints are made, they often concern availability of appropriate food and arbitrary decisions by the camp authorities in granting visiting rights.

Conditions of detention were of some concern to the CPT on its visit to Slovakia. Detainees at Bratislava Municipal Police Headquarters were reported to be confined to their cells for 23 hours a day, with no activities other than the daily walk in the secure corridor and the reading of occasional magazines offered by the police staff on duty. Some had been detained for nearly a month. The CPT commented that

CHAPTER 2   CENTRAL AND EASTERN EUROPE

"to be held under such conditions for weeks on end must be a stultifying experience", and recommended daily outdoor exercise and a supply of appropriate reading material in the short term, and in the long term that persons detained under the 1995 Act on the Stay of Foreigners be held in special centres.[32] The CPT received a positive response from the Slovak authorities, and was assured that on 1 April 1997, the Ministry of the Interior would open a refugee centre for foreigners staying illegally on the territory of the Slovak Republic that would meet the criteria of the CPT.

Some asylum seekers are also held in the Adamov-Gbely centre in Slovakia during a quarantine period, lasting normally between four and seven weeks. The CPT heard no allegations of ill-treatment – on the contrary, "it gained a favourable impression of the relations between staff and the asylum seekers" – and approved of the fact that there was no security perimeter fence and that the guards were unarmed. It did however express concern at the lack of special provisions for women and children and the absence of any activities (such as sports or reading materials). The Committee recommended that psychiatric/psychological care be offered to detainees and that they be informed of their rights in their own languages.

Hungarian camps and the centre in the transit area at Budapest airport are visited frequently by UNHCR, which is believed not to have made any objections to the conditions. NGOs have been more critical, however. As mentioned above, the Kistarcsa (Kerepestarcsa) camp was finally closed down in July 1995 following criticism of conditions by human rights organisations.[33] One of the main problems cited was the lack of information given to foreigners during the aliens police procedure, which meant that there were a large number of displaced people from areas of war or civil war, including Bosnians and Rwandans. Due to the lack of interpretation and information, and possibly as a result of psychological pressure by the authorities, the majority of foreigners did not challenge the decision to place them in compulsory residence. Other problems included lack of outdoor exercise (maximum half an hour per day), "very bad" hygienic conditions, insufficient food, and inadequate medical services. Foreigners required to stay at the camp were also obliged to reimburse the authorities for the costs of their stay before leaving the country. Since the closure of the Kistarcsa camp, the largest camp is now the one at Gyor, in the west of the country. In addition to the problems of obtaining permits to leave the camp and the lack of information mentioned above, human rights organisations have criticised the overcrowded conditions, the "deplorable" conditions of hygiene, the inadequate food, the failure to provide suitable accommodation for women and children and the racist and intolerant attitudes

---

32   1995 Report by the Committee for the Prevention of Torture on its Visit to Slovakia.
33   See the *Report on the Aliens' Police Shelter in Kistarcsa, supra* note 27.

(particularly where religion is concerned) on the part of the staff.[34] NGOs report that the airport detention centre, comprising two barracks with poor conditions – no freedom of movement, no public telephone, inadequate nutrition and only one shower – is isolated in practice, with even priests and diplomatic representatives experiencing difficulty in gaining access. Another general complaint about detention centres and shelters is the separation of family members, though according to a recent amendment to the Aliens Act (Cabinet Decree No. 145 of 1994), migrant families may be placed in shelters or detention centres without separation "if the possibilities in the building are provided".

In Poland, detainees awaiting deportation are kept strictly separate from persons imprisoned on criminal charges, and UNHCR monitoring has confirmed that they are held in separate units or wings of facilities. The situation in deportation facilities is the subject of regular inspections by UNHCR and its implementing partner, the Helsinki Foundation for Human Rights. Overcrowding of pre-deportation detention facilities has not been reported as of concern, unlike ordinary Polish prisons. There have been sporadic reports of failure to respect religious dietary requirements, in particular from Muslims, who have claimed that they have been served pork. The nutritional value of food has not been questioned, and food content and size of portions is subject to legal regulations. A review by the Polish Ombudsman has resulted in a number of concerns and recommendations. The Ombudsman criticised the use of deportation arrests for detention of any significant period of time, due to the facilities available in the arrests. It was recommended that persons detained for 90 days pending deportation be placed in guarded centres. A review by the Committee against Torture of detention conditions in Poland resulted in no major criticism concerning abuses of fundamental human rights.

In its report on its 1995 visit to Bulgaria, the CPT expressed concern over the length of detention in the Drouzhba-2 centre – the delegation was informed that the maximum period of detention was 30 days (Section 39 para. 2, of the Regulations implementing the Aliens' legislation), but an examination of the registers revealed that one person had been in the centre for nearly two months. Apart from criticism of the sanitary facilities, an area used for "disciplinary" purposes, the medical facilities and the fact that inmates wore pyjamas all day (the Committee said that this would be "degrading" for many detainees), the delegation's main concern was the lack of activities for the detainees. In addition, the Bulgarian Helsinki Committee mentions poor facilities for the detention of women and children (despite good relations between the organisation and the police in this respect), but considers the major problem to be the fact that the first authorities contacted by the Bulgarian police are often the representatives of the national embassy of the detainees, with a

---

34   OIP, *La détention et le traitement des demandeurs d'asile – Belgique, Hongrie, Suisse*, supra note 11, pp. 8–9.

view to facilitating their deportation. This can have serious consequences for persons wishing to apply for asylum. Until recently, there was no representative of the National Bureau for Territorial Asylum and Refugees permanently in contact with the detention centre.

Conditions of detention would seem to be worst in "unofficial" detention centres, notably airport transit zones. In Sofia and Bucharest there are frequent cases of people being held in transit zones for extended periods with totally inadequate facilities. In at least one well-attested case this has happened also at Bratislava airport. In Sofia people have been held in the transit lounge for extended periods with no access to facilities and without anywhere suitable to sleep. The Committee for the Prevention of Torture did not have access to the detention facility in the transit zone at Sofia international airport during its 1995 visit and requested more information on conditions there. The detention of asylum seekers in the transit zone has been described as "a cause for particular concern" by the International Helsinki Federation.[35] The IHF has described conditions of detention at Otopeni airport in Bucharest as "inhuman".[36] The detention facility, established in November 1994, comprises two rooms, a corridor and two toilets with a shower. Foreigners are locked up and are only allowed out into the transit hall when there are no other passengers in the airport – there is a guard on duty in the corridor. One of the main problems is overcrowding – there are 13 bunk beds in one of the rooms, but there are frequently more detainees than beds. The facility is also described as inadequately ventilated and dirty. The medical service is insufficient (detainees have to pay if they wish to see the airport doctor) and food is also reported to be inadequate (two meals per day served by the Romanian airline company, which is responsible for the costs of foreigners until their deportation).[37]

III   Eastern Europe – Russia and the Commonwealth of Independent States

III.1   Transit migration[38]

From the information available on asylum practice in Russia and the CIS countries (including Armenia, Azerbaijan, Belarus, Georgia, Moldova and Ukraine), it is clear that the majority of countries are transit countries for asylum seekers wishing to reach western Europe. In Russia, for example, stringent policies regulating

---

35   IHF, *1996 Annual Report, supra* note 13, p. 61.
36   *Ibid.*, p. 153.
37   APT, *Rapport sur les mauvais traitements et les conditions de détention en Roumanie, supra* note 13, p. 30.
38   Information based on the Danish Refugee Council's *Report on "Safe Third Country" Policies in Europe, supra* note 5.

admission into western Europe in conjunction with porous, weakly-controlled national borders have resulted in large groups of potential asylum seekers transiting through the country. The Russian authorities often claim that such groups have no intention of applying for asylum. Ukraine has a unique geographical position, having borders with seven different countries, and although the Ukrainian authorities are introducing stricter controls at the eastern borders, it is reported that it is still comparatively easy to cross without proper documents. In Belarus, officials of the State Migration Service fear that the lack of effective border controls with Russia and Ukraine and the position of Belarus as a gateway to the north and the west could result in a build-up of asylum seekers unable to continue to western Europe. It is also feared that the lack of an effective determination procedure in Russia could lead to a mass influx of asylum seekers if Belarus were to start processing asylum claims. State Migration Officials have therefore announced that they plan to protect the country from this eventuality by introducing very tough standards for obtaining refugee status.

III.2   Refugee legislation and the legal basis for detention

Generally speaking, there is at present no policy of detaining asylum seekers other than for reasons of illegal entry, state security or on criminal grounds. In Azerbaijan, for example, an asylum seeker may initially be detained if he has no valid passport, but if he applies for asylum he will be released unless he is considered a threat to state security. There is no systematic detention of rejected asylum seekers in the region, and expulsion orders are rare and are not enforced.

Although some countries have adopted refugee legislation, it is not fully implemented. Russia has ratified the 1951 Geneva Convention and the 1967 Protocol, and in March 1993 adopted a Law on Refugees and a Law on Forced Migrants (intended for persons who possess or have obtained Russian citizenship and are considered to be in a refugee-like situation). The present Law on Refugees does not specifically provide for detention of asylum seekers, and instances of detention occur largely as a result of failure to implement legislation on refugees – a criticism voiced more generally by the UN Human Rights Committee in its July 1995 Comments to the report submitted by Russia under Article 40 of the ICCPR.[39] Thus asylum seekers (referred to as "immigrants" in the Federal Migration Service regulations) may be detained at police stations or in prison for the time necessary (usually no more than two or three days) until their asylum application has been submitted at the nearest FMS office, in the transit zone of the airport (where detention has been known to last for up to 20 months) or when crossing the border

---

39 "The Committee is concerned that the profound legislative changes taking place within the State party have not been matched by the actual protection of human rights at the implementation level."

illegally. In the St. Petersburg detention centre for foreigners (see the section on conditions of detention below), registration of an asylum application will not secure release and asylum seekers remain in detention until a decision on the application has been taken, or, if it is a negative decision, until they can be deported.

Under the new draft Law on Refugees, currently pending before the State Duma (Parliament), no provision for detention of asylum seekers is envisaged. The draft law, like its predecessor, refers to a so-called Temporary Accommodation Centre (TAC) where the applicant has the right to reside during the determination procedure. If an asylum seeker has entered the country illegally or has no right to stay on Russian territory, he will be obliged to reside at the centre (again see the section on conditions of detention below).

A further related problem is the continuation of the *propiska* regime, despite the fact that it has been declared unconstitutional. This administrative measure, requiring a residence permit for a specific city or area, has been inherited from the Tsarist regime and is designed to prevent massive population flows to the cities. The system is still strictly enforced in Moscow (Ordinance No. 2154 issued by the Moscow city government), Krasnodar, St. Petersburg, Voronezh and elsewhere in Russia (over 25 regions out of Russia's 89). According to the International Helsinki Federation (IHF), *propiska* requirements are implemented "in a disproportionate measure against dark-skinned people", in particular from the Caucasus, Asia and Africa).[40] It has particularly severe consequences for asylum seekers: they will be denied access to a determination procedure if they have no *propiska*, and even if they are granted refugee status, it is only valid in the area or city for which they hold a *propiska*. This has reportedly affected "hundreds of thousands" of refugees from Chechnya, among others.[41]

Belarus has not yet signed the Geneva Convention or any other international or regional instrument concerning refugees, but a presidential decree of November 1994 authorised the Ministry of the Interior to grant asylum and a national Law on Refugees came into effect in July 1995. Neither are implemented, however, and there is still no status determination procedure. There is in fact a legal basis for detaining asylum seekers in Section 5 of the Law on Refugees ("Cooperation of the State institutions in relation to refugees"), which authorises the border guards to

---

40   IHF, *1996 Annual Report, supra* note 13, p. 159. Citing a report by Human Rights Watch/Helsinki, *Russia: Crime or Simply Punishment* (Newsletter, Volume 7 No. 12, September 1995), the IHF observes that measures introduced in a presidential decree to eliminate ethnic and racial intolerance are undermined by federal and municipal legislation ostensibly aimed at fighting organised crime – in fact, the latter has actually motivated racial attacks by the Moscow police. "This legislation restricts some basic civil rights such as the right to freedom of movement, the right to protection against arbitrary searches, and the right of a detainee to be informed promptly of the charges against him/her."
41   *Ibid.*, p. 162.

detain aliens who enter the country without authorisation and with the aim of acquiring refugee status, and to inform the State Migration Service of their presence. Asylum seekers are technically permitted to remain in the country on a temporary basis, but many have difficulty in registering in practice and may be subject to arbitrary fines or detention. UNHCR Minsk will intervene in cases brought to its attention. Thus, until refugee determination begins, the position of the Belarus government is that all asylum seekers in Belarus are illegal immigrants.

Ukraine, which is not party to the 1951 Geneva Convention or 1967 Protocol, but has signed the European Convention on Human Rights, adopted a Law on Refugees in December 1993. Asylum seekers are not normally detained during the determination procedure in Ukraine. The determination procedure has only begun to operate very recently and there is a considerable backlog of cases. The authorities have started by processing the cases of Afghans. The cases of Iranians and Iraqis are particularly sensitive, as there is technically no legal way of entering Ukraine from these countries and would-be asylum seekers are arrested and detained as illegal immigrants. In the first instance, detention usually lasts just a few days and they are released upon payment of a fine. However, if caught trying to cross the borders to the west, they may receive a prison sentence of up to 18 months. Foreigners detained under these circumstances may therefore include some people in need of protection. There is no special airport procedure for dealing with "quasi-detention" at the airport and UNHCR has only limited possibilities for monitoring practice. The fact that the new asylum legislation is not yet fully implemented means that asylum seekers who have not yet been able to legalise their status are considered to be illegal immigrants by the militia and the authorities, and, as in Belarus, may be subject to repeated fining, potential arrest and in some cases to police harassment.

III.3   Conditions of detention

Reports of prison conditions in the CIS countries vary from poor to "appalling"[42] – generally a reflection of the economic hardship experienced by these countries, rather than a deliberate policy of deprivation, though abuse of detainees is not uncommon.

In its July 1995 Comments on the report submitted by Ukraine (under Article 40 of the International Covenant on Civil and Political Rights), the UN Human Rights Committee is critical of cases of lengthy administrative detention and denial of access to detainees by legal representatives. The Committee is also concerned by the conditions of detention in Ukrainian prisons, especially overcrowding, and by continuing reports of torture and ill-treatment committed by the police and security forces.

---

42   IHF, *1996 Annual Report, supra* note 13, p. 155.

CHAPTER 2   CENTRAL AND EASTERN EUROPE

The Committee does however welcome the recognition by Ukraine of the Committee's competence to receive and consider individual communications under the Optional Protocol to the Covenant, and the enactment of the Act on Provisional Detention (June 1993) and the Decree of the Ukrainian Cabinet on Programmes for Bringing up to World Standards the Conditions of Detention (January 1994). The Committee also expresses approval of measures introduced to strengthen the independent status of the judiciary and improve judicial guarantees for individuals.

Of the 73 Temporary Accommodation Centres (TACs) in Russia, only one is used for asylum seekers from non-CIS countries. It is situated in the Perm region, in the town of Ocher in the eastern Urals, about 35 hours by train from Moscow. The camp accommodates approximately 100 persons, the majority of whom are Afghans. Asylum seekers are referred to the centre by regional migration services, in particular the Moscow Migration Service. According to UNHCR, conditions in the centre are adequate and asylum seekers are free to come and go, and may even travel for several days to Moscow. The centre's administrative authorities provide them with papers in order to facilitate their travel to Moscow. Other TACs are used by migrants and refugees from the CIS region, including displaced persons from Chechnya.

Russian human rights organisations have however criticised the centre because of its inaccessible location, and have said that TACs in reality operate as closed camps. They have pointed to the discrepancy between official and unofficial estimates of the numbers of refugees in the country (official figures suggest 500,000 persons, whereas unofficial estimates put the total number as high as two or three million), suggesting that many did not want to be registered because they would be forced to live in these closed camps and because Russia was in any case merely a transit country.[43]

A matter of the utmost gravity is the situation of detained asylum seekers in Moscow airport. Due to the absence of a Federal Migration Service (FMS) official in the airport, it is impossible for asylum seekers to register a claim for asylum – their only possibility of submitting an application is to contact UNHCR, which will then inform the FMS.[44] They are frequently deported to their country of origin before any decision on their asylum claim has been taken, without any consideration of the risk that this might constitute *refoulement*. When deportation proves to be impossible (due mostly to lack of documents, absence of a country prepared to accept the person or statelessness), asylum seekers can be stranded in the transit zone for considerable periods of time (as long as 20 months in one case). The transit

---

43   *Report on the NGO Consultation on Detention of Asylum Seekers in Europe*, Copenhagen 18 November 1995, p. 4.
44   UNHCR Moscow reports that a point of immigration control is currently being established at Sheremetyevo-2 airport to assess individual claims for asylum presented by arriving passengers.

lounge is unsuitable for such prolonged stays. UNHCR Moscow is aware of several cases of prolonged stay in the transit zone, including vulnerable cases such as unaccompanied minors, persons with mental health problems and women.[45] Food in the transit zone is provided three times a day by the national airline carrier (Aeroflot). Since July 1996 UNHCR has had periodic access to the transit zone. It provides blankets and supplies "long stayers" with necessary items such as soap, warm clothing and pocket money for telephone calls.

Apart from the transit zone of Moscow airport, asylum seekers are not systematically detained in Russia. The only exception known to UNHCR Moscow is the detention centre for foreigners in St. Petersburg which holds foreigners stopped at the western border of the Russian Federation, usually with forged documents or no documents at all. They are held in the detention centre prior to deportation, where a detention order has been issued by the city prosecutor. People are reported to have been detained for lengthy periods of time until funds can be obtained for their deportation. In several cases known to UNHCR, the detainees themselves have had to arrange for funds to pay for the ticket, either through friends or the municipal authorities in the city. In other cases, the authorities contacted the relevant embassies, asking them to pay for the ticket.

Recently, the St. Petersburg Immigration Control Department, responsible for refugee status determination in St. Petersburg and the region, has gained regular access to the detention centre. It interviews asylum seekers, registers their applications and ensures that no deportation is carried out until a decision has been taken. According to UNHCR, no positive decisions have yet been taken in the determination procedure.

Apart from detention for common crimes, asylum seekers can be detained arbitrarily by the police for violating the *propiska* system. If a person does not have the requisite registration for a city or region, he may be subject to an arbitrary fine, which may be followed by arbitrary detention at a police station (usually for brief periods of several hours, as opposed to days). There have been frequent reports of beatings and extortion of money by members of the police.[46]

---

45 UNHCR reported a number of individual cases of detention followed by deportation or *refoulement*, mostly to African countries, in 1995. One further case involved three Iraqi asylum seekers returned to Moscow from Athens by the Greek authorities, allegedly because they were holding forged documents. These cases have been documented in the DRC's *Report on "Safe Third Country" Policies in Europe*, *supra* note 5.

46 In its *1996 Annual Report* (*supra* note 13, p. 159), the International Helsinki Federation singles out state violence against dark-skinned people (including arbitrary arrests, ill-treatment and restrictions on freedom of movement) as a major area of concern in Russia. Quoting from a newsletter by Human Rights Watch/Helsinki (*supra* note 40), the organisation reports: "A typical experience for a dark-skinned male foreigner or resident in Moscow in 1995 was to be stopped on the street by road patrol officers and asked to provide documents to prove that he was in Moscow legally. If he failed to do that – and very often even if he did – he was made to come to the police station. The police would

CHAPTER 2 CENTRAL AND EASTERN EUROPE

In addition to suffering inhumane prison conditions, asylum seekers serving prison sentences are at risk of being returned to the countries where they fear persecution without any examination of their claims, according to Amnesty International. The organisation describes the case of Lee Sen Yen, a citizen of the Democratic People's Republic of Korea (DPRK), who was returned to the DPRK by the Russian authorities, reportedly under an agreement allowing prisoners to be sent to serve their sentences in their home country. He had requested asylum in the former Soviet Union on at least two occasions, but was deported before a decision on his most recent request (submitted in 1993) had been taken. Amnesty feared that the asylum seekers, who alleged to have been previously tortured in police detention in the DPRK, risked facing further human rights abuses.[47]

Conditions in prisons and detention centres in general in Russia are described by the UN Human Rights Committee as cruel, inhuman and degrading.[48] The Committee expresses concern at the increased length of pre-trial and temporary detention and the lack of monitoring of such detention. It also regrets the lack of familiarity of law enforcement and prison officers with the guarantees provided in the new Russian Constitution and in the Covenant. Commenting on the lack of independence and efficiency of the judiciary, the Committee observes that "the judicial system in the Russian Federation cannot be effective to ensure protection of rights until there is a sufficient number of well-trained and qualified judges and lawyers". The Committee concludes by recommending that the treatment of persons deprived of their liberty, whether in detention centres or penitentiary facilities, be effectively monitored. It calls for Visitors' Committees to be set up, and for consideration to be given to various other practical measures designed to reduce the overcrowding of pre-trial detention centres, particularly the greater use of release pending trial. Finally, it urges the Russian government to ensure that all persons held in detention are held for a legitimate cause, for a reasonable period of time, and under humane conditions.

---

insult, intimidate and often beat the detainee until he paid a fine for an alleged violation of the law. ... As a justification for such 'checks', the authorities cited an infringement of residence regulations or a traffic violation, suspicion of illegal possession of drugs, or suspected involvement in organised crime. In the overwhelming majority of cases, no formal charges were brought against a detainee."

47 Amnesty International, *1996 Annual Report*, p. 259.
48 See also the November 1994 Report of the Special Rapporteur (Mr Nigel Rodley) of the UN Commission on Human Rights for a detailed description of the human rights problems arising from the prison system in the Russian Federation.

IV The Baltic States

IV.1 The Baltic States in transition

In order to understand the present refugee policy in the Baltic States and the widespread use of detention of asylum seekers, the broader framework of the Baltic States, including historical, political and economic factors, must be taken into consideration.

In the 19th century the Baltic countries were part of the Tsarist Russia. The countries won independence after the First World War and were independent until 1940, when they were again occupied by Russia. After the Second World War, the Baltic countries were turned into republics and incorporated into the Soviet Union. The three countries regained their independence from the Soviet Union in August 1991. This new independence meant that the countries were faced with the colossal task of constructing a whole new political and economic system, including legislation and administration regarding foreigners, asylum seekers and refugees.

One particular problem common to all three of the Baltic States has been the great number of non ethnic-residents, especially of Russian origin, who had been settled in the countries over the years and became stateless persons once the Baltic countries regained independence.[49]

Owing to their historical background, with a relatively short period of independence in the wake of 50 years of foreign domination and the present economic, social and ethnic difficulties, the Baltic States have been reluctant to adopt and implement refugee legislation and adhere to the 1951 Geneva Convention. Furthermore the Baltic countries fear that if they implement a refugee law, many of the thousands of potential asylum seekers from third countries (especially the Middle East and Afghanistan) who are currently living more or less illegally in Russia in particular would enter the Baltic States and seek asylum.

This scenario would naturally pose a number of problems, including overloading of the asylum procedure, and these problems would be further exacerbated by the fact that, despite several attempts, it has been impossible for all three Baltic States to conclude readmission agreements with Russia and Belarus. Under the present circumstances, it is thus impossible for the Baltic countries to re-admit asylum seekers who have previously been in transit in Russia or Belarus.[50]

---

49 In Estonia about 65% of the population are ethnic Estonians, 25% are Russians, and 10% are other nationalities. In Latvia about 55% of the population are ethnic Latvians, 33% are Russians, and 12% are other nationalities. In Lithuania about 85% of the population are ethnic Lithuanians, 8% are Russians and 7% are Poles. Source: Danish Ministry of the Interior, *Second Report on the Baltic States*, 22 January 1996.

50 Moreover the return of asylum seekers to their previous countries of transit is problematic, as for the most part these countries have either not ratified or only partially

CHAPTER 2   CENTRAL AND EASTERN EUROPE

Finally the Baltic States have had many problems with so-called "illegal immigrants" who use the Baltic States as transit countries to the west; those of them who fail to reach a western country or are discovered by the police end up "trapped" in the Baltic States (see below). A number of politicians and officials from the Baltic countries have stated that it would be premature to implement a refugee law before solving the problem of "illegal immigrants".

As a result of the foregoing, the Baltic States have in the past few years prioritised tightening border controls and signing readmission agreements rather than the adoption and implementation of refugee legislation. To date, both Lithuania and Estonia have adopted a refugee law and have acceded to the 1951 Geneva Convention and its 1967 Protocol. However, these laws have not entered into force, and thus neither the laws nor the Convention are implemented in practice.

Although their failure to implement an acceptable refugee policy might pose a temporary obstacle, all the indications are that the Baltic States will, in the near future, become more closely integrated with the countries of western Europe[51] and, with assistance from the international community, will implement refugee legislation and determination procedures in compliance with the 1951 Geneva Convention.

IV.2   The Baltic States as transit countries

As mentioned above, one particular problem for the Baltic States is that since becoming independent they have been used as transit countries by asylum seekers and migrants seeking entry into western Europe, in particular the Nordic countries. This "human trafficking" has been criticised by the Nordic countries, which have received a large number of asylum seekers and refugees via the Baltic countries,[52] but it has also resulted in a number of asylum seekers who have failed to reach the Nordic countries becoming "stranded" in the Baltic States (see for example the situation of the group of asylum seekers in the Olaine camp in Latvia, described below). It has primarily been asylum seekers and migrants from the Middle East,

---

implemented the 1951 Geneva Convention – this is the case with Russia and Belarus, for example.

51   All three countries have stated that it is their intention to promote their integration into western economic and political structures. Estonia, Latvia and Lithuania are members of the Council of Europe and have signed the *European Convention on Human Rights and Fundamental Freedoms*. In 1995 they also applied for membership of the European Union and signed an association agreement with the EU.

52   In order to improve and strengthen the border control in the Baltic States, the Nordic countries have assisted by providing considerable financial and logistical support. For instance in 1994 the Danish government contributed to border controls in the Baltic States with a grant of DKR 9 million, and in 1996 a police liaison officer was posted to Vilnius, Lithuania.

Afghanistan and Sri Lanka who, after staying illegally for a period in Russia or Belarus, have travelled – often with costly assistance from human traffickers and agents – through the Baltic States and across the Baltic Sea to the Nordic countries.

As the Nordic countries do not for the time being, in view of the absence of acceptable refugee legislation, consider the Baltic States as "safe third countries", the asylum seekers in question are not rejected to the Baltic States, but have their asylum claims examined in the Nordic countries. This fact in itself has been a contributory factor to the widespread use of the Baltic States as transit countries.

Particularly in the years just after independence, a number of illegal boat crossings took place, with a large number of asylum seekers travelling by sea from the Baltic States to Sweden and Denmark.[53] In the night of 1 August 1995, a Danish ship picked up 73 asylum seekers from Sri Lanka, who were found drifting in four lifeboats in the Baltic Sea in international waters. The four lifeboats had previously been put out by a Latvian-registered ship, and it was nothing short of miraculous that the lifeboats were discovered by the Danish ship. The asylum seekers were later brought to Denmark, where all of them applied for asylum. The Danish police managed to apprehend the captain of the Latvian ship, and he was subsequently sentenced to one year's imprisonment in Denmark.

In addition to the absence of an acceptable refugee policy, the widespread use of the Baltic countries as transit countries can in particular be attributed to their geographical position at the Baltic Sea and inefficient border controls at the border crossings between the Baltic States and Russia and Belarus.

IV.3   Illegal immigrants and asylum seekers

In the absence of refugee legislation and determination procedures in force in the Baltic States, which would make it possible to distinguish between asylum seekers and immigrants, asylum seekers are considered to be illegal immigrants and are either rejected at the border or, if they manage to enter the Baltic States and are discovered by the police, are placed in detention in regular prisons or in special detention camps for foreigners.

Since the Baltic States, as mentioned above, have no readmission agreements with Russia or Belarus, it has been impossible for them to readmit migrants and asylum seekers who have previously been in transit in Russia or Belarus, unless there is evidence of a previous legal stay. As a result of this, many asylum seekers have been trapped in the Baltic countries and placed in detention, often under harsh

---

53   There have been seven landings altogether on Danish territory, the latest in 1994, and a total of 387 asylum seekers have arrived in Denmark in this way. These boat transports seems to be decreasing in recent years, possibly concurrently with the improvement and strengthening of the coast guard in the Baltic States.

conditions, for indefinite periods, without any possibility of having their asylum claims examined.[54]

Amnesty International stated in August 1996 that the organisation's main concerns in Estonia, Latvia and Lithuania in the period January 1995–July 1996 were the application of the death penalty and the detention of asylum seekers. It was stressed in this context that "Amnesty International believes that any asylum seeker who is detained should be given a prompt, fair, individual hearing before a judicial or similar authority to determine whether his or her detention is lawful and in accordance with international standards".[55]

Resettlement to countries in the west, as was the case with a group of asylum seekers in Estonia and Latvia (see below), would solve the immediate problem for the asylum seekers in question, but is viewed by UNHCR and many governments in the region as a solution which should only be resorted to in exceptional circumstances, as it is feared that a resettlement policy could create a "pull factor" encouraging additional arrivals. However, long-term detention without any prospect of a solution, combined with harsh, inhumane conditions, could according to UNHCR become the justification for a resettlement solution.[56]

As no clear distinction is made between migrants and asylum seekers, the exact number of asylum seekers in the Baltic States is not known, but it is roughly estimated that there might be between 4,000 and 5,000 potential asylum seekers.

The situation and developments in each of the three countries will be described in greater detail below.

IV.4 Lithuania

On 4 July 1995, Lithuania became the first of the Baltic States to pass a Refugee Law making it technically possible to distinguish between immigrants and asylum seekers in need of international protection. The refugee definition in the Law is based on the definition in Article 1 in the 1951 Geneva Convention, and the Law is, according to UNHCR, broadly in line with the Convention.[57] The Lithuanian Parliament ratified the Geneva Convention and New York Protocol in January 1997.

The Convention and the Refugee Law have not yet entered into force, but Lithuania has subsequently received financial and technical assistance from UNHCR, UNDP (United Nations Development Programme), IOM (International

---

54 It must be noted that many of the asylum seekers did not initially wish to seek asylum in the Baltic States, since their primary objective was to reach the Nordic countries.
55 *The Baltic States, a summary of recent concerns*, Amnesty International, International Secretariat, August 1996.
56 See *Note on developments regarding asylum seekers and refugees in the Baltic States*, UNHCR, ROBNC Stockholm, January 1996 and, as a possible example, the group of asylum seekers who are detained in Olaine detention camp in Latvia.
57 *Ibid.*

Organisation for Migration) and the Nordic countries for preparing the infrastructure for the implementation of the Convention and the Refugee Law.[58]

A refugee reception centre in Rukla was therefore opened in August 1996, a Refugee Board has been set up, the necessary staff have been recruited, workshops and training programmes on the provisions of the 1951 Geneva Convention and on refugee status determination have been arranged and various by-laws and regulations to enable the implementation of the Refugee Law have been adopted by the Lithuanian government.

In comparison with the other two Baltic States, Lithuania has in recent years had great difficulties with many larger groups of migrants and asylum seekers who have tried to cross the Lithuanian border on their way to the Nordic countries.[59] In December 1995 politicians in the Lithuanian Parliament proposed, without success, that due to the problem of transit migration, ongoing preparations for implementing the Refugee Law should be stopped or postponed until readmission agreements were concluded with Russia and Belarus.

According to the Refugee Law, a foreign national has the right to apply for asylum and obtain refugee status in Lithuania. The Migration Department of the Ministry of the Interior will be responsible for the first instance decisions in the asylum cases. A refusal from the Migration Department can be appealed to the Refugee Board within 14 days.[60] The Board must reach a decision on the asylum seeker's appeal within ten calendar days of receiving it.

In addition to hearing appeals, the Board has two other main tasks: to take care of the social integration of refugees into Lithuanian society and to take measures to prevent the violation of the human rights of refugees.[61]

Foreigners who apply for asylum and are accepted in the asylum procedure[62] will, while the request for refugee status is being examined, be provided with temporary asylum and will be ettled in the refugee reception centre in Rukla.

---

58   UNHCR made a financial contribution of US$ 134,000 in 1995, while a group of mostly Nordic donors supported the Lithuanian authorities in 1996 to the order of US$ 1.5 million, *ibid.*

59   Unlike Latvia and Estonia, Lithuania has, after concrete negotiations between the two countries' border police forces, succeeded in having a number of migrants and asylum seekers readmitted by Belarus.

60   The Board will consist of members of the Parliament, representatives from various Ministries, the Red Cross and the Centre for Human Rights. The 12 Members of the Board have been appointed; see government Resolution No. 455 of 15 April 1996, *On forming the Board on Refugee Matters.*

61   The Board shall in this way "investigate reports and appeals related to facts of human rights violations of refugees or asylum seekers, and cooperate in this sphere with other state institutions and NGOs"; see government Resolution No. 647 of 31 May 1996, *Regulations of the Refugee Board.*

62   According to Section 4 there might be reasons preventing foreigners from enjoying/seeking asylum in Lithuania, e.g. if "6) he or she has come from a country in

CHAPTER 2   CENTRAL AND EASTERN EUROPE

Asylum seekers will be allowed to leave the centre for no longer than 72 hours. If an asylum seeker leaves the centre without a permit for more than 72 hours, without valid reasons, investigation of his application for asylum may be terminated and the Migration Department may instruct the police to find the asylum seeker and issue him with a deportation order to leave the country.[63]

Asylum seekers with temporary asylum will, according to Section 13 of the Refugee Law, be guaranteed the right to use the services of an interpreter free of charge; to live in the refugee centre free of charge and use the services offered by it; to use medical services free of charge; and to receive a monthly allowance to cover minor expenses.

As mentioned above, the Refugee Law has not yet been implemented, and asylum seekers are as a consequence still considered to be illegal immigrants and are placed in detention in regular prisons or under lesser forms of restriction in the so-called Foreigners Registration Centre in Pabrade, a former USSR military barracks close to the Belarus border. According to UNHCR, a riot was started by asylum seekers in Pabrade Foreigners Registration Centre on 21 May 1997 in protest against restrictions of their rights and unsatisfactory living conditions.[64] They were also dissatisfied with the long period of waiting and recently implemented regulations prohibiting them from leaving the camp in order to go to the shops or the bank. The riot was stopped on 22 May following talks between high-ranking officials from the Lithuanian Ministry of Interior and representatives of the asylum seekers.[65]

In September 1996, however, the Lithuanian authorities, with assistance from UNHCR and the Danish government, began an "advance implementation" of the

---

which he or she could have received asylum" or if "8) he or she refuses to furnish information about him/herself or provides information that is clearly erroneous about the circumstances of his or her entrance into the Republic of Lithuania."

63   See government Resolution No. 421 of 3 April 1996, *Order on Restrictions on Freedom of Movement*.

64   According to the *Report prepared by the Danish delegation posted for the realisation of the project concerning an advanced implementation of the Lithuanian refugee act*, Danish Immigration Service, Copenhagen, February 1997, p. 14 *et seq.*, living conditions in the Pabrade camp posed the following problems *inter alia*: poor conditions of health and hygiene, including cold and damp resulting in illness and hospitalisation of some asylum seekers; insufficient supplies of bedding and warm clothing particularly for new arrivals in quarantine; no financial means (money and valuables are confiscated by the authorities, and no pocket money is provided) and poor relations with the *Greito Reaparimo Batalionas* (GRB) staff guarding the camp round the clock. The Lithuanian Red Cross is now responsible for distributing clothing, but the Danish delegation recommended that a humanitarian organisation be represented in the camp in order to attend to social problems.

65   See UNHCR's *Information Note on Refugee Issues in the Baltic Countries*, No. 41, June 1997.

Refugee Law. Officials from Denmark[66] and Lithuania, together with a consultant from UNHCR, carried out interviews in the registration centre in Pabrade in order to separate asylum seekers in need of international protection from those who could genuinely be described as "illegal immigrants".

The asylum seekers will subsequently be granted a temporary territorial asylum status and transferred to the reception centre in Rukla, where they must await the entry into force of the Refugee Law (believed to be imminent) and consideration of their claims for refugee status. The real migrants may on the other hand be returned, with possible assistance from IOM, to their native countries.

The first group of asylum seekers – 21 Afghans and one Iraqi – were moved from the registration centre in Pabrade to much better conditions in the reception centre in Rukla in March 1997.

IV.5　　Latvia

A group of 130 asylum seekers, mostly Iraqi Kurds, were kept in detention in the Olaine detention camp in Latvia for about two years after failing to reach Sweden in December 1994. The asylum seekers, including 49 children, were then sent back and forth from one Baltic State to another for several weeks, as no country would accept them. Finally the group was reluctantly accepted by the Latvian authorities and in the spring of 1995 were placed in Olaine prison camp.

Following a dispute arising out of a hunger-strike started in August 1995 by some of the group in protest at their continuing detention, police and prison guards were reported to have broken into the premises on 1 September 1995, indiscriminately beating detainees and destroying their personal possessions. A representative of Caritas, together with a Moslem Imam and a Caldean Catholic priest, was finally allowed to visit the detainees and found them in "... a deplorable situation. Many children, youngsters, old people, women and men, had wounds, scars and swellings from baton blows." The children in particular are described as being traumatised, and the group as a whole in the utmost despair. During the following weeks Caritas was not allowed to deliver its weekly food supplements to the detainees, and the local UNHCR representative was denied access to them.[67] Further reports on alleged beatings of some of the asylum seekers were received later in September 1995.

In July 1995, the Human Rights Committee (which met to consider Latvia's initial report on its compliance with the International Covenant on Civil and Political Rights (ICCPR)) stated that with regard to the issue of detention in general

---

66　The Danish Immigration Service assigned four officials to Lithuania for a period of three months.

67　When the local UNHCR representative finally, after almost three weeks, was allowed to visit the detainees, he could still see the unmistakable marks of the beatings.

CHAPTER 2   CENTRAL AND EASTERN EUROPE

it was particularly "concerned at allegations of mistreatment of detainees and at the conditions in places of detention". The Committee also expressed concern that "there do not seem to be clear mechanisms for dealing with complaints of violence by law-enforcement authorities and of conditions in detention centres and prisons".

In the autumn of 1995, the critical conditions in Olaine attracted considerable publicity in the Nordic countries and were criticised by a number of NGOs and authorities in the Nordic countries. The Latvian authorities denied the alleged ill-treatment of the asylum seekers, claiming that use of force could not be avoided and that, on the contrary, the asylum seekers themselves had organised several assaults on police officers and prison guards who were performing their duties.[68]

At the end of 1995, the group was transferred to improved premises inside the Olaine camp, but separate from the regular prison, and the prison staff was reorganised. Although the conditions for the asylum seekers subsequently improved significantly and the allegations of ill-treatments stopped, the detention regime remained unchanged. Furthermore, UNHCR still had difficulties in gaining access to the Olaine camp and many problems persisted regarding the asylum seekers' protection.[69]

In April 1996, the Commissioner of the Council of the Baltic Sea States on Democratic Institutions and Human Rights, Mr. Ole Espersen, stated during a visit to Latvia that refugees were a Latvian human rights problem and that detention of asylum seekers, including children, without opportunity for education and socialisation, was a serious human rights problem which had to be resolved in the immediate future.

Serious doubts were also raised in a number of quarters about the legality of the prolonged detention of the asylum seekers in Olaine.[70] It was thus questioned whether the detention had been sanctioned by a judge and on what legal basis the asylum seekers were being detained.

In May 1996, UNHCR decided to finance the legal assistance for one of the asylum seekers in Olaine who wanted to contest the legality of his detention in

---

68   *The Baltic States: a summary of recent concerns, supra* note 55.
69   See for example the sudden disappearance of a group of approximately 20 asylum seekers from the camp in Olaine; UNHCR's *Information Note on Refugee Issues in the Baltic Countries*, No. 20, 19 July 1996.
70   See Section 15 of the Latvian Constitutional Law, which states that: "Detainment, imprisonment, searches or other restrictions of a person's freedom are permissible only in accordance with the procedures stipulated by law. Each person is guaranteed the right to an attorney upon the moment of his or her detention. The law determines the maximum terms of detainment, imprisonment and preliminary investigation. Within 72 hours from a person's detention, a judge must issue a court order to sanction the person's arrest and further detention or to order the immediate release of such person ..."

court, but the asylum seeker in question subsequently decided to withdraw his complaint.[71]

In September 1996, UNHCR, in a one-off operation agreed with the Latvian government, conducted interviews with the asylum seekers in Olaine in order to determine their status. Subsequently, those who were found to be refugees (108 persons) were exceptionally accepted for resettlement by the Nordic countries in December 1996.

In July 1996 the Latvian government formed a long-awaited inter-ministerial working group to draft new refugee legislation. Representatives from the Ministry for Foreign Affairs, the Ministry of the Interior and the Ministry of Justice participated in the working group, and the National Human Rights Office and UNHCR provided assistance in drafting the law. The working group was also asked to assess the transitional period needed from the adoption of a refugee law to Latvia's readiness to accede to the 1951 Convention. A draft Refugee Law was submitted to the Cabinet of Ministers in November 1996. In February 1997 it was approved by the Cabinet and forwarded to the Parliament, where it passed the first reading on 8 May 1997.

In April 1997, the Foreign Minister was asked by the Cooperation Council of the Latvian government to explain why Latvia had concluded fewer visa-free travel agreements with *inter alia* the Nordic countries, than Estonia and Lithuania. He explained that the main obstacle was that Latvia, unlike the other two countries, had neither adopted a refugee law nor ratified the 1951 Geneva Convention.

The Ministry for Foreign Affairs has formed a working group with representatives from the Ministries of Justice, the Interior and Foreign Affairs which, in collaboration with UNHCR and the Latvian branch of Caritas, is going to prepare the implementation of the Refugee Law. It will also investigate possible sites for a refugee reception centre.

In April 1997, the Latvian government, in cooperation with UNDP and UNHCR, called a meeting of potential donors to present its plans for the forthcoming implementation of the Refugee Law.

IV.6   Estonia

Estonia routinely practises detention of asylum seekers, the stated purpose of which is to deter further transit migration. In August and September 1994, a group of 88 mostly Kurdish asylum seekers attracted considerable publicity in the region when they started a hunger-strike in protest at their prolonged detention, separated from their families and with no hope of a solution to their plight. Concern was voiced by UNHCR, the UN Working Group on Arbitrary Detention, Amnesty International

---

71   UNHCR, *Information Note on Refugee Issues in the Baltic States*, No. 17, 24 May 1996.

CHAPTER 2   CENTRAL AND EASTERN EUROPE

and a number of other NGOs. The group was finally accepted for resettlement by Finland in February 1995 on the basis of a bilateral agreement. Many of the asylum seekers had been in detention for over one year.

In the past few years Estonia has not experienced the same major problems with illegal migrants as Latvia and Lithuania,[72] probably due to relatively efficient Estonian border controls and the fact that the preferred land transit routes would appear to lie through Lithuania. It is understood to be very difficult to cross the Estonian border without being detected by the border guard or the police. In order to strengthen the border guard and combat "illegal immigration", the Board of the Estonian National Border Guard has improved cooperation with the border guard of Latvia and Russia and with Interpol, for instance by organising seminars and meetings for professional staff.

In connection with the resettlement of the group of asylum seekers to Finland, it was agreed that Estonia should pursue its efforts to establish a humane refugee policy, and an Estonian government commission suggested in September 1996 that Estonia should begin to make preparations for ratifying the 1951 Geneva Convention, drafting a refugee law and setting up reception centres.

In February 1997 the Estonian Parliament unanimously adopted a national Refugee Law and ratified the 1951 Geneva Convention and its 1967 Protocol.

The Law conforms to standards laid down in the Geneva Convention and grants refugee status to people fleeing persecution on political, racial or religious grounds. According to the Law, asylum can be denied to war criminals and to people who have committed crimes against humanity, who pose a threat to Estonia's security or who are seeking better economic conditions. However, there remain some questions as to how the Refugee Law will work in practice, particularly with regard to the right to appeal.

The Estonian government is now in the process of implementing the new legislation, by preparing the necessary accompanying statutes, establishing the necessary institutions and appointing and training the relevant staff.

V   Conclusion

At the present time, detention of asylum seekers in central and eastern Europe can largely be attributed to the continuing failure, despite the enactment of refugee legislation in many countries, to distinguish adequately between asylum seekers in need of protection and other aliens in the context of the struggle to contain transit migration. Local NGOs and international human rights and refugee organisations have expressed increasing concern at continuing detention of asylum seekers in

---

72   According to a report of 20 September 1996 by ECRE, Brussels, entitled *Asylum and Migration*, there were no illegal border crossings into Estonia in 1995.

airports, the increase in the phenomenon of pre-deportation detention, the detention-like conditions of some asylum seekers who are subject to restrictions on freedom of movement during the determination procedure and conditions of detention themselves.

States are obliged to conform to the standards contained in the international instruments to which they are party, regardless of the general economic situation – not all the desirable changes require capital outlay. Human rights organisations in the CEECs report that there are numerous training programmes for border guards, government officials and staff in detention centres, run in cooperation with a number of organisations (including UNHCR, the European Council on Refugees and Exiles, the EU and governments and NGOs in western European countries) which are already bringing about improvements for detained asylum seekers in the region.

Human rights representatives have also issued a clear call for vigilance: they warn that their emerging democracies are taking their cue from western Europe which, by detaining its own asylum seekers, is giving a dangerous signal that a return to a climate of arbitrary arrests, restrictions, detentions and imprisonments in central and eastern Europe might go uncondemned.[73]

---

73 Speaker from the Russian Federation, quoted in the *Report on the European Seminar on Detention of Asylum Seekers*, Danish Refugee Council and Danish Centre for Human Rights, Copenhagen, 17 November 1995, pp. 37–38.

Chapter 3 Detention of Asylum Seekers: The United States Perspective

By Paolo Morante

Contents

Part I   Introduction
Part II Legal aspects of detention: II.1 Legal provisions – II.2 Previous regime: Exclusion, deportation and the fiction of "entry" – II.3 New laws: Everyone excludable – II.4 Anti-terrorism laws
Part III Conditions of detention: III.1 Detention facilities – III.2 Service Processing Centers – III.3 State and local prisons – III.4 Private contract facilities
Part IV Detention by air carriers
Part V   Detention of minors
Part VI Conclusion

I   Introduction

Over the last 15 years, US policy on the detention of asylum seekers has become increasingly restrictive. Growing numbers of aliens seeking refuge in the US have prompted the government to employ detention as a deterrent to entry.[1] While budgetary constraints and the lack of detention beds have prevented the incarceration of aliens to the extent advocated by some of the nation's leaders, recent immigration reforms have reinforced this punitive approach and called for additional funds to be directed towards its implementation.

The use of detention as a deterrent to entry raises serious concerns about the ability of legitimate asylum seekers to obtain protection in the US. Commentators and critics[2] have attacked US detention policy for violating both domestic and

---

1   There were 26,512 asylum applications filed in 1980, 18,889 in 1986, 60,736 in 1988, 103,964 in 1992, 150,386 in 1993, 123,000 in 1994 and 53,000 in 1995. US Immigration and Naturalization Service, *Asylum Reform: A Year of Success* (1 April 1996).
2   See e.g. Lawyers Committee for Human Rights, *The Detention of Asylum Seekers in the United States: A Cruel and Questionable Policy* (1989) (hereinafter *Cruel and Questionable Policy*).

international law with respect to refugees' rights, including the right to apply for asylum, to be free from unnecessary restraints on their movements and to be safe from forcible return to places where persecution awaits them.[3]

This chapter looks at the principal ways in which detention has affected asylum seekers in the US. Part II addresses legal topics, comparing the state of the current law with the previous one and assessing the impact of some of the dramatic changes brought about by the sweeping legislative reforms of 1996. Part III provides an overview of detention conditions for asylum seekers in the US, emphasizing some of the system's most glaring shortcomings. Parts IV and V briefly address the responsibilities of air carriers and their impact on detention-related issues, and US policy on the detention of alien minors. They are followed by a few concluding remarks.

II   Legal aspects of detention

II.1   Legal provisions

In 1996, what survived of the traditional image of the US as a country of immigrants, built by immigrants, and open to immigrants was radically altered. The experience of life in the US changed for the worse for persons at virtually every level of the immigration chain, from illegal entrants to permanent residents. Beyond profound changes in the immigration laws, the new landscape was forged by Congress through sweeping legislation on several other fronts, including criminal law, anti-terrorism measures, and welfare law.[4]

While only a small portion of such legislation affects the rights of asylum seekers directly, the reforms as a whole sanctioned a new atmosphere in the country

---

[3]   See Art. 14, *Universal Declaration of Human Rights*, G.A. Res. 217, 3 GAOR UN Doc A/810, p. 71 (1948); Arts. 31, 33, *United Nations Convention relating to the Status of Refugees*, 28 July 1951, 19 U.S.T. 6259, T.I.A.S. No. 6577, 189 U.N.T.S. 150; *United Nations Protocol relating to the Status of Refugees*, 31 January 1967, U.S.T. 6223, T.I.A.S. No. 6577, 606 U.N.T.S. 267 (entered into force in the US on 1 November 1968); *Convention against Torture and Other Cruel, Inhuman or Degrading Treatment or Punishment*, opened for signature on 10 December 1984, Art. 3, Annex G.A. Res. 46 (XXXIX 1984), 23 I.L.M. 1027, as modified, 24 I.L.M. 535.

[4]   In addition to the *Illegal Immigration Reform and Immigrant Responsibility Act* of 1996, H.R. 2202, passed as part of an omnibus spending bill, H.R. 3610, Pub. L. No. 104–208, 110 Stat. 3009 (1996) (hereinafter IIRIRA), Congress passed the following Acts in 1996, which considerably affect the lives and status of aliens in the US: the *Antiterrorism and Effective Death Penalty Act* of 1996, Pub. L. No. 104–132, 110 Stat. 1214 (1996) (discussed below) (hereinafter AEDPA); and *the Personal Responsibility and Work Opportunity Reconciliation Act* of 1996, Pub. L. No. 104–193, 110 Stat. 2105 (1996) (taking away significant social benefits from several classes of aliens, including permanent residents).

CHAPTER 3   THE US PERSPECTIVE

and profoundly influenced public attitudes toward immigration. As shown below, the fate of individual asylum seekers is often dependent on the relatively unsupervised decisions of detention guards and Immigration and Naturalization Service (INS) officers at the local level. In this context, the general atmosphere in which the authorities operate becomes all-important, and the recent legislative changes went a long way toward making immigrants' lives in the US significantly worse. That said, what follows should not be understood as a comprehensive account of these changes, but rather as an introduction to the legal provisions directly affecting the paths of asylum seekers upon arrival in the US.

II.2   Previous regime: Exclusion, deportation and the fiction of "entry"

In the early 1980s, after over a quarter-century of a liberal release approach, US policy on the detention of improperly documented arriving aliens took a turn toward restrictiveness. Responding to the unanticipated arrival of more than 125,000 mostly undocumented Cubans in 1980, and in an effort to deter increasing numbers of Haitian boat people from seeking refuge in the US, in 1982 the Immigration and Naturalization Service (INS) adopted a new rule,[5] calling for the blanket detention of all aliens arriving without proper documentation. Under that rule, INS District Directors could parole some of those aliens into the country, but only "for emergent reasons or for reasons deemed strictly in the public interest".[6] "Emergent reasons" were understood to consist of medical reasons rendering continued detention inappropriate.[7] Under the "public interest" standard, aliens who posed "neither a security risk nor a risk of absconding," could be released if they were pregnant, a juvenile, an infant, the beneficiary of a visa petition filed by a close relative, or a witness to a judicial, administrative, or legislative proceeding.[8]

While initially intended to deter aliens without proper documentation from seeking entry into the US, the policy was disproportionately burdensome for asylum seekers. Then as now, individuals fleeing persecution were often either unable to obtain proper documentation or forced to resort to falsified papers in order to escape their oppressors. Unless they fell into one of the few, narrow categories described

---

5   47 Fed. Reg. 30044–46 (July 9, 1982), codified at 8 C.F.R. §§ 212.5, 235.3.
6   INA § 212(d)(5)(A); 8 C.F.R. § 212.5(a)(1995). In the early 1990s, at the urging of advocates such as the Lawyers Committee for Human Rights, and in an attempt to diminish the negative impact of this approach on genuine asylum seekers, the INS tentatively instituted the Asylum Pre-Screening Officer (APSO) Program (discussed further in this chapter's conclusion). Designed to expedite the release of aliens with genuine humanitarian grounds for admission, the Program got off to a shaky start and now faces an uncertain future in the new climate of hostility created by the recent legislation.
7   8 C.F.R. § 212.5(a)(1)(1995).
8   8 C.F.R. § 212.5(a)(2)(1995).

above, detention awaited them upon arrival in the US and could last up to several years, pending final resolution of their asylum applications.

The policy also penalized the relatively few undocumented asylum seekers who affirmatively presented their claims to the authorities upon arrival, while it rewarded those who succeeded in entering the US by misrepresentation or evading inspection. Before the recent legislative overhaul, US immigration law distinguished between "excludable" and "deportable" aliens based on the legal fiction of "entry". Excludable aliens were held not to have "entered" the US, thus not to have a sufficiently significant stake in remaining in the US, and were consequently denied many constitutional protections enjoyed by deportable aliens.[9] By categorizing aliens who arrived without proper documentation as excludable, the policy subjected them to detention without significant recourse to due process guarantees.[10] On the other hand, aliens without proper documentation who were apprehended after entering the US by subterfuge were considered deportable and not subject to the regulation. Thus, with no evidence that excludable aliens were any more likely to abscond than deportable ones, the rule arbitrarily differentiated between them and encouraged illegal entry, while inhibiting affirmative applications from aliens with compelling asylum claims but without the means to "enter" the US legally before applying.

For these reasons, both commentators and advocates for asylum seekers argued for substantial change. Proposals to remedy the situation ranged from the elimination of the fiction of entry in US immigration law to the expansion and improvement of procedures for the granting of parole to asylum seekers.[11] Sweeping

---

9   The attitude of US immigration law toward the availability of recourse to constitutional protections by excludable aliens is encapsulated in Supreme Court Justice Minton's 1950 pronouncement: "*Whatever* the procedure authorized by Congress is, *it is due process* as far as an alien denied entry is concerned." (Emphasis added) United States *ex rel. Knauff* v. *Shaughnessy*, 338 US 537, 544, 70 S.Ct. 309, 313, 94 L.Ed. 317 (1950). Conversely, "an alien who has entered the country [cannot be deported] without giving him all opportunity to be heard upon the questions involving his right to be and remain in the United States." *Kaoru Yamataya* v. *Fisher*, 189 US 86, 101, 23 S.Ct. 611, 615, 47 L.Ed. 721 (1903); see also *Landon* v. *Plasencia*, 459 US 21, 32, 103 S.Ct. 321, 329, 74 L.Ed.2d 21 (1982) ("an alien seeking admission to the United States requests a privilege and has no constitutional rights regarding his application. ... [H]owever, once an alien gains admission to our country ... his constitutional status changes accordingly."); *Fernandez-Roque* v. *Smith*, 734 F.2d 576, 582 (11th Cir. 1984) ("excludable aliens cannot challenge either admission or parole decisions under a claim of constitutional right").

10 Ibid.

11 Among others, the Lawyers Committee for Human Rights stressed the need to provide for the release of all "credible asylum applicants who pose no danger to the public and constitute little risk to abscond". Lawyers Committee for Human Rights, *Detention of Refugees: Problems in the Implementation of the Asylum Pre-Screening Officer Program*, pp. 14–15 (1994) (hereinafter *Asylum Pre-Screening Officer Program*); see also the US

CHAPTER 3   THE US PERSPECTIVE

reforms finally came in 1996. As shown below, however, they were a far cry from what asylum seekers' advocates had in mind.

II.3   New laws: Everyone excludable

The immigration reforms of 1996 came about in an atmosphere of political hostility toward immigrants. Part of the Republican Party's successful campaign to regain control of Congress in 1994 was predicated on strong anti-immigrant rhetoric, designed to inject into the American middle class a sense of impending crisis requiring stringent measures to "take back control of the border".[12] While illegal immigration was the reformers' principal target for demonization, generous asylum procedures were also attacked as being too susceptible to abuse by unscrupulous aliens.[13]

Accordingly, the new legislation narrowed in significant ways both an alien's access to asylum relief and the benefits available thereunder.[14] For example, an alien

---

Committee for Refugees, *Refugees at Our Border: The US Response to Asylum Seekers* pp. 14–16 (1989); and *Cruel and Questionable Policy, supra* note 2, p. 1.

12   Pat Buchanan, right wing commentator and sometime candidate in Republican presidential primaries, perhaps best exemplified the use of divisive rhetoric at the expense of immigrants: "Some of Buchanan's surest applause lines are for his promise to build 'a security fence along our southern border' and stop illegal immigration 'cold.' For a further freeze: 'a basic moratorium on legal immigration for five years because I think this country is in danger of pulling apart.'" Colman McCarthy, *Buchanan Versus the Bishops*, Wash. Post, 27 February 1996, at D20. Buchanan himself wrote: "As for illegal immigration, Congress could order a security fence built on the US southern border, beef up the Border Patrol, cut off welfare to illegals, and demand expulsion of all foreign officials who interfere in US politics the way those arrogant Mexican consul officials interfered with California's vote on Proposition 187, the ballot initiative to withdraw a wide range of benefits, including primary education for children, from illegal immigrants." Patrick J. Buchanan, *As the Republican Hour Begins, It's Time for GOP Audacity*, Houston Chronicle, 13 November 1994, p. 5.

13   Particularly effective was the conjuring of images of foreign terrorists taking advantage of generous asylum provisions to carry out their "dirty business"; see e.g. Celia W. Dugger, *Immigration Bill's Deadlines May Imperil Asylum Seekers*, N.Y. Times, 12 February 1996, at B1, Col. 2 (supporters of the immigration bill cite the notorious cases of Sheik Omar Abdel Rahman, an Egyptian cleric sentenced to life imprisonment for a plot to terrorize New York City, and Mir Amal Kansi, a Pakistani suspected of gunning down two people outside a CIA complex in Virginia, both of whom were able to prolong their stay in the US by filing applications for asylum).

14   A full account of the substantial changes to asylum procedures brought about by the 1996 reforms is beyond the scope of this paper. I have attempted here to give an overview of the principal provisions in order to contextualize the discussion of detention issues. To an observer of asylum legislation in Europe, some of the recent changes in the US will sound familiar. In the American context, however, some of these changes represent dramatic departures from the country's traditionally relatively open and optimistic attitude toward immigration. In particular, changes affecting the permanence of

is now ineligible for asylum if the INS determines that (1) a "safe third country" is available to receive the alien;[15] (2) the alien fails to demonstrate by clear and convincing evidence that the application has been filed within one year of the alien's arrival in the US;[16] or (3) the alien has had a prior application for asylum denied in the US.[17] Under the new law, a grant of asylum does not entitle an alien to permanent residence in the US, and may be rescinded if the Attorney General, through the INS, determines that (1) the alien no longer qualifies as a refugee, due to a "fundamental change in circumstances";[18] (2) the alien has fallen into one of the categories that would have made him or her ineligible for asylum in the first place;[19] (3) a third country, where the alien would not be subjected to persecution, has become available and is willing to grant the alien asylum or similar temporary

---

asylum relief and the grant of a genuine opportunity for refugees to rebuild their lives have significantly altered the landscape of immigration to the US; see *infra* note 18. With some exceptions, the new provisions will become effective on 1 April 1997. *Illegal Immigration Reform and Immigrant Responsibility Act* (IIRIRA) § 604(c).

15 A "safe third country" is defined as one other than the alien's country of nationality, where the alien's life or freedom would not be threatened and he or she would have access to a full and fair asylum procedure. IIRIRA § 604(a), INA § 208(a)(2)(A).

16 IIRIRA § 604(a), INA § 208(a)(2)(B). This provision, intended to deter so-called frivolous or fraudulent applications, actually presents certain difficulties for some *bona fide* asylum seekers, while fraudulent applicants may find it relatively simple to overcome them. Genuine refugees are often traumatized by the persecution they have suffered and may experience emotional trouble in formulating a claim within the established time limit. Conversely, fraudulent applicants experience no such emotional difficulties, and will therefore be able to comply with the time restrictions without problem. Similarly, while genuine circumstances of flight might make it difficult for *bona fide* asylum seekers to gather evidence of their date of arrival (especially if circumstances make it necessary for a victim of persecution to enter the US illegally), an alien coming to the country with the intention of staking a fraudulent claim will have no trouble gathering the necessary evidence in advance.

17 IIRIRA § 604(a), INA § 208(a)(2)(C). It should be noted that the new law permits an alien to apply anew, or to apply after one year from his or her date of arrival, if he or she can demonstrate either changed circumstances which materially affect his or her eligibility or extraordinary circumstances justifying the delay in submitting the application. IIRIRA § 604(a), INA § 208(a)(2)(D). It remains to be seen, however, how significant this provision will prove in practice in a climate of general hostility toward immigrants.

18 IIRIRA § 604(a), INA § 208(c)(2)(A).

19 These categories include: (1) having participated in any way in the persecution of others; (2) constituting a danger to the US by virtue of having been convicted of a particularly serious crime; (3) rousing serious suspicions of having committed a serious non-political crime abroad prior to arrival; (4) constituting a danger to the security of the US; (5) having been firmly resettled, prior to arrival in the US, in a country other than the one where persecution occurred; (6) being connected with any terrorist activity. IIRIRA § 604(a), INA § 208(c)(2)(B). For a more detailed treatment of the last category, see the discussion below relating to the provisions of the *Antiterrorism and Effective Death Penalty Act* of 1996.

CHAPTER 3   THE US PERSPECTIVE

protection pursuant to a multilateral agreement;[20] (4) the alien has voluntarily resettled, or attempted to resettle, in the country where persecution occurred;[21] or (5) the alien has acquired a new nationality.[22] Upon rescission of asylum status, the alien becomes removable from the US.[23]

The new legislation eliminates the fiction of "entry" by treating all aliens who are "unlawfully present" in the US as not yet admitted.[24] Under the prior legal regime, the INS was entitled to take aliens in deportation proceedings into custody.[25] In contrast to excludable aliens, however, an alien apprehended after entering without inspection or overstaying his or her visa was classified as deportable and could appeal the custody decision to an immigration judge, either for release or for bond reduction.[26] The judge then had to determine whether the applicant constituted a poor bail risk or a threat to national security, keep a written record and inform the parties of the reasons for the decision.[27] If necessary, the applicant could further appeal the judge's bond determination to the Board of Immigration Appeals, an appellate administrative tribunal.[28] The availability of judicial review in deportation proceedings sometimes led to earlier release for deportable aliens as compared to those in exclusion proceedings.[29]

In treating all "unlawfully present" aliens as not yet admitted, the new law relegates them all to the status previously described as "excludable" – which, for the purposes of recourse against detention, is equivalent to being deprived of any

---

20   IIRIRA § 604(a), INA § 208(c)(2)(C). By comparison to similar recent changes in some European countries' approach to asylum (e.g. Germany and other Schengen agreement signatories) this provision foreshadows the daunting possibility that groups of refugee-receiving countries around the world might attempt to set up structures to deal with regional fluctuations in the flow of refugees by periodically transferring "excess" numbers from one country to the other pursuant to international multilateral agreements. Such a scenario clearly runs the risk of failing to afford asylum seekers a genuine opportunity to rebuild their lives in permanent, meaningful ways.
21   IIRIRA § 604(a), INA § 208(c)(2)(D).
22   IIRIRA § 604(a), INA § 208(c)(2)(E).
23   IIRIRA § 604(a), INA § 208(c)(3).
24   The definition "unlawfully present" includes both aliens who have overstayed their visas and aliens who entered without inspection. INA § 235(a)(1); IIRIRA §§ 301(a), (b), 302(a).
25   8 C.F.R. § 242.2(c)(1995).
26   8 C.F.R. §§ 3.19(a), 242.2(d) (1995).
27   8 C.F.R. §§ 3.1(b)(7), 3.19(f)(1995).
28   *Ibid.*
29   It should be emphasized, however, that prohibitively high bonds often constituted insurmountable barriers for indigent aliens in detention, effectively limiting the release advantages deportable aliens may have had over excludable ones. Bond amounts were initially left to the discretion of INS District Directors, were often arbitrarily set and varied widely from one district to another. 8 C.F.R. § 242.2(c)(2)(1995); see *Cruel and Questionable Policy*, *supra* note 2, p. 17. Similarly situated asylum applicants could thus often be subjected to significantly different treatment, depending on the INS district within which they found themselves.

significant constitutional protections. While eliminating the prior irrational practice of favoring aliens who entered illegally over those who affirmatively presented asylum applications at the border, the new provisions simply put all unlawfully present aliens in as unfavorable a position as those in the worst case scenario under prior law.[30] As a result, no *bona fide* asylum applicant will be advantaged by the new provisions, but some (those who enter without inspection or overstay their visas) will be made worse off. All asylum seekers who are either arriving or are unlawfully present (in other words the vast majority) will be deprived of the favorable appeal provisions available to deportable aliens with respect to the INS decision to detain them.

The new law also provides for the "expedited removal" without a hearing of all aliens who arrive in the US with no documents or with fraudulent documents, unless they raise a credible fear of persecution before an INS asylum officer at the border.[31] A negative decision by the INS officer in this regard may be appealed to an immigration judge, who must review it within seven days of the INS officer's determination.[32] Detention of the alien is mandatory until a final determination of the credible fear question is reached.[33]

Further detention is automatic, pending consideration of his or her asylum application, for any alien who succeeds in establishing such a credible fear upon

---

30 American immigration case law is full of instances of aliens who, after living in the country for years, or even decades, were threatened with exclusion, often resulting from a technicality, upon returning after a brief trip abroad; see e.g. *Shaughnessy* v. *US ex rel. Mezei*, 345 US 206, 73 S.Ct. 625, 97 L.Ed. 956 (1953) (after living in the US for 25 years, the respondent went to Hungary for 19 months, was found excludable upon return and confined to indefinite detention at Ellis Island when no other country agreed to take him in). *Mezei* was only the first of a long string of cases, many of which are never reported.

31 A credible fear of persecution is defined as a "significant possibility" that the alien will establish eligibility for asylum. INA § 235(b)(1)(B). Immigration authorities are under no obligation to inform aliens subject to expedited removal of the availability of asylum relief. This raises a host of questions concerning the adequacy of requiring genuine victims of persecution to raise their claims affirmatively and immediately upon arrival. It is common knowledge that trauma, fear, or an understandable mistrust of authorities may prevent legitimate refugees from being capable of producing their stories or formulating their claims with such efficiency. These difficulties are compounded by the fact that the authorities' obligation to inform an alien that he or she may be represented by counsel, and to provide him or her with a list of available *pro bono* attorneys, does not arise until the time of actual filing of the asylum application. IIRIRA § 604(a), INA § 208(d)(4). It is possible that upcoming regulations, to be issued by the INS in conformity with the new laws, will create obligations to provide fuller information and attorney access to arriving aliens. Similar regulations have done so in the past, see e.g. 8 C.F.R. §§ 236.5 (1995), but need not do so in the future. No such obligations have been created as of this writing.

32 *Ibid.*

33 INA § 235(b)(1)(B)(iii)(IV).

arrival, or who applies for asylum while unlawfully present in the US.[34] Subsequently, the INS may release the alien, but only on bond of at least US$ 1,500 or on "conditional parole".[35] The authorities are under no obligation to release the alien, however, and may prolong detention indefinitely. Additionally, the alien has no recourse to judicial review of INS decisions concerning either the length of detention or the denial of bond or parole.[36] From a historical perspective, giving such extensive discretion to the INS in detention matters promises to lead to serious shortcomings in the treatment of asylum seekers. As shown below, detained aliens traditionally have had little opportunity to voice their concerns about conditions of detention, and the INS has shown no ability or inclination to correct its own missteps.[37]

By comparison to the previous regime, more stringent deadlines and scheduling requirements in the applications' adjudicatory process under the new law raise some hope for shorter detention periods. In the absence of exceptional circumstances, the initial interview or hearing on the merits of the application must begin within 45 days of filing, and a result must be reached no later than six months

---

34 INA § 235(b)(1)(B)(ii). The finality of this situation for some asylum seekers may be affected by the future of the APSO Program, discussed in the conclusion to this article.

35 INA § 236(a). The 1996 legislation does not elaborate on the substantive meaning of "conditional parole". In the past, the term has indicated the relatively favorable terms imposed on deportable aliens as a condition for the granting of parole; see *Matter of Patel*, 15 I. & N. December 666(1976). Further clarifications as to the term's meaning in this context, however, are left to regulations to be promulgated by the INS in the months to come. While substantive commentary on such provisions will have to wait until specific regulations are available, it is important here to underscore that Congress has chosen to leave the details of the granting of parole entirely in the hands of the Executive. This approach is permissible under watershed decisions of the federal courts in the 1980s, but it is by no means mandated by them. The policy of leaving ample room for the INS to administer the granting of parole has led in the past, and is likely to lead in the future, to substantial discrimination in the application of parole provisions among aliens of different classes and ethnic backgrounds; see e.g. *Jean v. Nelson*, 727 F.2d 957 (11th Cir. 1984), modified 472 US 846, 105 S.Ct. 2992, 86 L.Ed.2d 664 (1985) (INS practice of disproportionately denying parole to Haitian refugees as compared to others was acceptable without substantive inquiry as long as the INS could advance a "facially legitimate and *bona fide* reason").

36 INA § 236(e). Astonishing though it may seem, such treatment is not likely to meet with significant difficulties from a constitutional perspective. As explained above, by treating all unlawfully present aliens as not yet admitted, the new law relegates them to a status in which *habeas corpus* and due process challenges to parole or custody decisions are, for all practical purposes, of little use; see *supra* note 9, and particularly *Fernandez-Roque* v. *Smith*, 734 F.2d 576, 582 (11th Cir. 1984) ("excludable aliens cannot challenge either admission or parole decisions under a claim of constitutional right"). By contrast, an alien in deportation proceedings "should not be detained or required to post bond except on a finding that he is a threat to the national security or that he is a poor bail risk". *Matter of Patel*, 15 I. & N. December 666, 666 (BIA 1976).

37 See *infra*, section on conditions of detention.

after filing.[38] Administrative appeal against that decision must be taken within 30 days.[39] However, there are no explicit deadlines for reaching the decision on appeal, and the extent to which the system will be able to comply even with explicit scheduling requirements remains to be seen. Asylum adjudication resources are scarce, its institutions already suffering under the weight of considerable backlogs.[40] Success in complying with required deadlines in cases filed under the new law may also come at the expense of older cases which, not being subject to comparable timing requirements, may end up being postponed indefinitely and result in prolonged, equally indefinite detention periods.

The new law requires the INS to detain virtually all criminal aliens upon release from criminal custody and until termination of their removal proceedings.[41] However, in view of the foreseeable short-term insufficiency of currently available detention space and personnel, the new law allows for a one-year period of transition, effective from September 30, 1996 and extendable for one additional year.[42] During this time, the INS must take into custody all aliens who fall under the following categories upon release from their criminal sentences: (1) aggravated felons; (2) aliens not admissible because they committed crimes of moral turpitude, drug trafficking or abuse, prostitution, or violation of immigration conditions to a grant of immunity, and repeat offenders whose aggregate sentences exceeded five years; and (3) aliens deportable because they committed crimes of moral turpitude, aggravated felonies, drug-related or certain firearms offenses, or crimes against the State. Of these, the INS may release only aliens under categories (2) and (3), provided they either (1) were lawfully admitted to the US, pose no threat to the community and no risk of absconding; or (2) were not lawfully admitted, but cannot be removed because no country will accept them, and they pose no threat to the community and no risk of absconding.[43]

---

38 IIRIRA § 604(a), INA § 208(d)(5)(A)(ii) and (iii).
39 IIRIRA § 604(a), INA § 208(d)(5)(A)(iv).
40 Subject to availability of funds, the 1996 legislation calls for at least 300 additional Asylum Officers (for a total of at least 600) by fiscal year 1997. IIRIRA § 605. According to the INS, the backlog of asylum cases stood at 460,000 as of 1 April 1996. US Immigration and Naturalization Service, *Asylum Reform: A Year of Success* (1 April 1996). For fiscal year 1993, the Senate found the backlog of asylum cases to be up to 340,000. Conference Report on H.R. 3355, *Violent Crime Control and Law Enforcement Act* of 1993, 140 Cong. Rec. H8772–03, H8836 (21 August 1994). One proponent of reform estimated that backlog to have risen to 450,000 by August 1995. Rep. Bob Franks, NJ, *Introduction of a Bill to Reduce Political Asylum Abuse*, 141 Cong. Rec. E1635–01 (August 3, 1995).
41 IIRIRA § 303(a), INA § 236(c). The only exceptions are where release is necessary to facilitate witness protection or cooperation with justice, if the alien poses no danger to the community and no risk of absconding. IIRIRA § 303(a), INA § 236(c)(2).
42 IIRIRA § 303(b)(2).
43 IIRIRA § 303(b)(3).

CHAPTER 3   THE US PERSPECTIVE

While most asylum seekers are not affected legally by provisions pertaining to criminal aliens, the new impetus toward detention is likely to affect genuine refugees in several significant, if indirect, respects. As shown below, asylum seekers are often made to share detention space with seasoned criminals. This affects not only their immediate environment in terms of their relationship to fellow prisoners, but also their standing with respect to INS officers and private prison guards, who frequently have difficulty and make little effort in distinguishing between different classes of aliens. The treatment asylum seekers receive during detention is thus likely to be substantially worsened by the pervasive presence of criminal aliens in their immediate detention surroundings. Deprived of significant means to voice their concerns, asylum seekers are also at risk of having their histories, interests and goals lumped in with those of criminal aliens in the eyes of distant politicians and the general public.[44]

II.4   Anti-terrorism laws

The 26 February 1993 attack on the World Trade Center in New York City and the 19 April 1995 bombing of the federal building in Oklahoma City thrust the question of terrorism into the political limelight. The threat of radical anti-establishment violence on US soil and how to prevent it became hot issues, offering President Clinton and Congressional legislators an opportunity to show a capacity for strong, dynamic initiative with relatively little risk of disagreement. One result, among others, was a series of draconian measures at the border which, although unlikely to affect a large number of asylum seekers, is nevertheless indicative of the country's newfound mistrust of foreigners and Congress' willingness to sacrifice aliens' procedural rights to short-term political ends.[45]

Some genuine asylum seekers may be affected by the new anti-terrorism measures and detained as a result. Under prior law, a terrorist was defined as an alien who: (1) has engaged in terrorist activity, or (2) immigration officials know or

---

44   It should also be noted, however, that the severity of certain new criminal provisions, for example those designed to combat document fraud, could also affect asylum seekers directly. Frightened or inadvertent asylum seekers may slip into one of a number of "criminal" alien categories accidentally, and thereafter receive treatment ostensibly intended for presumptively undesirable criminals; see e.g. IIRIRA § 334 (pertaining to enhanced criminal penalties for failure to depart, illegal re-entry, and passport and visa fraud); IIRIRA §§ 211, 214 (pertaining to criminal penalties for fraudulent use of government-issued documents and for knowingly presenting documents which fail to contain a reasonable basis in law or in fact).

45   The *Antiterrorism and Effective Death Penalty Act* (AEDPA), *supra* note 4, was signed into law by President Clinton on 24 April 1996.

have reason to believe is likely to engage in terrorist activity.[46] The new measures substantially expand these categories to include any alien who has incited terrorist activity, or who is either a representative or simply a member of an organization designated as a terrorist organization by the Secretary of State.[47] Such designations are likely to be susceptible to foreign policy demands, but unlikely to be very sensitive to the needs of individual asylum seekers. As a result genuine, peaceful refugees may end up defined as terrorists because of political membership of the "wrong" organizations.[48]

With minor exceptions, an alien alleged to be a terrorist may not apply for asylum.[49] To determine whether he or she is a terrorist, the alien is subjected to special "Alien Terrorist Removal Proceedings," which sharply curtail his or her procedural rights.[50] In addition, the alien must be detained until he or she is either removed from the US or cleared of the charge of being a terrorist by a final judgment.[51] Although these provisions are too recent to provide any significant data on the duration of appeal procedures, it is conceivable that such a structure will lead

---

46 INA § 212(a)(3)(B)(i) (1995). In addition, any officer, official, representative or spokesman of the Palestine Liberation Organisation (PLO) was automatically considered a terrorist. *Ibid.*

47 IIRIRA § 342, AEDPA § 411, INA § 212(a)(3)(B).

48 The possibility of error is particularly great in the case of aliens from countries such as Algeria, for example, where violent factions like the *Groupe Islamique Armé* are frequently associated with, yet wholly separate from, *bona fide* political parties like the *Front Islamique du Salut*. While there is no reason to suspect a member of the political party of terrorism, the existence of the terrorist organization may lead inexperienced immigration officials to do so erroneously.

49 The exceptions cover situations in which the alien either falls under the category of mere member of a terrorist organization, or is deemed by the Attorney General, as a matter of discretion, not to constitute a danger to the security of the US. AEDPA § 431, INA § 208(a). I consider these exceptions minor because INS officers at ports of entry, to whom the Attorney General's discretion is delegated, are unlikely to look favorably upon aliens in the current climate.

50 A detailed description of the rules governing the conduct of the "Alien Terrorist Removal Proceedings" is beyond the scope of this paper. For a general flavor, however, it should be mentioned that a special court composed of federal district court judges is set up to determine whether the alien is in fact a terrorist. During the proceedings, which are open to the public, the alien has a right to counsel, but may be prevented from examining any adverse evidence or witnesses if these are considered classified, or if their disclosure would endanger national security. Where this is the case, the judge considers the evidence *ex parte, in camera* and, where possible, a summary of the evidence is provided to the alien. In addition, the Federal Rules of Evidence do not apply, and the alien has no recourse to exclude any evidence against him or her obtained by unlawful means or in violation of his or her rights. AEDPA § 401(a), INA § 504.

51 AEDPA § 401(a), INA §§ 506, 507. This requirement means that, where the hearing judge clears the alien of the charge of being a terrorist and the government appeals, the alien must remain in custody for the pendency of the appeal. AEDPA § 401(a), INA § 507(a)(2).

CHAPTER 3   THE US PERSPECTIVE

to substantial periods of detention. As shown below, for many asylum seekers such an option can turn into a harrowing experience.

III   Conditions of detention

III.1   Detention facilities

Detention facilities have often proved inadequate for the task at hand. Despite the civil nature of immigration proceedings, federal courts and commentators have frequently likened conditions of confinement for aliens to those reserved for serious criminals, or worse.[52] The INS holds detained aliens in three different kinds of facilities: those run by the INS directly, known as Service Processing Centers (SPCs);[53] those run by private companies under contract to the INS, known as "non-

---

52   The Tenth Circuit has compared detention conditions for Cuban *Marielitos* to prison conditions reserved for "our worst criminals", *Rodriguez-Fernandez* v. *Wilkinson*, 654 F.2d 1382, 1385 (10th Cir. 1981). In describing the prospective site for a detention facility at Fort Allen, Puerto Rico, a federal district court went so far as to declare that "[a]t other times and circumstances the so-called refugee facility would be referred to as a concentration camp", *Puerto Rico* v. *Muskie*, 507 F.Supp 1035, 1043 (D.P.R.), vacated per consent agreement *sub nom. Marquez-Colon* v. *Reagan*, 688 F.2d 611 (1st Cir. 1981). Perhaps most significantly, courts evaluating the constitutionality of detention conditions for aliens have paid lip service to the distinction between asylum seekers and convicts, but proceeded to analyze cases under standards applicable to criminals only; see e.g. *Imasuen* v. *Moyer*, 1995 WL 506055 (N.D.Ill.), available in WESTLAW, Allfeds Database (stating that detention of non-criminals is unconstitutional where it amounts to punishment under Due Process clause of Fifth Amendment, but proceeding to uphold detention of non-criminal aliens by applying Eighth Amendment cruel and unusual punishment standard, which is ostensibly applicable only to criminal prisoners). Commentators equating immigration detention facilities to correctional institutions include Arthur C. Helton, *The Legality of Detaining Refugees in the United States*, 14 N.Y.U. Rev. L. & Soc. Change 353, 364 (1987); Peter H. Schuck, *The Transformation of Immigration Law*, 84 Colum. L. Rev. 1, 28 n. 149 (1984); Margaret H. Taylor, *Detained Aliens Challenging Conditions of Confinement and the Porous Border of the Plenary Power Doctrine*, Hast. Const. L. Quart. 1087, 1113, n. 126 (1995) (hereinafter Taylor). Newspaper reports have found conditions of detention for aliens to be even worse than prisons. In particular, one report stated that "[o]f the 15 detention centers INS use[d] to hold detainees [in 1993], only two have met the minimum standards of the American Correctional Association". *Prison v. INS Detention: Convicts Have More Perks*, Miami Herald, 16 December 1993, p. 25A; see also *Is This Any Way to Treat People?*, Newsday, 1 December 1993, p. 50, Col. 1 (discussing evidence that detention conditions for asylum seekers are considerably below those for US criminals).

53   The INS operates nine detention facilities directly (located in Aguadilla, PR; Boston, Mass.; El Centro, Cal.; El Paso, Tex.; Florence, Ariz.; Miami, Fla.; New York, NY; Los Fresnos, Tex.; and San Pedro, Cal.), which account for 2,549 beds. James A. Puleo, Executive Associate Commissioner, Programs, Immigration and Naturalization Service, *Overall Detention Policy and Coordination: Testimony Before the House Appropriations Committee*, Subcommittee on Commerce, State and Justice (6 April 1995), available in

service" facilities;[54] and ordinary state or local criminal correctional facilities at which the INS rents available space for the detention of aliens.[55] In addition to these, the US government set up what were originally meant to be only temporary detention facilities at US naval bases in Guantanamo Bay, Cuba, and Empire Range, Panama, in response to unexpectedly high influxes of Haitian and Cuban refugees beginning in the 1980s.[56] While analytically distinguishable in some significant ways, these different types of detention facilities have shared serious shortcomings in regard to meeting acceptable standards in the conditions of detention.

WESTLAW, CONGHRT database (hereinafter *Overall Detention Policy*). The INS also operates one facility in Oakdale, La., jointly with the Bureau of Prisons (BOP), which dedicates approximately 1,000 beds to criminal aliens. Taylor, *supra* note 52, p. 1106, No. 99. The 1996 immigration reforms called on the INS to increase detention space to 9,000 beds by fiscal year 1997. IIRIRA § 386(a). An additional US$ 150 million was also added to the INS budget to cover the costs of removing inadmissible and deportable aliens, including detention costs. IIRIRA § 385. In February 1996, the INS announced plans to build a new detention facility in collaboration with the US Marshals Service in Batavia, New York, with 454 beds intended partly for aliens awaiting deportation hearings, but also for common criminals. 61 Fed. Reg. 6658 (21 February 1996).

54 The INS used five privately run facilities as of April 1995, accounting for 1,095 beds for aliens of all kinds; see *Overall Detention Policy*, *supra* note 53. Of these, the Corrections Corporation of America ran two in Houston and Laredo, Texas; Esmor Correctional Services ran two in Seattle, Washington and Elizabeth, New Jersey; and Wackenhut Corporation ran one facility in Denver, Colorado. *Ibid.*; INS Public Affairs Unit. An additional, privately run facility, used exclusively to house 500 criminal aliens, was located in Eloy, Ariz. *Ibid.*

55 The number of such facilities used by the INS is in the hundreds, but varies periodically. Americas Watch, *Brutality Unchecked: Human Rights Abuses Along the US Border With Mexico* 62 (1992) (hereinafter *Brutality Unchecked)*; see also Women's Commission for Refugee Women and Children, *A Cry for Help: Chinese Women in INS Detention* (1995) (hereinafter *A Cry for Help)*. According to James A. Puleo, "the INS reimburses state and local jails based on INS needs and the availability of bed space to acquire in excess of 600,000 detention days per year, or approximately 1,640 beds annually. As of 31 March 1995, about 1,700 beds were being used in state and local jails." *Overall Detention Policy*, *supra* note 53. In presenting the Justice Department's budget for 1997 to the Senate, Attorney General Janet Reno earmarked US$ 500 million to reimburse state and local correctional facilities for detention space used by the INS. Janet Reno, Attorney General of the United States, *Prepared Testimony before the Senate Appropriations Committee, Commerce, Justice, and State, the Judiciary and related Matters*, available in WESTLAW, CONGHRT database (2 May 1996) (hereinafter *Testimony of Janet Reno)*. As of January 1995, 69,926 aliens, not all asylum seekers, were incarcerated in state correctional facilities, and an unknown number were held in city or county jails around the country. Alexander T. Aleinikoff, General Counsel, Immigration and Naturalization Service, *Identification of Criminal Aliens and Removal of Deportable Aliens: Testimony Before the House Judiciary Committee*, Subcommittee on Immigration and Claims, available in WESTLAW, CONGHRT database (23 March 1995) (hereinafter *Identification and Removal)*.

56 Tracy Wilkinson, *Hitches Slow Panama-US Tent City Rush*, L.A. Times, 4 September 1994, p. A17, Col. 1.

CHAPTER 3   THE US PERSPECTIVE

III.2   Service Processing Centers

Facilities run by the INS directly have forced asylum seekers to share living space with experienced criminals, giving rise to frequent intimidation and abuse.[57] Overcrowding has been a chronic problem, occasionally reaching incredible and untenable proportions. In the words of one commentator:

> "Soon after the new policy of detaining undocumented excludable aliens was announced in 1981 . . . the Krome detention center in Florida was filled more than three times beyond its stated capacity. Over a thousand detainees (mostly Haitians) were crowded into makeshift shelters without adequate sanitation or medical care. Conditions at Krome were abhorrent during this period. Untreated sewage threatened to contaminate the drinking water. The Florida Health Department cited Krome for numerous health and safety violations, and the state sued to close the facility because of the severe overcrowding."[58]

Similar conditions plagued the Los Fresnos, Tex., facility in 1990, after the INS implemented a policy of increased detention as a deterrent against immigrants from Central America.[59] Two thousand detainees were forced to occupy a space designed for 425, and many were confined to tents or other temporary arrangements without access to showers or clean clothes.[60] In 1994, both Krome and Los Fresnos once again risked severe overpopulation as thousands of fleeing Haitians and Cubans approached US shores before being diverted to face similarly strenuous conditions at the US Naval Base in Guantanamo Bay.[61]

Detainees are often held for years at inadequately staffed SPCs designed for two to three month stays.[62] They are provided with few educational opportunities, translation services are scarce and facilities often isolated, making access to family and counsel impracticable. The joint INS/Bureau of Prisons (BOP) facility in Oakdale, La., for example, is located about three-and-a-half hours by car from both

---

57   According to one report, asylum seekers forced to share prison cells with seasoned criminals were subjected to severe verbal and physical abuse by their cell mates, including being severely beaten, prevented from sleeping for hours on end, or being set on fire while they slept. The same report indicates that often asylum seekers were wrongly accused and made to pay for the disciplinary infractions of their criminal cell mates; see *Brutality Unchecked*, supra note 55, p. 56; see also Arthur C. Helton, *The Detention of Asylum Seekers in the United States and Canada*, in Asylum Law and Practice in Europe and North America, p. 169 (1992).
58   Taylor, *supra* note 52, p. 1114.
59   Robert Suro, *US Is Renewing Border Detentions*, N.Y. Times, 8 February 8 1990, at A22.
60   *Brutality Unchecked*, supra note 55, pp. 58–59.
61   Taylor, *supra* note 52, p. 1116.
62   *Cruel and Questionable Policy*, supra note 2, p. 22; *Brutality Unchecked*, supra note 55, p. 57; Taylor, *supra* note 52, p. 1116.

New Orleans and Houston, the nearest cities. Detainees are thus dependent for legal services on the scant resources of the local bar, which consists of twelve lawyers unaccustomed to providing *pro bono* representation, and a few extraordinarily willing volunteer attorneys from New Orleans.[63]

Conditions are often unsanitary, medical care poor, and food provisions inadequate, while prison authorities frequently use segregation arbitrarily as an incentive for detainees to concede to deportation.[64] At some facilities, detainees are prevented from going outdoors for the entire length of their detention,[65] while in other cases they are deprived of the most basic shelter:

> "At the El Centro SPC, for example, detainees were forced to spend fourteen hours a day outside in the desert sun, where temperatures regularly exceeded one hundred degrees, simply because there were not enough guards to supervise the air-conditioned barracks during the day."[66]

Serious deficiencies in medical services plague detention facilities at all levels. In 1993, the deliberate refusal by the INS at Guantanamo to provide adequate medical care to HIV-positive Haitian detainees was condemned by a federal court as "outrageous, callous and reprehensible".[67] Beyond such high-profile cases, deficient basic medical services are a common feature of INS detention centers. A doctor visiting the El Centro SPC in 1981 found significant portions of the detainee population suffering from scabies, a highly contagious skin disease easily treated with over-the-counter medicines.[68] According to some reports, pregnant women and detainees suffering from chronic health or psychiatric problems (often occasioned or precipitated by the detention conditions themselves) have been among the most neglected.[69]

---

63 *Cruel and Questionable Policy, supra* note 2, p. 25.
64 See American Civil Liberties Union, Public Policy Report, *Justice Detained: Conditions at the Varick Street Immigration Detention Center* (1993) (hereinafter *Justice Detained); A Cry for Help, supra* note 55. Already in 1983, an unpublished study by Church World Service found that: "All of the [SPC] facilities in general are ill-equipped to handle the recreational, physical and especially mental-health needs of detainees ... Most facilities have poor medical care for detainees, food is barely adequate or poor, access to telephones is difficult to almost impossible. Visits by relatives and legal representatives are often restricted in general due to time or problems due to lack of space in the physical facility, or are arbitrarily denied by INS." M. Schrock, *Conditions and Needs in the INS Detention Facilities: A Report,* p. 2 (November 1983).
65 See e.g. *Justice Detained, supra* note 64, pp. 11 and 32–33
66 Taylor, *supra* note 52, pp. 1116–17.
67 *Haitian Centers Council* v. *Sale*, 823 F.Supp. 1028, 1038 (E.D.N.Y. 1993).
68 *Brutality Unchecked, supra* note 55, p. 57.
69 Taylor, *supra* note 52, p. 1117; see also *Justice Detained, supra* note 64, pp. 44–46; *Brutality Unchecked, supra* note 55, pp. 59–60; American Civil Liberties Union, *Detention of Undocumented Aliens* 56–60 (1990).

CHAPTER 3   THE US PERSPECTIVE

Physical abuse of detainees has also been a recurring problem at SPC detention facilities. Despite cooperation with the Bureau of Prisons (BOP), and the promulgation of minimum standards of conduct and respect for prisoners on the part of guards, the INS has failed to ensure compliance with such standards at individual facilities. Instead of leading to better treatment of detainees, this cooperation with BOP has sometimes led to such unwarranted intrusions into individual privacy as pat searches, metal detector examinations and phone call monitoring by guards.[70] Americas Watch has documented a consistent pattern of abuse at SPCs, resulting from attempts by guards to discipline detainees through punishment, to suppress protests about detention conditions, or simply to assert limitless power over detainees. The following passage concerning events at El Centro illustrates a commonly occurring pattern:

"In practically every case, a detention officer singled out a detainee for beating because he disliked his 'attitude' or for some other pretext. The detainee was then locked in the shower room at the Processing building and hit by the officer in the stomach, chest, and sometimes other parts of the body. In several cases, other officers watched passively. According to many detainees, verbal abuse is widespread at El Centro, and guards routinely use profanity in insulting detainees."[71]

While its efforts to set uniform acceptable standards of officer behavior at SPCs have been largely unsuccessful, the INS has also engaged in a widespread practice of hiring private guards to supplement an insufficient supply of government trained Detention Enforcement Officers.[72] These private guards exhibit many of the same shortcomings discussed below in connection with "non-service" facilities. In addition, complicated or non-existent complaint procedures at SPCs have made it practically impossible for isolated detainees to draw attention to their plight.[73] As a result, many detainees have resorted to extreme remedial measures, such as hunger-strikes and riots, to obtain redress of their grievances.[74]

---

70   *Cruel and Questionable Policy, supra* note 2, pp. 23–24.
71   *Brutality Unchecked, supra* note 55, p. 54; see also Judith Cummings, *Aliens Staging Hunger Strike at Detention Camp*, N.Y. Times, 4 June 1985, available in LEXIS, NEWS Library, NYT File (describing detainee grievances at El Centro to include human rights abuses, inadequate food and medical attention, poor sanitation facilities, physical abuse and lack of access to lawyers).
72   As of April 1995, approximately 40% of the detention staff at SPCs were private contract employees. *Overall Detention Policy, supra* note 53.
73   *Brutality Unchecked, supra* note 55, p. 55.
74   James Bennet, *Illegal Aliens and Guards Hurt in Melee*, N.Y. Times, 30 December 1991, available in LEXIS, NEWS Library, NYT File (25 asylum seekers planning hunger-strike to protest food quality at Varick Street are involved in fight with INS guards); Lydia Chavez, *Aliens Are Paying a Price for Honesty*, New York Times, 24 December 1987,

The dramatic inadequacy of detention conditions at SPCs is compounded by indications that widespread incompetence, or design, or both, have contributed to a lack of procedural transparency on the part of the INS in its management of the facilities. While abuses and inadequate conditions often go unaddressed due to a

---

available in LEXIS, NEWS Library, NYT File (17 asylum seekers staging hunger-strike at Varick Street facility were routinely forced by guards to walk through dining room at meal times); *Cuban Refugees in US: A Recent History*, N.Y. Times, 4 December 1987, available in LEXIS, NEWS Library, NYT File (thousands of Cuban refugees at four facilities (Krome, Florence, AZ, Oakdale and Atlanta federal penitentiary) riot, take hostages and stage hunger-strikes to protest policy of indefinite detention); Judith Cummings, *Aliens Staging Hunger Strike at Detention Camp*, N.Y. Times, 4 June 1985, available in LEXIS, NEWS Library, NYT File (180 Central American refugees at El Centro go on hunger-strike to protest inadequate food and medical attention, poor sanitation facilities, physical abuse and lack of access to lawyers); *Refugees Continue Hunger Strike*, N.Y. Times, 11 March 1985, available in LEXIS, NEWS Library, NYT File (23 Afghan asylum seekers go on hunger-strike to protest unwarranted ten month detention at Varick Street SPC); United Press International, *Aliens Held in Miami Go on a Hunger Strike*, N.Y. Times, 1 February 1984, available in LEXIS, NEWS Library, NYT File (Asylum seekers protesting detention conditions at Krome and excessively long application processing delays liken facility to concentration camp, call for "collective suicide" and go on hunger-strike); Joseph P. Fried, *Afghans Find Asylum Goal Hard to Gain*, N.Y. Times, 5 May 1983, available in LEXIS, NEWS Library, NYT File (40 Afghans stage hunger-strike to protest unjustifiably long (15 months) detention periods at INS facility in Brooklyn, N.Y.); Associated Press, *Court Order Cuts Haitian Total in Miami Detention Site to Two*, N.Y. Times, 13 October 1982, available in LEXIS, NEWS Library, NYT File (During the early 80s inadequate conditions for Haitian detainees at Krome led to several violent riots, 200 escapes, 29 suicide attempts and numerous hunger-strikes); *US Is Remaining Adamant as Detained Haitians Press Appeals for Asylum*, N.Y. Times, 24 April 1982, available in LEXIS, NEWS Library, NYT File (33 Haitian women asylum seekers go on hunger-strike in support of pending litigation to obtain their release from Krome); *Immigration Service Says Over 100 Fled from Haitian Camp*, N.Y. Times, 29 December 1981, available in LEXIS, NEWS Library, NYT File (600 Haitian detainees begin hunger-strike on Christmas Eve to protest conditions at Krome); Raymond Bonner, *US Transfers 120 Haitians to Prison in New York State*, N.Y. Times, 5 September 1981, available in LEXIS, NEWS Library, NYT File (about 1,000 Haitian detainees, including women, participate in hunger-strike to protest detention conditions at Krome); John M. Crewdson, *Salvadoran Says Fear of Death Pushed him on Hard Trek North*, N. Y. Times 6 March 1981, available in LEXIS, NEWS Library, NYT File (140 Salvadoran asylum seekers at El Centro protest authorities' withholding of information concerning the rumored murder of fellow Salvadorans recently deported to El Salvador).
Not surprisingly, similar developments are not the exclusive province of facilities run by the INS directly, but have taken place at non-service facilities as well: Matthew Purdy and Celia Dugger, *Legacy of Immigrants' Uprising: New Jail Operator, Little Change*, N.Y. Times, 24 August 1996, available in LEXIS, NEWS Library, NYT File; Kenneth B. Noble, *Golden Venture Refugees on Hunger Strike in California to Protest Detention*, N.Y. Times, 2 December 1995, available in LEXIS, NEWS Library, NYT; William E. Schmidt, *Atlanta Prison Lockup of Cubans Continues*, N.Y. Times, 25 October 1984, available in LEXIS, NEWS Library, NYT File; *Haitians at 2 Detention Sites Refusing to Eat and to Talk*, N.Y. Times, 25 December 1981, available in LEXIS, NEWS Library, NYT File.

lack of proper reporting mechanisms, there have also been signs of active concealment on the part of some officials. Most prominently, disgruntled INS employees revealed in 1996 that INS officers in charge of the Krome detention center in July 1995, actively deceived a visiting Congressional delegation about conditions at the center. Shortly before the delegation's arrival, the officers released large numbers of detainees to prevent discovery of overcrowded conditions, and destroyed incriminating computer records and evidence of further problems in the detention system.[75]

As this article goes to press, several class action lawsuits have been filed against the INS, alleging manifold constitutional violations of alien detainees' rights at SPCs.[76] Similar efforts in the past, however, have proved unsuccessful.[77]

III.3   State and local prisons

Alien detainees housed in state and local prison space rented by the INS endure similar conditions.[78] In these cases, asylum seekers are often treated like dangerous criminals, with no regard for the hardships they may have endured as a result of persecution, or for the particularly vulnerable condition in which they may find themselves.

> "A common problem at jails is that the INS contracts orally for the use of space and makes few or no special provisions regarding the treatment of INS detainees. Many jails take pride that INS detainees are treated just like other prisoners. They make no provision for the needs of INS detainees, such as Spanish [or other foreign] language materials, information regarding US immigration laws and procedures, lists of organizations that provide free or

---

75 Matthew Purdy and Celia Dugger, *Legacy of Immigrants' Uprising: New Jail Operator, Little Change*, N.Y. Times, 7 July 1996, available in LEXIS, NEWS Library, NYT File (hereinafter *Legacy of Uprising*). According to accusations by the 40 disgruntled INS employees, their bosses improperly released 149 detainees prior to the arrival of the congressional delegation, and instructed guards to remove their weapons belts, handcuffs and holsters "to present a kinder, gentler image". Subsequently, at least five senior INS officials refused to answer investigators' questions without the assistance of counsel. Mark Lacey, *INS Officials Are Balking at Inquiry Prompted by Gallegly*, L.A. Times, 26 October 1995, p. 5, available in WESTLAW, LATIMES Database.

76 The Los Angeles based Center for Human Rights and Constitutional Law, among others, has filed suit against the INS alleging violations at SPCs in San Pedro, Cal., and El Paso, Tex., as well as at other detention facilities in Forrest Park, Ga., and Houston and Laredo, Tex. Associated Press, *INS Detainees Say They're Treated Unfairly*, S.F. Chronicle, 4 July 1995, at A15; *Conditions at INS Lockups Unconstitutional, Suit Says*, L.A. Times, 30 September 1994, p. 2.

77 See e.g. *Imasuen*, supra note 52 and accompanying text.

78 The 1996 immigration reforms confirm the ability of the INS to make use of state and local detention facilities. IIRIRA § 305(a), INA § 241(g).

low-cost legal representation in immigration proceedings, and access to telephones during the evening."[79]

Detainees at local and state correctional institutions are even further removed from the pertinent authorities than their counterparts at SPCs or privately run facilities.[80] As a result, they are even more vulnerable to neglect and sometimes horrifying forms of abuse. In one recent instance, Chinese women refugees reaching the US after harrowing experiences at sea were held for over two years at a local prison where they allegedly became victims of sexual abuse by the prison guards.[81] In another, similarly appalling recent episode, twelve correction officers at a Union County, NJ, jail were prosecuted for beating and kicking alien detainees, dunking their heads in toilets and pulling out their hairs with pliers, while other officers attempted to cover up the incidents.[82]

III.4 Private contract facilities

"Non-service" facilities display many of the same inadequacies found at SPCs, compounded by the cost-cutting concerns and lack of appropriate supervision associated with the private sector. The INS maintains a few "nominal" officers at these facilities to perform governmental functions which legally may not be contracted out, but leaves the bulk of operational responsibilities to the private company in charge.[83] Under these conditions, severe understaffing, ignorance and disregard for the vulnerable condition of asylum seekers, poor health and meal services, and sorely deficient social, educational and recreational provisions are commonplace. Mental and physical suffering at these facilities has caused many

---

[79] *Brutality Unchecked, supra* note 55, p. 62.
[80] In this respect, it should be noted that the 1996 reforms require that an officer or employee of a state who is charged with performing tasks related to the investigation, apprehension or detention of aliens must be knowledgeable about relevant federal law provisions and have received "adequate training regarding the enforcement of relevant federal immigration laws". IIRIRA § 133, INA § 287(g)(2). Such officers must also be placed under the supervision of the INS. IIRIRA § 133, INA § 287(g)(3). However, the provisions say nothing about training with respect to understanding and catering to the particular needs of asylum seekers, or of detained aliens as individuals in general. At best, one can hope that the provisions will suffice to ensure that such state officers will have received a level of training approximating that of the lowest rank of INS personnel. As shown in the section devoted to conditions at SPCs, however, even that is not much of a guarantee.
[81] The New Orleans Parish Prison, the county facility where the women were held, had already been the subject of legal action alleging sexual abuse of inmates prior to the asylum seekers' arrival; see *A Cry for Help, supra* note 64, p. 4.
[82] *Legacy of Uprising, supra* note 75.
[83] *Overall Detention Policy, supra* note 53.

asylum seekers to opt in despair for returning to persecution in their countries of origin rather than endure further detention at the hands of the US government.[84]

Recent developments in connection with the Esmor Correctional Services Corporation's operation of a detention center in Elizabeth, New Jersey, provide a vivid illustration of the inadequacy of privately run detention facilities. According to one report, Esmor ran the center "with underpaid, poorly trained guards who harassed and degraded immigrants, and the immigration service fumbled its supervisory role".[85] Only three months after the center opened in August 1994, dozens of detainees went on a hunger strike to protest abusive treatment by guards, the arbitrary use of strip searches, unnecessary shackling, bad food, the authorities' failure to turn lights off at night and the indefinite duration of detention periods.[86] Despite the presence of INS supervisors, however, conditions did not improve. The layout of the facility itself was such that groups of 30 to 50 detainees, separated by gender, spent day after day in a single large room, where they ate, slept, and went to the bathroom. Toilet facilities and showers were open, in full view of the rest of the room but for clearly insufficient, three-foot-tall structures inappropriately called "privacy walls". These rooms, where detainees spent days on end, had only very narrow windows overhead, and the facility as a whole lacked adequate outdoor access, exercise space or equipment, and a proper library.[87] One woman described her existence there as "a mind-numbing routine, lived out in dirty clothes, on insect-infested beds, with no privacy".[88] Over the first few months of 1995, the abuse of detainees by guards escalated to include arbitrary beatings and the vengeful or unjustified use of solitary confinement, theft of personal property including money and jewelry, and the forcing of detainees to wear soiled clothing.[89]

On June 18, 1995, mounting frustration flared into violence when "the center erupted in a storm of broken glass, smashed furniture and fear. . . A ragtag band of detainees took over the building, demolished much of the interior and barricaded themselves inside for five hours before the center was stormed by law enforcement

---

84 Arthur C. Helton, *The Detention of Asylum Seekers in the United States and Canada*, supra note 57.
85 *Legacy of Uprising*, supra note 75.
86 *Ibid.* When contacted for comment on the strike, William Tillman, Deputy Director of the INS regional office in Newark, NJ, said: "There is a hunger strike, but our experience with aliens in custody is that there is almost always a hunger strike." Astonishingly William Slattery, President of Esmor, declared: "I am unaware of any ongoing problems. Conditions at the facility are excellent." Judy Peet, *Sikh Activists Protest at INS Center Citing Hunger Strike By Detainees*, Star Ledger, 16 November 1994, available in WESTLAW, STLGRN Database.
87 Author's visit to Elizabeth, NJ, facility on 20 June 1995.
88 Perez-Peña, *Illegal Aliens Overrun a Jail in New Jersey*, N.Y. Times, 19 June 1995, at A1, Col. 3 (hereinafter Perez-Peña).
89 *Legacy of Uprising*, supra note 75.

officers."[90] The incident attracted the attention of the media, the center was temporarily shut down, and the INS initiated an investigation which eventually produced a report. The report found that Esmor repeatedly breached its contract by consistently subjecting detainees to serious and unwarranted abuse, providing substantially sub-standard facilities and withholding crucial information from INS supervisors, and that the immigration service's efforts at supervision themselves were sorely lacking.[91] And yet, a year and a half later the disturbance has produced little change. Criminal and civil rights investigations into the guards' conduct have yielded no charges, no INS personnel connected to the events have been disciplined in any way, and Esmor was permitted to recoup its losses entirely by selling its contract for US$ 6.2 million to another private provider, which was scheduled to reopen the facility by the end of 1996.[92]

The events at Esmor seriously call into question the wisdom of relying on the private sector to provide adequate detention facilities for immigrants. The combination of profit-seeking incentives and the alien detainees' lack of voice consistently leads to substantial abuses of asylum seekers and others. Although by now a trend toward privatization in correctional services is clearly discernible across the US, there was considerable resistance at first where US citizen prisoners were

---

90   Perez-Peña, *supra* note 88.
91   Among the report's findings were the following: "cases of physical and verbal abuse by poorly trained guards, theft of detainee property by guards and frequent awakening of detainees in the middle of the night. . . guards routinely issu[ing] female detainees male underwear with large question marks drawn in the crotch and frequently refus[ing] to issue sanitary napkins to female detainees who were menstruating. [The facility] was understaffed, had unqualified and poorly trained guards and experienced 60 percent turnover rate, due in part to low salaries. [It] failed to provide adequate medical services, housed four juveniles in violation of INS regulations and failed to provide twice-weekly clean clothing or appropriate footwear to detainees as required. Esmor employees made a concerted effort to hide information and cover up abuses and problems. . . Willard Stovall, [the facility administrator] consistently referred to [it] as 'my house' in a manner indicative of his apparent belief that INS should not participate in day-to-day matters related to detainees. [He added:] 'Esmor's corporate policy is to keep the INS in the dark as much as possible.' [In addition, the report found that t]he pattern of physical abuse, corporal punishment, verbal abuse, harassment and other degrading actions against inmates was the result of a 'systematic methodology' by some Esmor guards to control, intimidate and discipline the detainee population. ... Detainees were at times placed into segregation or isolation cells without proper documentation, often as punishment for minor offenses or as a means of harassment in violation of Esmor's contract and correctional standards. Esmor personnel attempted to deport aliens without returning their funds, valuables and property[, and the facility] failed to meet some American Correctional Association standards including lack of privacy in some toilet areas, insufficient outdoor recreation area and lack of chairs and writing areas in segregation cells." Robert Cohen, *Immigrant Site Won't Reopen*, Star Ledger, 22 July 1995, available in WESTLAW, STLGRN Database.
92   *Legacy of Uprising*, *supra* note 75; author's conversations with staff members of the Lawyers Committee for Human Rights.

CHAPTER 3   THE US PERSPECTIVE

concerned. Conversely, the relative lack of public interest in the plight of immigrants and the fact that they enjoy fewer and narrower constitutional protections made it possible to use the detention of aliens as an experimental ground for testing the effectiveness of privatization in this field.[93] The results so far clearly indicate that the interests of detained asylum seekers would be far better served by abandoning reliance on the private sector altogether in the management of detention space.[94]

---

93   In the early 1980s, private corporations seeking to break into the market for "correctional" services tapped first into the INS' need for detention space, then gradually sought to provide low or at most medium security facilities for US citizens in the face of great scepticism from both governmental agencies and observers in the field; see Bob Wiedrich and Storer Rowley, *Prisons for Profit Trend Breaking Out*, Chic. Trib., 19 May 1985, at C1; Loretta Tofani, *More Correctional Facilities Operated by Private Firms*, Wash. Post, 18 February 1985, at A6. More recently, private enterprise has spread to provide services at all levels of the US correctional system; see Adrian Moore, *Privatize the Jail County System*, L.A. Times, 20 November 1996, at B9 ("In 1995, the number of privately operated adult prisons grew by 15%, to 109 facilities. New privately operated jails are in the works in Colorado, Florida, Indiana, Maryland, New Mexico, Michigan, Pennsylvania and Texas, and the Federal Bureau of Prisons is expanding its program of private operations contracts"); Kathy Walt and Polly Ross Hughes, *Private Prison Boom, Gloom*, Houston Chronicle, 1 September 1996, at State 1 (assessing the existence of 92 privately run prisons across 17 states and Puerto Rico, with Texas accounting for the greatest number by far). Despite the recent boom, the privatization of correctional and detention facilities is still a hotly debated issue; see e.g. Robert E. Pierre, *D.C. Corrections Deal Comes Under Scrutiny*, Wash. Post, 29 October 1996 (Correctional Corporation of America, a private company controlling almost 40,000 prison beds worldwide, comes under heavy scrutiny during its bid to take over Washington, D.C.'s Correctional Treatment Facility); Jeff Gerth and Stephen Labaton, *Prisons for Profit: A Special Report*, N.Y. Times, 24 November 1995, at A1, Col. 1 (questionable political and budgetary concerns criticized as principal justifications behind prison privatization effort).

94   Esmor Correctional Services Corporation, which in 1995 managed nine detention facilities (two of which were immigration-related), became a public corporation in February 1994, reported annual revenues of US$ 24.3 million and profits of US$ 1.5 million in 1994, and expected earnings in excess of US$ 36 million for 1995. One of the most financially successful and fastest growing companies in the field, it has achieved its results by running facilities at low cost. It won the contract for the Elizabeth, NJ, site from the INS by outbidding its closest competitor by US$ 20 million (Esmor's bid was US$ 54 million). While the expenditure involved in housing one detainee for one day has been estimated to be between US$ 25–60, in 1995 Esmor charged the INS US$ 75 to US$ 100 a day per detainee. John Sullivan, *Operator of Immigration Jail Has a History of Troubles*, N.Y. Times, 20 June 1995, at A1 (hereinafter *History of Troubles*); Maureen Castellano, *INS to Probe Conditions at Private Jail for Aliens*, N.J. Law J., 12 June 1995, p. 5, available in LEXIS, LEGNEW Library, ALLNWS File; Lizette Alvarez and Lisa Getter, *Coming to America: The Tangled Web of US Immigration*, Atlanta Constitution, 3 January 1994, at A5, available in WESTLAW, ATLNTAJC Database; *Housing Illegal Immigrants Pays Off for PA*, Baltimore Sun, 29 September 1996, at 10B, available in WESTLAW, BALTSUN Database.

IV Detention by air carriers

Recent controversies over air carrier custody of asylum seekers have heightened concerns about privately run detention facilities. Contractual agreements with the US government permit air carriers to bring passengers in transit to other countries into the US temporarily, provided that the carriers agree to pay for the custody of such passengers until departure from the US.[95] These expenses usually entail no more than the provision of a transit lounge at the airport. However, when passengers afforded such "transit without visa" (TWOV) status refuse to proceed with their scheduled travel plans in order to file an asylum application in the US, questions arise as to the manner and location in which they are to be held pending adjudication of their claims. Similar concerns arise in connection with stowaways whose presence on a carrier is discovered only upon arrival in the US.

When assigned responsibility for detaining these aliens, carriers typically resort to hotels and private security companies to carry out the job. Predictably, detention conditions in such instances vary greatly from case to case. Alarming reports of inhumane situations, however, are frequent. The Lawyers Committee for Human Rights has documented cases in which security companies forced detainees to sleep on transit lounge chairs for more than a week before taking them to a hotel. Widespread disregard for the asylum seekers' health has been coupled with failure to provide them with adequate food, sometimes for more than 24 hours at a time. When hotel rooms have been provided, security guards have often been abusive and afforded detainees no privacy. In one case, security guards regularly smoked and watched television in the detainees' room until very late at night, leaving one woman no place to dress in private. The asylum seekers' isolation and the lack of adequate translation services substantiate concerns that only a fraction of such instances ever get reported, allowing a far greater number to take place undetected.[96]

Before the 1996 immigration reforms, several affected airlines brought suits against the government to be rid of the responsibility to pay for the detention of TWOV asylum seekers and stowaways.[97] Principally, they claimed that the INS

---

95 As a condition of using US airports and other points of entry, air carriers and other "transportation lines" must also enter into contracts with the INS regarding the entry and inspection of aliens. IIRIRA § 362, INA § 233.

96 This information was gathered by individual staff members of the Lawyers Committee for Human Rights over a number of years of contact with countless asylum seekers detained by carriers in the vicinity of US airports (principally in the New York area).

97 For TWOV asylum seekers, see *Air Transport Association of America v. Reno*, 80 F.3d 477 (D.C. Cir. 1996); *Aerolineas Argentinas v. United States*, 77 F.3d 1564 (Fed. Cir. 1996); *Lan-Chile Airlines v. Meissner*, 65 F.3d 1034 (2d Cir. 1995). For stowaways, see *DIA Navigation Co. v. Pomeroy*, 34 F.3d 1255 (3d Cir. 1994); *Argenbright Security v. Ceskoslovenske Aeroline*, 849 F.Supp. 276 (S.D.N.Y. 1994); see also Kathleen T. Beesing, *Who Pays Detention Costs When Aliens Seek Asylum at the Borders of the*

CHAPTER 3   THE US PERSPECTIVE

violated the terms of a 1986 "user fee statute"[98] when it asked airlines to shoulder detention costs in addition to remitting the fee required under the statute, which was already intended to cover "detention, transportation, hospitalization, and all other expenses of detained aliens".[99] Appellate courts in two of the three principal lawsuits sided with the airlines[100] and, after considerable lobbying on both sides, the 1996 reforms addressed the issue directly.

As a result, the INS currently has sole responsibility for the actual, physical detention of an alien who has been permitted to land in the US.[101] This means that stowaways and TWOV passengers who apply for asylum are to be detained in the same facilities and under the same conditions as other asylum seekers, which should eliminate some of the problems mentioned above in connection with inadequate carrier-provided facilities. However, under certain conditions the INS may still pass on the costs of detaining such aliens to the carriers who brought them,[102] and substantial monetary penalties are imposed on carriers who fail to comply with the screening and removal requirements imposed by the new law.[103] In this way, the new provisions ensure that the INS bears direct responsibility for the detention conditions of asylum seekers who make it to the US, but the overall number of aliens who benefit from the improvement will probably drop as carriers concerned

---

   US?, 22 Transp.L.J. 495 (1995); *Airline Lawsuit Challenges INS Policy on Detention Costs for Excludable Aliens*, 69 Interpreter Releases 299, 300 (1992).
98   INA § 286 (1995).
99   INA § 286(a) (1995).
100 *Air Transport Association of America v. Reno*, 80 F.3d 477 (D.C. Cir. 1996); *Lan-Chile Airlines v. Meissner*, 65 F.3d 1034 (2nd Cir. 1995).
101 IIRIRA § 305(a), INA § 241(c); see *Joint Explanatory Statement of the Committees of Conference*, H.R. Conf. Rep. No. 828, 104th Cong., 2nd Sess. (1996), available in WESTLAW, LH Database (hereinafter Joint Statement).
102 IIRIRA and its legislative history are very clear as to the assignment of liability to carriers in the context of stowaways, and generally limit such liability to a period not to exceed 15 days after the arrival of the alien in the US, *Ibid*. In combination with substantial monetary penalties imposed on carriers for failing to comply with appropriate screening and removal procedures in this context (see *infra* note 103 and accompanying text), the provisions can be seen as intended to provide carriers with strong incentives to monitor access to their crafts at the source in order to reduce the incidence of unexpected arrivals of asylum seekers at US ports of entry. In this connection, the INS has proposed detailed regulations to govern the conduct of screening procedures to "prevent the boarding of improperly documented aliens destined for the United States." 61 Fed. Reg. 29,323 (1996) (to be codified at 8 C.F.R. § 273).
     Conversely, the provisions for assigning liability in the case of TWOV passengers are not explicitly spelled out in either the act or the legislative history and are thus less clear. However, the framers of IIRIRA did call on the INS to issue regulations in the matter in order to ensure that blanket provisions are uniformly applied across all districts. Joint Statement, *supra* note 101.
103 A US$ 2,000 penalty is imposed for each failure to comply with payment of detention costs of an alien under INA § 241(d), and a US$ 5,000 penalty is imposed for each failure to comply with the removal of a stowaway under 241(d)(2). IIRIRA § 307(a), INA § 243(c).

with shouldering detention costs and fines tighten screening procedures at foreign ports. Thus, legitimate asylum seekers, who often experience difficulty obtaining proper travel documents and visas to flee persecution, may be more likely to be denied access to the means of escape by airlines and other carriers in countries of origin.

V   Detention of minors

With regard to US citizens, the prevailing national policy concerning juveniles has been to limit the use of detention to the most serious or violent offenders, and even then to ensure that minors are detained separately from adults and are provided with supportive services and education.[104] In contrast to these practices, every year the INS arrests thousands of alien children, most of whom are unaccompanied by adults, on suspicion of being deportable.[105] These children are often held in custody with adult strangers, subjected to full-body strip-searches, and afforded no educational or recreational opportunities.[106]

In 1993, the Supreme Court upheld an INS regulation allowing detained alien juveniles to be released only to their parents, close relatives or legal guardians, except "in unusual and compelling circumstances".[107] Other adults who expressed an interest in taking the children in were not allowed to do so. Ironically, the Court grounded its decision in concern for the protection of the child: it found that the right of a detained minor who has no parent, guardian, or close relative, to be released into the custody of another adult is not sufficiently strong to warrant release and overcome the State's compelling interest in the child's welfare.[108] Opponents argued that far from promoting the welfare of alien children, the regulation instead served the INS as a means of identifying and apprehending alien parents and relatives of minors, who may also be refugees at risk of deportation.[109]

---

104   *Cruel and Questionable Policy, supra* note 2, p. 19.
105   For example in 1990, 8,500 were arrested, mostly teenage boys from Mexico and Central America, 70% of whom were unaccompanied by adults. *Supreme Court Upholds INS Regulation Restricting Juveniles' Release*, 70 Interpreter Releases 413, 414 (1993).
106   *Flores v. Meese*, 681 F. Supp. 665, 666 (1988).
107   *Reno v. Flores*, 507 US 292, 113 S.Ct. 1439, 123 L.Ed.2d 1 (1993); see 8 C.F.R. § 242.24 (1995).
108   507 US pp. 303–05, 113 S.Ct., p. 1447.
109   *Cruel and Questionable Policy, supra* note 2, p. 20. In some areas of the country, where legal representation for alien children with no means is not available, this state of things has had the perverse effect of keeping children in detention even after they have expressed a desire to return to their home countries, because no adult was available to whom the child could be released in order to undertake the return trip. Claudia Weinstein, *The Children San Diego Forgot*, American Lawyer, September 1987, p. 102.

CHAPTER 3   THE US PERSPECTIVE

VI   Conclusion

The use of detention as a deterrent to immigration is both irrational and in violation of international norms for the protection of refugees. It is irrational because there is no reason to believe that its deterrent effect can target only undeserving aliens seeking admission to the US. On the contrary, aliens intending to abuse the system may be able to prepare better in advance and avoid longer detention periods. It violates international norms because it deprives genuine refugees of an opportunity to obtain much needed protection, placing unnecessary restraints on their movements and often forcing them either to return to, or never to leave, places where they face persecution. Perhaps most importantly, the use of detention in the US often violates asylum seekers' rights under international law by subjecting them to further unwarranted, frequently harrowing suffering after they have successfully fled persecution in their countries of origin.

The problem of abuse of the US asylum system by unscrupulous aliens, to the extent that there is one, might find much more rational solutions in better, faster and more accurate procedures to determine the merits of individual applications. Similarly, efforts should be made to assess the extent to which detention is warranted in each individual case, with a view to the timely release or parole of as many legitimate asylum seekers as possible.

Under pressure from refugee advocate groups and others, the INS attempted such an approach in the early 1990s with the Asylum Pre-Screening Officer (APSO) Program. The Program set forth criteria to be applied by INS officers during pre-screening interviews at major airports and other ports of entry to determine whether particular asylum seekers should be paroled into the country pending the adjudication of their claims.[110] Although the INS experienced considerable practical

---

110   The criteria included the certainty of the alien's true identity, the credibility of the asylum claim, and the risk that the alien would abscond if paroled. Aliens had to have legal representation to qualify, and they could not have participated in the persecution of others, have been convicted of an aggravated felony abroad or of a particularly serious crime in the US, have been firmly resettled in another country or present a danger to the security of the US. INS District Directors reviewed the APSO's recommendations, determined whether the asylum seeker in question should be paroled and, if necessary, could require the posting of a bond. Lawyers Committee for Human Rights, Asylum Program, *Detention of Refugees: Problems in Implementation of the Asylum Pre-Screening Officer Program 8–9* (1994). (hereinafter *Asylum Pre-Screening Officer Program*). There was no administrative appeal of the District Director's parole decision, although judicial review could be had by *habeas corpus* petition. *Noorani* v. *Smith*, 810 F. Supp. 280, 285 (W.D. Wash. 1993); see also Lawyers Committee for Human Rights, *Representing Asylum Applicants: An Attorney's Guide to Law and Procedure 105* (Interim Edition 1994).

difficulties in implementing it,[111] significant efforts by advocate groups to keep the Program alive have been successful to some extent. As of this writing, it appears that an expansion is planned to install APSOs directly at some detention facilities, and an official manual providing advocates with information about the program is in the works.[112]

The vehemence of recent legislation, however, dramatically diminishes the likelihood of any substantive shifts in detention policy in the near future. If detention is to be used as a deterrent to immigration, the need for substantial improvements in the conditions of detention is all the more pressing. American immigration law deprives aliens who have not been formally admitted of the constitutional protections necessary to raise effective challenges to inhumane incarceration, and practical restrictions at individual facilities frequently deprive aliens of adequate alternative avenues to voice their complaints. At least with respect to asylum seekers, such a state of affairs is unpardonable under international law, as well as under basic humanitarian standards of fairness. The situation demands exposure, public debate and vigorous advocacy at every level.

---

111 According to the Lawyers Committee for Human Rights, the unaccountability of INS District Directors led to widespread non-compliance with the Program's criteria, as the APSOs' recommendations for release were often disregarded. Reports of discrimination on the basis of national origin, coupled with a failure to keep appropriate statistical records, substantiate a concern that certain districts (e.g. New York and Harlingen, Texas) have refused to implement the Program altogether. The failure of the INS to inform applicants of negative parole decisions, the frequent imposition of unaffordably high bonds, the failure to give the applicant an opportunity to obtain counsel before the interview, and substantial delays in the entire process are among other difficulties the program experienced in its first few years. *Asylum Pre-Screening Officer Program*, *supra* note 110, pp. 9–14.

112 This information was provided by Eleanor Acer, who currently directs the Asylum Program of the Lawyers Committee for Human Rights and has been involved directly in negotiations with the INS.

Chapter 4 Detention of Asylum Seekers: The Canadian Perspective

By Ron Poulton and Barbara Jackman

Contents

Part I   Introduction
Part II Detention criteria: II.1 Immigration Act, RSC 1985, Section 103 – II.2 Immigration Act, RSC 1985, Section 103.1
Part III Risk to national security: III.1 Immigration Act, RSC 1985, Section 40.1 – III.2 Immigration Act, RSC 1985, Section 19
Part IV Non-rights for non-citizens
Part V   Detention on the grounds of fear of persecution
Part VI Detention of children
Part VII Conditions of detention
Part VIII Conclusion

I   Introduction

On 15 August 1995, an adjudicator with the Canadian Immigration and Refugee Board ordered the continued detention of a 17 year old Kurdish girl who had entered Canada ten months earlier, on 22 October 1994, claiming political asylum. Detained on arrival, the girl was found eligible to make a refugee claim in Canada and streamed into the refugee determination process. But she was not released from detention. The reason: her political opinion.

At page 5 of the decision, the adjudicator states:

"Her lawyer (Ms Jackman) has argued that (the girl) has the right under the Charter of Rights and Freedoms to exercise free speech and freedom of association. She says that to rely on (the girl's) writings and even her alleged affiliation with the aims and objectives of the PKK[1] infringes on her rights in this respect. She argues ably that case law here, and in the United States as well, supports her contention that one's ideas and associations can't be held

---

1   Kurdish Workers' Party, Turkey.

against one in the manner proposed by counsel for the Minister. The Court has, however, in the past come to different conclusions in immigration matters specifically."[2]

If you are a political refugee claimant in Canada, according to the adjudicator's decision, your opinions may land you in prison. In the case considered, the Kurdish girl made the mistake of admiring the writings of Chairman Mao Tse Tung and Ocalon, current leader of the PKK. Her detention was so prolonged and difficult that she expressed a desire to leave Canada and abandon her asylum claim. Fortunately, though, she did continue with her claim, and was eventually granted refugee status and released. Deeply traumatized by her treatment in Canada, however, she left the country soon after to join her sick mother in Lebanon.

The case highlights an alarming development in Canadian asylum policy. Increasingly, whilst cognizant of Canada's humanitarian tradition and international commitments, the government has actively engaged in programs designed to restrict the admission into Canada of those seeking refuge. Interdiction at so called "departure" points has led to a reduction in the number of asylum claims being made in Canada, from estimates of over 36,000 in 1990 to approximately 17,000 in 1995.[3]

It appears that detention may be being used as a further weapon of deterrence. Although at present the numbers are not great – in fact most asylum seekers are not detained – they have been increasing over the past few years. The cases which exist suggest an unwritten policy of using confinement to force a claimant into submission and, finally, departure. Furthermore, those most commonly targeted are those who have been politically active in self-determination or liberation struggles – a factor highlighting the most troubling aspect of the process: the decision on detention is discretionary, and it is made on the basis of arbitrary political assessments.

II Detention criteria

A careful scrutiny of the procedures for detention and how they are used reveals a system which discriminates on the basis of political opinion, fails to live up to requirements of due process and which is, on the whole, inconsistent with Canada's international refugee and human rights obligations.

---

2   *In the matter of the Immigration Act and a detention review hearing held on 31 July 1995, 3 and 4 August 1995, concerning* (name withheld). This case is unpublished, and therefore there is no further reference.

3   Canadian Council of Refugees, July 1995.

CHAPTER 4   THE CANADIAN PERSPECTIVE

II.1   Immigration Act, RSC 1985, Section 103

Asylum claimants are initially subject to the same detention criteria as any other alien entering, or who has already entered, Canada. Posing a danger to the public and likelihood of appearance for examination, inquiry or removal are the criteria used. What differentiates the process for refugees is the nature of an asylum claim and the fears a claimant may have of being removed.

An asylum seeker informs immigration officials of his or her desire to claim refuge in Canada either at a point of entry into the country or in-land, at some date following successful crossing of the border. A determination of "eligibility" is undertaken, wherein a non-refugee related assessment is made (such matters as previous refugee determination and membership of an inadmissible class are considered in this assessment). A conditional removal order is then rendered, which converts into a removal order if the refugee claim is rejected or abandoned. At any point in this process, immigration officials are empowered to arrest and detain, if they hold the opinion that there are reasonable grounds to believe that the person may be a danger to the public or might not appear for an examination, inquiry or removal from the country.

Detention cases are referred to an adjudicator for review within 48 hours of detention, then after seven days and subsequently every 30 days. Section 103(7) of the Immigration Act directs an adjudicator to release an individual from detention if satisfied that he or she is not likely to pose a danger to the public and is likely to appear for further immigration proceedings. At this point, the onus of proof shifts to the detainee for all subsequent detention reviews. The person must demonstrate that his or her release will not pose a danger and that he or she will appear for immigration processes. This sometimes proves an impossible undertaking for the refugee claimant, given the earlier determination and apparent willingness to associate membership of a political group *per se* with constituting a danger.

II.2   Immigration Act, RSC 1985, Section 103.1

Section 103.1(1) requires the mandatory detention of every person unable to satisfy an immigration officer of his or her identity, or where – in the opinion of the Deputy Minister or a person designated by the Deputy Minister – there is reason to suspect that the person may be a member of one of six specified inadmissible classes, including suspected war criminals, individuals who have perhaps been members of groups which might have engaged in terrorism in the past, and senior members of governments that violated human rights. The detention must be reported forthwith to a senior immigration officer who may authorize its continuation for a period not exceeding seven days.

An additional period of detention may be ordered for persons detained under Section 103.1(1), where the Minister certifies that the person's identity has not been established, or that there is reason to suspect that he or she is a member of an inadmissible criminal or security class, requiring an additional period of detention in which to conduct investigations. The person will be brought before an adjudicator once during each seven day period thereafter, for a review of the reasons behind this continued detention. In cases involving criminal or security concerns, the review is held *in camera*.

Detention under these provisions may continue as long as an adjudicator is satisfied that the Minister is making reasonable efforts to investigate the matter. In these circumstances, the merits of detention are not subject to review. This provision has been harshly criticized by the Toronto-based Refugee Lawyers Association in its submissions with respect to Bill C-86 – the bill leading to the current legislation. Discussing Section 103.1, the Association commented: "The provision does not allow for the adjudicator to assess the reasonableness of the Minister's suspicion, which might be wholly spurious, or the basis of the detention in the first place, but only the reasonableness of the efforts to investigate."[4]

The reasonableness of the suspicion is subject to Federal Court review, *in camera*, with limited access by the person concerned, or his or her counsel, to government reports and allegations.

III Risk to national security

III.1 Immigration Act, RSC 1985, Section 40.1

Another provision of the Immigration Act mandating detention is Section 40.1, imposing what is referred to as a "security certificate" on a refugee claimant or other non-permanent resident in Canada. Under Section 40.1 of the Act, where a security certificate is imposed alleging that the person falls within one of the inadmissible security classes specified in Section 19 of the Act, the person is automatically detained without review by an adjudicator and remains so until a designated Federal Court judge determines whether or not the security certificate is reasonable. If the certificate is not deemed reasonable, the person may be freed on the regular grounds for release as determined by an adjudicator. If the certificate is upheld, the person will remain in confinement until removed from Canada, or until 120 days have passed since the issuance of a removal order against her or him, which has not been enforced. In this instance, a designated Federal Court judge may consider release if

---

[4] *A Submission With Respect to Bill 86: An End to Canada's Humanitarian Tradition?* Report of the Refugees Lawyers Association, 1992.

CHAPTER 4   THE CANADIAN PERSPECTIVE

satisfied that the person does not pose a danger to the public and that his or her removal is not likely to occur within a reasonable period of time.

III.2   Immigration Act, RSC 1985, Section 19

What constitutes an inadmissible class is listed in Section 19 of the Immigration Act. As well as persons with criminal intent or backgrounds, those who are or have been members of an organization that is or was engaged in espionage, subversion or terrorism are also deemed inadmissible and may be detained.

In addition to forming a basis for detention according to Sections 103.1(1) and 40.1, the Section 19 provisions may also be used to exclude a refugee claimant from the refugee determination process, effectively barring his or her right to make a claim.

The inadmissible security classes, particularly those listing membership or past membership of an organization that is or was engaged in acts of terrorism, raise particular problems because detention is premised solely on associational status and not on conduct – either past conduct giving rise to future safety concerns or future conduct arising from a person's purpose in coming to Canada.

It has been stated that "[i]f, for example, Nelson Mandela were to return to Canada, he could be barred as being a member of the African National Congress (the ANC having at one point in its history engaged in activities calculated to subvert the former so called democratically elected government of South Africa)."[5]

The opportunity for abuse available to a bureaucracy via Section 19 is clearly illustrated in the recent case of *Wahid Khalil Baroud* v. *Minister of Citizenship and Immigration.*[6] Baroud is a stateless Palestinian. He entered Canada in May 1991 and immediately claimed protection as a Convention refugee. He had been a member of the Palestinian Liberation Organization (PLO) and a member of Fatah, facts which he disclosed on arrival. He had left the PLO in 1990 and sought refuge in Canada. Baroud was detained on arrival in May 1991 for 41 days and then, following a determination that he was not a danger to the public, released. He was detained again three years later in June 1994 after contacting the immigration services to inquire about the status of his refugee claim, which he had not heard anything about for three years.

In 1994 the government filed a certificate alleging Baroud to have been a member of Fatah and Force 17, organizations which were known to engage in acts of terrorism. There was no allegation that Baroud personally engaged in the plotting or carrying out of any terrorist act, nor was it alleged that he was likely to engage in acts of terrorism or subversive activities at any point in the future. The judge

---

5   *Commentary on Bill C-86*, Barbara Jackman, July 1992.
6   Baroud v. *MCI*, (1995), 22 O.R. (3rd) Part 4, 255, (Ont CA).

designated to consider whether the security certificate against Baroud was reasonable concluded that it was, basing his decision solely on past political affiliation and not on the basis of any wrongful conduct on Baroud's part.[7] His past political affiliations and beliefs were enough to bar him from the refugee process, detain him – at this point indefinitely – and finally expel him from the country.

The Federal Court process provides for no timely, prompt review of detention. As a statutory court, it has not been given *habeas corpus* jurisdiction or detention review jurisdiction, except where 120 days have passed since the issuance of a deportation order and the person has not yet been removed from Canada. However, there may well be an indefinite lag before the detention is reviewed, because the security hearing in the Federal Court must take place first, followed by an inquiry to consider deportation – neither of which proceedings are subject to fixed time limits.

Such delays in detention review are inconsistent with international human rights standards, which require the right to prompt review of detention. The negation of *habeas corpus* as a right also violates international human rights norms, as it is generally viewed as being a non-derogable right.

Depressed and discouraged by his endless detention in the Don Jail, a short-term detention facility for criminals in downtown Toronto, Baroud decided to abandon his refugee claim and to leave Canada voluntarily. At the time of writing, he was still detained at the Toronto West Jail, another short-term criminal detention facility.

IV   Non-rights for non-citizens

It has not always been proven necessary to use the weighty security provisions in the Immigration Act to justify detention or to prevent or discourage refugee claims in Canada. Two prominent cases exemplify alternative means used by immigration officials, one made at the port of entry and the other in-land.

In *Dehghani* v. *Minister of Employment and Immigration*,[8] the asylum seeker arrived at Toronto's Pearson airport from Iran, indicating his intention to claim refugee protection. He was referred for secondary examination by an immigration officer and review by a senior immigration officer. After a four-hour wait, the examination took place. Throughout the time he waited, he did not feel free to leave. In fact, if he had tried to do so, he could – and probably would – have been detained by the immigration officer exercising his detention power.

The secondary examination was a detailed interrogation, dealing with the substantive elements of Dehghani's refugee claim. Only after the interview was

---

[7]   In *The Matter of a Certificate issued pursuant to Section 40.1 of the Immigration Act and in Relation to Wahid Khalil Baroud* (31 May 1995), unreported, Court File No: DES 3 94 (FCTD).

[8]   *Dehghani* v. *MEI*, (1993), 1 SCR 1053, (SCC).

CHAPTER 4 THE CANADIAN PERSPECTIVE

concluded was he told of his right to a lawyer. By that time, he had emphasized to the immigration officer that he had come to Canada to work – leaving out much of the basis for his refugee claim.

Dehghani failed to mention that the Iranian authorities had executed his daughter and confiscated his property because he and his family were "royalist sympathizers". Dehghani was unfamiliar with Canadian law and culture and believed that it was prudent to tell the immigration officer what he did. This proved fatal to his refugee claim. When later referred to an inquiry for the assessment of whether there was a credible basis for his refugee claim, the tribunal assessing the claim relied on the notes made by the immigration officer at the secondary examination to find Dehghani not credible.

On appeal to the Supreme Court, his counsel argued that Dehghani had been detained whilst waiting for the secondary examination, in that he was not free to leave and that, being detained, he should have been advised of his right to counsel, as Canada's Constitution requires. The Court disagreed, holding that "no detention of constitutional consequences" had occurred. The rationale for the decision was that there was an absence of stigma associated with referral to a secondary examination, that the mere statutory duty to answer questions and criminal sanctions for refusing to answer does not necessarily trigger a constitutional detention, and that the questioning in the secondary examination was merely routine – part of the general screening of persons seeking entry to Canada. Mr Dehghani was found inadmissible and ordered to be excluded from Canada, making him liable for removal to Iran, a country in which he reasonably feared persecution. Had he been informed of his right to counsel and chosen to exercise that right, a lawyer could have instructed him regarding the consequences of the answers he was giving to the immigration officer and advised him to be truthful and forthright.

What the *Dehghani* and *Baroud* cases highlight is that Canadian courts discriminate against persons in respect of their status in Canada. The starting point for the application of constitutional human rights standards to persons involved in status proceedings is that non-citizens have no right to remain in or enter Canada. From this point of view, it is an easy matter for the Courts to negate the existence of human rights for aliens, whilst recognizing the same rights for others. The high point in Canadian constitutional law for non-citizens came in 1985, when the Supreme Court of Canada, the highest appellate court, determined that refugee claimants had a right to adequately know the case against them and respond, normally by way of oral hearing, regarding the merits of their claim.[9] Since then, the composition of the Court has changed and there has not been a single decision which recognizes human rights for aliens. The Supreme Court of Canada has sanctioned the denial of a right to seek *habeas corpus* by non-citizens, the denial of

---

9   *Singh v. MEI, (*1985), 1 SCR177, (SCC).

a right to counsel when detained in instances where information relevant to later proceedings is obtained, the denial of a State obligation to protect the integrity of the family or to consider the best interests of children.[10] The leadership of the Supreme Court, of course, has its impact on the lower courts, although it is fair comment to note that the lower courts – both provincial and federal – are subject to the same xenophobic fears as the Supreme Court of Canada.

V Detention on the grounds of fear of persecution

The final case of note is that of a 13 year old Turkish citizen who arrived in Canada in July 1993 and made a refugee claim. He was interviewed at the airport by an immigration officer who ordered his detention. He remained in detention for over 15 months, throughout his refugee hearing and despite a decision by the Immigration and Refugee Board that he was a Convention refugee. The reason for his detention? His expressed fear of returning to Turkey and his statement that, because of this fear, he would not present himself for removal if required to do so. The immigration officers and subsequent adjudicators sitting at the detention reviews relied on this statement to justify continued detention. Following his successful refugee hearing, the government appealed against the refugee decision, and continued detention was ordered pending the appeal.[11]

The fundamental nature of a refugee claim is a fear of return to the country from which flight is made. Without this fear, compelling the refugee to take drastic and desperate action, there would be no claim. How can one expect that such a person would willingly state that they would return to this country if they must? Such a statement would obviously be prejudicial to later advancing a successful refugee claim. Yet immigration officers and adjudicators apparently believed this possible.

The government was successful on appeal and the boy's refugee claim was subsequently denied.

VI Detention of children

A depressing reality arising from two of the above cases, the detention of the Kurdish teenage girl and the Turkish teenage boy, is the absence in Canadian common law or constitutional norms of any distinct standards for the treatment of children. Article 37.2 of the Convention on the Rights of the Child, which Canada has ratified,[12] imposes an obligation on a State to detain a child only as a measure of

---

10 *Baroud v. MCI, supra* note 6; *Dehghani v. MEI, supra* note 8; *Langner v. MEI*, (August 1995), unreported (SCC).
11 *Sahin v. MCI*, (1995) 1 F.C. 214.
12 The *Convention on the Rights of the Child* entered into force on 2 September 1990.

CHAPTER 4   THE CANADIAN PERSPECTIVE

last resort and then only for the shortest appropriate period of time. In Canada, however, children – like adults – are detained indefinitely. The considerations applied to children are the same as for adults. There is no separate process for children. They are evaluated on credibility in the same way as adults, and subjected to extensive, harsh and frightening cross examination by immigration officials and Justice Department lawyers. No concessions are given or made on the basis of their young age. Whilst Canada has ratified the Convention on the Rights of the Child, in the immigration and refugee context it is mere "window dressing", since, as a matter of law, the best interests of the child are not taken into account as a justifiable consideration by decision makers.

VII   Conditions of detention

In December 1995, Michael Akhimien, a 40-year-old Nigerian refugee claimant, died in custody at the Celebrity Inn detention center in Toronto. After spending a month in detention awaiting a hearing, he withdrew his refugee claim and indicated that he wanted to return to Nigeria. Three weeks later he reported feeling ill. He was checked by a nurse when he was found lying on the floor of his room and again when he was found sitting in an overflowing bathtub. He died late that night. His death drew widespread attention to concerns about conditions and issues of medical attention in immigration detention.

A Coroner's Inquest was held into Mr. Akhimien's death. The jury concluded that the death was due to complications from untreated diabetes. The jury made 16 recommendations to improve medical treatment in immigration detention. A coalition of human rights and refugee-serving groups has criticized the jury's verdict and is demanding a public inquiry into wide-ranging concerns about immigration detention centers in Canada. The jury's verdict is being judicially reviewed. The coalition is considering raising its concerns with the UN Committee against Torture.[13] There have long been concerns about immigration detention practices and conditions, including medical treatment, forced drugging of deportees, overcrowding, inadequate privacy for women and children, holding detainees in penal facilities and racism. If the pressure that has developed around the Akhimien case continues, these immigration detention centers may finally receive the scrutiny they deserve.

---

13   *Recommendations Arising out of the Inquest into the Death of Michael Akhimien*, Chief Coroner's Office, Solicitor-General's Department, June 7, 1996; see generally Lila Sarick, *Detained man died of diabetes complications*, inquest told, Globe & Mail, 8 May 1996, at A7; Paulette Peirol, *Government accused of torture in refugee death*, Globe & Mail, 8 October 1996, at A7; Jim Rankin, *Canada may face "torture" probe*, Toronto Star, 8 October 1996, at A3.

VIII   Conclusion

The vast majority of asylum seekers in Canada are not held in detention. There is no policy of automatic detention for everyone seeking asylum on our shores. People come, claim protection as refugees and are usually allowed to leave the immigration centers and ports of entry where their claims are lodged. However, case by case discretion is exercised and decisions are made: this person poses a danger, this one does not; this person is a terrorist, this one not. And therein lies the danger. Immigration officials and adjudicators, bolstered by security reports, are allowed to decide which political organizations and which political opinions are threatening and which are not.

Instead of an individual analysis of particular and specific threats, the question is one of association – based on membership and organizational affiliation. Mere alliance with an organization which has a terrorist component – or worse, *had* a terrorist component, is enough – even if the alliance was in the person's distant past.

Detaining a person for his or her political beliefs alone, and not for his or her conduct, constitutes a denial of free speech and association: this is what Canada is practising. The risk of rights abuses of this nature has been amplified because, in the immigration context, our courts have ruled that the right to counsel at an examination at the entry port does not apply and that *habeas corpus* or other prompt, effective remedies for a person detained under security provisions in the Immigration Act do not apply.

Once these models have been established and sanctioned by the courts, the attitude of restriction and denial expands. Officials get the taste for detention and how to exclude people from the asylum process, or at least discourage them from continuing in it. When a 13 year old boy says he is afraid to return to his country, he is imprisoned. When a 17 year old girl keeps a diary with writings from her favorite political personages, she is classified as dangerous and detained.

In closing we refer again to the words of the adjudicator in her decision to continue the detention of the 17 year old Kurdish girl. In casting doubt on the girl's purpose in being in Canada and her membership of the PKK, the adjudicator writes:

> "Much of what she testified to regarding the materials in her possession has been said before on her behalf by counsel. For example, it has been said that material in her notebook comes from the essays of Chairman Mao and other scholars of like philosophy. Ms Schweitzer (her lawyer) produced extracts from Mao's writings and there is no doubt that the passages shown in (the girl's) notebooks are taken, in whole or in part, from these writings authored by Mao. I would point out however, that these are not taken from one page, or one paragraph; they seem to have been copied from the essay in a logical order. This suggests ... that she has read and understood the entire essay and

CHAPTER 4   THE CANADIAN PERSPECTIVE

has taken from them the salient quotes, in connection with her purpose in reading this material."[14]

The girl had actually read and understood what Mao had said. Therefore, according to the adjudicator, she must be a terrorist.

---

14   *Supra* note 2.

Chapter 5 Detention of Asylum Seekers: The Australian Perspective

By Fedor Mediansky

Contents

Part I   Introduction
Part II The rationale for immigration detention
Part III Detention and the law
Part IV Detention centres
Part V   The politics of immigration detention in Australia
Part VI Current reform initiatives
Part VII Conclusion – Table

I   Introduction

By western comparison the Australian refugee intake is not large. The annual intake under the humanitarian categories averages below 15,000 per annum in recent years. Yet Australia is alone among western countries in having mandatory non-reviewable detention of asylum seekers. Such provisions as exist for release from detention are very limited, falling short of the guidelines on detention set by the United Nations High Commissioner for Refugees. Efforts to modify the detention regime have met with little success.

This paradox needs to be understood against the background of Australia's historic experience and its geographic circumstances. The colonial settlements, established along a vast coastline, felt isolated and vulnerable in an alien environment. Such perceptions engendered a deep sense of insecurity. In this context immigration control became closely linked to national security and survival. Among the first acts of the newly established Federal government was the enactment of restrictive immigration laws which sought to ensure a homogenous (and essentially British) population. Thus immigration detention was provided for in the Migration Restriction Act 1901.

The breach of basic human rights, a central feature of immigration detention, tended to sit uneasily (at least in recent times) with a political culture which is deeply egalitarian and largely committed to liberal values. The conflict between liberal values and a historically based concern with immigration control remains at the core of the debate on immigration detention. During the earlier post-war decades Australia followed a relatively humane course towards asylum seekers, and thus over half a million refugees and displaced persons have been resettled under humanitarian programs. This trend extended to the early boat arrivals from southeast Asia in the 1970s. Some 52 boats arrived between 1975 and 1981. All were allowed to stay and the approach to the detention regime was liberal.

The pendulum shifted from liberal policies to an emphasis on immigration control in the late 1980s. Between 1989 and mid-1996, some 55 boats arrived with about 2,600 people; a further 71 children were born in Australia. Most were treated as unauthorised arrivals; those who sought to stay were held in detention and only 521 were allowed to remain in Australia. Since 1989 all "illegals" have been subject to mandatory detention. The boat arrivals were detained for the entire period of the determination process, in some cases for up to five years. Recent statistics are given in the table at the end of this chapter.

II   The rationale for immigration detention

The principal rationale for detention is immigration control. Australia maintains a universal visa system and a large-scale migration program, which includes humanitarian categories. Broadly speaking, any non-citizen who enters the country without a visa is deemed an unauthorised arrival and is liable to immigration detention. Thus all asylum seekers who arrive directly by sea, "the boat people", are subject to mandatory detention until their status is determined. On the other hand, those who enter the country with a visa and then seek asylum are not usually kept in detention. Thus the rationale for detention is immigration control: namely to uphold the universal visa requirement and to guard against unauthorised arrivals undermining the immigration program.

A further rationale for detention is to facilitate the processing of unauthorised border arrivals. A related reason is guarding against absconding. Yet it is difficult to see why asylum seekers would abscond under Australian circumstances. Those on bridging visas have an incentive to keep in contact with the authorities in the hope of a favourable decision. Asylum seekers who abscond are not excluded from the determination procedure, but they are liable to have their bridging visas cancelled and without a visa, they face mandatory detention. The immigration authorities have acknowledged that there has been little difficulty in maintaining contact with applicants during the determination procedures.[1] The problem of absconding arises after an application has failed and the applicant no longer has legal means of

---

1   Australian Parliament, Joint Standing Committee on Migration, *Asylum, Border Control and Detention*, AGPS Canberra, 1994, p. 110.

remaining in the country. Failed asylum seekers who abscond are liable to police action.

Detention has also been justified on economic grounds. Yet detailed figures on the costs of detention are not available. The Department of Immigration and Multicultural Affairs (DIMA) estimates that the annual cost of the detention facilities for boat people is AU$ 6 million. The economic rationale for detention is that it enables the government to provide the asylum seekers with a range of services, including accommodation, food, health care, counselling and education, which would not be available to them outside the detention centres. Non-government organisations have contested this argument. They point to the Asylum Seeker Assistance Scheme (ASAS) which has proved a viable form of support for asylum seekers who are in the country legally and thus not in detention. The ASAS is funded by the government and administered by the Australian Red Cross. Normally, ASAS support is not available for the first six months. Without this source of financial support, most asylum seekers have no alternative to detention as community organisations are unable to meet the basic needs of detainees without government subvention.

Much of the economic argument for detention hinges on estimates of the costs of detention against the costs of community release programs. The data on costs is incomplete and so the argument cannot be resolved conclusively. It seems fair to say that the remote location of the principal detention centre, together with the mounting security provisions in recent years, makes the case for detention on economic grounds very doubtful. Furthermore, there is no evidence to suggest that asylum seekers prefer the security of detention centres to community release with support from the existing government programs as well as from the NGOs.

DIMA has also acknowledged that detention serves as a form of deterrence against the violation of the universal visa system. The more severe detention practices, begun in mid-1996 (outlined below), will undoubtedly serve to further deter those who would seek asylum in Australia.

III   Detention and the law

Immigration to Australia is regulated by the Migration Act 1958 (as amended) and the Migration Regulations.

Immigration detention in Australia is a form of administrative detention which refers to the deprivation of personal liberty for reasons other than conviction of an offence. Administrative detention is not contrary to the Australian Constitution and is recognised under international law. Furthermore, the High Court of Australia has observed in the 1992 *Lim* case[2] that the rights and immunities of aliens differ in significant respects from those of Australian citizens, an important difference being the vulnerability of aliens to exclusion or deportation. The High Court also observed that the Constitution provides significantly diminished protection to aliens "against imprisonment otherwise than pursuant to judicial process".[3] In the *Lim* case, Justice McHugh elaborated on the characteristics of administrative detention. He said that in the case of detention pending the determination of an alien's application to enter the country, detention is non-punitive and legitimate because the purpose is to prevent the applicant from entering the community until a determination is made. The judge also reasoned that detention has a non-punitive and legitimate objective when imposed on an unsuccessful applicant who is subject to deportation.[4] In general terms, the rights and immunities of aliens are fewer than those of citizens because the former can be held in immigration detention. The legal safeguards that apply to administrative detention are, in some respects, inferior to those that apply to persons held under criminal proceedings. For example, asylum seekers in detention can be kept incommunicado and there is no requirement to inform them of their right to legal representation.

The overwhelming number of asylum seekers who are detained are those arriving by boat from southeast Asia without an entry visa (see the statistical table at the end of the chapter). Such people are regarded as unauthorised border arrivals who must be held in detention until they are granted a visa or leave the country. Immigration detention is mandatory for all those who are "unlawfully" in Australia; these include undocumented border arrivals, most of whom seek asylum when given the opportunity to do so, as well as overstayers and those whose visas have been cancelled. The rationale for detention is breach of immigration regulations. Thus not all asylum seekers are subject to detention. Those who enter the country "lawfully" can apply for protection while they hold a valid visa; if their application is declared admissible, they are issued a bridging visa on the expiry of their valid visa which entitles them to remain until the determination of their application. If they fail to apply for protection while still holding a valid visa, they are treated as overstayers when the visa expires. As such they are subject to supervised departure and, in some cases, immigration detention. Overstayers are not subject to criminal charges.

While asylum seekers who are not immigration cleared are subject to mandatory detention, some categories are eligible for release while their application for asylum is under consideration. The mechanism for release from detention is a bridging visa which enables the holder to live in the community while their

---

2 *Chu Kheng Lim and Others* v. *Minister for Immigration, Local Government and Ethnic Affairs and Another*, High Court of Australia, 6, 7 August , 9 December 1992, Canberra.
3 *Ibid.*, p. 50.
4 *Ibid.*, p. 51.

CHAPTER 5   THE AUSTRALIAN PERSPECTIVE

application for "lawful" entry is being determined. Those eligible for bridging visas are in prescribed categories which include:

- children up to the age of 18;
- victims of torture and trauma;
- those 75 years of age or over.

In practice very few boat arrivals are granted bridging visas. This includes children born in Australia of parents held in detention. Likewise, families with children under 18 years are usually denied a bridging visa on the grounds of maintaining family unity.

According to the Migration Regulations 1994, persons can be released from detention when they "cannot be cared for in a detention environment". This "special needs" category applies to torture and trauma victims and can be extended to those with health requirements. The primary consideration for release is access to services. While figures are unavailable, it seems that few torture and trauma victims are released from detention because of their "special needs". Potential torture and trauma victims are identified in several ways: by DIMA officers in the course of interviews, by legal advisers, by the medical staff at the detention centre, or by self-referral. Once identified, they are referred by the detention centre medical staff for assessment by independent specialist agencies in the various states, such as the Service for the Rehabilitation of Torture and Trauma Survivors in New South Wales. Treatment is provided in several settings: within the detention centre by the medical staff or by consultant therapists. They can also be treated outside detention centres, usually by escorted visits to specialist agencies.

The refusal of a bridging visa is reviewable by the Refugee Review Tribunal (RRT) for certain categories of detained persons but not for those detained at the border. Detained persons cannot be released even by the courts (a practice declared unlawful by the UN Human Rights Commmittee in its 1997 ruling on Communication No. 560/1993, referred to below in Chapter 8) unless they meet the criteria for a visa.

Determination of refugee status is a two-stage process. At the primary stage, DIMA examines claims against the Convention and Protocol and a decision on granting a protection visa is made. Unsuccessful applicants can apply for a merits review by the RRT which can uphold or set aside the primary decision to deny a protection visa. Under major revisions introduced in 1992 to the Migration Reform Act 1958, the right to appeal immigration decisions through the courts has been substantially reduced. The new laws, effective since 1994, seek to limit the judicial review of adverse DIMA decisions by extending the right to review by the RRT - decisions of the RRT are not subject to judicial review except in tightly defined cases which are set out in the Act as "judicially reviewable decisions". In the main, these are defined narrowly and applied exclusively to cases involving the failure to observe prescribed procedures and errors of law.

The legislative basis for detaining rejected asylum seekers is in the Migration Act 1958, which states that aliens without valid visas are subject to detention. Rejected in-country asylum applicants are subject to supervised departure (as opposed to deportation). Rejected applicants who abscond can be placed in detention while awaiting supervised departure. There is no maximum period for detention before departure, although the usual practice is to effect supervised departure as soon as possible (usually within days).

In principle, Australian immigration law and practice should be influenced by the international instruments to which it is a signatory. In practice, these instruments exercise limited influence because domestic legislation takes precedence. Attempts to challenge domestic legislation in the courts on the grounds of Australia's international obligations have met with limited success. For example, the High Court (in the 1992 *Lim* case) refused to rule on a submission that the duration of detention was contrary to the plaintiff's rights under the 1951 Geneva Convention and the ICCPR.[5]

The relevant international instruments are as follows:

- the 1951 UN Convention relating to the Status of Refugees (acceded to by Australia in 1954) and its 1967 Protocol (acceded to in 1973). Adherence to the Convention is complicated by the fact that most of Australia's regional neighbours in southeast Asia, via which large numbers of refugee applicants arrived by boat, have not acceded to the Convention. Thus they are not obliged to allow, and on occasion have not allowed, asylum seekers to land. When allowed to land, the regional countries provide a level of protection that is often lower than that provided in Australia. It is doubtful, however, that most Asian asylum seekers are aware of the level of protection in Australia and thus it is unlikely that Australia acts as a regional "magnet" for refugees;
- UNHCR Executive Committee Conclusions;
- the International Covenant on Civil and Political Rights (ratified in 1980);
- the Convention Against Torture and Other Cruel, Inhuman or Degrading Treatment or Punishment (ratified in 1989);
- the Convention on the Rights of the Child (ratified in 1990).

International practice, especially in comparable western countries such as Canada, the US and western Europe, is also taken into account.

References to these instruments are frequently made in the domestic refugee debate and many advocacy groups have sought modifications to detention practice

---

5   *Ibid.*, p. 53.

CHAPTER 5   THE AUSTRALIAN PERSPECTIVE

by such references. For example the Human Rights Commissioner has argued that the lack of provision for individual circumstances of detainees is in breach of Article 9 of the ICCPR.[6]

UNHCR has expressed concern about the imposition of prolonged detention on asylum seekers and argued that such practice was not in accord with the Geneva Convention (Article 31) and Executive Committee Conclusion No. 44.[7] Again, it argued that the prolonged detention of children is contrary to the Convention on the Rights of the Child. While such criticism has undoubtedly proved politically embarrassing to the Australian government, not least because its foreign policy is formally committed to "good international citizenship", it does not seem that international norms have led to modification of detention practice. The reason is partly because government departments have tended to argue that current practice is not seriously at odds with the relevant international instruments. The Parliamentary Committee on Migration sought advice in 1994 from the Attorney General's Department on this issue and the advice it received is that "overall ... the existing detention arrangements comply with the international obligations Australia has assumed". The Attorney General's Department stated that:

"Detention for the purposes of exclusion from Australia, investigation of claims for protection, satisfactorily identifying the detainee, processing refugee or entry permit applications within a reasonable time and protecting public security is unobjectionable."[8]

Underlying these judgements was the observation that administrative detention is not, in itself, contrary to international law.

There were, however, some reservations about this judgement. The Attorney General's advisers expressed reservation about mandatory detention for all uncleared asylum seekers and advised that in some cases, prolonged detention and the detention of children, "may" be in breach of international law.[9] Again, the Department of Foreign Affairs and Trade has argued that while detention practice generally complies with Australia's international obligations, greater discretion in implementing the regulations would diminish the prospects of a challenge. The Department stated that:

"there would be less likelihood that our compliance with our international obligations could be challenged ... if there were more discretion under

---

6   *Ibid.*, p. 112.
7   *Ibid.*, p. 113.
8   *ibid.*, p. 114.
9   *Ibid.*, pp. 114–116.

regulations relating, in particular, ... to cases in which detention has been prolonged for whatever reason and in cases which involve children."[10]

IV Detention centres

The Migration Act provides for the establishment of immigration detention centres. The Act also establishes the principle of mandatory detention and sets out different detention arrangements for immigration clearance, unlawful non-citizens and for questioning.

By the early 1990s, almost all unauthorised boat arrivals in long-term detention were held at two centres: the Westbridge Stage 2 Centre in Sydney and the remotely located Immigration Reception and Processing Centre at Port Hedland, in northwest Australia. The Port Hedland facility is exclusively for boat arrivals who land on Australia's northern coastline.

These centres are managed by DIMA, which is responsible for day-to-day operations. DIMA is also responsible for the overall conditions at the centres as well as for the level of services provided. The DIMA detention staff are not responsible for the determination of asylum claims; this is the responsibility of a Canberra based section of the Department. The extensive security regime is the responsibility of the Australian Protection Service (APS), a unit of the government's security service.

The security protocol at the two long-term detention centres isolates the detainees from the community and consequently various services are provided within the detention centres. Health facilities at Port Hedland include resident general and psychiatric nurses and visits by medical and dental practitioners. Some educational services are provided for long-term detainees as well as vocational and English language classes. There is also a small welfare staff, an interpreter service and access to telephone and postal services. Detainees have access to legal advisers who provide assistance with asylum applications and advice on appeals, though access to these provisions were seriously curtailed in mid-1996 (see below). While the level of services (for those who have lodged asylum claims) has undoubtedly been improved, advocacy groups argue that they still fall short of acceptable Australian standards and that in some cases, they are below the standards laid down by international instruments. The contention that most services would be at a higher level (and in some cases less costly) if detainees had direct access to mainstream services holds most weight when the point of comparison is with services available in the populated areas of the country rather than in remote places like Port Hedland. Yet policy seems firmly committed to keeping unauthorised asylum seekers in remote northwestern Australia. The mothballed Curtin air force base (in the same region) was used in 1995 to accommodate the overflow from Port Hedland.

---

10 *Ibid.*, p. 117.

CHAPTER 5   THE AUSTRALIAN PERSPECTIVE

Advocacy groups have repeatedly questioned the justification for keeping border arrivals at remote locations in northwestern Australia. It has been argued that the location of the Port Hedland facility hinders access to fully qualified legal advisers, interpreters with the necessary languages, culturally appropriate medical practitioners, counsellors and religious leaders, as well as to ethnic and cultural support groups. It has also been argued that the cost of legal services are substantially increased by the location of Port Hedland. It can also be added that the administrative costs are increased with the regular use of Canberra-based DIMA and APS staff. These observations notwithstanding, DIMA has shown no interest in relocating detainees to centres closer to the more populated parts of the country. The main justification for the location of Port Hedland is the logistic convenience of having a facility close to where boat arrivals land. The deterrent value of the facility is reflected in the departmental comment that it avoids a premature indication of acceptance into the community.[11]

Several organisations have investigated the detention centres in recent years. Their reports expressed serious reservations about the use of long-term immigration detention. The report of the Australian Institute of Criminology recommended that maximum use be made of conditional release as an alternative to detention and that only those detainees with criminal convictions should be kept in penal institutions. The report of the Human Rights Commission recommended the review of detention policy and the granting of temporary residence to those detained for more than two years. This report also expressed concern with the process of "inculturation"– a consequence of prolonged detention – whereby detainees lose contact with their own culture. The report of the Australian Council of Churches identified a number of deficient services at Port Hedland. It also criticised the practice of detaining asylum seekers for over two years and pointed to the depressed psychological state of many detainees who had been held in long-term detention.

In her dissenting report, Senator Christabel Chamarette noted that the majority report of the Parliamentary Committee on Migration paid little attention to the psychological effects of long-term detention.[12] Yet the evidence clearly points to the psychologically harmful effects of detention, even when the detention regime is humane.

Senator Chamarette argued that placing asylum seekers in detention tended to reinforce the traumatic experiences which led to the search for asylum in the first place. She argued that the physical conditions in detention centres – deprivation of liberty, living behind barbed wire under the direction of uniformed guards in regimented and prison-like conditions – was stressful, as was the prolonged

---

11   *Ibid.*, p. 189.
12   *Ibid.*, p. 206.

uncertainty while awaiting the determination of the application in a strange and isolated environment.[13]

These observations were reinforced by the Victorian Foundation for Survivors of Torture. The Foundation undertook psychological assessments for DIMA of Cambodians held in long-term detention. It found severe levels of depression and anxiety of all the assessed detainees. While other contributing factors have to be recognised, there is no doubt that long-term detention was a major (and ongoing) cause of stress, contributing to the extreme levels of anxiety and depression which were found to be a common condition of the detainees. Though funded by public money, the results of the consultancy are tightly held by DIMA, perhaps because of the politically embarrassing nature of the findings. While statistical data is not available, it is widely known that self-mutilation and attempted suicide have occurred from time to time at Australian refugee detention centres.

The socially damaging effects of long-term detention have been reported by several NGOs. The Australian Red Cross (with a full time representative at the Port Hedland centre) noted changes in behaviour caused by prolonged detention. It reported behavioural traits including:

"apathy, anger, violence, anxiety, depression and withdrawal. ... Their ability to take control of their future, to make decisions, to articulate logical argument ... diminishes with the increase in this dependency syndrome. This dependency is all too prevalent within the Port Hedland facility."[14]

It appears that the "dependency syndrome" noted by the Red Cross persists well after release and severely limits the ability of long-term detainees to resume normal lives. A report of a committee of the Saint Vincent de Paul Society, working with Cambodian boat people who had experienced long-term detention, noted a high level of dependency and a reluctance to assume initiative. The report linked such behaviour to the experience of prolonged detention.[15]

The effects of prolonged detention on children have also been noted by the Red Cross.[16] The NSW Child Protection Council, in its submission to the parliamentary inquiry, argued that conditions in detention had an adverse effect on the development of children. The Victorian Foundation for Survivors of Torture has also expressed concern about the psychological impact of long-term detention on children.

---

13 *Ibid.*, p. 207.
14 *Ibid* , p. 206.
15 Saint Vincent de Paul, Eastern Suburbs Migrant & Refugee Committee, *Sponsorship Programs for Returning Cambodian Boat People*, Sydney, 1995. Unpublished, pp. 11–14.
16 *Asylum, Border Control and Detention, supra* note 1, p. 207.

CHAPTER 5   THE AUSTRALIAN PERSPECTIVE

V   The politics of immigration detention in Australia

While immigration detention has aroused controversy in Australia, it is not a major political issue. Committed minorities maintain an ongoing debate, while mainstream public opinion remains unengaged.

Advocacy groups in the NGO community have lobbied against long-term immigration detention. While their criticisms have led to improvements in the conditions at detention centres, they have not succeeded in modifying detention practice. Funding arrangements undoubtedly mute critical comment from many organisations. Major NGOs working in the refugee field, including the Refugee Council, Red Cross, Saint Vincent de Paul Society and the Australian Council of Churches, play significant roles in the government's refugee and migration programs. This work is funded by the government and represents a significant funding source which could be jeopardised if criticism were to breach the accepted boundaries.

Eminent persons have criticised the long-term detention of asylum seekers. These include the Human Rights Commissioner; practising judges, including Alastair Nicholson, Chief Justice of the Family Court and Justice Michael Kirby who was recently elevated to the High Court; and a former Prime Minister, Malcolm Fraser. Though criticism from such people is undoubtedly embarrassing to the government, its commitment to mandatory detention for boat people has not eased. Indeed, the attitude of the Howard government (elected in March 1996) has hardened.

The major source on detention issues in Australia is undoubtedly the 1994 parliamentary report entitled: Asylum, Border Control and Detention.[17] The report framed its recommendation on detention within the government's current policy framework as set out in the Migration Act of 1958 and the Migration Reform Act of 1992. Its recommendations include:

- public funding of legal advice for border refugee claimants when preparing primary claims and appeals to the Refugee Review Tribunal;
- giving priority to applications from asylum seekers who are held in detention (as a means of minimising time spent in detention);
- endorsement of the practice of holding border refugee claimants in detention during the initial determination and review process, including legal appeals, but a recommendation "that there be a possibility for considering release where the period of detention exceeds six months";
- the designation of a "prescribed class" of detainees who would be eligible for a bridging visa (and thus release) for those held in detention for more than six

---

17   See *supra* note 1.

months; this recommendation was aimed at vulnerable groups, torture and trauma victims and those with special needs based on age or health;
– endorsement of the continued operation of the Port Hedland facility, subject to a number of recommendations aimed at improving its operations and services.

The position of the major NGOs is set out in the 1994 Charter of Minimum Requirements for Legislation Relating to the Detention of Asylum Seekers. The Charter sets out norms on the treatment of detained asylum seekers by major representative organisations including the Australian Council of Churches, the Human Rights and Equal Opportunity Commission, the International Commission of Jurists, the Australian Red Cross and the Refugee Council of Australia. The minimum requirements of the Charter call for:

– unrestricted access to independent legal advice;
– the right of all detained asylum seekers to apply for bridging visas and the right to review when the application is refused;
– presumption in favour of granting bridging visas and the limitation of refusal to prescribed grounds;
– regular reviews for those held in detention;
– the location of detention facilities near metropolitan centres to ensure better access to support services and facilities;
– establishment of an Immigration Detention Advisory Committee, with representatives of both the government and non-government sectors, as well as detainees, in order to monitor services in detention centres including health care, torture and trauma counselling, education, interpreting services, access to legal advice, recreational facilities and pastoral care.

VI   Current reform initiatives

Government resistance to detention reform has not deterred advocacy groups from pressing for change.

In June 1993, a communication was sent to the UN Human Rights Committee (HRC) on behalf of a Cambodian national who was held in detention at Port Hedland. The applicant arrived by boat in Australia in November 1989. Asylum was refused after some three and a half years in detention. Though attempts to challenge the decision in the courts were frustrated by DIMA, the case reached the High Court of Australia which upheld the legislative power of the federal authorities. This decision opened the way for an appeal to the UN Human Rights Committee (HRC), under the individual complaints procedure (Optional Protocol to the International Covenant on Civil and Political Rights). The appeal thus challenged Australian detention practice by bringing it before the authoritative UN agency. It was an

CHAPTER 5   THE AUSTRALIAN PERSPECTIVE

entirely private initiative, made on behalf of the applicant, in the knowledge that any finding would have relevance for other detainees.

The basis of the communication was essentially twofold: arbitrary detention while the applicant's status was under determination (Article 9(1) of the ICCPR) and the lack of access to the legal process by virtue of isolation while being held in detention (Article 9(4) of the ICCPR). The communication was submitted on 20 June 1993 and was declared admissible in May 1995. The HRC adopted its views on 30 April 1997.[18] The HRC found a violation on the first count, finding that the applicant's detention for a period of over four years was not proportional to the aim of preventing him from absconding and was therefore arbitrary within the meaning of Article 9(1). With regard to Article 9(4), the HRC found a violation of the applicant's rights because the courts had no power to review the continued detention of an individual and to order his release. However, regarding the complaint that the applicant had not been adequately informed of his rights, had been forcibly removed from a state jurisdiction without adequate notice being given to his legal advisers and had been held at a remote location which had prevented him from obtaining legal advice, the HRC found that this part of the communication did not raise an issue as the applicant had been informed in Kampuchean of his right to legal assistance a fortnight after his arrival in Australia and that his relocation to several detention centres throughout Australia did not "detract from the fact that he retained access to legal advisers". Furthermore, the HRC did not find that there had been a violation of Article 2(1) on the grounds of discrimination against "boat people", but did find that there had been a violation of Article 2(3) (right to an effective remedy) and that the applicant should be compensated for the period he had spent in detention.

Concerned with the slow pace of reform, the recently formed Detention Reform Coordinating Committee has drawn up an Alternative Detention Model.[19] The model incorporates the principal requirements of the Charter of Minimum Requirements and sets these out in operational terms to facilitate the reform of the current detention provisions. The alternative model envisages a number of modifications to the detention regime. It sets out five grounds for detention and presumes that most detained asylum seekers would be released within three months of arrival on bridging visas. The alternative model proposes a simple three-stage regime moving from more severe restrictions on personal liberty to increasingly liberal provisions. These are closed detention, open detention and three forms of community release. The model also provides for ongoing review to ensure equitable case management for asylum seekers. Having completed the Alternative Detention

---

[18]   *A (name deleted)* v. *Australia*, Communication No. 560/1993, UN Doc. CCPR/C/59/D/560/1993 (30 April 1997); see also Chapter 8 for a further description of this case and Appendix I.2, which reproduces relevant articles of the ICCPR.

[19]   Reproduced in full in Appendix VII.3 to this book.

Model in 1996, the Detention Reform Committee is embarking on a program of advocacy aimed at the adoption of its proposals by the government.

The Human Rights and Equal Opportunity Commission is conducting a wide ranging inquiry into detention practices in Australia as a result of numerous complaints received from persons in detention and from refugee advocacy groups. Its report was due in the second part of 1996, but appeared to be delayed.

The outlook for reform had taken an alarming direction by mid-1996. The conservative Howard government took steps to make Australia significantly less open to asylum seekers and to further isolate and marginalise those held in detention.

The government further isolated asylum seekers at Port Hedland by curtailing their access to legal advice and community support. In a report to the Catholic Bishops Conference, the Catholic chaplain to the detention centre outlined the deteriorating conditions at Port Hedland and accused the authorities of restricting religious freedom and access to pastoral care.

The recently instituted practice of holding detainees incommunicado at Port Hedland was challenged in the courts by the Human Rights Commissioner when he attempted to send a sealed letter to detainees, in accordance with his enabling legislation. When the challenge was upheld by the Federal Court, the Minister for Immigration introduced legislation (in June 1996) to amend the Migration Act so as to deny persons held in immigration detention access to the Human Rights Commissioner and the Ombudsman unless the persons in detention initiate a complaint in writing. Prior to this amendment, the Human Rights Commissioner and the Ombudsman had the right to contact detainees even when these persons had not requested contact. The amended legislation also states that immigration officials are not obliged to provide detainees with an application form for a visa or with information as to their eligibility to apply for a visa or access to advice (legal or otherwise) in relation to an application for a visa.[20] These changes would further isolate detainees and curtail the exercise of their legal rights to seek asylum. In a stinging attack on the new bill, the Human Rights Commissioner said that this would place the Immigration Department outside Australia's human rights law.

The government's concern to expedite applications has led to the adoption of procedures that, in practice, severely curtail the prescribed rights of asylum seekers to information. New arrivals are not told about their rights unless they specifically request to be informed. As they are held in isolation on entering detention, the likelihood that they will learn of their rights is seriously diminished. Asylum seekers have access to free and independent legal advice after their application for asylum is declared admissible by DIMA.

---

20 Because of representations by the Human Rights Commissioner the legislation was on hold as at November 1996.

Asylum seekers will have their access to the courts severely restricted as a result of cost-cutting measures. The Minister for Immigration expressed concern about the costs of asylum applicants seeking the review of adverse decisions by the Immigration Review Tribunal, claiming that in mid-1996 there were 559 immigration cases before the courts and 60% of these related to asylum claims. The Minister established a review to identify ways of restricting appeals to the courts, a report was to be published and legislative changes have been foreshadowed. Further cost-cutting measures under way include cutting the refugee intake to 12,000 and reducing the funding for the legal aid for asylum seekers who appeal an adverse primary determination.

VII   Conclusion

The mandatory detention of unauthorised asylum seekers (arriving spontaneously) is not a major political issue in Australia. However, a nationwide political debate surfaced in the latter part of 1996 on Asian immigration. This debate undoubtedly hardened the resolve of the government to tighten its procedure on boat arrivals.

The use of detention as an instrument of immigration control is deeply rooted in history and it is still widely accepted. Advocacy groups have not focused on the issue of detaining unauthorised asylum seekers on arrival. Again, there has been little objection to detention prior to expulsion. On the other hand, detention during the determination procedure, especially over a prolonged period, has attracted criticism. There has been widespread concern expressed about long-term (more than six months) detention as well as about the detention of vulnerable groups (children, the aged and infirm, and torture and trauma victims).

On the whole, Australian governments have not responded to these concerns and are unlikely to while bipartisan consensus persists on these issues. Until recently, officials have been more receptive to criticism of internal conditions in detention and here there has been some headway. The pendulum is now shifting towards immigration control and deterrence; and the voices of reform have become more isolated. Under the present government the treatment of asylum seekers in detention has deteriorated seriously.

The outlook for humane reforms is not encouraging. During the 1990s the major parties have all supported arrangements that discourage asylum. Their position on refugee issues is influenced by domestic concerns with unemployment and government cost-cutting policies. There is also rising concern over the growing numbers of asylum seekers worldwide. Thus, while Australia continues with a significant immigration program, its policies toward asylum seekers are falling in line with the more restrictive practices prevailing in other western countries.

Table

Detained asylum seekers as a percentage of total asylum seekers:

Financial year	Total number asylum seekers	Number in detention	Percentage
1993/94	7,662	209 boat people*	2.72
1994/95	7,399	265	3.58
1995/96	7,915	287	3.62

* Figures are not available for categories other than boat people for 1993/94, since recorded asylum seeker information did not indicate whether they were held in detention.

Chapter 6 Comments on the UNHCR Position on Detention of Refugees and Asylum Seekers

By Karin Landgren[1]

Contents

Part I   Introduction
Part II   UNHCR's role: II.1 Increasing use of detention: The 1995 Survey – II.2 The use of detention: Executive Committee Conclusion No. 44
Part III The 1951 Convention relating to the Status of Refugees: III.1 Article 31 – III.2 Article 26 – III.3 Article 8 – III.4 Article 9
Part IV   The scope of protection: IV.1 Protected persons – IV.2 Distinguishing refugees and asylum seekers from other aliens – IV.3 The exceptional nature of detention – IV.4 The elements of necessity and proportionality – IV.5 What constitutes detention? – IV.6 Alternatives to detention – IV.7 Procedural safeguards – IV.8 Access to UNHCR – IV.9 Segregation from offenders – IV.10 The detention of minors
Part V   Detention and international solidarity

I   Introduction

The very purpose of refugee protection is to protect human rights. Refugees and asylum seekers are supposed to be treated in accordance not only with the refugee law regime, but also in accordance with human rights standards. This may seem to be stating the obvious, but a bifurcation continues to make itself felt, emphasising the separateness of refugees rather than the universality of human rights. One illustration of this is found in the detention of refugees and asylum seekers. Even as the rights to liberty and security of person, and freedom of movement, are strengthened through human rights instruments and mechanisms, the detention of refugees and asylum seekers risks becoming regarded, increasingly, as a matter of administrative practice, perhaps even a routine. The circumstances under which such

---

1   The views expressed here are those of the author alone and do not necessarily represent those of UNHCR or the United Nations.

detention is permissible are narrow, and when it takes place beyond that framework, it should be challenged.

According to the prevailing international consensus, the detention of refugees and asylum seekers should normally be avoided. And yet, detention of refugees, asylum seekers and stateless persons appears to have increased in the western world. In 1996, the European Court of Human Rights found that France had violated the right to liberty and security of person in detaining asylum seekers within an international airport transit zone, for 19 days, without judicial review.[2] Notwithstanding this welcome development, political imperatives in favour of detention still hold the upper hand. Nearly half a century after the drafters of the Refugee Convention debated imposing "penalties ... on account of illegal entry or presence" and not applying to the movements of refugees "restrictions other than those which are necessary",[3] practice and interpretation varies widely.

In 1986, UNHCR's advisory body, the Executive Committee (ExCom), adopted a Conclusion on the detention of refugees and asylum seekers. The annual Conclusions on International Protection by the Executive Committee are without binding force; however, they are an indicator of current State practice, and reflect the consensus of a broad group of States, including non-signatories to the international refugee instruments. Conclusion No. 44 on Detention of Refugees and Asylum Seekers states that detention should normally be avoided, in view of the hardship which it involves.

While UNHCR and human rights advocates seek a new consensus strengthening refugees' and asylum seekers' protection from detention, the current climate is a harsh one. In western Europe, the view that asylum seekers' claims are largely abusive prevails. Given the widespread use of narrow, restrictive interpretations of the refugee definition by decision-makers, the percentages of applicants recognised there as refugees under the Refugee Convention ranges from modest to microscopic. These recognition rates rarely reflect the genuine protection needs of the asylum seeker, and are subsequently cited to buttress assertions of fraudulent and abusive claims[4] – which in turn prompt recourse to more restrictive measures.

---

2 Case of *Amuur v. France*, application No. 19776/92, report of the Commission of 10 January 1995, judgment No. 17/1995/523/609 of 25 June 1996, to be published in Reports of Judgments and Decisions for 1996, Carl Heymans Verlag, Köln.
3 Art. 31, 1951 *Convention relating to the Status of Refugees*.
4 "Evidence from Canada and Denmark, two States where abbreviated asylum procedures are well-resourced and relatively objective, demonstrates that less than eight percent and twenty percent respectively of all asylum claims are without credible basis in the 1951 Geneva Convention. It is reasonable to presume that fewer still involve cases of intentional fraud. Blanket characterisations tend to serve a rhetorical purpose, painting a uniform image of unworthy migrants ...", Shacknove, Andrew, and Byrne, Rosemary, *The*

CHAPTER 6   COMMENTS ON THE UNHCR POSITION

II   UNHCR's role

Under its Statute, UNHCR is to provide for the international protection of refugees by, among other things, supervising the application of international conventions for the protection of refugees.[5] States parties to the 1951 Convention are committed, under Article 35, to facilitating UNHCR's duty in this regard. In view of these responsibilities, and relying also on relevant principles of international law, UNHCR has developed certain positions in relation to the detention of asylum seekers. In 1995, following an in-depth survey of European legislation and practice in respect of the detention of refugees and asylum seekers,[6] UNHCR issued Guidelines on the Detention of Asylum Seekers. These Guidelines address some of the lacunae in the existing standards on refugee detention, notably with regard to the definition of detention, the nature of the judicial or administrative review to which it should be subject, and the use of detention against minors.[7] They also seek to reflect international legal developments: in the period since the 1986 Executive Committee Conclusion, human rights law has progressed and been further refined, particularly through the organs of the Council of Europe.

II.1   Increasing use of detention: The 1995 Survey

Asylum seekers risk detention principally at two stages: upon entry or at the time of making their request, and upon the failure of their application, pending deportation. These comments will largely address the first instance. With regard to the second instance, despite the ostensibly greater claim to "necessity" in pre-deportation detention, its use in respect of stateless persons, persons of indeterminate nationality, and persons whose countries of origin decline to readmit them is cause for concern.

Following indications of an increase in the use of detention – indeed, suggestions that in a few countries, it had become routine in respect of asylum seekers at borders – UNHCR undertook a survey of European legislation and practice in this respect. The results confirmed empirical and anecdotal evidence of

---

Safe Country Notion in European Asylum Law, Harvard Human Rights Journal, Volume 9, Spring 1996, p. 199.

5   *Statute of the Office of the United Nations High Commissioner for Refugees,* UNGA Res. 428(V), para. 8(a).

6   *Detention of Asylum-Seekers in Europe,* European Series, Volume 1 No. 4, October 1995, UNHCR Geneva.

7   The following Conclusions are relevant: Nos. 7(e), *Expulsion,* 1977; 22(II)(B)2(a), *Protection of Asylum Seekers in Situations of Large-Scale Influx,* 1981; 36(f) *General,* 1985; 46(f) *General,* 1987; 47(e) *Refugee Children,* 1987; 50(I), *General,* 1988; 55(g), *General,* 1989; 65(c), *General,* 1991; 68(e), *General,* 1992, 71(f), *General,* 1993; 72, *Personal Security of Refugees,* 1993, 73, *Refugee Protection and Sexual Violence,* 1993.

widespread recourse to detention, as well as turning up other factors in States' use of detention which make monitoring and supervision problematic. For one thing, the concept of detention denotes different things in different countries. Secondly, even allowing for variations in interpretation of the term, governments were rarely able to provide accurate statistical data on the numbers detained, the duration of detention, or a breakdown by age and gender.

Finally, the UNHCR survey identified serious obstacles in obtaining effective access to legal counselling, the lack of suspensive effect of appeals and onerous bail conditions as being among the principal difficulties facing detained asylum seekers.

II.2   The use of detention: Executive Committee Conclusion No. 44

In 1986, several years after UNHCR had begun to highlight the problem of detention of asylum seekers, the Executive Committee adopted Conclusion No. 44 (XXXVII) on Detention of Refugees and Asylum Seekers. This Conclusion reflects minimum standards, without prejudice to applicable higher standards established by domestic law or international law as, for example, through the European Human Rights Convention.

The starting-point of Conclusion No. 44 is an expression of deep concern at the large numbers of refugees and asylum seekers in the world who are the subject of detention "or similar restrictive measures". The Executive Committee then expressed the opinion that in view of the hardship which it involves, detention should normally be avoided. If necessary, detention may be resorted to only on grounds prescribed by law to verify identity; to determine the elements on which the claim to refugee status or asylum is based; to deal with cases where refugees or asylum seekers have destroyed their travel and/or identity documents or have used fraudulent documents in order to mislead the authorities of the State in which they intend to claim asylum; or to protect national security or public order.[8]

The concepts of penalties for illegal entry or presence, of necessity, and of measures to protect national security or public order as expressed here mirror discussions at the Ad Hoc Committee of Plenipotentiaries during the drafting of the 1951 Convention. The elaboration of those articles relevant to detention of refugees (in particular, Article 31 on penalties for illegal entry, and to a lesser degree Article 26 on freedom of movement, Article 8 on exceptional measures, and Article 9 on provisional measures) shows the acute awareness on the part of the drafters of the seriousness of such restrictions, and the limited use to which they should, therefore, be put.

---

[8]   ExCom Conclusion No. 44, *Detention of Refugees and Asylum Seekers*, 1986, para. b, reproduced in Appendix V.2 to this book.

CHAPTER 6   COMMENTS ON THE UNHCR POSITION

III   The 1951 Convention relating to the Status of Refugees

III.1   Article 31[9]

Under the first paragraph of this Article, States are not to impose penalties, on account of their illegal entry or presence, on refugees coming directly from a territory where their life or freedom was threatened, provided they present themselves without delay to the authorities and show good cause for their illegal entry or presence. According to Robinson, this article "was inspired by the notion of 'enjoying asylum', and the necessity of distributing the burden of refugees more or less evenly among the States"[10] – an early reflection on the need for burden-sharing. During the discussion, the representative of France stated that:

> "If States were not prepared to take into account article 14 of the Universal Declaration of Human Rights and if countries far from those whence the refugees were coming were not prepared to make some effort to relieve the burden assumed by initial reception countries, the latter would be unable to support indefinitely the considerable commitments resulting from their liberal policy ..."[11]

Refugees would not be required to show that they had been unable to find asylum in any other country, specifically including countries adjacent to the country they had fled, "... because every State could claim that the refugee should have tried first another country and thus, in most instances, Article 31 would become a dead letter".[12]

---

[9]   Article 31: Refugees unlawfully in the country of refuge
   1. The Contracting States shall not impose penalties, on account of their illegal entry or presence, on refugees who, coming directly from a territory where their life or freedom was threatened in the sense of Article 1, enter or are present in their territory without authorisation, provided they present themselves without delay to the authorities and show good cause for their illegal entry or presence.
   2. The Contracting States shall not apply to the movements of such refugees restrictions other than those which are necessary and such restrictions shall only be applied until their status in the country is regularised or they obtain admission into another country. The Contracting States shall allow such refugees a reasonable period and all the necessary facilities to obtain admission into another country.

[10]   Robinson, Nehemiah, *Convention Relating to the Status of Refugees: Its History, Contents and Interpretation,* Institute of Jewish Affairs, New York, 1953, p. 151.

[11]   *Ad Hoc* Committee on Statelessness and Related Problems, Summary record of the Seventh Meeting, E/AC.32/SR.7, 2 February 1950, pp. 4-5, in Collected Travaux Préparatoires (Takkenberg), Volume 1, p. 188.

[12]   Robinson, *supra* note 10, p. 153.

The meaning to be given to "coming directly" has been the subject of considerable scrutiny and interpretation in recent years. According to Paul Weis, it "refers also to persons who have been in an intermediary country for a short time without having received asylum there".[13] No fixed duration can be applied mechanically to the concept of a short time. Some guidance is to be found in Executive Committee Conclusion No. 15 on Refugees Without an Asylum Country (1979), which – perhaps optimistically – invokes concepts of fairness and reasonableness in determining whether the asylum seeker may be called on first to request asylum from another State.[14]

Robinson continues: "'Good cause' for illegal entry must be assumed if the refugee could not have entered legally this or any other country in time to avoid persecution, unless, of course, he chose an obviously distant or overcrowded country for no good reason."[15]

Asylum seekers are protected under Article 31, notably the provisions of paragraph 2, which limits States in restricting refugees' freedom of movement (necessarily including those whose status is not yet determined). In particular, States are not to apply restrictions to refugees' movements "other than those which are necessary". Commentary on the Convention is consistent in interpreting necessity narrowly. According to Robinson, the Ad Hoc Committee had in mind security or special circumstances, "such as a great and sudden influx of refugees".[16] Weis further noted that "[i]n the case of asylum seekers, proceedings on account of illegal entry or presence should be suspended pending examination of their request". Hathaway has commented that when this is read in conjunction with Article 31(1), "it is clear that illegal entry alone cannot legitimate the detention of asylum seekers".[17]

13　*The Refugee Convention, 1951: The Travaux Préparatoires analysed with a commentary by Dr. Paul Weis,* Cambridge International Documents Series, Volume 7, p. 302.
14　ExCom Conclusion No. 15, para. h(iii) The intentions of the asylum seeker as regards the country in which he wishes to request asylum should as far as possible be taken into account;
(iv) regard should be had to the concept that asylum should not be refused solely on the ground that it could be sought from another State. Where, however, it appears that a person, before requesting asylum, already has a connection or close links with another State, he may *if it appears fair and reasonable* be called upon first to request asylum from that State (emphasis added).
The Conclusion continues:
Para. i While asylum seekers may be required to submit their asylum requests within a certain time limit, failure to do so, or the non-fulfilment of other formal requirements, should not lead to an asylum request being excluded from consideration.
15　Robinson, *supra* note 10, p. 154.
16　*Ibid.*
17　Hathaway, James C., and Dent, John A., *Refugee Rights: Report on a Comparative Survey,* York Lanes Press, Toronto, 1995, p. 19.

CHAPTER 6   COMMENTS ON THE UNHCR POSITION

Grahl-Madsen states that:

"... the drafters of the Conventions were agreed that that paragraph does not prohibit detention for the purpose of investigation. It may undoubtedly be deemed necessary for the authorities to check the identity of a person whose entry or presence is unauthorised and who claims to be a refugee, and to investigate into the details of the story he tells. For this purpose it may – just may – also be necessary to detain him. ... Such a measure must, in order to be legal, really be deemed necessary ..."[18]

The use of detention in the context of Article 31 appears to have attracted surprisingly little debate during the Convention's drafting. What constituted necessary restrictions to the movement of refugees was not defined; and the question of whether a State could keep an illegally-entered refugee in custody was asked, but was not answered.[19]

III.2   Article 26[20]

This article concerns the rights of refugees "lawfully" in the territory.[21] During drafting, the Danish delegate noted that restrictions on the freedom of movement of a refugee were to occur only when absolutely necessary, were to be decided on the merits of each individual case, and were to be implemented under conditions "both morally and materially ... consistent with human dignity ...".[22] The right of refugees to choose their place of residence and to move freely is subject only to any regulations applicable "to aliens generally in the same circumstances" – a proviso that refugees are not to be discriminated against on account of being refugees.

Some 13 States have entered reservations to Article 26, generally reserving the right to designate the place of residence of refugees and referring to considerations of national security. This consideration finds explicit expression in the Organisation of African Unity (OAU) Refugee Convention, which provides that countries of asylum shall, as far as possible, settle refugees at a reasonable distance from the

---

18   Grahl-Madsen, Atle, *The Status of Refugees in International Law,* Sijthoff, Leiden, 1972, p. 418.
19   Robinson, *supra* note 10, p. 154.
20   Article 26: Freedom of movement
     Each Contracting State shall accord to refugees lawfully in its territory the right to choose their place of residence and to move freely within its territory, subject to any regulations applicable to aliens generally in the same circumstances.
21   *Résidant régulièrement* – "understood to refer to refugees either lawfully admitted or whose illegal entry was legalised", Robinson, *supra* note 10, p. 111.
22   E/AC.32/L.15 of 30 January 1950.

147

frontier of their country of origin, for reasons of security.[23] This imperative is reiterated in the Executive Committee Conclusion No. 22 on the Protection of Asylum Seekers in Situations of Large-Scale Influx (1981).

III.3   Article 8[24]

Article 8 envisaged measures which might be taken in wartime, or post-war, against nationals of enemy States, and which would affect refugees of that nationality unless provision were made for their exemption. Measures such as internment or sequestration of property were foreseen in time of crisis, and for reasons of State security; the inclusion of this article was based on Article 44 of the Geneva Convention of August 12, 1949 relating to the Protection of Civilian Persons in Time of War.[25]

The wording of Article 8 might fairly be described as flaccid or, as the Canadian delegate is reported to have said, as giving with one hand what it takes away with the other.[26] The fact that it is envisaged for use in times of war or extreme tension between two States limits its scope of application, and its relevance to the broader detention debate.

III.4   Article 9[27]

As with Article 8, Article 9 is couched in terms of exceptionality: it pertains to times of "war or other grave and exceptional circumstances" and provisional measures which may be justified in the interests of national security. The purpose of this

---

23 *OUA Convention Governing the Specific Aspects of Refugee Problems in Africa*, 1969, Article 2(6): "For reasons of security, countries of asylum shall, as far as possible, settle refugees at a reasonable distance from the frontier of their country of origin." Similar provisions are made in ExCom Conclusion No. 72, *Personal Security of Refugees*, 1993.

24 Article 8: Exemption from exceptional measures
With regard to exceptional measures which may be taken against the person, property or interests of nationals of a foreign State, the Contracting States shall not apply such measures to a refugee who is formally a national of the said State solely on account of such nationality. Contracting States which, under their legislation, are prevented from applying the general principle expressed in this Article, shall, in appropriate cases, grant exemptions in favour of refugees.

25 Robinson, *supra* note 10, p. 90.

26 *Ibid.*, p. 91.

27 Article 9: Provisional measures
Nothing in this Convention shall prevent a Contracting State, in time of war or other grave and exceptional circumstances, from taking provisionally measures which it considers to be essential to the national security in the case of a particular person, pending a determination by the Contracting State that that person is in fact a refugee and that the continuance of such measures is necessary in his case in the interests of national security.

CHAPTER 6   COMMENTS ON THE UNHCR POSITION

article, according to Robinson, "is to permit the wholesale provisional internment of refugees in times of war, followed by a screening process".[28]

IV   The scope of protection

IV.1   Protected persons

Executive Committee Conclusion No. 44 states that while its use of the term "refugee" has the same meaning as that in the 1951 Convention and 1967 Protocol relating to the Status of Refugees, it is without prejudice to wider definitions applicable in different regions. The same protection with respect to detention is owed to asylum seekers, who may be refugees within the Convention, the Statute, or other relevant instruments. It is also owed to persons rejected for asylum or refused access to the refugee status determination procedure on purely formal grounds, without an examination of the merits of the case.

In examining the scope of protection, it is important to note that the Executive Committee has acknowledged that there exists a gap between the scope of UNHCR's mandated protection activities, and the obligations formally assumed by States to provide international protection. There are a number of reasons for this state of affairs: one illustrative example is the large number of persons who have been forced to flee due to conflict. While it is generally acknowledged that such persons require international protection, they will not necessarily be granted refugee status under the 1951 Convention – or, indeed, other suitable forms of protection. UNHCR was called on to explore further measures to ensure international protection to all who need it. Where refugees in need of international protection are detained, and even refused entry and/or returned to countries which may interpret *refoulement* very narrowly, the stated objective of ensuring protection to all who need it is likely to be undermined.[29]

Following findings that annual asylum applications in 13 European States dropped, in 1994, to around 318,000 (roughly on a par with 1989 levels), the Inter-governmental Consultations on Asylum, Refugee and Migration Policies examined the "significant illegal population, living on the margins of society, [which] is a matter of increasing concern to many governments". Their preliminary study noted that this population "can also involve persons fleeing war or conflict areas, who fall

---

28   Robinson, *supra* note 10, p. 95.
29   It should be recalled that the Conference of Plenipotentiaries on the Status of Refugees and Stateless Persons – which met in Geneva in 1951 to finish work on the Convention – also unanimously adopted the following recommendation: "The Conference expresses the hope that the Convention relating to the Status of Refugees will have value as an example exceeding its contractual scope and that all nations will be guided by it in granting so far as possible to persons in their territory as refugees and who would not be covered by the terms of the Convention, the treatment for which it provides."

outside the asylum system, and may be difficult or impossible to return to the country or area of origin".[30] The fact that persons fleeing war or conflict can and frequently do fall outside the asylum system, and may be classed as illegal immigrants, is part of the problem in securing their international protection.

IV.2   Distinguishing refugees and asylum seekers from other aliens

In Conclusion No. 44, the Executive Committee stressed the importance for national legislation and/or administrative practice to make the necessary distinction between the situation of refugees and asylum seekers, and that of other aliens. What distinguishes the asylum seeker from the ordinary alien is the need, or search, for international protection.

IV.3   The exceptional nature of detention

Dictionary definitions of "exceptional" propose synonyms such as extraordinary; unusual; peculiar. The use of the word "exceptional" reinforces the general rule that asylum seekers shall not be detained, the fact that the purposes for which detention may be used are enumerated exhaustively, and that even these may be invoked only if the detention is necessary for those purposes to be met.

Exceptional bases for detention include, if necessary, cases where refugees or asylum seekers have destroyed their travel and/or identity documents or have used fraudulent documents "in order to mislead the authorities of the State in which they intend to claim asylum". Even so, the Executive Committee regularly calls on States to ensure that measures to discourage the abuse of asylum procedures have no detrimental effect on the fundamental principles of international protection, including the institution of asylum. In particular, the Executive Committee has underlined that circumstances may compel a refugee or asylum seeker to have recourse to fraudulent documentation when leaving a country in which his physical safety or freedom are threatened.[31]

This logic is put into effect in Italian practice, among others. While the use of false passports is punishable under the Italian Penal Code, asylum seekers are deemed to have acted "in a state of necessity," and therefore not to have committed an offence.[32]

---

30   *Illegal Aliens: A Preliminary Study*, Secretariat of the Inter-governmental Consultations on Asylum, Refugee and Migration Policies in Europe, North America and Australia, June 1995, p. 2.

31   Conclusion No. 58, *Problem of Refugees and Asylum Seekers who Move in an Irregular Manner From a Country in Which They Had Already Found Protection*, 1989, para. i.

32   UNHCR, *Detention of Asylum-Seekers in Europe*, supra note 6, p. 146.

CHAPTER 6   COMMENTS ON THE UNHCR POSITION

The increase in visa requirements and the widespread use of carrier sanctions may spur the use of fraudulent measures by the asylum seeker. It is ironic that both the use of fraudulent travel documents and the use of genuine travel documents may be invoked as elements impugning the credibility of the asylum seeker. The very use of restrictive measures (including increased recourse to detention) may itself cast asylum seekers in a negative light, contributing to a hardened climate in which persons in need of protection are inadequately distinguished from illegal aliens generally.

IV.4   The elements of necessity and proportionality

Underlining its exceptional character, the Executive Committee in its Conclusion No. 44 spelled out the situations in which resort might be had to detention (only on grounds prescribed by law: to verify identity; to determine the elements on which the claim to refugee status or asylum is based; to deal with cases where refugees or asylum seekers have destroyed their travel and/or identity documents or have used fraudulent documents in order to mislead the authorities of the State in which they intend to claim asylum; or to protect national security or public order); and further qualified all these with the words "if necessary".

That an action is necessary means that it is essential or indispensable:

"[I]t ... may not be resorted to just for the convenience of the authorities. Such a measure must, in order to be legal, really be deemed necessary ... It does not suffice that detention is considered convenient for the police or immigration authorities. Under the terms of Article 31(2), the authorities have to accept inconvenience ..."[33]

Even when the circumstances under which detention might be invoked are present – such as, for example, where travel or identity documents have been destroyed or are fraudulent in order to mislead the authorities in the State where asylum is claimed – the element of necessity, in relation to the particular case, must still be present, as an additional dimension. Conversely, "necessity" modifies only the stated purposes, and cannot be invoked on extraneous grounds. Thus, the use of detention for other purposes, such as deterring would-be asylum seekers, is always inconsistent with these standards.

While different considerations may apply in cases of mass influx of asylum seekers,[34] according to Weis, "[i]t results from the history of the provision that refugees should not be kept behind barbed wire. A short period of custody may be

---

33   Grahl-Madsen, *supra* note 18, p. 418.
34   See Executive Committee Conclusion No. 22, *Protection of Asylum Seekers in Situations of Large-Scale Influx*, 1981.

151

necessary in order to investigate the identity of the person. Refugees may also be placed in a camp, particularly in cases of mass influx."[35]

It is interesting to note, in this connection, the findings of a study by Amnesty International of the use of detention against asylum seekers in the United Kingdom, which revealed that a significant proportion of detained asylum seekers, relative to other asylum seekers, withdrew their claims prior to a final decision.[36] This may, of course, be an unintended effect of detention, and merits further study.

To give meaning to the requirement that detention be for the "minimum period necessary", the purpose of detention in any particular case must be known. In Conclusion No. 44, the Executive Committee "recognised the importance of fair and expeditious procedures for determining refugee status or granting asylum in protecting refugees and asylum seekers from unjustified or unduly prolonged detention". As Guy Goodwin-Gill has noted, "[t]he detention of refugees and asylum seekers is never an appropriate solution to their plight. The power to detain must be related to a recognised object or purpose, and there must be a reasonable relationship of proportionality between the end and the means."[37]

IV.5   What constitutes detention?

"... [S]till it is argued that ... the detention is not indefinite, because it may be terminated by the individual's voluntary departure from the country. [This] argument is not worthy of comment."[38]

Dismissing the suggestion that asylum seekers are not in detention because they are free to return to their country of origin at any time, little did the commentator know that it was to be a full decade before international law caught up, laying the issue to rest.[39] The *Amuur* Case concerned four Somali nationals who arrived in France (via Kenya and Syria) in March 1992, were held at Paris Orly

---

35   Weis, *supra* note 13, p. 303.
36   "... the study strongly suggested that the debilitating effects of such prolonged incarceration induces a disproportionately large number of detained asylum seekers to abandon their asylum claim before it has been fully resolved. ... Six of the 50 detainees (12 percent) withdrew their asylum application and made a voluntary departure from the United Kingdom, having spent an average of 130 days in detention. According to Home Office figures, in 1993 only 2.7 percent of all asylum seekers withdrew their asylum application, while in 1994 the figure was 3.0 percent." *Cell Culture: The Detention & Imprisonment of Asylum Seekers in the United Kingdom*, Amnesty International, London, December 1996, p. 7.
37   Goodwin-Gill, Guy, *International Law and the Detention of Refugees and Asylum Seekers*, International Migration Review, Volume 20 No. 2, 1986, p. 211.
38   *The Detention of Non-Nationals*, *infra* note 48, p. 150.
39   Judgment in the case of *Amuur v. France*, *supra* note 2; see also Chapter 7 of this book for an analysis of this judgment.

CHAPTER 6   COMMENTS ON THE UNHCR POSITION

airport, and were then returned to Syria. This was in conformity with the Law of 6 September 1991 (amending an earlier Ordinance on aliens' conditions of entry into France) which allowed aliens who had been refused leave to enter France, or who had sought asylum, to be held in transit zones of ports and airports for no more than 20 days. Presenting this draft to Parliament, the Minister of the Interior stated that: "Aliens in that situation are not detained [*retenus*], since they are not on French territory, as they are free to leave at any time."[40]

Two weeks before the *Amuur* applicants landed at Orly, the French *Conseil Constitutionnel* had declared this provision to be unconstitutional, as the degree to which it impinged on personal liberty would have to attract "appropriate provision for the courts to intervene".

The European Human Rights Commission found by 16 votes to 10 that in this case, the measures concerned lacked the degree of physical constraint required to constitute a deprivation of liberty.[41] The European Court of Human Rights found otherwise. While Contracting States had the undeniable sovereign right to control aliens' entry into and residence in their territory, this right must be exercised in accordance with the provisions of the Convention. Referring to both the European Human Rights Convention and the Refugee Convention, the Court stated that:

> "States' legitimate concern to foil the increasingly frequent attempts to get round immigration restrictions must not deprive asylum seekers of the protection afforded by these Conventions. ... Above all, such confinement must not deprive the asylum seeker of the right to gain effective access to the procedure for determining refugee status."[42]

The Court noted that the applicants had been placed under strict and constant police surveillance, without legal or social assistance – particularly with regard to lodging an asylum request – for 15 days. For 17 days, neither the length nor necessity of their confinement had been reviewed by a court. The Court then addressed the argument that the applicants could depart from the transit zone – and from France – at any time, finding that this possibility could not exclude a restriction on liberty. The possibility became theoretical, moreover, "if no other

---

40   Official Gazette, Proceedings of the National Assembly, 19 December 1991, p. 8256, cited in judgement *Amuur v. France, ibid.*
41   *Ibid*, pp. 21 and 24. Article 5(1): Everyone has the right to liberty and security of person. No one shall be deprived of his liberty save in the following cases and in accordance with a procedure prescribed by law:
(f) the lawful arrest or detention of a person to prevent his effecting an unauthorised entry into the country or of a person against whom action is being taken with a view to deportation or extradition."
42   *Ibid.*, p. 25.

country offering protection comparable to the protection they expect to find in the country where they are seeking asylum is inclined or prepared to take them in".[43]

The fact that detention may take various forms was not explored by the Executive Committee, although UNHCR has noted that there is a qualitative difference between detention and other restrictions on freedom of movement; thus, persons subject to limitations on domicile and residency are not generally considered to be in detention. The recent UNHCR Guidelines specify that the confinement of asylum seekers within a narrowly bounded or restricted location, including prisons, closed camps, detention facilities, or airport transit zones, where the only opportunity to leave the limited area is to leave the territory, should be subject to the same protections. When considering whether confinement constitutes detention, the intensity and the cumulative impact of the restrictions should be assessed.[44]

IV.6   Alternatives to detention

Whereas the 1986 Executive Committee Conclusion No. 44 is silent in respect of alternatives to detention, the Guidelines specify that viable alternatives should be applied first. Grahl-Madsen notes that:

> "... if a less severe measure, such as ordering the person in question to stay in a particular town or district, can be considered sufficient, the authorities are debarred from applying more severe measures, such as requiring the refugee to stay in a certain house or camp, or outright detaining him."[45]

In any case, other measures which may be adequate to verify identity, the destruction of travel documents, and so on, should be explored as part of fair and expeditious procedures for refugee status determination. Monitoring and guarantee mechanisms are employed in a number of countries, and recourse should first be had to these, in the absence of evidence to suggest that they will fail. Alternative measures need to be genuinely accessible to the applicant. The UNHCR survey on detention in Europe revealed numerous examples of such measures, including asylum seekers being required to remain at a particular address; to deposit a passport, other travel documents and ticket; to furnish a bond; or to report to the police at specified times, in order to ensure that he or she does not abscond.[46]

---

43   *Ibid.*, p. 26.
44   See case of *Amuur* v. *France, ibid.*, and *Guzzardi* v. *Italy*, judgment of 6 November 1980, Series A No. 39.
45   Grahl-Madsen, *supra* note 18, p. 419.
46   UNHCR, *Detention of Asylum Seekers in Europe, supra* note 6, pp. 101 and 106.

CHAPTER 6   COMMENTS ON THE UNHCR POSITION

As with assessments of necessity and proportionality, an examination of alternatives to detention must start from the aims to be achieved. Rather than this logic-based review of the utility of detention, mere perceptions of its usefulness may be setting the agenda. A large number (15) of European countries were reported as having introduced or amended legislation in 1994 which allowed for detention or increased existing powers to detain asylum seekers or rejected refugees. UNHCR offices could not identify an overt correlation, however, between asylum seekers absconding and increased use of detention:

> "... when the [UNHCR] Offices were asked whether there was a 'tradition' of ... persons failing to appear for appointments or to properly comply with the asylum procedure, for the most part, the answer was no. ... Those countries which responded by saying that there *was* such a tradition were not those countries which registered an increase in the use of restrictive measures against asylum seekers." (Emphasis added)[47]

The fact that the numbers of persons seeking asylum in Europe continue to fall should put paid to perceptions of the continent being overrun via the asylum mechanisms. The fall in the number of asylum seekers may be attributable to numerous measures, including visa restrictions, carrier sanctions, manifestly unfounded procedures, "safe third country" policies, and readmission agreements, among others.

IV.7   Procedural safeguards

The UNHCR Guidelines elaborate on the notion of "prescribed by law" to specify that this means a law which is in conformity with general norms and principles of international human rights law. This underlines that the strongest check on the use of detention lies in subjecting it to review – a review which examines both the lawfulness of the measure, and the substantive issue of whether detention is and continues to be necessary in the particular case. To be meaningful, it is not sufficient if such reviews simply acknowledge the exercise of a discretion to detain.

Under Conclusion No. 44, the Executive Committee "recommended that detention measures taken in respect of refugees and asylum seekers should be subject to judicial or administrative review". One omission of this Conclusion was its failure to specify the need for independent judicial or administrative review. Goodwin-Gill has noted:

---

47   *Ibid*, p. 55.

"... the insistence with which human rights instruments require that all forms of detention be in accordance with and authorised by law. Implicit in this principle, which itself constitutes the first protection against arbitrary treatment, is the further requirement that the practice of detention be subject to effective control by independent judicial authority."[48]

Conclusion No. 44 also omits mention of the need for review to be prompt. The new Guidelines therefore identify, as one of the three minimum procedural safeguards, the right to challenge the lawfulness of the deprivation of liberty promptly before a competent, independent and impartial authority. The Guidelines go on to state: that this right should extend to all aspects of the case (that is, not only the technical legality of the detention); that the detainee should receive legal assistance; and that there should be the possibility of periodic review. UNHCR has further recommended that States should develop criteria having the force of law strictly limiting the situations in which detention will be imposed.[49]

In a number of cases, the review requirement is overlooked, or such review as is available fails to offer an effective remedy. Commenting on the United Kingdom, Amnesty International has stated that:

"In practice, ... most asylum seekers detained under Immigration Act powers have no effective means of challenging the basis for their detention, and of seeking their release – a position markedly different from that of accused persons in the United Kingdom's criminal justice system."[50]

The Amnesty study points to the absence of a presumption in favour of liberty, on the one hand, and the practice of seeking large sums of money as bail guarantees as reasons why the mechanism has failed.

IV.8   Access to UNHCR

The right of the asylum seeker to contact UNHCR or other refugee assistance agencies becomes especially important in the context of detention. The two other minimum procedural guarantees enumerated under the UNHCR Guidelines, in addition to prompt and independent review, are the right for the detained asylum seekers to be informed of the reasons for detention and of their rights in this connection, in a language and in terms which they understand, and the right to contact the local UNHCR office, national refugee or other agencies and a lawyer –

---

48 Goodwin-Gill, Guy, *The Detention of Non-Nationals, with Particular Reference to Refugees and Asylum Seekers*, in *Defence of the Alien*, Volume IX, 138–151, 1986.
49 UNHCR inter-office Memorandum 28/92, *Current Asylum Issues*, 13 March 1992.
50 *Cell Culture, supra* note 36, p. 17.

CHAPTER 6   COMMENTS ON THE UNHCR POSITION

and, of course, the means to make such contact. The reality is that asylum seekers often fail to understand why they have been detained. In many cases, also, while the right to contact UNHCR or another agency exists, asylum seekers are not explicitly informed of this possibility.

IV.9   Segregation from offenders

Conclusion No. 44 of the Executive Committee, in specifying that the conditions of detention of refugees and asylum seekers must be humane, singles out two elements: segregation from common criminals, and the need to ensure their physical safety. The Guidelines expand on the notion of "humane", referring to the inherent dignity of the person, and also to existing norms and principles of international law and standards on the treatment of detainees.

IV.10   The detention of minors

The rights of children, and especially their rights in the context of conflict, persecution, and asylum seeking, have received heightened attention in the past decade.[51] A particularly firm position is called for in respect of the detention of minor asylum seekers. In this context, the conditions of detention, where it does occur, are also important. In practice, however, specific provision is rarely made in European legislation in respect of the detention of minors.

UNHCR's policy on this issue is to the point: "Refugee children should not be detained."[52] Citing the relevant provisions of the 1989 Convention on the Rights of the Child (CRC), UNHCR Guidelines note that the detention of minors must be used as a measure of last resort, for the shortest appropriate period of time. As with any action taken by States parties concerning minors, a primary consideration shall be the best interests of the child. Under the CRC, moreover, children have the right not to be separated from their parents against their will (Article 9), and States parties are obliged to provide special measures of protection to refugee children and asylum seekers who are minors, whether accompanied or not (Article 22).[53]

The UNHCR Guidelines state that if children who are asylum seekers are detained in airports, immigration holding centres or prisons, they must not be held under prison-like conditions. Special arrangements must be made for living quarters which are suitable for children and their families. Strong efforts must be made to have them released from detention and placed in other accommodation. Detained

---

51 *Impact of Armed Conflict on Children*, Report of the expert of the Secretary-General, Ms Graça Machel, submitted pursuant to UNGA Res 48/157; A/51/306, 26 August 1996.
52 *Refugee Children: Guidelines on Protection and Care*, UNHCR, 1994, p. 86; see Appendix VI.2 to this book.
53 See Appendix I.5.

157

children have the right to education. Children who are detained benefit from the same minimum procedural guarantees as adults. In addition, a legal guardian should be appointed for unaccompanied minors.

V Detention and international solidarity

For several years, UNHCR has in its annual protection reports noted waning international solidarity with countries most affected by refugee flows. Generous refugee admission policies need to go hand in hand with – and are to an extent synonymous with – such solidarity. One cannot escape the conclusion that restrictive measures taken by industrialised countries have repercussions elsewhere, and these can undermine refugee protection far and wide, through the so-called "ripple effect".

This is noticeable in the detention practices of a number of states who find themselves on the "front line", receiving asylum seekers in transit to more developed countries. The UNHCR survey notes, for example, that the three Baltic countries (Estonia, Latvia, Lithuania) make no legal distinction between asylum seekers and illegal migrants; these are routinely detained and, sometimes, removed from the country (usually back to the country of transit). A group of more than a hundred asylum seekers was returned from Estonia to Latvia in December 1994. Following a decision by the Latvian cabinet, the group was detained for two years in Olaine prison centre in Latvia, where "the conditions in the detention centre are very harsh and UNHCR received reliable reports of repeated mistreatment of this group by the Latvian police authorities".[54]

Nor are harsh detention practices limited to "front-line", newly-democratic States. A recent report on an industrialised country reveals detention practices and policies which challenge the concepts of necessity and proportionality:

> "Australia has a policy of automatically detaining asylum seekers who arrive without prior authorisation of their entry ... The majority of 'boat people' who arrived from 1989 onwards were detained during the entire asylum procedure, which could take months and sometimes years. More than 800 children, among them more than 70 babies born in detention, spent up to two years behind barbed wire. ... In order to be able to pursue an asylum claim effectively, asylum seekers need to be informed of their rights under Australian and international law. International standards also require that any detained person be given an explanation of their rights and how to exercise them. However, the government recently moved to limit detained asylum seekers' access to this

---

54 UNHCR, *Detention of Asylum-Seekers in Europe, supra* note 6, p. 83; see also Chapter 2 of this book.

CHAPTER 6 COMMENTS ON THE UNHCR POSITION

information. ... [having] proposed legislation to remove certain existing rights of detained asylum seekers and to effectively exclude its officials from independent scrutiny under Australian human rights laws."[55]

What can be done to reverse the growing recourse to detention? For one thing, human rights and refugee advocates, and those working for greater tolerance within communities, can emphasise the universality of human rights. The primordial right to life, liberty and security of person is equally primordial for asylum seekers. Secondly, there is a dangerously self-fulfilling aspect of detaining asylum seekers, which can only demean and diminish the refugee protection regime. The increased use of detention against asylum seekers enhances the perception that there is something amiss with that group of people. It contributes to animosity towards asylum seekers as a whole, perhaps even subconsciously, particularly in the context of prominence given to unfounded asylum claims, which are routinely described as "abuses" of the asylum system. Such perceptions can trump sober analysis in policy formulation, leading to the use of detention in response to political pressure, rather than as a last resort.

In addition to lobbying and advocacy, practical assistance in the form of rights awareness and legal and social counselling is essential, to prevent such detention as does occur from being prolonged and to ensure recourse to review. Asylum processing is extremely expensive in most western European countries, as is detention. Suggestions that alternatives to detention could reduce the cost of asylum processing, while not detracting from effectiveness, should be tested, and the "best practice", derived from other countries, be publicised and emulated.

As Arthur Helton has pointed out:

"Detention policies are fundamentally inconsistent with the universal approach needed to achieve any kind of solution, and threaten to retard development of the international refugee regime and impose arbitrary abuse on large numbers of individuals."[56]

The international community has committed itself to seeking solutions, and international solidarity and burden-sharing have consistently been identified as core features of this quest. Should these arguments, as well as respect for human rights, be found unpersuasive, a case can also be made on the basis of self-interest. The standards which western Europe applies in dealing with difficult issues will be

---

55 Amnesty International, FOCUS, *Australia: A Champion of Liberty?* 9 January 1997, p. 6; see also Chapter 5 of this book.
56 Helton, Arthur C., *The Detention of Refugees and Asylum Seekers*, in *Refugees and International Relations,* ed. Loescher and Monahan, Oxford University Press, New York, 1989, p. 140.

scrutinised, adapted and applied further afield. If western governments would wish to encourage refugees and asylum seekers to remain in their own regions, it is imperative that they present standards to be emulated.

Chapter 7 Detention of Asylum Seekers in the light of Article 5 of the European Convention on Human Rights

By Christos Giakoumopoulos[1]

Contents

Part I   Asylum seekers and the European Convention on Human Rights
Part II Applicability of Article 5 of the European Convention on Human Rights to detained asylum seekers
Part III Rights guaranteed to detained asylum seekers under the European Convention on Human Rights: III.1 The requirement of lawfulness – III.2 Guarantees as to the duration of the detention – III.3 The right to appeal – III.4 The right to compensation – III.5 Conditions of detention
Part IV Conclusion: A statement from the *Amuur* judgment

I Asylum seekers and the European Convention on Human Rights

An initial reading of the European Convention on Human Rights does not necessarily reveal the utility of this international instrument for the protection of foreigners and more particularly of asylum seekers. In comparison to the arsenal of specialised conventions and agreements, the European Convention on Human Rights appears to be no more than a marginal protection instrument providing some general safeguards already secured by domestic legislation. This is all the more so since the Convention as such refers to aliens on two occasions, namely in Article 5 para. 1(f) and in Article 16, only with a view to restricting rather than protecting their rights. Article 16 provides that the Convention does not prevent the Contracting States from imposing restrictions on the political activities of aliens; Article 5 para. 1(f) envisages and authorises the detention of aliens with a view to preventing their unauthorised entry into a country or with a view to removing them from it. One has difficulty in seeing these provisions as securing any rights to aliens or to asylum seekers.

---

1   The views expressed here are those of the author alone.

However, there are indeed at least three reasons why the Convention is an important instrument for the protection of asylum seekers.

Firstly, the Convention enshrines the very essential principles of a democratic society based on the rule of law, principles which are also to be found at the origin of the protection afforded under humanitarian law. In this respect, one should note that the Convention appears to be "a constitutional instrument of the European public order"[2] and in addition "a living instrument which must be interpreted in the light of present day conditions".[3] As the European Court of Human Rights repeatedly stated, "unlike [other] international treaties, the Convention comprises more than mere reciprocal engagements between Contracting States. It creates over and above a network of mutual, bilateral undertakings, objective obligations, which, in the words of [its] Preamble, benefit from a collective enforcement."[4]

The second reason lies in the way the Convention is construed: as stated in its Article 1, the rights set out in the Convention are guaranteed to "everyone within [the] jurisdiction" of the Contracting Parties. Every Contracting Party has therefore to secure these rights not only to its own nationals, but also to aliens and stateless persons.[5] This is a fundamental principle which is inherent in the very notion of the international protection of human rights, namely that the protection applies to all human beings, regardless of their nationality. Moreover, this principle is expressly mentioned in Article 14 of the Convention which obliges Contracting Parties to recognise the rights and freedoms it contains "without discrimination on any ground such as ... race, colour, ... national or social origin, association with a national minority, ... birth or other status".[6] Where exceptions to this principle are permitted, these are specifically stipulated in the text of the Convention (see for example, the above-mentioned Article 16). Moreover, the Convention does not simply spell out the declaration that a fundamental right or freedom is guaranteed, but also sets out the conditions under which restrictions to this right or freedom are permitted.

The third reason – and perhaps the most obvious from a practical point of view – is the unique procedure that is available for the enforcement of that Convention, namely the individual application procedure under Article 25 of the Convention. It

---

2   Eur. Court H.R., case of *Loizidou* v. *Turkey* (Preliminary objections), judgment of 23 March 1995, para. 75.

3   Eur. Court H.R., *Tyrer* judgment of 25 April 1978, Series A No. 26, pp. 15–16, para. 31.

4   Eur. Court H.R. *Ireland* v. *United Kingdom*, judgment of 18 January 1978, Series A No. 25, p. 90, para. 239.

5   J. Velu, R. Ergec, *The European Convention on Human Rights*, p. 67, para. 76 *et seq.*; G Cohen Jonathan, *The European Convention on Human Rights*, ed. Economica, p. 38; No. 288/57, Yearbook I, p. 209; No. 788/60, *Austria* v. *Italy*, 11 January 1961, Yearbook IV, pp. 139–141.

6   For a detailed interpretation of the significance of Article 14 for detained asylum seekers, see Working Document No. 7 by Pia Justesen (researcher at the Danish Centre for Human Rights), 1995 European Seminar on Detention of Asylum Seekers, available from the Danish Refugee Council.

is actually this procedure that has enabled the European Human Rights Commission and European Court of Human Rights – the bodies established to ensure the observance of the engagements undertaken by the Contracting States – to develop a case law concerning the situation of aliens and of asylum seekers – often qualified as "jurisprudential boldness"[7] – which gives this instrument particular relevance to international protection of asylum seekers.

The utility of the Convention for cases concerning asylum seekers, pointed out in the 1980s,[8] has been exploited, in particular, after the *Soering* judgment of the European Court of Human Rights[9] and has given some interesting results.[10] In most cases, an alien requesting asylum in a Contracting State will derive certain advantages from Article 3 of the Convention. Admittedly, the Convention does not give him the right of asylum, but indirectly it could prohibit his removal to a country when serious grounds have been shown for believing that he runs a genuine risk of being subjected to torture or inhuman or degrading punishment or treatment there, that treatment being prohibited by Article 3 of the Convention. This principle, first established in an extradition case, was extended to include asylum seekers in the *Cruz Varas and Others* judgment of 20 March 1991.[11] In that judgment the Court asserted that the expulsion of an asylum seeker can raise a problem from the standpoint of Article 3 and engage the responsibility of a Contracting State. This case law was since confirmed in the *Vilvarajah and Others* judgment of 30 October 1991.[12]

---

7   F. Sudre, *Le contrôle des mesures d'expulsion et d'extradition par les organes de la Convention Européenne des Droits de l'Homme*, in *Immigrés et Réfugiés dans les Démocraties Occidentales: Défis et Solutions*, Colloque Montpellier, 27–29 April 1987, Ed. Economica, p. 253.

8   See *inter alia* R. Plender, *Problems raised by certain aspects of the present situation of refugees from the standpoint of the European Convention on Human Rights*, Council of Europe, 1984; J.A. Carillo, *The European Convention on Human Rights and Asylum Seekers*, 16th Colloquy on European Law, p. 27, Council of Europe, Strasbourg 1987.

9   *Soering* judgment of 7 July 1989, Series A No. 161; see also T. Vogler, *The scope of extradition in the light of the European Convention on Human Rights*, in Mélanges Wiarda, p. 663 ; M. O'Boyle, *Extradition and expulsion under the European Convention on Human Rights – Reflections on the Soering case*, in J. O'Reilly, *Essays in Honour of B.Walsh*, The Round Hall Press, p. 93 ; C. van de Wyngaert, *Applying the European Human Rights Convention to extradition: opening Pandora's box?*, ICLQ 1990, p. 757.

10 See *inter alia* M. Bossuyt and I. Lammerant, *La conformité à la Convention européenne des droits de l'homme des mesures d'éloignement du territoire de demandeurs d'asile déboutés*, RTDH 1993, p. 417. An overview of the Convention organs' case law on asylum seekers can be found in N. MOLE, *Problems raised by certain aspects of the present situation of refugees from the standpoint of the European Convention on Human Rights*, Council of Europe, 1995; see also O. de Schutter, *La Convention européenne des droits de l'homme et l'asile*, Revue du droit des étrangers 1994, No. 80/81, p. 471 *et seq.*

11 Series A No. 201, p. 28, paras. 69–70.

12 Series A No.215.

Until recently, however, the question of detention of asylum seekers had not been brought before the organs of the European Convention on Human Rights. In fact, why should an asylum seeker rely on a legal provision which explicitly authorises his detention, rather than on other provisions of international instruments aimed precisely at protecting him from arbitrary detention?

To answer this question, one must have regard to the rights guaranteed under the European Convention on Human Rights, bearing in mind the nature of the protection offered by the Convention's control mechanism and its effectiveness.

Article 5 of the Convention reads as follows:

1. Everyone has the right to liberty and security of person. No one shall be deprived of his liberty save in the following cases and in accordance with a procedure prescribed by law:
   a. The lawful detention of a person after conviction by a competent court;
   b. The lawful arrest or detention of a person for non-compliance with the lawful order of a court or in order to secure the fulfilment of any obligation prescribed by law;
   c. The lawful arrest or detention of a person effected for the purpose of bringing him before the competent legal authority on reasonable suspicion of having committed an offence or when it is reasonably considered necessary to prevent his committing an offence or fleeing after having done so;
   d. The detention of a minor by lawful order for the purpose of educational supervision or his lawful detention for the purpose of bringing him before the competent legal authority;
   e. The lawful detention of persons for the prevention of the spreading of infectious diseases, of persons of unsound mind, alcoholics or drug addicts or vagrants;
   f. The lawful arrest or detention of a person to prevent his effecting an unauthorised entry into the country or of a person against whom action is being taken with a view to deportation or extradition.

2. Everyone who is arrested shall be informed promptly, in a language which he understands, of the reasons for his arrest and of any charge against him.

3. Everyone arrested or detained in accordance with the provisions of paragraph 1(c) of this Article shall be brought promptly before a judge or other officer authorised by law to exercise judicial power and shall be entitled to trial within a reasonable time or to release pending trial. Release may be conditioned by guarantees to appear for trial.

4. Everyone who is deprived of his liberty by arrest or detention shall be entitled to take proceedings by which the lawfulness of his detention shall be

decided speedily by a court and his release ordered if the detention is not lawful.
5. Everyone who has been the victim of arrest or detention in contravention of the provisions of this Article shall have an enforceable right to compensation.

The general declaration of the right to liberty and security of person in paragraph 1 is followed by an exhaustive list of cases in which deprivation of liberty is permitted. It expressly provides that where deprivation of liberty is permitted this must occur in accordance with a procedure prescribed by law. Thus, the lawfulness of any measure amounting to a deprivation of liberty becomes a Convention requirement. Paragraphs 2 and 4[13] of the same Article guarantee specific rights to individuals arrested and detained, namely the right to appeal and to be informed of the reasons for their arrest. Finally, paragraph 5 ensures the right to compensation for everyone deprived of his liberty in violation of paragraphs 1 to 4. These provisions, to the extent that they apply to asylum seekers, supplement and even strengthen the protection granted to them either by the 1951 Convention or by other "soft law" provisions such as the Conclusions of the UNHCR Executive Committee or the Recommendations of the Committee of Ministers of the Council of Europe.

The 1951 Geneva Convention prohibits criminal prosecution of asylum seekers for having illegally entered the territory of the Contracting States. It forbids asylum seekers being sentenced to imprisonment after criminal conviction for having illegally entered the territory of a Contracting State. However, Article 31 of the Geneva Convention does not, as such, exclude deprivation of or restrictions on the right to liberty pending the asylum procedure. Such measures are often imposed on asylum seekers upon their arrival in the country of asylum and these measures are not a "penalty" within the meaning of Article 31 but an administrative measure not connected with the offence of illegal entry. Therefore, Article 31 of the 1951 Convention might not offer the expected protection in a large number of cases of detention of asylum seekers. Moreover, the UNHCR Executive Committee already noted, in 1986, that large numbers of asylum seekers in different areas of the world were the subject of detention by reason of their illegal entry or presence in search of asylum, pending resolution of their situation.[14]

Furthermore, Conclusion No. 44 does not exclude the possibility of detaining asylum seekers in order to verify their identity or to determine the elements on which their claim for refugee status is based. The Conclusion even allows detention pending the asylum procedure, since it recognises the need for fair and expeditious procedures for determining the refugee status with a view to "protecting refugees and asylum seekers from unjustified and unduly prolonged detention". Above all,

---

13 Para. 3 only relates to pre-trial detention in the context of criminal proceedings.
14 ExCom Conclusion No. 44 (XXXVII).

Conclusion No. 44 expressly provides that "detention may be resorted to only on grounds prescribed by law ... to deal with cases where refugees or asylum seekers have destroyed their travel and/or identity documents ... or to protect national security or public order". This is however an important element since it appears that the number of undocumented asylum seekers is increasing due to the difficulties they face in obtaining travel documents from the authorities of their country of origin. Most of them travel on false documents as it may be the only opportunity they have to flee from persecution and they destroy their papers before arrival, in an attempt to conceal their route so that a "country of first asylum" cannot be identified. Undocumented asylum seekers will be most often held in the so-called international or transit zones of airports before having access to normal asylum procedures.[15] Combined with the accelerated procedures provided for the determination of the so-called "manifestly unfounded cases", the international zone practice[16] has led to systematic "airport detention" of asylum seekers while a procedure is pending as to whether their asylum request is to be regarded as a genuine one or not.

Governmental and non-governmental organisations felt concerned by this phenomenon and this concern has led to the adoption by the Committee of Ministers of the Council of Europe of "guidelines to inspire practices of Council of Europe Member States concerning the arrival of asylum seekers at European airports".[17] The guidelines stress that, in order to secure treatment in conformity with human dignity for the asylum seeker, it is important not to prolong the stay of the applicant at the airport beyond a strictly necessary period of time. Furthermore, the Recommendation provides that it is only possible to hold the asylum seeker in the airport under the conditions and for the maximum duration provided for by law. The Recommendation adds a number of guarantees such as: the right to be received and accommodated under the best possible conditions; the right of the asylum seeker to be informed about his situation; the right to an interpreter; and the right to enter into contact with certain authorities. However, these rights are not directly granted to asylum seekers. They are "guidelines" which the Committee of Ministers recommends to Council of Europe Member States.

The guarantees offered by the European Convention on Human Rights are, on the other hand, individual rights which benefit from a collective enforcement and

---

15   See Council of Europe, Parliamentary Assembly, Recommendation 1163 (1991) and report by Lord Mackie of Benshie on the arrival of asylum seekers at European airports (2 September 1991, Doc. 6490).
16   D. Joly, *Refugees – Asylum in Europe?*, Minority Rights Group, London 1992, p. 123 *et seq.*; see also *Frontières du droit – Frontières des Droits: l'introuvable statut de la "zone internationale"*, Actes du Colloque sur le statut de la zone internationale organisé par l'ANAFE, L'Harmattan, Paris 1993.
17   Recommendation No. R (94) 5 of the Committee of Ministers of the Council of Europe, adopted on 21 June 1994.

their effective implementation can be pursued by actions before an international tribunal.[18]

II   Applicability of Article 5 of the European Convention on Human Rights to detained asylum seekers

The conclusion that the European Convention on Human Rights may offer asylum seekers concrete protection against detention contrasts with the extremely poor results achieved in this field before the Convention organs.

There are several reasons for this. Probably, one of them is the complexity of the structure of Article 5 of the Human Rights Convention – the main provision of the Convention coming into play as regards detention – compared with the most explicit and apparently sufficient protection accorded under Article 31 of the Geneva Convention relating to the Status of Refugees and under Conclusion No. 44 (XXXVII) on Detention of Refugees and Asylum Seekers of the Executive Committee of the UNHCR and other texts. Moreover, the rather negative wording of Article 5 para. 1 explicitly allows the detention of aliens with a view to preventing their unauthorised entry into a country, and one might think that in these circumstances any protection under this provision would be illusory or futile.[19] But there is a further reason, and this concerns the uncertainty as to the applicability of Article 5 in the case of detention of asylum seekers. In several countries, asylum seekers who are held for a period at the airport or under a strict regime in a reception centre/refugee camp are not usually regarded as being in detention.[20] In France, for example, a distinction is made between *"détention"* and *"rétention"*. The principal question raised here is whether being "held" upon arrival in a country of asylum in an international or transit zone or a camp constitutes a deprivation of liberty within the meaning of Article 5 para. 1.

Under the system of the Convention, the notion of deprivation of liberty is somewhat uncertain, and the case law offers no definition of it. It should be noted that Article 5 concerns only "deprivation" of liberty, not the restrictions on freedom of movement covered by Article 2 of Protocol No. 4. But the distinction between "deprivation" and "restriction" can prove particularly awkward. The case law of the

---

18   Also before a national tribunal, where the Convention is incorporated in domestic law.
19   For example, H. Lambert seems to compare Article 5 of the Human Rights Convention to Article 31 of the Geneva Convention in the following terms: "The detention of asylum seekers in Europe is directly covered by Article 5 of the ECHR, while Article 31 of the 1951 Convention states that refugees unlawfully in the country of refuge shall not be subject to any penalties nor their movements to restrictions. Lawful arrest and detention of an alien is justified by Article 5 of the ECHR when s/he entered a country illegally", in *Seeking asylum*, Martinus Nijhof 1995, p. 104.
20   UNHCR, *Detention of Asylum seekers in Europe*, European Series, Volume 1 No. 4, Geneva 1995, p. 53.

Strasbourg organs contains certain borderline cases such as the following: a curfew imposed at night constitutes a restriction on freedom of movement; house arrest constitutes a deprivation of liberty.[21] In the *Guzzardi* case, the Court considered that house arrest on a small island constituted a deprivation of liberty. It took account of the facts that the space available to the applicant was very restricted, that his social contacts were extremely limited, that he was placed under close surveillance and that the period concerned exceeded 16 months. The Court has repeatedly stated that in proclaiming the "right to liberty", paragraph 1 of Article 5 is contemplating the physical liberty of the person. Its aim is to ensure that no-one should be dispossessed of this liberty in an arbitrary fashion. In order to determine whether someone has been "deprived of his liberty" within the meaning of Article 5, the starting point must be his concrete situation and account must be taken of a whole range of criteria such as the type, duration, effects and manner of implementation of the measure in question.[22]

Holding aliens in the international zone can also raise major problems. The conditions in which the alien is held can vary from one country to another, or even from one airport to another.[23] The manner in which the zone is defined, the facilities available to persons "held" there, the extent to which such individuals can contact the persons of their choice, and above all the length of time they are held in the international zone are the chief factors determining the degree of constraint and hence the reply to the question concerned.

In its decision of 16 October 1992 on the admissibility of application No. 18560/91 (*S., N. & T.* v. *France*), the Commission declared admissible a complaint under Article 5 submitted by three women of Tamil origin and citizens of Sri Lanka who had been refused entry into France and had been kept in Paris Roissy airport for more than one month. The applicants complained that their detention in the airport had no legal basis in French law and that they had no possibility of challenging the legality of the measure complained of before a domestic judicial authority. A complaint under Article 3 of the Convention that if returned to Sri Lanka the applicant would be subjected to torture or inhuman treatment was also declared admissible. This application was later struck off the list of cases before the Commission, the applicants having failed to pursue the prescribed procedure.

In contrast to this decision, the Commission declared inadmissible, as manifestly ill-founded, a similar complaint by three Lebanese citizens who had been kept in Vienna airport for one week, before their admission into Austria (application

---

21 Case of *Cyprus* v. *Turkey*, applications Nos. 6780/74 and 6950/75, Commission's report of 10 July 1976, p. 82, para. 235, and p. 100, para. 286.
22 Eur. Court H.R., *Guzzardi* judgment of 6 November 1980, Series A No. 39, p. 33, para. 92; *Engel and others* judgment of 8 June 1976, Series A No. 22, p. 24, paras. 58–59.
23 See on this point Council of Europe Parliamentary Assembly, report by Lord Mackie of Benshie on the arrival of asylum seekers at European airports, *supra* note 15.

CHAPTER 7   ARTICLE 5 ECHR

No. 19066/91, *S., M. & Y.* v. *Austria*, decision of 5 April 1993). The Commission observed the following:

> "The Commission notes that the applicants arrived of their own free will at Vienna airport on 9 March 1990. Thereupon they were housed in the transit area until 16 March 1990. During this period they were free at any time to leave Austria. Indeed, they were offered the possibility of boarding a plane to leave Austria on 11, 14 and twice on 15 March 1990, but they refused.
> It is true that in their submissions the applicants claim that they could not leave the transit area as, upon their return to Lebanon they would have been exposed to the danger of torture and inhuman treatment.
> However, the Commission notes that the Austrian authorities offered the applicants the possibility of returning to Larnaca in Cyprus from where they had left on 9 March 1990 when they flew to Vienna. In the Commission's opinion the applicants have not sufficiently demonstrated that, upon their return to Cyprus, the Cypriot authorities would have expelled them immediately to Lebanon. In any event the Commission has (previously) found that the applicants have failed to show that in Lebanon they would face a real risk of being subjected to treatment contrary to Article 3 of the Convention.
> In these circumstances it cannot be said that during their stay at the airport transit area the applicants were deprived of their liberty within the meaning of Article 5 para. 1 of the Convention."

The reasoning in this decision as well as the comparison between it and the decision in the above-mentioned application No. 18560/91 shows clearly the tendency in the Commission's case law to link the issue of deprivation of liberty with that of the risk of being subjected to treatment prohibited by Article 3 in case of return to the country of origin. For the Commission, where this risk is not established, the asylum seeker is free to leave the airport and consequently his stay there cannot be regarded as a deprivation of liberty.

This approach, which was not unanimously accepted and has already been criticised,[24] was brought before the European Court of Human Rights in the context of the case of *Mahad, Lahima, Abdelkader and Mohamed Amuur* v. *France*.[25]

This case concerned the fact that the applicants, who were asylum seekers from Somalia, were held in the "international zone" (before the Act of 6 July 1992 turned it into a so-called "waiting zone") of Paris Orly airport from 9 to 29 March 1992. The applicants invoked Article 5 para. 1 of the Convention. They had also

---

24 See O. de Schutter, *supra* note 10, p. 476.
25 Case of *Amuur* v. *France*, application No. 19776/92, report of the Commission of 10 January 1995, judgment No. 17/1995/523/609 of 25 June 1996, to be published in Reports of Judgments and Decisions for 1996, Carl Heymans Verlag, Köln.

169

complained, invoking Article 3, Article 5 para. 4, 6, and Articles 13 and 25 of the Convention, of the fact that the French authorities had refused to admit them to French territory and had sent them back to Syria. This part of the application was declared inadmissible. As regards the Article 5 issue, the Commission observed the following:

> "The four applicants were held in the international zone of Paris Orly airport from 9 to 29 March 1992, that is for a period of twenty days. During this time they stayed at the Arcade Hotel, which has been declared an extension of the so-called international zone of the airport. As indicated in the Report of the Parliamentary Assembly of the Council of Europe, those who are held in this zone have no contact with the outside world, rarely have even access to a telephone, and are under the surveillance of the border police.[26] Having regard to the conditions described above, the period which the applicants spent in the international zone, particularly given its length, does not appear essentially distinguishable from measures categorised as 'detention' in the ordinary sense of the word."

In the Commission's view, the fact that the applicants were kept on one floor of a hotel and not in a typical place of detention is irrelevant, as their situation displayed the essential characteristics of a deprivation of liberty.

However, this *prima facie* finding was overturned by further considerations relating to the applicants' possibility of leaving the airport and returning to a country where they ran no risk of being subjected to torture or to other treatment prohibited by Article 3. In the Commission's view, the consideration that the applicants were free to leave the Arcade Hotel at any time, provided that they immediately left

---

26 The report of the Parliamentary Assembly of the Council of Europe indicated as regards the situation in Paris Roissy airport: "Asylum seekers are detained in a so-called international zone at the airport, which means that they are not yet on French territory. During detention, no access to social workers and in fact no communication with the outside world exists. Moreover, asylum seekers do not always have access to telephones. On permission from the border police, a chaplain can visit asylum seekers. No recreational or educational facilities are put at the asylum seekers' disposal. No legal basis for detention exists and a maximum term is not prescribed by law. The French authorities claim that asylum seekers stay in the international zone for a maximum of one week and that children are seldom held. Some asylum seekers claim to have spent six weeks waiting for the Ministry of the Interior to decide whether their application is to be passed on to OFPRA or whether they will be sent back. Asylum seekers in the international zone sleep on the floor and on the plastic chairs. The airport provides them with meals and there are a few showers for their use in the middle of the night when they are not being used by others. Due to lack of space at the airport itself, the international zone is extended to one of the floors of the nearby Arcade Hotel."

French soil, could cure the deprivation of liberty inherent in the applicants' situation.

The Commission recalled that in addition to factors such as the living conditions, the restricted nature of the contact available and the police surveillance, in order for a measure of restriction to qualify as a "deprivation of liberty" under the Convention, it must reach a certain level of physical constraint. The question was therefore raised as to what extent the applicants could free themselves from the effects of the measure in issue. Of course, in the Commission's view, it is totally insufficient to find that the applicants had a theoretical and illusory ability to go to a third country; it was necessary to examine whether the applicants had a real possibility of freeing themselves from detention in the international zone and going to a country which was neither their country of origin, nor a country likely to hand them over to the authorities from whom they were fleeing. The Commission then observed that the applicants arrived at Orly airport, of their own free will, from Damascus and that they went back to Syria, which agreed to accept them. They had not shown that their life or their physical security were in danger in Syria. Nor had they claimed that the French authorities prevented them from leaving the international zone of the airport in order to fly to Syria. Consequently, the degree of constraint required before the measure to which the applicants were subjected could be described as a "deprivation of liberty" was not present. By this reasoning, the Commission's majority concluded that Article 5 was not applicable in the applicants' case.

However, there were convincing arguments in favour of applying Article 5 in general, as shown in the opinion expressed by the Commission's minority.[27]

Article 5 para. 1(f) of the Convention expressly refers to the detention of a person "to prevent his effecting an unauthorised entry into the country". The situation at which this provision appears to be aimed is that of a person who has been detained for the sole purpose of excluding him from the State in question. It does not seem to imply that that State intends to prevent him generally from leaving its territory voluntarily for another country. The very wording of the Convention therefore supports the opinion that airport detention involves a case of detention covered by Article 5.

Moreover, as regards the assertion that a person may be free to leave the airport, the dissenting Commission members observe that this may prove rather theoretical if the only State willing to admit the asylum seeker is the one from which he fled and where, in his view, he will be in grave danger on his return. At the very least, a certain amount of time is often needed in order to clarify the situation of the person concerned and to decide any applications he may make.

---

27   See the common dissenting opinion of ten members of the Commission in the above-mentioned report, *supra* note 25.

In addition, the position that holding asylum seekers in transit areas in airports amounts to a measure of administrative detention seems to be accepted at both national and international level.

In recent years there have been discussions in a number of countries about how to characterise, in law, the situation where foreigners are held in special zones attached to airports. With regard to France, the *Conseil Constitutionnel* ruled in its judgment of 25 February 1992 that holding a foreigner in the transit zone did encroach upon that person's individual liberty, because of the combined effect of the degree of restriction and length of time involved.[28] The same finding was made by the Paris *tribunal de grande instance* in a judgment of 25 March 1992.[29] This court added that total deprivation of freedom of movement is not essential to a finding that this freedom has been encroached upon; it suffices that the person has had his liberty seriously restricted.

In the Netherlands the *Hoge Raad* has further admitted that Article 5 applies to persons held in the airport transit zone.[30]

At the international level the European Committee for the Prevention of Torture and Inhuman or Degrading Treatment or Punishment, which is authorised under Article 2 of the European Convention against Torture to visit places "where persons are deprived of their liberty", felt entitled to include places such as the Arcade Hotel at Roissy airport in its visits. Similarly, the Committee visited the transit zone of Brussels airport and the special transit room at Schwechat airport in Vienna. These places were regarded as places of detention just like the Snarova

---

28   The reasoning of the *Conseil Constitutionnel* is the following: an alien held in the transit zone does not experience a degree of personal restriction comparable to that which he would if placed in a holding centre. Nevertheless, the degree of restriction involved, combined with the length of the detention, means that holding an alien in the transit zone does encroach upon the individual freedom of the person detained within the meaning of Section 66 of the Constitution.

29   Paris *tribunal de grande instance, Levelt* v. *Ministre de l'Intérieur* judgment of 25 March 1992. The Court held that "holding an alien on the premises of the Arcade Hotel, given the degree of confinement and the length of detention – which is not defined by any legislative provision but by a mere administrative decision, without any judicial supervision whatsoever – does constitute an encroachment on the individual liberty of the person held. Total deprivation of freedom of movement is not essential to a finding that this freedom has been encroached upon; it is enough if, as in the instant case, the person has had his liberty seriously restricted as a result of the relevant decision .... Further, in the absence of a specific legal rule governing the detention in the international zone of an asylum seeker for such time as is strictly necessary for the administrative authorities to consider whether his application is admissible, those authorities are not entitled to invoke in their support a general and automatic right to hold an alien in this zone, which is under surveillance."

30   *Hoge Raad der Nederlanden*, 9 December 1988, *Shokuh* v. *NL*, Revue du droit des étrangers, No. 52, p. 16, with comments by L. Denys, *Applicabilité de l'article 5 CEDH au centre d'accueil des demandeurs d'asile à l'aéroport de Schiphol.*

Holding Centre for Asylum Seekers located in the vicinity of Fornebu airport in Norway.

In the dissenting opinion expressed in the Commission's report these elements were taken into consideration. The dissenting members of the Commission found that the applicants in the *Amuur* case were deprived of their liberty during the period they were held in Orly airport. They further noted that at the material time, the detention of foreigners in the transit zone had no legislative basis in French law and that therefore the deprivation of liberty of the applicants was not effected "in accordance with a procedure prescribed by law" within the meaning of Article 5 of the Convention.

In its *Amuur* judgment given on 25 June 1996, the European Court of Human Rights found that the applicants were detained in breach of Article 5 of the Convention.

The Court dismissed the government's argument that the applicants could at any time have removed themselves from the sphere of application of the restrictive measures applied in the international zone. The mere fact that it is possible for asylum seekers to leave voluntarily the country where they wish to take refuge cannot exclude a restriction on the right of liberty. Furthermore, "this possibility becomes theoretical if no other country offering protection comparable to the protection they expect to find in the country where they are seeking asylum is inclined or prepared to take them in".[31] The Court concluded that holding the applicants in the transit zone of the Paris airport was equivalent in practice, in view of the restrictions suffered, to a deprivation of liberty and that, consequently, Article 5 was applicable to this case.

For the Court, as a matter of principle, holding asylum seekers in the international zone involves a restriction upon liberty. Such a restriction is inevitable while the application of an alien for leave to enter the territory with the purpose of seeking asylum is considered. However, such holding, when it exceeds the time necessary for this consideration, turns into a deprivation of liberty.

III   Rights guaranteed to detained asylum seekers under the European Convention on Human Rights

The applicability of Article 5 having been established under the conditions indicated in the above judgment, one should question whether the rights guaranteed under the Convention provide sufficient protection to detained asylum seekers.

---

31   *Amuur* judgment, *supra* note 25, para. 48.

III.1   The requirement of lawfulness

The requirement of lawfulness appears in litt. (b) of Conclusion No. 44 ("... detention may be resorted to only on grounds prescribed by law ...") of the Executive Committee of UNHCR as well as in Guideline 10 of Recommendation No. R (94) 5 of the Committee of Ministers of the Council of Europe:

> "The asylum seeker can be held in [an appropriate place of accommodation] only under the conditions and for the maximum duration provided for by law."

Equally, under Article 5, a measure amounting to a deprivation of liberty will only comply with the requirements of the Convention if it is legal in domestic law. Article 5 para. 1 lays down that any arrest or detention must be carried out "in accordance with a procedure prescribed by law". On this point the Convention first and foremost requires that any deprivation of liberty must have a legal basis in domestic law. Deprivation of liberty cannot occur in the absence of a domestic legal provision expressly authorising it. It further refers back to this national law and lays down the obligation to conform to both the substantive and procedural rules thereof.

In some cases the Court has checked whether the national authorities have observed the relevant provisions of domestic law.[32]

In its *Winterwerp* judgment, the Court stated that underlying the term "in accordance with a procedure prescribed by law" is the notion of fair and proper procedure, namely that any measure depriving a person of his liberty should issue from an appropriate authority and should not be arbitrary.[33]

Moreover, the national law authorising the deprivation of liberty must also be sufficiently accessible and precise,[34] elements which may be of particular importance for aliens.

The recent *Amuur* judgment goes even further in this direction:

> "Where the 'lawfulness' of detention is in issue, including the question whether 'a procedure prescribed by law' has been followed, the Convention refers essentially to national law and lays down the obligation to conform to the substantive and procedural rules of national law, but it requires in addition that any deprivation of liberty should be in keeping with the purpose of Article

---

32   See e.g. *Monnell and Morris* judgment of 2 March 1988, Series A No. 115, p. 20, para. 50; *Bouamar* judgment of 29 February 1988, Series A No. 129, p. 20, para. 47; *van der Leer* judgment of 21 February 1990, Series A No. 170.
33   Judgment of 24 October 1979, Series A No. 33, p. 19, para. 45.
34   See No. 9403/81, *Zamir* v. *United Kingdom*, 5 May 1982, DR 28 p. 235.

5, namely to protect the individual from arbitrariness.[35] In laying down that any deprivation of liberty must be effected 'in accordance with a procedure prescribed by law', Article 5 para. 1 primarily requires any arrest or detention to have a legal basis in domestic law. However, these words do not merely refer back to domestic law; like the expressions 'in accordance with the law' and 'prescribed by law' in the second paragraphs of Articles 8 to 11, they also relate to the quality of the law, requiring it to be compatible with the rule of law, a concept inherent in all the articles of the Convention.

In order to ascertain whether a deprivation of liberty has complied with the principle of compatibility with domestic law, it therefore falls to the Court to assess not only the legislation in force in the field under consideration, but also the quality of the other legal rules applicable to the persons concerned. Quality in this sense implies that where a national law authorises deprivation of liberty – especially in respect of a foreign asylum seeker – it must be sufficiently accessible and precise, in order to avoid all risk of arbitrariness. These characteristics are of fundamental importance with regard to asylum seekers at airports, particularly in view of the need to reconcile the protection of fundamental rights with the requirements of States' immigration policies."[36]

The Court further noted that at the material time the texts applicable did not allow the ordinary courts to review the conditions under which aliens were held or, if necessary, to impose a limit on administrative authorities as regards the length of time for which they were held. They did not provide for legal, humanitarian and social assistance, nor did they lay down procedures and time limits for access to such an assistance so that asylum seekers could take the necessary steps. The Court concluded that the legal rules in force at the time "did not sufficiently guarantee the applicant's right to liberty" and that accordingly there had been a breach of Article 5 para. 1.[37] In this way, the Court indirectly indicated the basic elements that a law regulating detention of asylum seekers should contain and the guarantees it should offer: judicial review, provisions setting time limits for the detention and regulation concerning access to legal, humanitarian and social assistance are the necessary elements which would make the law compatible with the rule of law, as required by the Convention.

---

35 See e.g. *Kemmache* v. *France* (No. 3) judgment of 24 November 1994, Series A No. 296-C, pp. 19–20, para. 42.
36 *Amuur* judgment, *supra* note 25, para. 50.
37 *Ibid.*, para. 53 *in fine*.

III.2   Guarantees as to the duration of the detention

Neither the Geneva Convention nor the Committee of Ministers Guidelines provide for a maximum duration of the detention of persons seeking asylum. In its Conclusion No. 44, the UNHCR Executive Committee recognises the importance of expeditious procedures in protecting asylum seekers from unduly prolonged detention. Article 5 para. 1(f) does not set any "reasonable time" or other express limit as to the length of an alien's detention pending extradition or deportation.[38] Therefore, the guarantees it offers might seem irrelevant: this provision will not set any limit to the prolongation of the detention nor can it prevent detention as such. Nevertheless, Article 5 para.1(f), as interpreted by the Court, should be understood as containing a safeguard as to the duration of the detention authorised, since the purpose of Article 5 as a whole is to protect the individual from arbitrariness. In its *Bozano* judgment, the Court considered that this principle was of particular importance with respect to Article 5 para.1(f) of the Convention.[39] This provision certainly implies – though it is not made explicit – that detention of an alien which is justified by the fact that proceedings concerning him are in progress can cease to be justified if the proceedings concerned are not conducted with due diligence.[40]

It is true that there are not many cases in which a serious problem has arisen as to the length of the detention under Article 5 para. 1(f). This is however due to the fact that almost all complaints under this provision were submitted by persons detained pending extradition procedures. It has been argued in these cases that persons opposing extradition may have good reasons to prolong the procedure and to delay execution of extradition. Thus, rather lengthy detentions have been found in conformity with the Convention's requirements since the government concerned could not be held responsible for the duration of the detention.[41]

This reasoning seems inapplicable to deportation cases, however, and should not apply to asylum seekers who have in principle good reasons to obtain a speedy examination of their cases. The Commission's recent report in the case *Chahal* v. *United Kingdom* – a case concerning deportation of a Sikh militant to India – confirms this position. The Commission found that five years was excessive in that the proceedings had not been pursued with the requisite speed. It also noted that

---

38   Application No. 9174/80, Commission's report of 1983, D.R. 40, p. 42.
39   Judgment of 18 December 1986, Series A No. 111, p. 23, para. 54.
40   See also the Commission's report in the case of *Kolompar* v. *Belgium* (judgment of 24 September 1992, Series A No. 235-C), in which the Commission found that the government had not acted with the diligence required under Article 5 para. 1(f) ; the Court, however, found no violation on the ground that the time spent in detention was due to the conduct of the applicant.
41   See S. Trechsel, *Liberty and security of person*, in R. Macdonald, F. Matscher, H. Petzold (ed.), *The European System for the Protection of Human Rights*, Martinus Nijhof, 1993, p. 314.

there was no abuse of judicial review process by the applicant in order to delay his deportation. Interestingly, the Commission took into account the fact that a person detained pending deportation is unconvicted and without charge, and stated that in these circumstances "it is important that proceedings to challenge the decision to deport should be handled with the utmost expedition". As regards the argument that the person facing deportation may profit from the delays in returning him to his country of origin, the Commission observed that the complaint was not that he was not sent back more quickly but rather that he was kept in detention pending the decision being taken as to whether he should or should not be deported.[42]

The above remarks clearly show that despite the *prima facie* negative wording of Article 5 para. 1(f), the Convention as a "living instrument" does contain guarantees against arbitrary prolongation of detention of aliens.

III.3   The right to appeal

According to Article 5 para. 4, everyone who is deprived of his liberty is entitled to take proceedings by which the lawfulness of his detention is decided speedily by a court and his release ordered if the detention is not lawful. Moreover, this provision is closely related to Article 5 para. 2, according to which "everyone who is arrested shall be informed promptly, in a language which he understands, of the reasons for his arrest". As emphasised by the Court, no-one entitled to lodge an appeal with a view to a speedy decision on the lawfulness of detention could possibly enforce that right effectively unless he is informed, speedily and adequately, of the facts and the legal rules relied upon to deprive him of his freedom.[43] The fact that proceedings making it possible to contest the lawfulness of the detention exist in domestic law is not enough to satisfy the requirements of Article 5 para. 4. The proceedings must also be "effective", which implies that a number of procedural rights must be granted to the alien. The right to free linguistic assistance, the right of access to the case file and the right to legal aid are among the minimum procedural safeguards that must be observed. Furthermore, the mere fact that such safeguards are provided for by law is not enough for the State to fulfil its obligations under this provision. These safeguards must also have been effectively implemented and the person concerned must have been given an opportunity to avail himself of them. This is required by the principle that the rights safeguarded by the Convention must be real and practical, not theoretical or illusory. When aliens reach the borders of Contracting States in total ignorance of the procedures of the countries in which they have arrived and being unaccustomed to claiming procedural rights from the

---

42   Application No. 22414/93, Commission's report of 27 June 1995, para 121. The final judgment of the court was rendered on 15 November 1996, and is described in Chapter 1 (Section V.2).
43   *X v. United Kingdom*, Series A No. 46, p. 27, para. 66.

authorities, the need for real and practical accessibility is one aspect of the requirements of the Convention which deserves emphasis.[44] It should finally be noted that Article 5 para. 4 is not wholly applicable to detentions of very short duration, i.e. of a few hours only.[45]

In the *Amuur* judgment the Court made two interesting observations. The first refers to the judicial nature of the review and to the impact of the detention on the asylum seeker's access to asylum procedures. The Court stated that:

"Although by the force of circumstances the decision to order holding must necessarily be taken by the administrative or police authorities, its prolongation requires speedy review by the courts, the traditional guardians of personal liberties. Above all, such confinement must not deprive the asylum seeker of the right to gain effective access to the procedure for determining refugee status." (Paragraph 43 *in fine*)

In requiring a judicial review of measures amounting to deprivation of liberty, Article 5 of the Human Rights Convention goes further than the recommendation of litt. (e) of ExCom Conclusion No. 44. According to the latter "detention measures taken in respect of refugees and asylum seekers should be subject to *judicial or administrative* review" (emphasis added). Recommendation R (94) 5 of the Council of Europe does not expressly provide for a right to appeal. Moreover, the requirements of Article 5 paras. 2 and 4 at least coincide with the guidelines in Recommendation R (94) 5 according to which asylum seekers held in airports shall be informed about the procedure followed and about their rights and obligations, and shall be given adequate linguistic and legal assistance and be allowed to contact the UNHCR representatives.

The second observation made by the Court relates to the effectiveness of the review proceedings. The French government had argued that since the Créteil *tribunal de grande instance* had given judgment in the applicants' favour on 31 March 1992 (after the applicants' deportation), they could not reasonably maintain that the remedy before that court was not effective and that, consequently, they could no longer claim to be victims of a violation of the Convention within the meaning of Article 25. The Court rejected this argument. Despite the ruling of the Créteil *tribunal* that holding the applicants in the transit zone at Paris Orly airport was unlawful and the order for their release, the Court noted that the applicants had

---

44 For an extensive analysis of the procedural requirements of Article 5 paras. 2 and 4 see S. Trechsel, *supra* note 41, pp. 314 *et seq.*; R. de Goutes, *Article 5 para. 2* in *La Convention Européenne des Droits de l'Homme*, sous la direction de L.E. Petiti, E. Decaux & P.H. Imbert, Economica 1995, pp. 203 *et seq.*; R. Koering-Joulin, *Article 5 para. 4, ibid.*, pp. 229 *et seq.*

45 No. 7376/76, DR 7, p. 123.

been held in the transit zone since 9 March and, above all, had been sent back to Syria on 29 March. Neither the decision of the Créteil *tribunal* nor the merely theoretical possibility of obtaining compensation for the prejudice they had suffered were regarded as effective redress of the situation of which the applicants complained. Indirectly, but certainly, the Court admitted that only proceedings by which the applicants could have obtained their actual release on the territory of the defendant State could be regarded as "effective".[46]

III.4   The right to compensation

Finally, under Article 5 para. 5, an asylum seeker who has been deprived of his liberty in breach of Article 5 paras. 1 to 4, shall have an enforceable right to compensation.[47] No similar provision is contained in either ExCom Conclusion No. 44 or the Council of Europe's Recommendation R (94) 5.

III.5   Conditions of detention

In contrast to Conclusion No. 44 and Recommendation R (94) 5, Article 5 does not guarantee any rights concerning *inter alia* the conditions of detention. However, under the Human Rights Convention conditions of detention must also comply with several requirements: the alien therefore has the right, under Articles 2 and 3 of the Convention, to appropriate medical assistance and also, under Article 8 (guaranteeing the right to respect for family life), the right, as soon as detained, to contact his family to inform them of his situation.

Article 3 of the Convention prohibiting ill treatment may be invoked by detained applicants claiming that the conditions of detention were such as to amount to inhuman treatment. In the *Greek Case*,[48] the Commission found that by reason of overcrowding, inadequate heating, inadequate sleeping and toilet facilities, insufficient food, recreation and contacts with the outside world, the conditions of detention of political detainees violated Article 3. Withholding of food and water and insufficient medical treatment were found to constitute inhuman treatment contrary to Article 3 in the *Cyprus* v. *Turkey* case.[49] The need to provide medical treatment – including psychiatric treatment[50] which may be extremely important, as

---

46 See *contra* the Commission's decision on the admissibility of the application, declaring inadmissible the applicants' complaint under Article 5 para. 4.
47 See S.Trechsel, *supra* note 41, pp. 341 *et seq.*
48 *The Greek Case*, Yearbook 12, 1969.
49 See *supra* note 21.
50 D.J. Harris, M. O'Boyle and C. Warbrick, *Law of the European Convention on Human Rights*, Butterworths, London, Dublin, Edinburgh, 1995, p. 71.

is shown in the recent report by Dr. Christina Pourgourides *et al.*[51] – was further stressed in the case of *Hurtado* v. *Switzerland*, in which the Commission found a breach of Article 3 when a person arrested by force was not given appropriate medical care (an X-ray which revealed a fractured rib) until six days after his arrest.[52]

It is true that the standards of Article 3 as interpreted by the Strasbourg bodies seem to be lower than the requirements in other European instruments. In its report in the case of *Eggs* v. *Switzerland*,[53] the Commission indicated that conditions of detention that do not comply with the 1973 Council of Europe Minimum Rules for the Treatment of Prisoners[54] do not necessarily amount to a breach of Article 3 of the Convention. Similarly, the standards between Article 3 and the European Convention for the Prevention of Torture and Inhuman or Degrading Treatment or Punishment are not equivalent: it is very probable that conditions and places of detention which were criticised by the Committee for the Prevention of Torture (CPT) would not give rise to a successful application under the Convention for Human Rights.[55] The CPT actually visited and criticised a number of places where asylum seekers were detained upon their arrival or awaiting deportation. As regards the places in France where aliens were held awaiting deportation, the Committee made recommendations concerning improvement of sanitary equipment, property and opportunities for physical exercise.[56] As regards the transit zone of Brussels airport, the Committee requested that urgent measures be taken to improve the accommodation conditions of persons who were obliged to stay in the airport for more than a few hours. Persons kept in the airport should be allowed to take their luggage and be given opportunities for physical exercise.[57] In its report on the special transit room at Schwechat airport in Vienna, the Committee recommended that access to transit rooms be guaranteed for persons whom asylum seekers might wish to contact, such as lawyers, interpreters or family members already in Austria.[58] As regards the Snarova Holding Centre for Asylum Seekers located in the

---

51 *A Second Exile: The Mental Health Implications of Detention of Asylum Seekers in the United Kingdom*, C.K. Pourgourides, S.P. Sashidharan and P.J. Bracken. Northern Birmingham Mental Health NHS Trust, 1996; see also Chapter 9 of this book.
52 *Hurtado* case, Series A No. 280-A, Commission's report. The case ended with an amicable settlement before the European Court of Human Rights.
53 Application No. 7341, DR 6, p. 170.
54 These Rules were replaced in 1987 by the European Prison Rules; see Recommendation R (87) 3 of the Committee of Ministers of the Council of Europe.
55 J. Murdoch, *The work of the Council of Europe's Torture Committee*, European Journal of International Law, Volume 5 (1994), p. 220.
56 See the Report of the CPT on its visit to France from 27 October to 8 November 1991, paras. 65–80.
57 See Report of the Committee to the Government of Belgium, 14 October 1994.
58 Report of the Committee to the Austrian Government, 3 October 1991, para. 92 of the Report, CPT/Inf (91) 10.

vicinity of Fornebu airport in Norway, the Committee recommended *inter alia* that an information booklet be given to the persons held there in order to explain to them their rights, the procedure applicable to them and the rules of the detention centre. The booklet should be made available in an appropriate range of languages.[59] Of course, non-compliance with the above recommendations of the Committee for the Prevention of Torture will only exceptionally amount to a breach of Article 3.[60] This, however, should not minimise the importance of rights guaranteed under Articles 3 and 8 for detained asylum seekers.

IV   Conclusion: A statement from the *Amuur* judgment

Having regard to the above, the answer to the question "Why should an asylum seeker seek protection under Article 5?" becomes obvious: Article 5 does not of course prohibit detention of asylum seekers, but subjects this detention to strict conditions and requirements while at the same time securing concrete, enforceable substantive and procedural rights for detained asylum seekers.[61]

There seems to exist a general consensus on the rights which should be granted to asylum seekers kept in various places upon their arrival in the country of asylum. These are included in various international texts such as ExCom Conclusion No. 44 and Recommendation R (94) 5 of the Council of Europe. Essentially these texts require that measures imposed on asylum seekers restricting or depriving them of their liberty have a legal basis in domestic law and that they are taken in accordance with this law; that a procedure is provided for judicial review of the legality of these measures ; that effective access to this procedure be secured to asylum seekers through appropriate legal and linguistic assistance. Applying Article 5 of the European Convention on Human Rights to detained asylum seekers adds to this network of provisions the element they are mainly lacking, namely the enforceable

---

59   See the Report of the Committee to the Government of Norway, 21 September 1994 (para. 49 of the Report, CPT/Inf (94) 11).

60   See for example the Commission's decision declaring inadmissible application No. 19066/91 (*S., M. and Y.* v. *Austria*), concerning conditions of detention in Schwechat airport in Vienna.

61   See P. Van Dijk and G.J.H. Van Hoof, *Theory and practice of the European Convention on Human Rights*, Kluwer 1990, p. 269: "The great importance of the provisions under (f) consists in that, although the Convention does not grant to aliens a right of admission to or residence in the Contracting States, Article 5 nevertheless contains certain guarantees in case the authorities proceed to arrest or detain an alien pending the decision on his admission, deportation or extradition. These consist first of all in a guarantee that such arrest or detention must be lawful and must therefore be in conformity with the relevant regulations of domestic law, coupled with the right of the person in question under paragraph 4 to have this lawfulness reviewed by a court and ultimately, if necessary, by the Strasbourg organs."

character of the rights concerned and the international control mechanism. To sum up, relying on Article 5 could make these rights more effective.

Since the *Amuur* judgment, Article 5 can be added to the human rights provisions which are of particular relevance in cases of asylum. In this respect it is perhaps interesting to note that the European Court of Human Rights took into consideration the more general question of human rights implementation in cases of asylum seekers. It recognised that many Member States of the Council of Europe have been confronted for a number of years now with an increasing flow of asylum seekers and recalled that States have the undeniable sovereign right to control aliens' entry into and residence in their territory. It emphasised, however, that this right must be exercised in accordance with the provisions of those international instruments that constitute the basis of a free democratic society: States' legitimate concern to foil the increasingly frequent attempts to get round immigration restrictions must not deprive asylum seekers of the protection afforded by the 1951 Geneva Convention relating to the Status of Refugees and the European Convention on Human Rights.[62]

---

62 Above mentioned *Amuur* judgment, *supra* note 25, para. 43.

Chapter 8 The Relevance of Key UN Instruments for Detained Asylum Seekers

By Anne-Marie Tootell, Jane Hughes and David Petrasek

Contents

Part I   Introduction
Part II Substantive criteria: II.1 Beneficiaries – II.2 Definition of deprivation of liberty – II.3 Legality of detention – II.4 Lawfulness and the prohibition of arbitrariness – II.5 Length of detention
Part III Procedural aspects: III.1 The right to information regarding grounds for detention – III.2 The right to challenge detention – III.3 Impartiality of the reviewing authority – III.4 The right to legal assistance – III.5 Timing and nature of the review
Part IV Implementing mechanisms
Part V   Conclusion

I   Introduction

This chapter offers an analysis of a number of key UN instruments in order to assess their relevance for detained asylum seekers.[1]

There is a substantial body of international standards and rules offering protection to detained persons, emanating from Article 3 of the 1948 Universal Declaration of Human Rights: "No-one shall be subjected to arbitrary arrest, detention or exile." This is a fundamental principle which all UN Member States have agreed to respect. It has been incorporated into a number of binding human rights instruments not only at global but also at regional level, including the 1950 European Convention on Human Rights and Fundamental Freedoms, the 1969 American Convention on Human Rights and the 1981 African Charter on Human and People's Rights.

The chapter refers primarily to Article 9 of the 1966 International Covenant on Civil and Political Rights (ICCPR) and Article 37 of the 1989 Convention on the Rights of the Child (CRC). Both of these instruments are binding on States Parties and both provide some form of implementing or monitoring body – in the case of the

---

1   The texts referred to in this chapter are reproduced in the Appendices to this book.

ICCPR, the Human Rights Committee (HRC), and in that of the CRC, the Committee on the Rights of the Child. Under each instrument, parties have periodic reporting obligations and under the terms of the Optional Protocol to the ICCPR individuals may also bring alleged breaches of the ICCPR for consideration before the Human Rights Committee.

In addition to the above, there are a number of texts which introduce more detailed safeguards elaborating upon those contained in the ICCPR and the CRC. These comprise the Standard Minimum Rules for the Treatment of Prisoners, first adopted in 1955 and extended in 1977 to ensure that persons arrested or imprisoned without charge should benefit from most of the provisions of these Rules, the 1988 Body of Principles for the Protection of All Persons under Any Form of Detention or Imprisonment (BOP) and the 1990 Rules for Juveniles Deprived of their Liberty (JDL). The JDL rules were adopted just one year after the adoption of the CRC. They regulate the management of facilities where juveniles are held, taking into account their special needs and entitlements. They apply to any person under the age of 18 who has been deprived of his or her liberty in an institution for any purpose, and therefore cover minor asylum seekers in administrative detention.

All the above instruments were adopted by consensus by UN Member States, in most cases after lengthy negotiations, and may thus be considered to have authoritative value even though they are not strictly speaking legally binding, except insofar as some of the rules they contain reflect customary international law.

Two further UN conventions should be mentioned at this point: the 1966 International Convention on the Elimination of All Forms of Racial Discrimination and the 1984 Convention against Torture and Other Cruel, Inhuman or Degrading Treatment or Punishment (CAT). Whilst they do not deal directly with detention and therefore do not fall within the scope of this paper, they may nevertheless prove useful for certain detained asylum seekers. The CAT, in particular, may be used to challenge deportation orders where asylum seekers risk being returned to a country where they would be in danger of being tortured. Indeed an increasing number of complaints submitted to the Committee against Torture concern alleged violations of Article 3 of the CAT.[2]

Before embarking on an analysis of the substantive and procedural aspects of Article 9 of the ICCPR and Article 37 of the CRC, it should be pointed out for the sake of clarity that this paper focuses exclusively on the fact of deprivation of liberty as set

---

2 Article 3(1) of the CAT states that: "No State Party shall expel, return (*refouler*) or extradite a person to another State where there are substantial grounds for believing that he would be in danger of being subjected to torture"; see for example the case of *Balabou Mutombo* v. *Switzerland* (Communication No. 13/1993), submitted to the Committee against Torture in October 1993. On 27 April 1994, the Committee found that for Switzerland to expel Mr Mutombo, a rejected Zaïrean asylum seeker, and return him to Zaire would constitute a violation of Article 3. This information was provided by Professor Bent Sørensen, Vice-Chairman of the Committee against Torture.

out in those articles and the observance of minimum guarantees formulated in this context, such as the right to be informed of the reasons for arrest. It does not deal with conditions of detention, which fall within the remit of Articles 7 and 10 of the CCPR (prohibition of torture or cruel, inhuman or degrading treatment or punishment, and humane treatment of all persons in detention respectively) and Article 16 of the CAT (cruel, inhuman or degrading treatment or punishment).

In the same way, all lesser restrictions on freedom of bodily movement, such as compulsory accommodation in certain areas or expulsion from State territory, come within the scope of Article 12 (freedom of movement) and Article 13 (expulsion) of the Covenant and will not be dealt with here.

Finally, it should be noted that the most important regional instrument in this area, the European Convention on Human Rights (ECHR), will be referred to only where it differs significantly from the Covenant. Article 5 of the ECHR is discussed in detail in Chapter 7.

II Substantive criteria

II.1 Beneficiaries

The scope of Article 9 here is clarified by the HRC in its General Comment 8/16[3] which, in the light of the narrow interpretations sometimes given by States Parties, explicitly states that "paragraph 1 is applicable to all deprivations of liberty, whether in criminal cases or in other cases, such as ... immigration control", and that "the important guarantee laid down in paragraph 4, i.e. the right to court control of the legality of the detention, applies to all persons deprived of their liberty by arrest or detention". The Committee adds, in paragraph 4 of its General Comment, that "if so-called preventive detention is used, for reasons of public security, it must be controlled by these same provisions".

Under Article 9 of the ICCPR, all detainees benefit from the provisions of paragraphs 1, 2, 4 and 5. However, paragraph 3 refers only to the right of persons arrested or detained on a criminal charge "to be brought promptly before a judge ... and entitled to trial within a reasonable time or to release", which would ironically appear to exclude persons detained on other, non-criminal grounds – such as asylum seekers – from these rights.

Significant for asylum seekers is the fact that although detention for immigration control purposes is a recognised form of deprivation of liberty within the meaning of Article 9 of the ICCPR, and immigration detainees thus technically enjoy the

---

3 The purpose of the General Comments is to provide definitive interpretation of the terms of the Covenant in the light of its implementation by States. They are adopted under Article 40(4) of the Covenant. The full text of General Comment 8/16, which relates to Article 9 of the Covenant, is reproduced in the Appendix IV.2 to this book.

protection of international standards regarding detention, it would nevertheless appear that they do not automatically benefit from the full range of safeguards accorded to persons detained on criminal charges.

Article 9 of the ICCPR, like Article 37 of the CRC, does not make any distinction between nationals and aliens (including asylum seekers) as regards the right not to be arbitrarily detained. The principle of non-discrimination between aliens and nationals is clearly stated in Article 2 of the ICCPR: "Each State Party to the present Convention undertakes to respect and to ensure to all individuals within its territory and subject to its jurisdiction the rights recognised in the present Covenant, without distinction of any kind, such as race, colour, sex, language, religion, political or other opinion, national or social origin, property, birth or other status."

This has been underlined by the HCR in its General Opinion 15/27 to Article 2 of the ICCPR, which states that "[t]he general rule is that each one of the rights of the Covenant must be guaranteed without discrimination between citizens and aliens. ... Aliens have the full right to liberty and freedom of the person. If lawfully deprived of their liberty, they shall be treated with humanity and with respect for the inherent dignity of the person."

II.2   Definition of deprivation of liberty

The guarantees set out in Article 9 of the ICCPR are reserved for persons who are forcibly detained within the boundaries of prisons, detention centres or other buildings designated for this purpose.

Unlike Article 5 of the European Convention on Human Rights (ECHR), Article 9 does not give an exhaustive list of situations in which detention is permissible.[4]

The question of detention is currently of particular relevance to asylum seekers held at border points, in transit/international zones at airports or in other alien detention centres. For several years, a number of European States considered that this qualified as "retention" rather than "detention" as defined by Article 5 of the ECHR on the grounds that the persons concerned were free to leave the country at any time. This premise has now been rejected by the European Court of Human Rights, which has deemed that such "zones" are a legal technicality[5] and that those detained there are to all intents and purposes deprived of their liberty in the conventional sense.

---

4   The draft produced by a working group in 1947 listed a number of permissible grounds similar to those laid down in Article 5 of the ECHR. There were subsequent proposals from a number of States, adding a further 40 grounds for detention. As it proved impossible to agree on such an exhaustive and unwieldy list, the idea was finally abandoned and an Australian proposal prohibiting anyone from being arbitrarily arrested or detained was unanimously adopted in 1949.

5   See also F. Julien-Laferrière, *Frontières du droit – Frontières des droits: l'introuvable statut de la "zone internationale"*, l'Harmattan/ANAFE, 1993.

CHAPTER 8 KEY UN INSTRUMENTS

The issue of detention in transit zones at airports has generated a considerable amount of debate in Strasbourg in respect of Article 5 of the ECHR. A report in January 1995 by the European Commission on Human Rights found that there had been no deprivation of liberty in the case of four Somali asylum seekers held in the international zone at the Paris Orly airport for 20 days because they had a safe third country (Syria) which would accept them.

This view was not supported, however, by the European Court of Human Rights, which examined the nature of the restrictions placed upon the individuals in question. The applicants were placed under strict and constant police surveillance. Legal and social assistance was only made available after two weeks, and neither the length nor the necessity of their confinement were reviewed by a court until two weeks later. The Court concluded that given the applicable restrictions, holding the applicants in the transit zone of Paris Orly airport was equivalent in practice to a deprivation of liberty. The Court also dismissed the argument that the existence of a so-called "safe third country" excluded the reality of a deprivation of liberty.[6]

The question of definition has not in itself given rise to lengthy discussions within the Human Rights Committee. A broad application of Article 9 is called for in the HRC's General Comment 8/16, and, as we have seen, detention for the purposes of immigration control is specifically mentioned. Moreover, the Working Group on Arbitrary Detention, a monitoring mechanism established by the UN Commission on Human Rights in 1991, and which bases its work on Article 9 of the ICCPR as well as on the Body of Principles, has repeatedly indicated that the detention of asylum seekers (and immigration detention generally) is a matter within its mandate.

II.3   Legality of detention

The requirement that deprivation of liberty be in accordance with procedures established by law is contained in Article 9(1) of the ICCPR and in Article 37(b) of the CRC. This refers to the domestic law of States, which, in accordance with Article 2(2) of the ICCPR, are required to "take the necessary steps ... to adopt such legislative or other measures as may be necessary to give effect to the rights recognised in the Covenant". In this case, States are required in their national legislation to stipulate all permissible grounds for detention to enable the legality of detention to be ascertained in all cases.

According to Nowak, the term "law" is to be interpreted in the strict sense of a parliamentary statute or an unwritten norm of common law accessible to persons

---

[6] Case of *Amuur* v. *France*, application No. 19776/92, report of the Commission of 10 January 1995, judgment of the European Court of Human Rights No. 17/1995/523/609 of 25 June 1996, to be published in Reports of Judgments and Decisions for 1996, Carl Heymans Verlag, Köln; see Chapter 7 for a detailed account of this case.

subject to the State's jurisdiction. He explicitly makes the point that administrative provisions are therefore not sufficient:

> "A restriction on liberty of person by an administrative act is permissible only when this takes place in enforcement of a law that provides for such interference with adequate clarity and regulates the procedure to be observed. The principle of legality is violated if somebody is either arrested or detained on grounds which are not clearly established in a domestic law, or which are contrary to such law ..."[7]

This comment is clearly of significance with respect to States which detain aliens, including asylum seekers, purely on the basis of internal administrative instructions.[8] Such instructions should always be public and approved by law.

II.4 Lawfulness and the prohibition of arbitrariness

Article 9(1) of the ICCPR[9] prohibits arbitrariness, as does Article 37(b) of the CRC. According to the HRC, the term "arbitrary" is to be given a broad application which is not to be equated with "against the law". Inherent in the term are "elements of inappropriateness, injustice and lack of predictability". This suggests that the scope of the prohibition of arbitrariness is a guarantee, aimed at both the national legislature (government) and the organs of enforcement (police and immigration services), to ensure that the law will not be applied arbitrarily.

The definition of "arbitrary" is therefore broader than that of "unlawful", and covers situations characterised by the absence of requirements such as appropriateness, necessity, proportionality to the ends to be achieved, predictability and justice.

The HCR has found that the prohibition of arbitrariness has been violated in a number of cases, including one where it held that "remand in custody pursuant to lawful arrest must not only be lawful but reasonable and necessary in all the circumstances, for example, to prevent flight, interference with evidence or the recurrence of crime".[10]

A relationship is therefore required between the use of detention and the ends to be achieved. No persons should be detained unless strictly necessary. In the case of asylum seekers and refugees, this is also underlined in Conclusion No. 44 of the

---

7   M. Nowak, *UN Covenant on Civil and Political Rights: Commentary to the CCPR*, Engell, 1993, p. 171.
8   In paragraph 15 of its July 1995 Comments to the Report submitted by the United Kingdom under Article 40 of the ICCPR, the HRC "notes with concern that adequate legal representation is not available for asylum seekers effectively to challenge administrative decisions."
9   Again, see Article 37(b) of the CRC and Principle 2 of the BOP.
10 Communication No. 305/1988.

CHAPTER 8   KEY UN INSTRUMENTS

UNHCR Executive Committee, which acknowledges a need for detention only under limited circumstances: to verify identity; to determine elements on which the claim to refugee status is based; to deal with cases where travel documents have been destroyed or where fraudulent documents are being deliberately used to mislead the authorities; and for reasons of public security.[11]

In a landmark decision in April 1997, the HRC dealt with the case of a Cambodian asylum seeker in Australia who was detained for over four years.[12] Essentially, the HRC considered whether the applicant's detention had been proportional to the desired ends, i.e. to prevent him absconding if left in liberty. While recognising that the detention of an asylum seeker was not *per se* arbitrary, the HRC determined that:

> "... detention should not continue beyond the period for which the State can provide appropriate justification. For example, the fact of illegal entry may indicate a need for investigation and there may be other factors particular to the individual such as the likelihood of absconding and lack of cooperation, which may justify detention for a period. Without such factors detention may be considered arbitrary, even if entry was illegal."

In reaching its conclusion that there had been a breach of Article 9(1) in this case and that the asylum seeker's detention was arbitrary, the Committee took into account the lack of a periodical review and the absence of State justification for the prolonged detention. In fact no reasons particular to the asylum seeker's case, as opposed to more general justifications, had been advanced to justify detention. It was common knowledge that the Australian government's policy of detaining Cambodian and other asylum seekers who arrived by boat was intended as a measure of deterrence.[13]

Article 9 of the ICCPR provides everyone with the fundamental right to liberty and security of person. The fundamental nature of this right cannot be forfeited for political or administrative purposes. Therefore, where detention is used as a deterrent to other asylum seekers or, in cases of rejected asylum seekers where the authorities experience difficulty in obtaining the necessary travel documents from the asylum seekers' consulates, it can be argued that such detention is disproportional, unpredictable and discriminatory.

---

11   See Chapter 6 for a detailed explanation of ExCom Conclusion No. 44 and other UNHCR texts.
12   *A. (name deleted)* v. *Australia*, Communication No. 560/1993, UN Doc. CCPR/C/59/D/560/1993 (30 April 1997).
13   See Chapter 5 for an account of Australian policy and practice regarding detention of asylum seekers.

The prohibition on arbitrary detention which also appears in the CRC is reinforced and emphasised by the strict requirement that detention for minors only be used as a measure of last resort and for the shortest possible period of time.

II.5   Length of detention

Article 9(3) of the Covenant provides that persons detained on criminal charges should be brought "promptly" before a judge and should be entitled to trial "within a reasonable time". Article 37(b) of the CRC is more specific and provides that detention of minors should be for the shortest appropriate period of time.

The second sentence of Article 9(3) states that "[i]t shall not be the general rule that persons awaiting trial shall be detained in custody". The HRC in General Comment 8/16 also acknowledges the very serious nature of pre-trial detention and specifically states that it should be "an exception and as short as possible".

As regards an asylum seeker, who after all has not committed any crime, the applicability of Article 9(3) and its attendant benefits (pre-trial detention under exceptional circumstances only and the right to release on bail) is questionable.

It has been observed that nearly all European States detain non-criminal asylum seekers in penal institutions under conditions akin to those of pre-trial detention, despite the fact that there is no question of their innocence and there are no criminal proceedings involved.[14] It would thus seem unlikely that the drafters of the ICCPR could have intended that asylum seekers should benefit from less favourable guarantees than those available to persons detained on criminal charges. Moreover, the ability of asylum seekers to secure release through payment of sureties (bail) is severely restricted by the fact that the majority of asylum seekers in foreign countries lack financial resources of their own and have no friends or family members to stand bail for them.

Rodley also notes the problematic wording of Article 9(3): "A restrictive reading of this language might be that, as long as formal charges are not preferred, the obligation to produce a detainee before the judicial authority does not apply. Such a reading would, of course, deprive the paragraph of purpose and should therefore be discarded."[15] This position is strengthened by Principle 11 of the Body of Principles, which requires that all persons held in detention (not just those detained on criminal charges) be given "an effective opportunity to be heard *promptly* by a judicial or other authority" (emphasis added).

The length of detention (both the uncertainty as to the total length and the frequently prolonged nature of detention in practice) is a major problem in respect of asylum seekers today. This only renders more important the observance and ability to

---

14 *Detention of Asylum Seekers in Europe*, European Series, Volume 1 No. 4, October 1995, UNHCR Geneva.
15 N. Rodley, *The Treatment of Prisoners Under International Law*, 1987, p. 199.

enforce the accompanying legal guarantees under Article 9 of the ICCPR and Article 37 of the CRC. In the decision concerning the asylum seeker in Australia, referred to above, the HRC held that a period of over four years in detention was "arbitrary" and a violation of Article 9(1) of the ICCPR in the absence of individual reasons particular to the case justifying such a detention.

In its July 1995 Comments to the Report submitted by the United Kingdom under Article 40 of the Covenant, the HRC states in paragraph 15 that "[t]he treatment of illegal immigrants, asylum seekers and those ordered to be deported gives cause for concern. The Committee observes that the incarceration of persons ordered to be deported and particularly the length of their detention may not be necessary in every case ..."

Also, the Committee on the Rights of the Child (CRC) has often expressed concern when considering State reports about the detention of child asylum seekers. Regarding Hong Kong, the CRC commented:

"The broad question of the treatment of Vietnamese children in detention centres in Hong Kong deeply concerns the Committee. It is the observation of the Committee that these children have been and continue to be the victims of a policy designed to discourage further refugees from coming into the area. While it is granted that the situation is a complex one, the policy of the continued detention of these children is incompatible with the Convention."

III   Procedural aspects

III.1   The right to information regarding grounds for detention

Article 9(2) of the ICCPR requires that anyone who is arrested be informed, at the time of arrest, of the reasons for the arrest. This is crucial in order to be able to effectively exercise the right to challenge the deprivation of liberty (Article 9(4)).

Unlike the ECHR (Article 5(2)) and the Body of Principles (Principles 10–14), Article 9(2) of the Covenant does not specify the form in which this information is to take. Thus it requires neither that the information be provided in writing, nor that it be in a language understood by the person concerned.

In one communication, the Human Rights Committee has stated that such language should contain sufficient detail to enable the person concerned to tell if his arrest was in accordance with the law.[16]

This procedural right is of particular importance for asylum seekers who are unfamiliar with European asylum and other administrative procedures and the languages in which they are conducted.

---

16   Communication No. 132/1988.

Two problems with respect to this procedural guarantee have emerged: firstly, in many countries it is not observed at all and secondly, where it is observed, the information is often not in a language or in terms which the asylum seeker understands. Whilst the Covenant cannot of course be held responsible for deficient State practice, its wording is insufficiently precise on this point. However, since the purpose of Article 9(2) is to allow for the exercise of other fundamental rights, it would seem logical to conclude that there is a positive obligation on the detaining authority to make the information available in a language the detainee understands, as clearly required in Principle 14 of the Body of Principles.

III.2   The right to challenge detention

The right to challenge detention (the right to *habeas corpus*) is common to many international instruments, and is set out in Article 9(4) of the ICCPR and Article 37(d) of the CRC.[17]

The right to have the lawfulness of detention reviewed by a court exists regardless of the grounds for detention. It is an independent right and may be violated if not observed, even where the detention is lawful. Thus asylum seekers as a category of detained person also have the right to petition and to have their detention reviewed by a court.

In General Comment 8/16, the HRC states that delays in bringing a detained person before a judge or other officer authorised by law to exercise judicial power must not exceed "a few days". The Committee points out that whilst more precise time limits are fixed by law in most States Parties, "many States have given insufficient information about the actual practices in this respect".

Habeas corpus proceedings are normally at the initiative of the detainee or his or her legal counsel. However, international standards require a separate, automatic review of detention. Principle 11 of the BOP provides that those detained have the right "to be heard promptly by a judicial or other authority" and such an authority "shall be empowered to review as appropriate the continuance of detention". This automatic right of review (independent of the right of petition to a court contained in Principle 32) is crucial. Asylum seekers are often prevented from exercising their legal rights by lack of information concerning these rights, lack of access to legal assistance and a fear of challenging the authorities.

The decision in remand proceedings relates exclusively to the lawfulness of deprivation of liberty. Where deprivation of liberty is found to be unlawful, the detainee should be released.[18] In addition, Article 9(5) provides for an enforceable right to compensation for anyone who has been wrongfully arrested or detained.

---

17   See also Principles 4, 9, 11, 17, 18 and 32 of the BOP.
18   Under Article 2(3) of the ICCPR, States are required to ensure that an effective remedy exists by law.

CHAPTER 8   KEY UN INSTRUMENTS

III.3   Impartiality of the reviewing authority

An important element of an effective review of detention is the relative independence and impartiality of the authority responsible.

While *habeas corpus* petitions must be heard by a court (under Article 9(4) of the ICCPR), international standards do allow for detention of asylum seekers to be under the control and review of "judicial or other authorities". Article 37 of the CRC states that review of detention should be before a "court or other competent, independent and impartial authority". In practice, under many national laws it is administrative bodies such as immigration adjudicators that are authorised by law to confirm an order to detain and to review the detention. In other cases, the authority might be a senior civil servant or even a minister.

The Body of Principles (Principle 32) defines a "judicial or other authority" as meaning those "whose status and tenure afford the strongest possible guarantees of competence, impartiality and independence". The independence of judges is (or should be) assured by their explicit separation from legislative and executive branches of government, the special rules regarding their appointment and removal, and their specific mandates to act in an independent manner. Similarly, while "other authorities" might be empowered to order and review the detention of asylum seekers, such authorities must be able to act independently and thus must be free of any real or perceived bias, or of the undue influence of government officials, civil servants or police forces.

At a minimum, the competent authority should be independent of the detaining authority. This is illustrated in the practice of the Human Rights Committee, which found in the case of *Mario Ines Torres* v. *Finland* that a police decision to detain a Spanish citizen could only be reviewed by the Ministry of the Interior, and was therefore declared to be a violation of Article 9(4).[19]

III.4   The right to legal assistance

The ICCPR is silent on this point. The question of legal advice was discussed in the HRC communication involving the Cambodian asylum seeker in Australia, mentioned above, who complained that its absence had resulted in a violation of Article 9(4). The asylum seeker had been moved on several occasions to remote locations, claiming that this had made it difficult to remain in contact with his lawyer. However, the HRC found that such assistance had been available to him and that he had been advised of his entitlement to it in his own language. Accordingly there was no issue under this provision. Although not an issue in this case, it would seem reasonable to infer from this decision, however, that the availability of legal advice and the explanation of an

---

19   Communication No. 291/1988.

individual's rights in a language which he or she understands are elements to be taken into account when discussing the adequacy of review rights under Article 9(4).

However, as regards minor asylum seekers, Article 37(d) of the CRC is explicit: "Every child deprived of his or her liberty shall have the right to prompt access to legal and other appropriate assistance."

Principle 17 of the Body of Principles also provides a right to legal assistance for all those detained, and in addition mandates that "where the interests of justice so require" a legal counsel will be assigned free of charge to represent detainees who do not have legal counsel of their own. Principle 32(2) adds that procedures regarding a challenge to the lawfulness of detention should be "simple and expeditious and at no cost for detained persons without adequate means". This is of particular relevance to asylum seekers, who are unlikely to have sufficient knowledge of the legal system, the language of the country concerned, or sufficient funds in order to be able to act alone.

III.5   Timing and nature of the review

According to Article 9(4) of the ICCPR, the decision of the reviewing body must be "without delay". Like the Strasbourg institutions, the Human Rights Committee has not given a fixed time schedule, stating that "the question of whether a decision was reached without delay must be assessed on a case by case basis". According to its previous determinations, however, it is clear that the review should be within a matter of weeks rather than months. In one case, a period of three months was found to be "in principle too extended", and in another, a period of five weeks without access to a judge was found to constitute a violation of Article 9(4).[20]

Although there are no provisions in the international treaties specifying that review should be periodic, Principle 11 of the BOP provides that "[a] judicial or other authority shall be empowered to review as appropriate the continuance of detention".

Article 9(1) of the ICCPR and Article 37(b) of the CRC prohibit arbitrary and unlawful deprivations of liberty. Any review of detention should therefore look beyond procedural legality under national legislation and consider the substantive reasons for detention in order to determine whether there has been abuse by the national authorities. The possibility of applying for release on bail or applications for judicial review which only provide limited grounds for challenging the legality of detention may not therefore be in conformity with this requirement.

In a significant development, in the same Australian case referred to above, the HRC ruled that the review of detention must be "in its effects, real and not merely formal". The court must be empowered to grant release where the detention is arbitrary, and not merely to assess the legality of the detention against the narrow requirements of domestic law. In that case, the Australian government had passed

---

20   Communications Nos. 291/1988 and 253/1987 respectively.

legislation prohibiting courts from ordering the release of certain classes of detained asylum seekers, although it did not prevent the asylum seekers from appealing to those courts. While this legislation was a particularly egregious example of making the review of detention a mere formality, the decision of the HRC might have wider implications. For example, where the review of detention never, or only rarely, in practice leads to release, it might be argued that such a review is a mere formality and not real in its effects.

IV   Implementing mechanisms

As previously stated, the ICCPR implementing body consists of the 18-member group of experts making up the Human Rights Committee (HCR), which has been operating for over 18 years. A similar body has been set up under the CRC, but there is no parallel mechanism for admitting inter-State complaints or individual petitions. There is a reporting system, however, which allows active participation by UN agencies and other specialist organisations.

Under Article 40 of the ICCPR, States are required to submit periodic reports (every five years) to the HRC on progress in implementing the provisions of the Covenant. Recently, the HRC has also begun to accept evidence in the form of written reports submitted by human rights and other organisations from the country concerned.[21] The HRC has no fact-finding powers of its own and is therefore dependent on the papers submitted, which can make it difficult to verify whether violations of the Covenant have taken place.

The HRC's consideration of the State reports are subsequently made public, usually in the form of a transcript of the hearings of officials representing the country, but sometimes in the form of a report. There is no enforcement mechanism (unlike the European Court of Human Rights, which can require a State to make changes to its legislation), and NGOs have described the procedure as merely an exercise in public embarrassment. Nevertheless, decisions reached by the HRC are generally complied with even though they are not legally binding.[22] The HRC can also order States to pay compensation and to undertake measures to prevent similar violations in future.

---

21   In its July 1995 Comments to the Report submitted under Article 40 of the Covenant by the United Kingdom (see *supra* note 8), the HRC states in paragraph 3 that: "The detailed information submitted by a wide range of non-governmental organisations has not only greatly assisted the Committee but is also a tribute to the democratic nature of United Kingdom society. These organisations play an essential role in furthering protection of human rights in the country."

22   For example, the case of 192 Haitian asylum seekers detained at the US Naval Base at Guantanamo Bay for up to 18 months was brought before the Working Group on Arbitrary Detention. The asylum seekers were detained because they had been tested positive for HIV and the US government argued that it was not in a position to provide them with

Under the 1966 Optional Protocol to the Covenant an additional monitoring mechanism was established, that of an individual communications procedure allowing individuals to submit complaints against ratifying States Parties. Article 1 of the Optional Protocol states that:

> "A State Party to the Covenant that becomes a party to the present Protocol recognises the competence of the Committee to receive and consider communications from individuals subject to its jurisdiction who claim to be victims of a violation by that State Party of any of the rights set forth in the Covenant. No communication shall be received by the Committee if it concerns a State Party to the Covenant which is not a party to the present Protocol."

As at December 1996, 134 States (two thirds of the world community) had ratified the Covenant. Of these, however, only 89 had become parties to the Optional Protocol. In the European context today, this effectively bars all detainees, including of course asylum seekers, from seeking justice and compensation under the provisions of Article 9 in certain countries, such as Albania, Azerbaijan, Greece, Turkey (the latter two countries have not ratified the Covenant either), Switzerland and the United Kingdom.

A further constraint in terms of implementation of the Covenant lies in the fact that a number of countries have submitted reservations, some of them immigration-related. Although the purpose of these reservations is to specify in greater detail how the provisions will be implemented in the State concerned, States are in effect exempting themselves from fulfilling certain obligations.[23]

V   Conclusion

From the foregoing we have seen that Article 9 of the ICCPR and Article 37 of the CRC recognise the fundamental right of every person to liberty and security. Individuals may only be detained if this is carried out in accordance with national legislation and their detention is not arbitrary; that is, where detention is necessary, proportional and is imposed without discrimination. When asylum seekers are detained, they deserve special attention, bearing in mind the fact that they may already have been incarcerated for lengthy periods of time, tortured or forced to endure other forms of persecution prior to arrival in the country of asylum. This element should also be taken into account when determining the length of detention.

---

appropriate medical care. In response to a report by the Working Group (21 December 1994), this practice was discontinued.

23 The UK government has also entered reservations to the CRC, stating that it will continue to apply provisions relating to UK immigration and nationality law.

Ideally, asylum seekers who are children/minors should not be detained at all, and if detention is necessary it should, in accordance with Article 37(b) of the CRC, be used only as "a measure of last resort and for the shortest appropriate period of time".

All the provisions of Article 37 of the CRC should be seen in the light of the guiding principle which appears in its Article 3:

"In all actions concerning children, whether undertaken by public or private social welfare institutions, courts of law, administrative authorities or legislative bodies, the best interests of the child shall be a primary consideration."

The provisions of Article 37 of the CRC should also be read in conjunction with Article 22 of the CRC, which grants refugee children or asylum seekers who are minors appropriate protection and humanitarian assistance in the enjoyment of rights set out in the CRC and any other international agreement to which the State is a party, whether the children are accompanied or not. To this effect, States are urged to cooperate with relevant organisations which can provide such protection and assistance.

Furthermore, according to Article 9 of the CRC, States should not separate children from their parents unless this is in the best interests of the child. This principle is used on some occasions by the authorities as a reason to justify detention of whole families of asylum seekers. It is, however, submitted that this would represent an argument not to detain any member of the family. This view is supported by reference to Article 37 of the CRC, which, as mentioned above, only permits detention of minors as a measure of last resort.

Asylum seekers are neither criminals nor suspected criminals; they have not forfeited their right to liberty in any way. The procedural safeguards provided for in Article 9 of the ICCPR and Article 37 of the CRC should therefore be rigorously observed in their case. In particular, the reasons for their detention should be explained to them in a language and in terms which they understand. Anything less than this seriously undermines their ability to fully exercise their right to challenge their detention under Article 9(4) of the ICCPR and Article 37(d) of the CRC. In accordance with Article 9(4), such an appeal should be made to a body independent of the detaining authority on a periodic basis and ideally the asylum seeker should receive some form of legal assistance.

States which have not done so should be encouraged to ratify both the ICCPR and its Optional Protocol, and incorporate their provisions into their domestic legislation to ensure that they are fully effective. Continued failure on the part of States to ratify the Covenant and/or the Optional Protocol may be construed as tacit admission that national practices could not withstand comparison with internationally accepted standards of protection. Moreover, the rights of asylum seekers would already be greatly enhanced under the existing Covenant were those States which have entered immigration-related reservations to withdraw them.

Despite the fact that the individual communications procedure provided for under the ICCPR is relatively straightforward, it is considered by some experts to be under-utilised. The opportunities for remedy contained in this and similar mechanisms under other instruments should be publicised and explored in order to encourage lawyers and others acting on behalf of detained asylum seekers to challenge their detention before supranational bodies. National NGOs could also play a more prominent role by submitting written evidence to the Human Rights Committee when it is scrutinising a State's performance under the periodic reporting procedure.

Ultimately, however, as Rodley observes, "law is only one tool for improving the lot of humanity. It can regulate only the society that has absorbed its values."[24] The challenge of the future is, then, to ensure that human rights are applied and enforced in the daily practice of States, and that effective international action is taken against States which fail to comply with their obligations.

---

24 See *supra* note 15.

Chapter 9 The Mental Health Implications of the Detention of Asylum Seekers

By Christina Pourgourides

Contents

Part I   Introduction
Part II   Selected case studies
Part III Detention and the current reception of asylum seekers in Europe
Part IV   Research into the mental health of refugees and detainees
Part V   The 1995–96 research project on the mental health of detained asylum seekers in the United Kingdom: Methodology
Part VI   Findings of the research project: VI.1 Information vacuum – VI.2 Detention conditions – VI.3 Need for external support – VI.4 Effect of detention on the asylum process – VI.5 Medical care – VI.6 General observations
Part VII Concluding comments

I   Introduction

"... Yes, at the very first beginning when I came to the UK I felt that I would be prepared to go through whatever came, even if dangerous. I prepared myself mentally to go through anything, but after two or three months I started thinking: Where was I? Why? What were the reasons I was being detained, if I just came to the UK to seek asylum? After all the things I have been through in my country, and of course I came expecting that you give me protection and freedom. The protection I was never given in my country because the situation was so bad that you had no freedom to speak about anything.

And then I come to your country and suddenly I realise I see myself in detention, in prison being moved from one place to another and I was very young and down and disgusted. I start to think, what is the human race, you know?

Many people were being treated like animals, I don't know how to describe it ... life was always eating the same food and sleeping and going to interviews. You get a lot of things in your mind from your country, you become broken and down ... After two months I started taking tablets, starting to think a lot, crying ... Just four walls, just walking and keep talking and being watched by the cameras whatever move you do, listening for the time they call you to come to interviews, calling for whatever thing they want, even the most insignificant thing, an interview or coming to take your photo for reasons they never say.

I mean, you get upset. This is not a reception that people who seek asylum except. No one can expect this."

Former detainee

This chapter provides a short summary of a report entitled "A Second Exile: The Mental Health Implications of Detention of Asylum Seekers in the United Kingdom", published by the North Birmingham Mental Health Trust in 1996.[1] It presents the findings of a research project developed in response to the increased demand for psychiatric assessments of detained asylum seekers received by a number of psychiatrists in the West Midlands.

In 1995, a picture had begun to emerge of a beleaguered group of people, many of whom had already experienced detention, torture and persecution in their country of origin, presenting in detention with what appeared to be symptoms of mental illness including depression, anxiety, psychosis and deliberate self harm.

The research project was set up to investigate the experiences of this group in greater detail in an attempt to establish why they presented as they did, how their symptoms arose, the response to such symptoms and the ways in which these could be prevented. The project was initiated by a group of concerned psychiatrists and the research work was carried out by the author, also a qualified psychiatrist, over a period of 12 months from July 1995 to July 1996. The project was funded jointly by the Barrow Cadbury Trust and the North Birmingham Mental Health Trust, with the grant being made available through the University of Birmingham's Department of Psychiatry.

The chapter begins with two selected case studies, which are then set in the context of the current climate of reception of asylum seekers in Europe. The chapter goes on to assess existing literature and research into the mental health of refugees, before outlining the methodology used by the 1995–96 research project and its principal findings. These findings will certainly be of relevance to detained asylum seekers in many other countries. The chapter concludes with a summary of the key recommendations of the research project.

---

[1] Copies of the full report (115 pages, including summaries of individual interviews and a comprehensive list of references) may be obtained from the Academic Unit, 71, Fentham Road, Erdington, Birmingham B23 6AL, UK.

CHAPTER 9   THE MENTAL HEALTH IMPLICATIONS

II   **Selected case studies**

Case No. 1: Ali is a 30 year old single Muslim from Algeria seen in detention in August 1995. He had been held for five months.
He grew up within a close-knit, stable family, training as a teacher and completing his military service before embarking on a career. He had a stable personality and no past psychiatric history.
He became increasingly politically active and campaigned on behalf of a party banned by the ruling regime, whose forces visited his home searching for him. He was arrested and imprisoned for several months. During this time he was denied visits from his family or access to a solicitor. He was severely tortured, including being severely beaten, and being forced to drink contaminated water. Electric shocks were applied over his body, including his genitalia. He was burnt with cigarettes, frequently losing consciousness whilst being tortured. He was at times held in solitary confinement, at times in overcrowded cells with others. His arms, shoulder and skull were fractured. He was transferred to hospital and following an operation he was returned to custody for the torture to be continued.
In the most shattering experience of his ordeal, he was tied to a bed and raped by one of the prison guards. This was painful, humiliating and terrifying.
He was eventually released, went into hiding and then fled Algeria. Following his arrival in the UK, where he sought asylum, he was detained by the authorities.
In prison he described his situation as a "living hell". He was unable to understand why he had been detained and why he was being treated like a criminal having committed no crime. Following an exchange with a fellow inmate he was punished by being held in solitary confinement for a three day period. He was particularly disturbed inside his cell, which resembled the one he had been held in whilst in Algeria. The uniformed guards acted as a constant reminder of his torturers. He found it difficult to communicate his needs in English. He felt suspicious of the prison authorities and of other inmates who mimicked the Muslim call to prayer as he tried to pray.
When interviewed in detention, he was severely agitated, trembling from top to toe. He was restless, made little eye contact and at times became extremely distressed, when he would gesticulate and hyperventilate. Later he became irritable and angry. He described feeling low, unable to sleep. Food had no taste and he did not feel hungry. He could not concentrate and felt he was losing his memory. He felt constantly afraid and was easily startled. He felt desperate, hopeless and helpless.
He had been troubled by voices speaking to him when alone and had seen blood on the walls of his cell as well as feeling a sinister presence in the room

which appeared to be a figure of a man dressed in black. He expressed a fear that he was going mad in prison.
He could see no future for himself and felt no hope of resuming a normal life. He had considered suicide and had made an attempt to hang himself in his cell, which was prevented by a guard carrying out a routine check. He said: "How can you give back life to a dead man?"

Case No. 2: Jose is a 24 year old Angolan man born to refugee parents in Zaire. He and his family walked back overland to Angola when he was aged five in a journey which he recalls vividly. They returned to their native village where he described a poverty-stricken but relatively happy childhood despite the fact that his mother was chronically ill with tuberculosis. When he was aged 13, his village was ambushed by the ruling government forces. During the attack, a rocket landed on the family home, killing his mother and two sisters whilst they slept. He described the horror of seeing their mutilated bodies and being unable to go to them as the only option was to flee.
He was captured by soldiers and held captive over the next two years in a military school. He escaped, living in derelict houses and in hiding over the next two years before managing to flee the country.
On arrival in the UK he claimed asylum. He was provided with accommodation, received benefits and embarked on English language classes. He began to rebuild his life, participating in sport and beginning to make friends. He formed a relationship with a British girl and her family. Some time later he was arrested and detained. His asylum application was refused and he was threatened with deportation.
At interview, he was in an agitated state, experiencing vivid and disturbing recollections of the bombing of his village and the killing of his family triggered by loud bangs or by film footage of war, such as news bulletins from Bosnia. During these episodes of recall, the images of the past were so vivid that he felt they were real. He awoke frequently from nightmares of the bombing. He told the prison doctor of the problem, and was given sleeping tablets which were unhelpful. A further prescription of anti-depressant tablets made him drowsy and dizzy.
Despite the ongoing support of his friends and girlfriend, he felt that perhaps it would have been better if he had been killed along with his family in Angola.

III Detention and the current reception of asylum seekers in Europe

In recent years the "climate of receptiveness" towards asylum seekers has cooled in Europe as a whole. There have been ongoing intergovernmental consultations regarding Europe's response to asylum seekers. This response is becoming more hostile. The increasing use of detention is one manifestation of this hostility. Since the 1993 Asylum and Immigration Appeal Act, the number of detentions in the UK has tripled. Approximately 11,000 people are detained in total over the course of a year, and 850 may be detained at any one time. UNHCR has indicated that asylum seekers should not normally be held in detention: "[I]n view of the hardship which it involves, detention should normally be avoided." The Home Office has said that detention is used only as "a last resort". It has also said that "all personal factors, including an individual's state of health, are taken into account in the decision to detain".

Detention is thought to be required for a number of apparently clear reasons, but the problem appears to be that in practice, detention appears arbitrary and is used too widely. Immigration officers are empowered to detain by the Immigration Act 1971. They are not required to give written reasons for their decision, and the examination prior to detention can be cursory. People consequently do not know why they are being detained or for how long they will be held. The average period of detention is 154 days. That is longer than the average period in remand in the UK and is a long time to be held under such uncertainty.

UNHCR has said that "the conditions of detention must be humane. Asylum seekers shall, wherever possible, not be accommodated with persons detained as common criminals." There are specially designated immigration detention centres, such as Campsfield House in Oxfordshire, but prisons are also being used to detain asylum seekers. In June 1994, 39% of detainees were held in prison. This is particularly distressing and bewildering for asylum seekers who have not been charged with or convicted of any offence.

Her Majesty's Chief Inspector of Prisons has said that prisons are "not suitable" for the holding of asylum seekers, having "insufficient staff and facilities to meet their particular needs". He has also been critical of the detention centres. In a report in 1995 he concluded that:

> "... [D]etention without time limit, no matter how reasonable the conditions, is extremely stressful. When combined with an uncertain future, language difficulties, a perceived or real lack of information, and the fact that some detainees appear to be terrified at the prospect of being deported, the stress increases."

IV   Research into the mental health of refugees and detainees

A wealth of psychiatric literature exists on the mental health problems of refugees and a smaller body of work on the experiences of detainees, but the plight of detained refugees or asylum seekers is a phenomenon which has received little attention by health professionals.

Numerous studies have established that refugees carry with them experiences of oppression and trauma that often go well beyond the individual experiences common to western urban societies. They have experienced military harassment, the death of family or friends, violence, rape and torture, occurring in climates of fear, mistrust and threat in which they are deprived of control over their own lives and overwhelmed by feelings of powerlessness. They have experienced the destruction of their society, culture and community. As a consequence, they undergo the experience of "cultural bereavement" where they grieve for multiple losses which touch every area of their lives.

In such a context, people who take flight may also experience the stress of an unpredictable and dangerous journey. On arrival in a host country, as well as relief they experience a range of emotions including homesickness, nostalgia, guilt for having fled and anxiety about loved ones left behind. They experience profound discontinuity in their lives, where they have to adapt to a change of role and status within an unknown context, where their status is uncertain and where language and cultural difficulties place them in marginal positions of isolation.

All these experiences predispose to the development of mental illness. Multiple studies have shown that refugees may experience depression, anxiety, morbid thoughts, psychosomatic symptoms and so on. They may feel pain, and if traumatic memories fade, they may find constant images of the past intruding into daily life. This can sometimes manifest as symptoms of Post Traumatic Stress Disorder (PTSD), first described in survivors of Cambodian refugee camps.

Further, it is well established that captivity is stressful in any context, but particularly so in pre-trial detention or remand, where a person has made a rapid transition from being at liberty to being in captivity. The initial stages are particularly stressful and we know that symptoms of psychological disturbance are more likely during the relatively early stages of incarceration, with suicide rates particularly high among those recently taken into custody and those on remand. Where there is no termination date the situation is even more stressful. The normal prison population can pace themselves through a sentence or towards a trial. In studies on political detention in South Africa, detention of unknown duration has been found to be particularly stressful. Detainees experience sleep disturbance, depression, withdrawal, anxiety and so on. They are undermined by debility, dependence and dread in an environment which is uncontrollable, unpredictable and unaccountable. These conditions are similar to the predicaments people face in torture situations, and detention has been called "torture without violence".

CHAPTER 9   THE MENTAL HEALTH IMPLICATIONS

V   **The 1995–96 research project on the mental health of detained asylum seekers in the United Kingdom: Methodology**

As mentioned above, the 1995–96 research project set out to document the experiences of detained asylum seekers and to explore the systems in place to meet their mental health needs and the problems which existed in practice. The project used a qualitative research methodology and involved extensive consultations with both detainees and other relevant individuals and organisations.

A series of fifteen in-depth, semi-structured interviews thus took place with detainees themselves, while they were in detention. They had been referred by legal representatives who had become concerned about their mental state and were requesting a psychiatric assessment.

The other individuals and organisations who were consulted during the course of the project were divided into broad categories: health professionals (including the Medical Foundation for the Care of Victims of Torture), legal representatives, volunteer visitors (including the Association of Visitors to Immigration Detainees), campaigning groups (including the British Refugee Council, the Asylum Rights Campaign, the European Council for Refugees and Exiles (ECRE) and the Joint Council for the Welfare of Immigrants), refugee community organisations, relatives of detainees and former detainees. These are all people who know something of the phenomenon being studied. They were invited to come together in a series of seven "focus groups". A focus group capitalises on communication between research participants to generate the data. They can ask questions to each other, exchange anecdotes and comment on experiences, without the imposition of *a priori* categories imposed by the researcher.

The interviewed population did not represent a random sample, and thus the findings cannot be extrapolated to the whole detained population. But the cases illustrate, with real life examples, many of the key issues. People seemed to cope in the first one–two months of detention and they would break down in the third or fourth month when their legal representative would note problems. They were all male, and they were young – the average age was 29 years. They had been detained for an average period of eight months (range 3–22 months). They had suffered multiple previous traumatic experiences with one third suffering bereavement, one third previous detention and one third torture. They were desperate and hopeless overall, with one third of them having made attempts at deliberate self harm (DSH), including ingestion of glass, self mutilation, attempted hanging and overdose. They presented with depressive and post traumatic symptoms, with one third fulfilling diagnostic criteria for PTSD and two thirds for depression. They were a vulnerable group. As a result of the reports produced, ten of the fifteen persons were released. One required in-patient treatment and three went on to receive counselling. Six of the ten went on to be given refugee status or exceptional leave to remain (ELR).

These findings give the lie to the government line that people's health is taken into consideration in the decision to detain, and the assurance that people likely to be given asylum are immediately released. There had been no screening, or only inadequate screening, prior to detention. Subsequent examination in detention failed to identify problems correctly. No-one had actually detected their distress and their symptoms in detention.

VI Findings of the research project

VI.1 Information vacuum

The focus groups revealed a wide range of themes. The most debilitating aspect of detention is the "information vacuum" in which detainees are placed. This is particularly so given the language problems in detention. The unknown duration, reasons and outcome of detention are particularly stressful for detainees. It renders them hopeless and helpless. They cannot pace themselves through a fixed period of time. They face the threat of transfer to another detention location and the fear of deportation, alongside the constant hope of release.

VI.2 Detention conditions

Detention conditions are harsh, especially in prisons, with long periods when detainees are actually locked into their cells for up to 14–22 hours a day. Lack of privacy, visiting restrictions and limits on making and receiving telephone calls make life particularly difficult. Although detention centres are more comfortable and have greater freedom of association than common prisons, they lack some of the facilities and resources available in prison, such as access to education, opportunities for worship and a culturally appropriate diet.

VI.3 Need for external support

Immigration officers and detention centre staff are seen as intimidating or combative. There is solidarity and mutual support between detainees, but there may also be some hostility among detainees along ethnic divisions or simply because of the close proximity in which they live.

Detained asylum seekers rely on positive contact and support with outside agencies, particularly legal representatives who are seen as the main hope of release, though unreliable legal representatives generated frustration amongst detainees. Volunteer visitors were also seen as a source of support. In the UK, an organisation called the Association of Visitors to Immigration Detainees has established a national network of volunteers who coordinate visits, liaise with each other and are now taking part in training programmes to improve the service they provide. It is a valuable non-statutory source of support. Visitors cited lack of clarity over their role and confusion of boundaries as creating complex emotional situations between themselves and detainees. Difficulties identified included detainees being placed in positions of unavoidable dependency. Detainees also rely heavily on services such as the Samaritans, a charity run volunteer telephone helpline providing counselling for crises such as suicidal ideation.

VI.4   Effect of detention on the asylum process

The asylum process was seen as an inseparable part of the experience of detainees. The procedure is a complex one. Interviews with the immigration authorities are an integral part of this procedure. Such interviews may be difficult for asylum seekers, necessitating the disclosure of often sensitive, detailed personal information. Establishing trust in the setting of such an interview is difficult. Asylum seekers may have had previously negative contacts with officials in their country of origin. It was recognised that the scrutiny of asylum claims can be undermining, where it focuses on questioning the credibility of an individual's testimony through identifying inconsistencies. There is a lack of acknowledgement on the part of the authorities that traumatic memories may be suppressed and therefore difficult to recall in their entirety.

VI.5   Medical care

Medical provision in detention centres and prisons is currently unsatisfactory. Detention centres lack 24 hour medical cover and have no facilities to deal with serious illness. Communication with medical staff is complicated by language difficulties, with the practice of using fellow detainees as interpreters deemed unacceptable. There is a failure to identify psychological symptoms. There is a high use of medication, even for underlying psychological problems. Screening for the physical and psychological sequelae of torture is limited. Examination of mental state and screening for suicidal ideas is rudimentary. Suicidal persons and others requiring treatment may be transferred from a detention centre to a prison hospital, which is punitive and unfair. It compounds the stress and despair of detainees, particularly suicidal detainees. Access to specialist medical opinion and psychiatric opinion in particular is not always readily available. Medical care in prisons is provided by the Prison Medical Service. In detention centres care is provided by a private agency in a contract with the Immigration Service. There is no transparency in this arrangement, with no information on accountability, no training and no protocols for managing suicide attempts, hunger-strikes etc.

The Home Office has made somewhat contradictory statements regarding medical care. It has insisted that medical staff are "employed to look after the general health and well being of detainees and are not equipped to make judgements on whether people have suffered torture". This is to seriously overlook the impact of torture on health. The Home Office further insists that "[d]octors are vigilant in identifying cases of serious concern". This does not appear to be the case in practice.

VI.6   General observations

General themes to emerge included the notion that detention deprives asylum seekers of access to the sources of support and the coping strategies which aid psychological healing and adaptation to the host society, such as family and community relationships, education and employment. Thus equipped people can rebuild in the aftermath of loss. In detention such building blocks are not available. Detention halts adaptation completely and is therefore the ultimate hostile reception. It constitutes a total denial of refugee experiences which are therefore invalidated.

The context of the experience was seen as important. Detention may be the last straw for someone who has been previously detained or tortured. But paradoxically, detention back home was seen as secondary to political activity or struggle and it was somehow more understandable, meaningful and easier to bear than arbitrary detention in the UK. Asylum seekers feel a profound ambivalence in seeking sanctuary in an environment of ongoing threat and hostility. In detention they lack landmarks to their identity and sense of self. In captivity they have copious time to contemplate traumatic past, unendurable present and unknown future. The concept of post traumatic stress is a misnomer when trauma is ongoing and not consigned to the past. Coping with the effects of institutionalisation was seen as a major problem upon release from detention.

Detainees are rendered hopeless and powerless in detention and their responses, which include distress, despondency, demotivation, anxiety and so on are normal responses to an abnormal situation. They can manifest in groups of symptoms consistent with psychiatric diagnoses but can also be seen as manifestations of suffering. This suffering and misery are generated by the practice of detention. A number of commentators feel that this is intentional, and that detention serves a deterrent function.

VII   Concluding comments

Detention results in severe psychological problems and is harmful to the mental health of detainees. It is abusive and inhumane. It recreates the environment of oppression, fear and uncertainty from which people have fled. In doing so, it compounds the stress they have endured, deprives them of their capacity to survive

CHAPTER 9 THE MENTAL HEALTH IMPLICATIONS

and creates new and pressing problems in host countries which are currently not being adequately dealt with.

The annual cost of detention runs to some GBP 20 million per year in the UK. However, the human cost in terms of misery and suffering is far greater. Release from detention would go a long way to ameliorating or preventing mental health problems and alleviating suffering. This is a powerful argument against detention. There is sufficiently compelling evidence that detention is a noxious practice which should be opposed on medical and humanitarian grounds.

The research team concluded the 1996 report on the mental implications of detention of asylum seekers with the following five key comments and recommendations:

1. The findings from our research on the impact of detention on the mental health of asylum seekers show that detention is likely to result in severe psychological problems and is harmful to the mental health of those detained.
2. We strongly recommend, therefore, that the current policy of detaining asylum seekers be abandoned because of the significant risk it poses to the mental health of the people involved, and that more humane and workable alternatives to detention be sought as a matter of priority.
3. As this is unlikely in the short term, and as long as detention is continued as part of government policy in dealing with asylum seekers, we recommend that appropriate safeguards be introduced to minimise the psychological damage on those detained. We recommend a review of the current procedures with this specific objective. A number of measures could be implemented immediately which would go some way to improving the situation of those currently in detention.[2]
4. Given that this research has pointed to detention as damaging to the mental health of asylum seekers, this should increase the urgency of attempts to bring about an end to the practice of detention. Networking, campaigning, liaison and information exchange between groups and individuals should focus on this primary objective.
5. Our enquiry was in the form of preliminary qualitative research. It has brought to light the substantial suffering associated with detention. There is now a need for further research into this area, to document the longer term effects of detention and its impact on adjustment in the host country. This is particularly urgent in view of the recent changes in legislation in this area.

---

[2] These are listed on pp. 101–103 of the full report; see also the recommendations contained in the 1996 ECRE *Position Paper on the Detention of Asylum Seekers*, in Appendix VII.1 to this book.

Appendices

APPENDICES

Table of Contents

Appendix I	**Universal Instruments**	**215**
I.1	1951 Convention relating to the Status of Refugees	215
I.2	1966 International Covenant on Civil and Political Rights	217
I.3	1966 Optional Protocol to the International Covenant on Civil and Political Rights	220
I.4	1984 Convention against Torture and Other Cruel, Inhuman or Degrading Treatment or Punishment	221
I.5	1989 Convention on the Rights of the Child	223
Appendix II	**Universal Standards**	**225**
II.1	1948 Universal Declaration on Human Rights	225
II.2	1955 Standard Minimum Rules for the Treatment of Prisoners, Economic and Social Council Resolution 663 C (XXIV) of 31 July 1957 and 2076 (LXII) of 13 May 1977	226
II.3	1988 Body of Principles for the Protection of All Persons under any Form of Detention or Imprisonment	245
Appendix III	**Regional Instruments**	**255**
III.1	1950 European Convention for the Protection of Human Rights and Fundamental Freedoms	255
III.2	1963 Protocol No. 4 to the European Convention for the Protection of Human Rights and Fundamental Freedoms, securing certain Rights and Freedoms other than those already included in the Convention and in the First Protocol thereto	257
III.3	1987 European Convention for the Prevention of Torture and Inhuman or Degrading Treatment or Punishment	258
III.4	1969 American Convention on Human Rights	262
III.5	1981 African Charter on Human and People's Rights	264
Appendix IV	**General Comments by the UN Human Rights Committee**	**267**
IV.1	General Comment 7, Article 7 (Sixteenth Session, 1982)	267

IV.2   General Comment 8, Article 9 (Sixteenth Session, 1982)   269
IV.3   General Comment 15 (Twenty-seventh Session, 1986)   270
IV.4   General Comment 21, Article 10 (Forty-fourth Session, 1992) ...   273

Appendix V   UNHCR Executive Committee Conclusions   277

V.1   Conclusion No. 22 (XXXII) – 1981 – Protection of Asylum
       Seekers in Situations of Large-Scale Influx   277
V.2   Conclusion No. 44 (XXXVII) – 1986 – Detention of Refugees
       and Asylum Seekers   281
V.3   Conclusion No. 58 (XL) – 1989 – Problem of Refugees and
       Asylum Seekers Who Move in an Irregular Manner from a
       Country in Which They Had Already Found Protection   283

Appendix VI   UNHCR Guidelines   287

VI.1   1995 UNHCR Guidelines on Detention   287
VI.2   1994 UNHCR Guidelines on Refugee Children   294

Appendix VII NGO recommendations   297

VII.1 1996 ECRE Position Paper on Detention   297
VII.2 1997 ECRE Research Paper on Alternatives to Detention –
       Practical alternatives to the administrative detention of asylum
       seekers and rejected asylum seekers   310
VII.3 The Australian Alternative Detention Model   324

Appendix I   Universal Instruments

I.1   1951 Convention relating to the Status of Refugees

Article 8: Exemption from exceptional measures

With regard to exceptional measures which may be taken against the person, property or interests of nationals of a foreign State, the Contracting States shall not apply such measures to a refugee who is formally a national of the said State solely on account of such nationality. Contracting States which, under their legislation, are prevented from applying the general principle expressed in this article, shall, in appropriate cases, grant exemptions in favour of such refugees.

Article 26: Freedom of movement

Each Contracting State shall accord to refugees lawfully in its territory the right to choose their place of residence and to move freely within its territory subject to any regulations applicable to aliens generally in the same circumstances.

Article 31: Refugees unlawfully in the country of refuge

1. The Contracting States shall not impose penalties, on account of their illegal entry or presence, on refugees who, coming directly from a territory where their life or freedom was threatened in the sense of article 1, enter or are present in their territory without authorization, provided they present themselves without delay to the authorities and show good cause for their illegal entry or presence.
2. The Contracting States shall not apply to the movements of such refugees restrictions other than those which are necessary and such restrictions shall only be applied until their status in the country is regularized or they obtain admission into another country. The Contracting States shall allow such refugees a reasonable period and all the necessary facilities to obtain admission into another country.

Article 33: Prohibition of expulsion or return ("refoulement")

1. No Contracting State shall expel or return ("refouler") a refugee in any manner whatsoever to the frontiers of territories where his life or freedom would be

2. The benefit of the present provision may not, however, be claimed by a refugee whom there are reasonable grounds for regarding as a danger to the security of the country in which he is, or who, having been convicted by a final judgment of a particularly serious crime, constitutes a danger to the community of that country.

Article 35: Co-operation of the national authorities with the United Nations

1. The Contracting States undertake to co-operate with the Office of the United Nations High Commissioner for Refugees, or any other agency of the United Nations which may succeed it, in the exercise of its functions, and shall in particular facilitate its duty of supervising the application of the provisions of this Convention.

2. In order to enable the Office of the High Commissioner, or any other agency of the United Nations which may succeed it, to make reports to the competent organs of the United Nations, the Contracting States undertake to provide them in the appropriate form with information and statistical data requested concerning:
(a) The condition of refugees,
(b) The implementation of this Convention, and
(c) Laws, regulations and decrees which are, or may hereafter be, in force relating to refugees.

APPENDIX I   UNIVERSAL INSTRUMENTS

I.2   1966 International Covenant on Civil and Political Rights

Article 2

1. Each State Party to the present Covenant undertakes to respect and to ensure to all individuals within its territory and subject to its jurisdiction the rights recognized in the present Covenant, without distinction of any kind, such as race, colour, sex, language, religion, political or other opinion, national or social origin, property, birth or other status.

2. Where not already provided for by existing legislative or other measures, each State Party to the present Covenant undertakes to take the necessary steps, in accordance with its constitutional processes and with the provisions of the present Covenant, to adopt such laws or other measures as may be necessary to give effect to the rights recognized in the present Covenant.

3. Each State Party to the present Covenant undertakes:
(a) To ensure that any person whose rights or freedoms as herein recognized are violated shall have an effective remedy, notwithstanding that the violation has been committed by persons acting in an official capacity;
(b) To ensure that any person claiming such a remedy shall have his right thereto determined by competent judicial, administrative or legislative authorities, or by any other competent authority provided for by the legal system of the State, and to develop the possibilities of judicial remedy;
(c) To ensure that the competent authorities shall enforce such remedies when granted.

Article 7

No one shall be subjected to torture or to cruel, inhuman or degrading treatment or punishment. In particular, no one shall be subjected without his free consent to medical or scientific experimentation.

Article 9

1. Everyone has the right to liberty and security of person. No one shall be subjected to arbitrary arrest or detention. No one shall be deprived of his liberty except on such grounds and in accordance with such procedure as are established by law.

2. Anyone who is arrested shall be informed, at the time of arrest, of the reasons for his arrest and shall be promptly informed of any charges against him.

3. Anyone arrested or detained on a criminal charge shall be brought promptly before a judge or other officer authorized by law to exercise judicial power and shall

be entitled to trial within a reasonable time or to release. It shall not be the general rule that persons awaiting trial shall be detained in custody, but release may be subject to guarantees to appear for trial, at any other stage of the judicial proceedings, and, should occasion arise, for execution of the judgment.

4. Anyone who is deprived of his liberty by arrest or detention shall be entitled to take proceedings before a court, in order that court may decide without delay on the lawfulness of his detention and order his release if the detention is not lawful.

5. Anyone who has been the victim of unlawful arrest or detention shall have an enforceable right to compensation.

Article 10

1. All persons deprived of their liberty shall be treated with humanity and with respect for the inherent dignity of the human person.

2. (a) Accused persons shall, save in exceptional circumstances, be segregated from convicted persons and shall be subject to separate treatment appropriate to their status as unconvicted persons;

(b) Accused juvenile persons shall be separated from adults and brought as speedily as possible for adjudication.

3. The penitentiary system shall comprise treatment of prisoners the essential aim of which shall be their reformation and social rehabilitation. Juvenile offenders shall be segregated from adults and be accorded treatment appropriate to their age and legal status.

Article 12

1. Everyone lawfully within the territory of a State shall, within that territory, have the right to liberty of movement and freedom to choose his residence.

2. Everyone shall be free to leave any country, including his own.

3. The above-mentioned rights shall not be subject to any restrictions except those which are provided by law, are necessary to protect national security, public order (*ordre public*), public health or morals or the rights and freedoms of others, and are consistent with the other rights recognized in the present Covenant.

4. No one shall be arbitrarily deprived of the right to enter his own country.

Article 13

An alien lawfully in the territory of a State Party to the present Covenant may be expelled therefrom only in pursuance of a decision reached in accordance with law and shall, except where compelling reasons of national security otherwise require, be allowed to submitt the reasons against his expulsion and to have his case reviewed by, and be represented for the purpose before, the competent authority or a person or persons especially designated by the competent authority.

Article 40

1. The States Parties to the present Covenant undertake to submit reports on the measures they have adopted which give effect to the rights recognized herein and on the progress made in the enjoyment of those rights:
(a) Within one year of the entry into force of the present Covenant for the States Parties concerned;
(b) Thereafter whenever the Committee so requests.
2. All reports shall be submitted to the Secretary-General of the United Nations, who shall transmit them to the Committee for consideration. Reports shall indicate the factors and difficulties, if any, affecting the implementation of the present Covenant.
3. The Secretary-General of the United Nations may, after consultation with the Committee, transmit to the specialized agencies concerned copies of such parts of the reports as may fall within their field of competence.
4. The Committee shall study the reports submitted by the States Parties to the present Covenant. It shall transmit its reports, and such general comments as it may consider appropriate, to the States Parties. The Committee may also transmit to the Economic and Social Council these comments along with the copies of the reports it has received from States Parties to the present Covenant.
5. The States Parties to the present Covenant may submit to the Committee observations on any comments that may be made in accordance with paragraph 4 of this article.

I.3 1966 Optional Protocol to the International Covenant on Civil and Political Rights

Article 1

A State Party to the Covenant that becomes a Party to the present Protocol recognizes the competence of the Committee to receive and consider communications from individuals subject to its jurisdiction who claim to be victims of a violation by that State Party of any of the rights set forth in the Covenant. No communication shall be received by the Committee if it concerns a State Party to the Covenant which is not a Party to the present Protocol.

APPENDIX I   UNIVERSAL INSTRUMENTS

I.4   1984 Convention against Torture and Other Cruel, Inhuman or Degrading Treatment or Punishment

Article 3

1. No State Party shall expel, return ("refouler") or extradite a person to another State where there are substantial grounds for believing that he would be in danger of being subjected to torture.

2. For the purpose of determining whether there are such grounds, the competent authorities shall take into account all relevant considerations including, where applicable, the existence in the State concerned of a consistent pattern of gross, flagrant or mass violations of human rights.

Article 16

1. Each State Party shall undertake to prevent in any territory under its jurisdiction other acts of cruel, inhuman or degrading treatment or punishment which do not amount to torture as defined in article I, when such acts are committed by or at the instigation of or with the consent or acquiescence of a public official or other person acting in an official capacity. In particular, the obligations contained in articles 10, 11, 12 and 13 shall apply with the substitution for references to torture of references to other forms of cruel, inhuman or degrading treatment or punishment.

2. The provisions of this Convention are without prejudice to the provisions of any other international instrument or national law which prohibits cruel, inhuman or degrading treatment or punishment or which relates to extradition or expulsion.

Article 22

1. A State Party to this Convention may at any time declare under this article that it recognizes the competence of the Committee to receive and consider communications from or on behalf of individuals subject to its jurisdiction who claim to be victims of a violation by a State Party of the provisions of the Convention. No communication shall be received by the Committee if it concerns a State Party which has not made such a declaration.

2. The Committee shall consider inadmissible any communication under this article which is anonymous or which it considers to be an abuse of the right of submission of such communications or to be incompatible with the provisions of this Convention.

3. Subject to the provisions of paragraph 2, the Committee shall bring any communications submitted to it under this article to the attention of the State Party to this Convention which has made a declaration under paragraph I and is alleged to

be violating any provisions of the Convention. Within six months, the receiving State shall submit to the Committee written explanations or statements clarifying the matter and the remedy, if any, that may have been taken by that State.

4. The Committee shall consider communications received under this article in the light of all information made available to it by or on behalf of the individual and by the State Party concerned.

5. The Committee shall not consider any communications from an individual under this article unless it has ascertained that:
(a) The same matter has not been, and is not being, examined under another procedure of international investigation or settlement;
(b) The individual has exhausted all available domestic remedies; this shall not be the rule where the application of the remedies is unreasonably prolonged or is unlikely to bring effective relief to the person who is the victim of the violation of this Convention.

6. The Committee shall hold closed meetings when examining communications under this article.

7. The Committee shall forward its views to the State Party concerned and to the individual.

8. The provisions of this article shall come into force when five States Parties to this Convention have made declarations under paragraph 1 of this article. Such declarations shall be deposited by the States Parties with the Secretary-General of the United Nations, who shall transmit copies thereof to the other States Parties. A declaration may be withdrawn at any time by notification to the Secretary-General. Such a withdrawal shall not prejudice the consideration of any matter which is the subject of a communication already transmitted under this article; no further communication by or on behalf of an individual shall be received under this article after the notification of withdrawal of the declaration has been received by the SecretaryGeneral, unless the State Party has made a new declaration.

I.5 1989 Convention on the Rights of the Child

Article 3

1. In all actions concerning children, whether undertaken by public or private social welfare institutions, courts of law, administrative authorities or legislative bodies, the best interests of the child shall be a primary consideration.
2. States Parties undertake to ensure the child such protection and care as is necessary for his or her well-being, taking into account the rights and duties of his or her parents, legal guardians, or other individuals legally responsible for him or her, and, to this end, shall take all appropriate legislative and administrative measures.
3. States Parties shall ensure that the institutions, services and facilities responsible for the care or protection of children shall conform with the standards established by competent authorities, particularly in the areas of safety, health, in the number and suitability of their staff, as well as competent supervision.

Article 9

1. States Parties shall ensure that a child shall not be separated from his or her parents against their will, except when competent authorities subject to judicial review determine, in accordance with applicable law and procedures, that such separation is necessary for the best interests of the child. Such determination may be necessary in a particular case such as one involving abuse or neglect of the child by the parents, or one where the parents are living separately and a decision must be made as to the child's place of residence.
2. In any proceedings pursuant to paragraph 1 of the present article, all interested parties shall be given an opportunity to participate in the proceedings and make their views known.
3. States Parties shall respect the right of the child who is separated from one or both parents to maintain personal relations and direct contact with both parents on a regular basis, except if it is contrary to the child's best interests.
4. Where such separation results from any action initiated by a State Party, such as the detention, imprisonment, exile, deportation or death (including death arising from any cause while the person is in the custody of the State) of one or both parents or of the child, that State Party shall, upon request, provide the parents, the child or, if appropriate, another member of the family with the essential information concerning the whereabouts of the absent member(s) of the family unless the provision of the information would be detrimental to the well-being of the child. States Parties shall further ensure that the submission of such a request shall of itself entail no adverse consequences for the person(s) concerned.

Article 22

1. States Parties shall take appropriate measures to ensure that a child who is seeking refugee status or who is considered a refugee in accordance with applicable international or domestic law and procedures shall, whether unaccompanied or accompanied by his or her parents or by any other person, receive appropriate protection and humanitarian assistance in the enjoyment of applicable rights set forth in the present Convention and in other international human rights or humanitarian instruments to which the said States are Parties.

2. For this purpose, States Parties shall provide, as they consider appropriate, co-operation in any efforts by the United Nations and other competent intergovernmental organizations or non-governmental organizations co-operating with the United Nations to protect and assist such a child and to trace the parents or other members of the family of any refugee child in order to obtain information necessary for reunification with his or her family. In cases where no parents or other members of the family can be found, the child shall be accorded the same protection as any other child permanently or temporarily deprived of his or her family environment for any reason , as set forth in the present Convention.

Article 37

States Parties shall ensure that:
(a) No child shall be subjected to torture or other cruel, inhuman or degrading treatment or punishment. Neither capital punishment nor life imprisonment without possibility of release shall be imposed for offences committed by persons below eighteen years of age;
(b) No child shall be deprived of his or her liberty unlawfully or arbitrarily. The arrest, detention or imprisonment of a child shall be in conformity with the law and shall be used only as a measure of last resort and for the shortest appropriate period of time;
(c) Every child deprived of liberty shall be treated with humanity and respect for the inherent dignity of the human person, and in a manner which takes into account the needs of persons of his or her age. In particular, every child deprived of liberty shall be separated from adults unless it is considered in the child's best interest not to do so, and shall have the right to maintain contact with his or her family through correspondence and visits, save in exceptional circumstances;
(d) Every child deprived of his or her liberty shall have the right to prompt access to legal and other appropriate assistance, as well as the right to challenge the legality of the deprivation of his or her liberty before a court or other competent, independent and impartial authority, and to a prompt decision on any such action.

Appendix II   Universal Standards

II.1   1948 Universal Declaration on Human Rights

Article 3

Everyone has the right to life, liberty and security of person.

Article 14

1. Everyone has the right to seek and to enjoy in other countries asylum from persecution.
2. This right may not be invoked in the case of prosecutions genuinely arising from non-political crimes or from acts contrary to the purposes and principles of the United Nations.

II.2 1955 Standard Minimum Rules for the Treatment of Prisoners, Economic and Social Council Resolution 663 C (XXIV) of 31 July 1957 and 2076 (LXII) of 13 May 1977

Preliminary observations

1. The following rules are not intended to describe in detail a model system of penal institutions. They seek only, on the basis of the general consensus of contemporary thought and the essential elements of the most adequate systems of today, to set out what is generally accepted as being good principle and practice in the treatment of prisoners and the management of institutions.

2. In view of the great variety of legal, social, economic and geographical conditions of the world, it is evident that not all of the rules are capable of application in all places and at all times. They should, however, serve to stimulate a constant endeavour to overcome practical difficulties in the way of their application, in the knowledge that they represent, as a whole, the minimum conditions which are accepted as suitable by the United Nations.

3. On the other hand, the rules cover a field in which thought is constantly developing. They are not intended to preclude experiment and practices, provided these are in harmony with the principles and seek to further the purposes which derive from the text of the rules as a whole. It will always be justifiable for the central prison administration to authorize departures from the rules in this spirit.

4. (1) Part I of the rules covers the general management of institutions, and is applicable to all categories of prisoners, criminal or civil, untried or convicted, including prisoners subject to "security measures" or corrective measures ordered by the judge.
(2) Part II contains rules applicable only to the special categories dealt with in each section. Nevertheless, the rules under section A, applicable to prisoners under sentence, shall be equally applicable to categories of prisoners dealt with in sections B, C and D, provided they do not conflict with the rules governing those categories and are for their benefit.

5. (1) The rules do not seek to regulate the management of institutions set aside for young persons such as Borstal institutions or correctional schools, but in general part I would be equally applicable in such institutions.
(2) The category of young prisoners should include at least all young persons who come within the jurisdiction of juvenile courts. As a rule, such young persons should not be sentenced to imprisonment.

APPENDIX II   UNIVERSAL STANDARDS

Part I   Rules of general application

Basic principle

6. (1) The following rules shall be applied impartially. There shall be no discrimination on grounds of race, colour, sex, language, religion, political or other opinion, national or social origin, property, birth or other status.
(2) On the other hand, it is necessary to respect the religious beliefs and moral precepts of the group to which a prisoner belongs.

Register

7. (1) In every place where persons are imprisoned there shall be kept a bound registration book with numbered pages in which shall be entered in respect of each prisoner received:
(a) Information concerning his identity;
(b) The reasons for his commitment and the authority therefor;
(c) The day and hour of his admission and release.
(2) No person shall be received in an institution without a valid commitment order of which the details shall have been previously entered in the register.

Separation of categories

8. The different categories of prisoners shall be kept in separate institutions or parts of institutions taking account of their sex, age, criminal record, the legal reason for their detention and the necessities of their treatment. Thus,
(a) Men and women shall so far as possible be detained in separate institutions; in an institution which receives both men and women the whole of the premises allocated to women shall be entirely separate;
(b) Untried prisoners shall be kept separate from convicted prisoners;
(c) Persons imprisoned for debt and other civil prisoners shall be kept separate from persons imprisoned by reason of a criminal offence;
(d) Young prisoners shall be kept separate from adults.

Accommodation

9. (1) Where sleeping accommodation is in individual cells or rooms, each prisoner shall occupy by night a cell or room by himself. If for special reasons, such as temporary overcrowding, it becomes necessary for the central prison administration to make an exception to this rule, it is not desirable to have two prisoners in a cell or room.

(2) Where dormitories are used, they shall be occupied by prisoners carefully selected as being suitable to associate with one another in those conditions. There shall be regular supervision by night, in keeping with the nature of the institution.

10. All accommodation provided for the use of prisoners and in particular all sleeping accommodation shall meet all requirements of health, due regard being paid to climatic conditions and particularly to cubic content of air, minimum floor space, lighting, heating and ventilation.

11. In all places where prisoners are required to live or work,
(a) The windows shall be large enough to enable the prisoners to read or work by natural light, and shall be so constructed that they can allow the entrance of fresh air whether or not there is artificial ventilation;
(b) Artificial light shall be provided sufficient for the prisoners to read or work without injury to eyesight.

12. The sanitary installations shall be adequate to enable every prisoner to comply with the needs of nature when necessary and in a clean and decent manner.

13. Adequate bathing and shower installations shall be provided so that every prisoner may be enabled and required to have a bath or shower, at a temperature suitable to the climate, as frequently as necessary for general hygiene according to season and geographical region, but at least once a week in a temperate climate.

14 All pans of an institution regularly used by prisoners shall be properly maintained and kept scrupulously clean at all times.

Personal hygiene

15. Prisoners shall be required to keep their persons clean, and to this end they shall be provided with water and with such toilet articles as are necessary for health and cleanliness.

16. In order that prisoners may maintain a good appearance compatible with their self-respect, facilities shall be provided for the proper care of the hair and beard, and men shall be enabled to shave regularly.

APPENDIX II   UNIVERSAL STANDARDS

Clothing and bedding

17. (1) Every prisoner who is not allowed to wear his own clothing shall be provided with an outfit of clothing suitable for the climate and adequate to keep him in good health. Such clothing shall in no manner be degrading or humiliating.

(2) All clothing shall be clean and kept in proper condition. Underclothing shall be changed and washed as often as necessary for the maintenance of hygiene.

(3) In exceptional circumstances, whenever a prisoner is removed outside the institution for an authorized purpose, he shall be allowed to wear his own clothing or other inconspicuous clothing.

18. If prisoners are allowed to wear their own clothing, arrangements shall be made on their admission to the institution to ensure that it shall be clean and fit for use.

19. Every prisoner shall, in accordance with local or national standards, be provided with a separate bed, and with separate and sufficient bedding which shall be clean when issued, kept in good order and changed often enough to ensure its cleanliness.

Food

20. (1) Every prisoner shall be provided by the administration at the usual hours with food of nutritional value adequate for health and strength, of wholesome quality and well prepared and served.

(2) Drinking water shall be available to every prisoner whenever he needs it.

Exercise and sport

21. (1) Every prisoner who is not employed in outdoor work shall have at least one hour of suitable exercise in the open air daily if the weather permits.

(2) Young prisoners, and others of suitable age and physique, shall receive physical and recreational training during the period of exercise. To this end space, installations and equipment should be provided.

Medical services

22. (1) At every institution there shall be available the services of at least one qualified medical officer who should have some knowledge of psychiatry. The medical services should be organized in close relationship to the general health

administration of the community or nation. They shall include a psychiatric service for the diagnosis and, in proper cases, the treatment of states of mental abnormality.

(2) Sick prisoners who require specialist treatment shall be transferred to specialized institutions or to civil hospitals. Where hospital facilities are provided in an institution, their equipment, furnishings and pharmaceutical supplies shall be proper for the medical care and treatment of sick prisoners, and there shall be a staff of suitable trained officers.

(3) The services of a qualified dental officer shall be available to every prisoner.

23. (1) In women's institutions there shall be special accommodation for all necessary pre-natal and post-natal care and treatment. Arrangements shall be made wherever practicable for children to be born in a hospital outside the institution. If a child is born in prison, this fact shall not be mentioned in the birth certificate.

(2) Where nursing infants are allowed to remain in the institution with their mothers, provision shall be made for a nursery staffed by qualified persons, where the infants shall be placed when they are not in the care of their mothers.

24. The medical officer shall see and examine every prisoner as soon as possible after his admission and thereafter as necessary, with a view particularly to the discovery of physical or mental illness and the taking of all necessary measures; the segregation of prisoners suspected of infectious or contagious conditions; the noting of physical or mental defects which might hamper rehabilitation; and the determination of the physical capacity of every prisoner for work.

25. (1) The medical officer shall have the care of the physical and mental health of the prisoners and should daily see all sick prisoners, all who complain of illness, and any prisoner to whom his attention is specially directed.

(2) The medical officer shall report to the director whenever he considers that a prisoner's physical or mental health has been or will be injuriously affected by continued imprisonment or by any condition of imprisonment.

26. (1) The medical officer shall regularly inspect and advise the director upon:
(a) The quantity, quality, preparation and service of food;
(b) The hygiene and cleanliness of the institution and the prisoners;
(c) The sanitation, heating, lighting and ventilation of the institution;
(d) The suitability and cleanliness of the prisoners' clothing and bedding;
(e) The observance of the rules concerning physical education and sports, in cases where there is no technical personnel in charge of these activities.

(2) The director shall take into consideration the reports and advice that the medical officer submits according to rules 25 (2) and 26 and, in case he concurs

with the recommendations made, shall take immediate steps to give effect to those recommendations; if they are not within his competence or if he does not concur with them, he shall immediately submit his own report and the advice of the medical officer to higher authority.

Discipline and punishment

27. Discipline and order shall be maintained with firmness, but with no more restriction than is necessary for safe custody and well-ordered community life.

28. (1) No prisoner shall be employed, in the service of the institution, in any disciplinary capacity.
 (2) This rule shall not, however, impede the proper functioning of systems based on self-government, under which specified social, educational or sports activities or responsibilities are entrusted, under supervision, to prisoners who are formed into groups for the purposes of treatment.

29. The following shall always be determined by the law or by the regulation of the competent administrative authority:
(a) Conduct constituting a disciplinary offence;
(b) The types and duration of punishment which may be inflicted;
(c) The authority competent to impose such punishment.

30. (1) No prisoner shall be punished except in accordance with the terms of such law or regulation, and never twice for the same offence.
 (2) No prisoner shall be punished unless he has been informed of the offence alleged against him and given a proper opportunity of presenting his defence. The competent authority shall conduct a thorough examination of the case.
 (3) Where necessary and practicable the prisoner shall be allowed to make his defence through an interpreter.

31. Corporal punishment, punishment by placing in a dark cell, and all cruel, inhuman or degrading punishments shall be completely prohibited as punishments for disciplinary offences.

32. (1) Punishment by close confinement or reduction of diet shall never be inflicted unless the medical officer has examined the prisoner and certified in writing that he is fit to sustain it.
 (2) The same shall apply to any other punishment that may be prejudicial to the physical or mental health of a prisoner. In no case may such punishment be contrary to or depart from the principle stated in rule 31.

(3) The medical officer shall visit daily prisoners undergoing such punishments and shall advise the director if he considers the termination or alteration of the punishment necessary on grounds of physical or mental health.

Instruments of restraint

33. Instruments of restraint, such as handcuffs, chains, irons and strait-jacket, shall never be applied as a punishment. Furthermore, chains or irons shall not be used as restraints. Other instruments of restraint shall not be used except in the following circumstances:
(a) As a precaution against escape during a transfer, provided that they shall be removed when the prisoner appears before a judicial or administrative authority;
(b) On medical grounds by direction of the medical officer;
(c) By order of the director, if other methods of control fail, in order to prevent a prisoner from injuring himself or others or from damaging property; in such instances the director shall at once consult the medical officer and report to the higher administrative authority.

34. The patterns and manner of use of instruments of restraint shall be decided by the central prison administration. Such instruments must not be applied for any longer time than is strictly necessary.

Information to and complaints by prisoners

35. (1) Every prisoner on admission shall be provided with written information about the regulations governing the treatment of prisoners of his category, the disciplinary requirements of the institution, the authorized methods of seeking information and making complaints, and all such other matters as are necessary to enable him to understand both his rights and his obligations and to adapt himself to the life of the institution.
(2) If a prisoner is illiterate, the aforesaid information shall be conveyed to him orally.

36. (1) Every prisoner shall have the opportunity each week day of making requests or complaints to the director of the institution or the officer authorized to represent him.
(2) It shall be possible to make requests or complaints to the inspector of prisons during his inspection. The prisoner shall have the opportunity to talk to the inspector or to any other inspecting officer without the director or other members of the staff being present.

(3) Every prisoner shall be allowed to make a request or complaint, without censorship as to substance but in proper form, to the central prison administration, the judicial authority or other proper authorities through approved channels.

(4) Unless it is evidently frivolous or groundless, every request or complaint shall be promptly dealt with and replied to without undue delay.

Contact with the outside world

37. Prisoners shall be allowed under necessary supervision to communicate with their family and reputable friends at regular intervals, both by correspondence and by receiving visits.

38. (1) Prisoners who are foreign nationals shall be allowed reasonable facilities to communicate with the diplomatic and consular representatives of the State to which they belong.

(2) Prisoners who are nationals of States without diplomatic or consular representation in the country and refugees or stateless persons shall be allowed similar facilities to communicate with the diplomatic representative of the State which takes charge of their interests or any national or international authority whose task it is to protect such persons.

39. Prisoners shall be kept informed regularly of the more important items of news by the reading of newspapers, periodicals or special institutional publications, by hearing wireless transmissions, by lectures or by any similar means as authorized or controlled by the administration.

Books

40. Every institution shall have a library for the use of all categories of prisoners, adequately stocked with both recreational and instructional books, and prisoners shall be encouraged to make full use of it.

Religion

41. (1) If the institution contains a sufficient number of prisoners of the same religion, a qualified representative of that religion shall be appointed or approved. If the number of prisoners justifies it and conditions permit, the arrangement should be on a full-time basis.

(2) A qualified representative appointed or approved under paragraph (1) shall be allowed to hold regular services and to pay pastoral visits in private to prisoners of his religion at proper times.

(3) Access to a qualified representative of any religion shall not be refused to any prisoner. On the other hand, if any prisoner should object to a visit of any religious representative, his attitude shall be fully respected.

42. So far as practicable, every prisoner shall be allowed to satisfy the needs of his religious life by attending the services provided in the institution and having in his possession the books of religious observance and instruction of his denomination.

Retention of prisoners' property

43. (1) All money, valuables, clothing and other effects belonging to a prisoner which under the regulations of the institution he is not allowed to retain shall on his admission to the institution be placed in safe custody. An inventory thereof shall be signed by the prisoner. Steps shall be taken to keep them in good condition.
 (2) On the release of the prisoner all such articles and money shall be returned to him except in so far as he has been authorized to spend money or send any such property out of the institution, or it has been found necessary on hygienic grounds to destroy any article of clothing. The prisoner shall sign a receipt for the articles and money returned to him.
 (3) Any money or effects received for a prisoner from outside shall be treated in the same way.
 (4) If a prisoner brings in any drugs or medicine, the medical officer shall decide what use shall be made of them.

Notification of death, illness, transfer, etc.

44. (1) Upon the death or serious illness of, or serious injury to a prisoner, or his removal to an institution for the treatment of mental affections, the director shall at once inform the spouse, if the prisoner is married, or the nearest relative and shall in any event inform any other person previously designated by the prisoner.
 (2) A prisoner shall be informed at once of the death or serious illness of any near relative. In case of the critical illness of a near relative, the prisoner should be authorized, whenever circumstances allow, to go to his bedside either under escort or alone.
 (3) Every prisoner shall have the right to inform at once his family of his imprisonment or his transfer to another institution.

APPENDIX II   UNIVERSAL STANDARDS

Removal of prisoners

45. (1) When the prisoners are being removed to or from an institution, they shall be exposed to public view as little as possible, and proper safeguards shall be adopted to protect them from insult, curiosity and publicity in any form.

(2) The transport of prisoners in conveyances with inadequate ventilation or light, or in any way which would subject them to unnecessary physical hardship, shall be prohibited.

(3) The transport of prisoners shall be carried out at the expense of the administration and equal conditions shall obtain for all of them.

Institutional personnel

46. (1) The prison administration, shall provide for the careful selection of every grade of the personnel, since it is on their integrity, humanity, professional capacity and personal suitability for the work that the proper administration of the institutions depends.

(2) The prison administration shall constantly seek to awaken and maintain in the minds both of the personnel and of the public the conviction that this work is a social service of great importance, and to this end all appropriate means of informing the public should be used.

(3) To secure the foregoing ends, personnel shall be appointed on a full-time basis as professional prison officers and have civil service status with security of tenure subject only to good conduct, efficiency and physical fitness. Salaries shall be adequate to attract and retain suitable men and women; employment benefits and conditions of service shall be favourable in view of the exacting nature of the work.

47. (1) The personnel shall possess an adequate standard of education and intelligence.

(2) Before entering on duty, the personnel shall be given a course of training in their general and specific duties and be required to pass theoretical and practical tests.

(3) After entering on duty and during their career, the personnel shall maintain and improve their knowledge and professional capacity by attending courses of in-service training to be organized at suitable intervals.

48. All members of the personnel shall at all times so conduct themselves and perform their duties as to influence the prisoners for good by their example and to command their respect.

49. (1) So far as possible, the personnel shall include a sufficient number of specialists such as psychiatrists, psychologists, social workers, teachers and trade instructors.

(2) The services of social workers, teachers and trade instructors shall be secured on a permanent basis, without thereby excluding part-time or voluntary workers.

50. (1) The director of an institution should be adequately qualified for his task by character, administrative ability, suitable training and experience.

(2) He shall devote his entire time to his official duties and shall not be appointed on a part-time basis.

(3) He shall reside on the premises of the institution or in its immediate vicinity.

(4) When two or more institutions are under the authority of one director, he shall visit each of them at frequent intervals. A responsible resident official shall be in charge of each of these institutions.

51. (1) The director, his deputy, and the majority of the other personnel of the institution shall be able to speak the language of the greatest number of prisoners, or a language understood by the greatest number of them.

(2) Whenever necessary, the services of an interpreter shall be used.

52. (1) In institutions which are large enough to require the services of one or more full-time medical officers, at least one of them shall reside on the premises of the institution or in its immediate vicinity.

(2) In other institutions the medical officer shall visit daily and shall reside near enough to be able to attend without delay in cases of urgency.

53. (1) In an institution for both men and women, the part of the institution set aside for women shall be under the authority of a responsible woman officer who shall have the custody of the keys of all that part of the institution.

(2) No male member of the staff shall enter the part of the institution set aside for women unless accompanied by a woman officer.

(3) Women prisoners shall be attended and supervised only by women officers. This does not, however, preclude male members of the staff, particularly doctors and teachers, from carrying out their professional duties in institutions or parts of institutions set aside for women.

54. (1) Officers of the institutions shall not, in their relations with the prisoners, use force except in self-defence or in cases of attempted escape, or active or passive physical resistance to an order based on law or regulations. Officers who have

recourse to force must use no more than is strictly necessary and must report the incident immediately to the director of the institution.

(2) Prison officers shall be given special physical training to enable them to restrain aggressive prisoners.

(3) Except in special circumstances, staff performing duties which bring them into direct contact with prisoners should not be armed. Furthermore, staff should in no circumstances be provided with arms unless they have been trained in their use.

Inspection

55. There shall be a regular inspection of penal institutions and services by qualified and experienced inspectors appointed by a competent authority. Their task shall be in particular to ensure that these institutions are administered in accordance with existing laws and regulations and with a view to bringing about the objectives of penal and correctional services.

Part II   Rules applicable to special categories

A. Prisoners under sentence

Guiding principles

56. The guiding principles hereafter are intended to show the spirit in which penal institutions should be administered and the purposes at which they should aim, in accordance with the declaration made under Preliminary Observation I of the present text.

57. Imprisonment and other measures which result in cutting off an offender from the outside world are afflictive by the very fact of taking from the person the right of self-determination by depriving him of his liberty. Therefore the prison system shall not, except as incidental to justifiable segregation or the maintenance of discipline, aggravate the suffering inherent in such a situation.

58. The purpose and justification of a sentence of imprisonment or a similar measure deprivative of liberty is ultimately to protect society against crime. This end can only be achieved if the period of imprisonment is used to ensure, so far as possible, that upon his return to society the offender is not only willing but able to lead a law-abiding and self-supporting life.

59. To this end, the institution should utilize all the remedial, educational, moral, spiritual and other forces and forms of assistance which are appropriate and available, and should seek to apply them according to the individual treatment needs of the prisoners.

60. (1) The regime of the institution should seek to minimize any differences between prison life and life at liberty which tend to lessen the responsibility of the prisoners or the respect due to their dignity as human beings.

(2) Before the completion of the sentence, it is desirable that the necessary steps be taken to ensure for the prisoner a gradual return to life in society. This aim may be achieved, depending on the case, by a pre-release regime organized in the same institution or in another appropriate institution, or by release on trial under some kind of supervision which must not be entrusted to the police but should be combined with effective social aid.

61. The treatment of prisoners should emphasize not their exclusion from the community, but their continuing part in it. Community agencies should, therefore, be enlisted wherever possible to assist the staff of the institution in the task of social rehabilitation of the prisoners. There should be in connection with every institution social workers charged with the duty of maintaining and improving all desirable relations of a prisoner with his family and with valuable social agencies. Steps should be taken to safeguard, to the maximum extent compatible with the law and the sentence, the rights relating to civil interests, social security rights and other social benefits of prisoners.

62. The medical services of the institution shall seek to detect and shall treat any physical or mental illnesses or defects which may hamper a prisoner's rehabilitation. All necessary medical, surgical and psychiatric services shall be provided to that end.

63. (1) The fulfilment of these principles requires individualization of treatment and for this purpose a flexible system of classifying prisoners in groups; it is therefore desirable that such groups should be distributed in separate institutions suitable for the treatment of each group.

(2) These institutions need not provide the same degree of security for every group. It is desirable to provide varying degrees of security according to the needs of different groups. Open institutions, by the very fact that they provide no physical security against escape but rely on the self-discipline of the inmates, provide the conditions most favourable to rehabilitation for carefully selected prisoners.

(3) It is desirable that the number of prisoners in closed institutions should not be so large that the individualization of treatment is hindered. In some countries

it is considered that the population of such institutions should not exceed five hundred. In open institutions the population should be as small as possible.

(4) On the other hand, it is undesirable to maintain prisons which are so small that proper facilities cannot be provided.

64. The duty of society does not end with a prisoner's release. There should, therefore, be governmental or private agencies capable of lending the released prisoner efficient after-care directed towards the lessening of prejudice against him and towards his social rehabilitation.

Treatment

65. The treatment of persons sentenced to imprisonment or a similar measure shall have as its purpose, so far as the length of the sentence permits, to establish in them the will to lead law-abiding and self-supporting lives after their release and to fit them to do so. The treatment shall be such as will encourage their self-respect and develop their sense of responsibility.

66. (1) To these ends, all appropriate means shall be used, including religious care in the countries where this is possible, education, vocational guidance and training, social casework, employment counselling, physical development and strengthening of moral character, in accordance with the individual needs of each prisoner, taking account of his social and criminal history, his physical and mental capacities and aptitudes, his personal temperament, the length of his sentence and his prospects after release.

(2) For every prisoner with a sentence of suitable length, the director shall receive, as soon as possible after his admission, full reports on all the matters referred to in the foregoing paragraph. Such reports shall always include a report by a medical officer, wherever possible qualified in psychiatry, on the physical and mental condition of the prisoner.

(3) The reports and other relevant documents shall be placed in an individual file. This file shall be kept up to date and classified in such a way that it can be consulted by the responsible personnel whenever the need arises.

Classification and individualization

67. The purposes of classification shall be:
(a) To separate from others those prisoners who, by reason of their criminal records or bad characters, are likely to exercise a bad influence;
(b) To divide the prisoners into classes in order to facilitate their treatment with a view to their social rehabilitation.

68. So far as possible separate institutions or separate sections of an institution shall be used for the treatment of the different classes of prisoners.

69. As soon as possible after admission and after a study of the personality of each prisoner with a sentence of suitable length, a programme of treatment shall be prepared for him in the light of the knowledge obtained about his individual needs, his capacities and dispositions.

Privileges

70. Systems of privileges appropriate for the different classes of prisoners and the different methods of treatment shall be established at every institution, in order to encourage good conduct, develop a sense of responsibility and secure the interest and co-operation of the prisoners in their treatment.

Work

71. (1) Prison labour must not be of an afflictive nature.
(2) All prisoners under sentence shall be required to work, subject to their physical and mental fitness as determined by the medical officer.
(3) Sufficient work of a useful nature shall be provided to keep prisoners actively employed for a normal working day.
(4) So far as possible the work provided shall be such as will maintain or increase the prisoners' ability to earn an honest living after release.
(5) Vocational training in useful trades shall be provided for prisoners able to profit thereby and especially for young prisoners.
(6) Within the limits compatible with proper vocational selection and with the requirements of institutional administration and discipline, the prisoners shall be able to choose the type of work they wish to perform.

72. (1) The organization and methods of work in the institutions shall resemble as closely as possible those of similar work outside institutions, so as to prepare prisoners for the conditions of normal occupational life.
(2) The interests of the prisoners and of their vocational training, however, must not be subordinated to the purpose of making a financial profit from an industry in the institution.

73. (1) Preferably institutional industries and farms should be operated directly by the administration and not by private contractors.
(2) Where prisoners are employed in work not controlled by the administration, they shall always be under the supervision of the institution's

personnel. Unless the work is for other departments of the government the full normal wages for such work shall be paid to the administration by the persons to whom the labour is supplied, account being taken of the output of the prisoners.

74. (1) The precautions laid down to protect the safety and health of free workmen shall be equally observed in institutions.
(2) Provision shall be made to indemnify prisoners against industrial injury, including occupational disease, on terms not less favourable than those extended by law to free workmen.

75. (1) The maximum daily and weekly working hours of the prisoners shall be fixed by law or by administrative regulation, taking into account local rules or custom in regard to the employment of free workmen.
(2) The hours so fixed shall leave one rest day a week and sufficient time for education and other activities required as part of the treatment and rehabilitation of the prisoners.

76. (1) There shall be a system of equitable remuneration of the work of prisoners.
(2) Under the system prisoners shall be allowed to spend at least a part of their earnings on approved articles for their own use and to send a part of their earnings to their family.
(3) The system should also provide that a part of the earnings should be set aside by the administration so as to constitute a savings fund to be handed over to the prisoner on his release.

Education and recreation

77. (1) Provision shall be made for the further education of all prisoners capable of profiting thereby, including religious instruction in the countries where this is possible. The education of illiterates and young prisoners shall be compulsory and special attention shall be paid to it by the administration.
(2) So far as practicable, the education of prisoners shall be integrated with the educational system of the country so that after their release they may continue their education without difficulty.

78. Recreational and cultural activities shall be provided in all institutions for the benefit of the mental and physical health of prisoners.

Social relations and after-care

79. Special attention shall be paid to the maintenance and improvement of such relations between a prisoner and his family as are desirable in the best interests of both.

80. From the beginning of a prisoner's sentence consideration shall be given to his future after release and he shall be encouraged and assisted to maintain or establish such relations with persons or agencies outside the institution as may promote the best interests of his family and his own social rehabilitation.

81. (1) Services and agencies, governmental or otherwise, which assist released prisoners to re-establish themselves in society shall ensure, so far as is possible and necessary, that released prisoners be provided with appropriate documents and identification papers, have suitable homes and work to go to, are suitably and adequately clothed having regard to the climate and season, and have sufficient means to reach their destination and maintain themselves in the period immediately following their release.
(2) The approved representatives of such agencies shall have all necessary access to the institution and to prisoners and shall be taken into consultation as to the future of a prisoner from the beginning of his sentence.
(3) It is desirable that the activities of such agencies shall be centralized or co-ordinated as far as possible in order to secure the best use of their efforts.

B. Insane and mentally abnormal prisoners

82. (1) Persons who are found to be insane shall not be detained in prisons and arrangements shall be made to remove them to mental institutions as soon as possible.
(2) Prisoners who suffer from other mental diseases or abnormalities shall be observed and treated in specialized institutions under medical management.
(3) During their stay in a prison, such prisoners shall be placed under the special supervision of a medical officer.
(4) The medical or psychiatric service of the penal institutions shall provide for the psychiatric treatment of all other prisoners who are in need of such treatment.

83. It is desirable that steps should be taken, by arrangement with the appropriate agencies, to ensure if necessary the continuation of psychiatric treatment after release and the provision of social-psychiatric after-care.

APPENDIX II UNIVERSAL STANDARDS

C. Prisoners under arrest or awaiting trial

84. (1) Persons arrested or imprisoned by reason of a criminal charge against them, who are detained either in police custody or in prison custody (jail) but have not yet been tried and sentenced, will be referred to as "untried prisoners" hereinafter in these rules.
   (2) Unconvicted prisoners are presumed to be innocent and shall be treated as such.
   (3) Without prejudice to legal rules for the protection of individual liberty or prescribing the procedure to be observed in respect of untried prisoners, these prisoners shall benefit by a special regime which is described in the following rules in its essential requirements only.

85. (1) Untried prisoners shall be kept separate from convicted prisoners.
   (2) Young untried prisoners shall be kept separate from adults and shall in principle be detained in separate institutions.

86. Untried prisoners shall sleep singly in separate rooms, with the reservation of different local custom in respect of the climate.

87. Within the limits compatible with the good order of the institution, untried prisoners may, if they so desire, have their food procured at their own expense from the outside, either through the administration or through their family or friends. Otherwise, the administration shall provide their food.

88. (1) An untried prisoner shall be allowed to wear his own clothing if it is clean and suitable.
   (2) If he wears prison dress, it shall be different from that supplied to convicted prisoners.

89. An untried prisoner shall always be offered opportunity to work, but shall not be required to work. If he chooses to work, he shall be paid for it.

90. An untried prisoner shall be allowed to procure at his own expense or at the expense of a third party such books, newspapers, writing materials and other means of occupation as are compatible with the interests of the administration of justice and the security and good order of the institution.

91. An untried prisoner shall be allowed to be visited and treated by his own doctor or dentist if there is reasonable ground for his application and he is able to pay any expenses incurred.

92. An untried prisoner shall be allowed to inform immediately his family of his detention and shall be given all reasonable facilities for communicating with his family and friends, and for receiving visits from them, subject only to restrictions and supervision as are necessary in the interests of the administration of justice and of the security and good order of the institution.

93. For the purposes of his defence, an untried prisoner shall be allowed to apply for free legal aid where such aid is available, and to receive visits from his legal adviser with a view to his defence and to prepare and hand to him confidential instructions. For these purposes, he shall if he so desires be supplied with writing material. Interviews between the prisoner and his legal adviser may be within sight but not within the hearing of a police or institution official.

D. Civil prisoners

94. In countries where the law permits imprisonment for debt, or by order of a court under any other non-criminal process, persons so imprisoned shall not be subjected to any greater restriction or severity than is necessary to ensure safe custody and good order. Their treatment shall be not less favourable than that of untried prisoners, with the reservation, however, that they may possibly be required to work.

E. Persons arrested or detained without charges

95. Without prejudice to the provisions of article 9 of the International Covenant on Civil and Political Rights, persons arrested or imprisoned without charge shall be accorded the same protection as that accorded under part I and part II, section C. Relevant provisions of part II, section A, shall likewise be applicable where their application may be conducive to the benefit of this special group of persons in custody, provided that no measures shall be taken implying that re-education or rehabilitation is in any way appropriate to persons not convicted of any criminal offence.

APPENDIX II UNIVERSAL STANDARDS

II.3 1988 Body of Principles for the Protection of All Persons under any Form of Detention or Imprisonment

Scope of the Body of Principles

These principles apply for the protection of all persons under any form of detention or imprisonment.

Use of terms

For the purposes of the Body of Principles:

(a) "Arrest" means the act of apprehending a person for the alleged commission of an offence or by the action of an authority;
(b) "Detained person" means any person deprived of personal liberty except as a result of conviction for an offence;
(c) "Imprisoned person" means any person deprived of personal liberty as a result of conviction for an offence;
(d) "Detention" means the condition of detained persons as defined above;
(e) "Imprisonment" means the condition of imprisoned persons as defined above;
(f) The words "a judicial or other authority" means a judicial or other authority under the law whose status and tenure should afford the strongest possible guarantees of competence, impartiality and independence.

Principle 1

All persons under any form of detention or imprisonment shall be treated in a humane manner and with respect for the inherent dignity of the human person.

Principle 2

Arrest, detention or imprisonment shall only be carried out strictly in accordance with the provisions of the law and by competent officials or persons authorized for that purpose.

Principle 3

There shall be no restriction upon or derogation from any of the human rights of persons under any form of detention or imprisonment recognized or existing in any State pursuant to law, conventions, regulations or custom on the pretext that this

Body of Principles does not recognize such rights or that it recognizes them to a lesser extent.

Principle 4

Any form of detention or imprisonment and all measures affecting the human rights of a person under any form of detention or imprisonment shall be ordered by, or be subject to the effective control of, a judicial or other authority.

Principle 5

1. These principles shall be applied to all persons within the territory of any given State, without distinction of any kind, such as race, colour, sex, language, religion or religious belief, political or other opinion, national, ethnic or social origin, property, birth or other status.

2. Measures applied under the law and designed solely to protect the rights and special status of women, especially pregnant women and nursing mothers, children and juveniles, aged, sick or handicapped persons shall not be deemed to be discriminatory. The need for, and the application of, such measures shall always be subject to review by a judicial or other authority.

Principle 6

No person under any form of detention or imprisonment shall be subjected to torture or to cruel, inhuman or degrading treatment or punishment[*]. No circumstance whatever may be invoked as a justification for torture or other cruel, inhuman or degrading treatment or punishment.

[*The term "cruel, inhuman or degrading treatment or punishment" should be interpreted so as to extend the widest possible protection against abuses, whether physical or mental, including the holding of a detained or imprisoned person in conditions which deprive him, temporarily or permanently, of the use of any of his natural senses, such as sight or hearing, or of his awareness of place and the passing of time.]

Principle 7

1. States should prohibit by law any act contrary to the rights and duties contained in these principles, make any such act subject to appropriate sanctions and conduct impartial investigations upon complaints.

2. Officials who have reason to believe that a violation of this Body of Principles has occurred or is about to occur shall report the matter to their superior authorities and, where necessary, to other appropriate authorities or organs vested with reviewing or remedial powers.

3. Any other person who has ground to believe that a violation of this Body of Principles has occurred or is about to occur shall have the right to report the matter to the superiors of the officials involved as well as to other appropriate authorities or organs vested with reviewing or remedial powers.

Principle 8

Persons in detention shall be subject to treatment appropriate to their unconvicted status. Accordingly, they shall, whenever possible, be kept separate from imprisoned persons.

Principle 9

The authorities which arrest a person, keep him under detention or investigate the case shall exercise only the powers granted to them under the law and the exercise of these powers shall be subject to recourse to a judicial or other authority.

Principle 10

Anyone who is arrested shall be informed at the time of his arrest of the reason for his arrest and shall be promptly informed of any charges against him.

Principle 11

1. A person shall not be kept in detention without being given an effective opportunity to be heard promptly by a judicial or other authority. A detained person shall have the right to defend himself or to be assisted by counsel as prescribed by law.

2. A detained person and his counsel, if any, shall receive prompt and full communication of any order of detention, together with the reasons therefor.

3. A judicial or other authority shall be empowered to review as appropriate the continuance of detention.

Principle 12

1. There shall be duly recorded:
(a) The reasons for the arrest;

(b) The time of the arrest and the taking of the arrested person to a place of custody as well as that of his first appearance before a judicial or other authority;
(c) The identity of the law enforcement officials concerned;
(d) Precise information concerning the place of custody.

2. Such records shall be communicated to the detained person, or his counsel, if any, in the form prescribed by law.

Principle 13

Any person shall, at the moment of arrest and at the commencement of detention or imprisonment, or promptly thereafter, be provided by the authority responsible for his arrest, detention or imprisonment, respectively with information on and an explanation of his rights and how to avail himself of such rights.

Principle 14

A person who does not adequately understand or speak the language used by the authorities responsible for his arrest, detention or imprisonment is entitled to receive promptly in a language which he understands the information referred to in principle 10, principle 11, paragraph 2, principle 12, paragraph 1, and principle 13 and to have the assistance, free of charge, if necessary, of an interpreter in connection with legal proceedings subsequent to his arrest.

Principle 15

Notwithstanding the exceptions contained in principle 16, paragraph 4, and principle 18, paragraph 3, communication of the detained or imprisoned person with the outside world, and in particular his family or counsel, shall not be denied for more than a matter of days.

Principle 16

1. Promptly after arrest and after each transfer from one place of detention or imprisonment to another, a detained or imprisoned person shall be entitled to notify or to require the competent authority to notify members of his family or other appropriate persons of his choice of his arrest, detention or imprisonment or of the transfer and of the place where he is kept in custody.

2. If a detained or imprisoned person is a foreigner, he shall also be promptly informed of his right to communicate by appropriate means with a consular post or the diplomatic mission of the State of which he is a national or which is otherwise entitled to receive such communication in accordance with international law or with

the representative of the competent international organization, if he is a refugee or is otherwise under the protection of an intergovernmental organization.

3. If a detained or imprisoned person is a juvenile or is incapable of understanding his entitlement, the competent authority shall on its own initiative undertake the notification referred to in the present principle. Special attention shall be given to notifying parents or guardians.

4. Any notification referred to in the present principle shall be made or permitted to be made without delay. The competent authority may however delay a notification for a reasonable period where exceptional needs of the investigation so require.

Principle 17

1. A detained person shall be entitled to have the assistance of a legal counsel. He shall be informed of his right by the competent authority promptly after arrest and shall be provided with reasonable facilities for exercising it.

2. If a detained person does not have a legal counsel of his own choice, he shall be entitled to have a legal counsel assigned to him by a judicial or other authority in all cases where the interests of justice so require and without payment by him if he does not have sufficient means to pay

Principle 18

1. A detained or imprisoned person shall be entitled to communicate and consult with his legal counsel.

2. A detained or imprisoned person shall be allowed adequate time and facilities for consultation with his legal counsel.

3. The right of a detained or imprisoned person to be visited by and to consult and communicate, without delay or censorship and in full confidentiality, with his legal counsel may not be suspended or restricted save in exceptional circumstances, to be specified by law or lawful regulations, when it is considered indispensable by a judicial or other authority in order to maintain security and good order.

4. Interviews between a detained or imprisoned person and his legal counsel may be within sight, but not within the hearing, of a law enforcement official.

5. Communications between a detained or imprisoned person and his legal counsel mentioned in the present principle shall be inadmissible as evidence against the detained or imprisoned person unless they are connected with a continuing or contemplated crime.

Principle 19

A detained or imprisoned person shall have the right to be visited by and to correspond with, in particular, members of his family and shall be given adequate opportunity to communicate with the outside world, subject to reasonable conditions and restrictions as specified by law or lawful regulations.

Principle 20

If a detained or imprisoned person so requests, he shall if possible be kept in a place of detention or imprisonment reasonably near his usual place of residence.

Principle 21

1. It shall be prohibited to take undue advantage of the situation of a detained or imprisoned person for the purpose of compelling him to confess, to incriminate himself otherwise or to testify against any other person.
2. No detained person while being interrogated shall be subject to violence, threats or methods of interrogation which impair his capacity of decision or his judgment.

Principle 22

No detained or imprisoned person shall, even with his consent, be subjected to any medical or scientific experimentation which may be detrimental to his health.

Principle 23

1. The duration of any interrogation of a detained or imprisoned person and of the intervals between interrogations as well as the identity of the officials who conducted the interrogations and other persons present shall be recorded and certified in such form as may be prescribed by law.
2. A detained or imprisoned person, or his counsel when provided by law, shall have access to the information described in paragraph 1 of the present principle.

Principle 24

A proper medical examination shall be offered to a detained or imprisoned person as promptly as possible after his admission to the place of detention or imprisonment, and thereafter medical care and treatment shall be provided whenever necessary. This care and treatment shall be provided free of charge.

Principle 25

A detained or imprisoned person or his counsel shall, subject only to reasonable conditions to ensure security and good order in the place of detention or imprisonment, have the right to request or petition a judicial or other authority for a second medical examination or opinion.

Principle 26

The fact that a detained or imprisoned person underwent a medical examination, the name of the physician and the results of such an examination shall be duly recorded. Access to such records shall be ensured. Modalities therefore shall be in accordance with relevant rules of domestic law.

Principle 27

Non-compliance with these principles in obtaining evidence shall be taken into account in determining the admissibility of such evidence against a detained or imprisoned person.

Principle 28

A detained or imprisoned person shall have the right to obtain within the limits of available resources, if from public sources, reasonable quantities of educational, cultural and informational material, subject to reasonable conditions to ensure security and good order in the place of detention or imprisonment.

Principle 29

1. In order to supervise the strict observance of relevant laws and regulations, places of detention shall be visited regularly by qualified and experienced persons appointed by, and responsible to, a competent authority distinct from the authority directly in charge of the administration of the place of detention or imprisonment.

2. A detained or imprisoned person shall have the right to communicate freely and in full confidentiality with the persons who visit the places of detention or imprisonment in accordance with paragraph 1 of the present principle, subject to reasonable conditions to ensure security and good order in such places.

Principle 30

1. The types of conduct of the detained or imprisoned person that constitute disciplinary offences during detention or imprisonment, the description and duration of disciplinary punishment that may be inflicted and the authorities competent to impose such punishment shall be specified by law or lawful regulations and duly published.
2. A detained or imprisoned person shall have the right to be heard before disciplinary action is taken. He shall have the right to bring such action to higher authorities for review.

Principle 31

The appropriate authorities shall endeavour to ensure, according to domestic law, assistance when needed to dependent and, in particular, minor members of the families of detained or imprisoned persons and shall devote a particular measure of care to the appropriate custody of children left without supervision.

Principle 32

1. A detained person or his counsel shall be entitled at any time to take proceedings according to domestic law before a judicial or other authority to challenge the lawfulness of his detention in order to obtain his release without delay, if it is unlawful.
2. The proceedings referred to in paragraph 1 of the present principle shall be simple and expeditious and at no cost for detained persons without adequate means. The detaining authority shall produce without unreasonable delay the detained person before the reviewing authority.

Principle 33

1. A detained or imprisoned person or his counsel shall have the right to make a request or complaint regarding his treatment, in particular in case of torture or other cruel, inhuman or degrading treatment, to the authorities responsible for the administration of the place of detention and to higher authorities and, when necessary, to appropriate authorities vested with reviewing or remedial powers.
2. In those cases where neither the detained or imprisoned person nor his counsel has the possibility to exercise his rights under paragraph 1 of the present principle, a member of the family of the detained or imprisoned person or any other person who has knowledge of the case may exercise such rights.

3. Confidentiality concerning the request or complaint shall be maintained if so requested by the complainant.

4. Every request or complaint shall be promptly dealt with and replied to without undue delay. If the request or complaint is rejected or in case of inordinate delay, the complainant shall be entitled to bring it before a judicial or other authority. Neither the detained or imprisoned person nor any complainant under paragraph 1 of the present principle shall suffer prejudice for making a request or complaint.

Principle 34

Whenever the death or disappearance of a detained or imprisoned person occurs during his detention or imprisonment, an inquiry into the cause of death or disappearance shall be held by a judicial or other authority, either on its own motion or at the instance of a member of the family of such a person or any person who has knowledge of the case. When circumstances so warrant, such an inquiry shall be held on the same procedural basis whenever the death or disappearance occurs shortly after the termination of the detention or imprisonment. The findings of such inquiry or a report thereon shall be made available upon request, unless doing so would jeopardize an ongoing criminal investigation.

Principle 35

1. Damage incurred because of acts or omissions by a public official contrary to the rights contained in these principles shall be compensated according to the applicable rules or liability provided by domestic law.

2. Information required to be recorded under these principles shall be available in accordance with procedures provided by domestic law for use in claiming compensation under the present principle.

Principle 36

1. A detained person suspected of or charged with a criminal offence shall be presumed innocent and shall be treated as such until proved guilty according to law in a public trial at which he has had all the guarantees necessary for his defence.

2. The arrest or detention of such a person pending investigation and trial shall be carried out only for the purposes of the administration of justice on grounds and under conditions and procedures specified by law. The imposition of restrictions upon such a person which are not strictly required for the purpose of the detention or to prevent hindrance to the process of investigation or the administration of justice, or for the maintenance of security and good order in the place of detention shall be forbidden.

Principle 37

A person detained on a criminal charge shall be brought before a judicial or other authority provided by law promptly after his arrest. Such authority shall decide without delay upon the lawfulness and necessity of detention. No person may be kept under detention pending investigation or trial except upon the written order of such an authority. A detained person shall, when brought before such an authority, have the right to make a statement on the treatment received by him while in custody.

Principle 38

A person detained on a criminal charge shall be entitled to trial within a reasonable time or to release pending trial.

Principle 39

Except in special cases provided for by law, a person detained on a criminal charge shall be entitled, unless a judicial or other authority decides otherwise in the interest of the administration of justice, to release pending trial subject to the conditions that may be imposed in accordance with the law. Such authority shall keep the necessity of detention under review.

General clause

Nothing in this Body of Principles shall be construed as restricting or derogating from any right defined in the International Covenant on Civil and Political Rights.

Appendix III   Regional Instruments

III.1   1950 European Convention for the Protection of Human Rights and Fundamental Freedoms

Article 1

The High Contracting Parties shall secure to everyone within their jurisdiction the rights and freedoms defined in Section I of this Convention.

Article 3

No one shall be subjected to torture or to inhuman or degrading treatment or punishment.

Article 5

1. Everyone has the right to liberty and security of person. No one shall be deprived of his liberty save in the following cases and in accordance with a procedure prescribed by law:
(a) the lawful detention of a person after conviction by a competent court;
(b) the lawful arrest or detention of a person for non-compliance with the lawful order of a court or in order to secure the fulfilment of any obligation prescribed by law;
(c) the lawful arrest or detention of a person effected for the purpose of bringing him before the competent legal authority on reasonable suspicion of having committed an offence or when it is reasonably considered necessary to prevent his committing an offence or fleeing after having done so;
(d) the detention of a minor by lawful order for the purpose of educational supervision or his lawful detention for the purpose of bringing him before the competent legal authority;
(e) the lawful detention of persons for the prevention of the spreading of infectious diseases, of persons of unsound mind, alcoholics or drug addicts or vagrants;
(f) the lawful arrest or detention of a person to prevent his effecting an unauthorised entry into the country or of a person against whom action is being taken with a view to deportation or extradition.

3. Everyone arrested or detained in accordance with the provisions of paragraph 1(c) of this article shall be brought promptly before a judge or other officer authorised by law to exercise judicial power and shall be entitled to trial within a reasonable time or to release pending trial. Release may be conditioned by guarantees to appear for trial.
4. Everyone who is deprived of his liberty by arrest or detention shall be entitled to take proceedings by which the lawfulness of his detention shall be decided speedily by a court and his release ordered if the detention is not lawful.
5. Everyone who has been the victim of arrest or detention in contravention of the provisions of this article shall have an enforceable right to compensation.

Article 14

The enjoyment of the rights and freedoms set forth in this Convention shall be secured without discrimination on any ground such as sex, race, colour, language, religion, political or other opinion, national or social origin, association with a national minority, property, birth or other status.

Article 16

Nothing in Articles 10, 11 and 14 shall be regarded as preventing the High Contracting Parties from imposing restrictions on the political activity of aliens.

Article 25

The Commission may receive petitions addressed to the Secretary General of the Council of Europe from any person, non-governmental organisation or group of individuals claiming to be the victim of a violation by one of the High Contracting Parties of the rights set forth in this Convention, provided that the High Contracting Party against which the complaint has been lodged has declared that it recognises the competence of the Commission to receive such petitions. Those of the High Contracting Parties who have made such a declaration undertake not to hinder in any way the effective exercise of this right.
Such declarations may be made for a specific period.
The declarations shall be deposited with the Secretary General of the Council of Europe who shall transmit copies thereof to the High Contracting Parties and publish them.
The Commission shall only exercise the powers provided for in this article when at least six High Contracting Parties are bound by declarations made in accordance with the preceding paragraphs.

APPENDIX III   REGIONAL INSTRUMENTS

III.2   1963 Protocol No. 4 to the European Convention for the Protection of Human Rights and Fundamental Freedoms, securing certain Rights and Freedoms other than those already included in the Convention and in the First Protocol thereto

Article 2

Everyone lawfully within the territory of a State shall, within that territory, have the right to liberty of movement and freedom to choose his residence.

Everyone shall be free to leave any country, including his own.

No restrictions shall be placed on the exercise of these rights other than such as are in accordance with law and are necessary in a democratic society in the interests of national security or public safety, for the maintenance of ordre public, for the prevention of crime, for the protection of health or morals, or for the protection of the rights and freedoms of others.

The rights set forth in paragraph 1 may also be subject, in particular areas, to restrictions imposed in accordance with law and justified by the public interest in a democratic society.

III.3 1987 European Convention for the Prevention of Torture and Inhuman or Degrading Treatment or Punishment

Article 1

There shall be established a European Committee for the Prevention of Torture and Inhuman or Degrading Treatment or Punishment (hereinafter referred to as the "Committee"). The Committee shall, by means of visits, examine the treatment of persons deprived of their liberty with a view to strengthening, if necessary, the protection of such persons from torture and from inhuman or degrading treatment or punishment.

Article 2

Each party shall permit visits, in accordance with this Convention, to any place within its jurisdiction where persons are deprived of their liberty by a public authority.

Article 4

1. The Committee shall consist of a number of members equal to that of the Parties.
2. The members of the Committee shall be chosen from among persons of high moral character, known for their competence in the field of human rights or having professional experiences in the areas covered by this Convention.
3. No two members of the Committee may be nationals of the same State.
4. The members shall serve in their individual capacity, shall be independent and impartial, and shall be available to serve the Committee effectively.

Article 5

1. The members of the Committee shall be elected by the Committee of Ministers of the Council of Europe by an absolute majority of votes, from a list of names drawn up by the Bureau of the Consultative Assembly of the Council of Europe; each national delegation of the Parties in the Consultative Assembly shall put forward three candidates, of whom two at least shall be its nationals.
2. The same procedure shall be followed in filling casual vacancies.
3. The members of the Committee shall be elected for a period of four years. They may only be re-elected once. However, among the members elected at the first election, the terms of three members shall expire at the end of two years. The members whose terms are to expire at the end of the initial period of two years shall

be chosen by lot by the Secretary General of the Council of Europe immediately after the first election has been completed.

Article 6

1. The Committee shall meet in camera. A quorum shall be equal to the majority of its members. The decisions of the Committee shall be taken by a majority of the members present, subject to the provisions of Article 10, paragraph 2.
2. The Committee shall draw up its own rules of procedure.
3. The Secretariat of the Committee shall be provided by the Secretary General of the Council of Europe.

Article 7

1. The Committee shall organise visits to places referred to in Article 2.
Apart from periodic visits, the Committee may organise such other visits as appear to it to be required in the circumstances.
2. As a general rule, the visits shall be carried out by at least two members of the Committee. The Committee may, if it considers it necessary, be assisted by experts and interpreters.

Article 8

1. The Committee shall notify the Government of the Party concerned of its intention to carry out a visit. After such notification, it may at any time visit any place referred to in Article 2.
2. A Party shall provide the Committee with the following facilities to carry out its task: a. access to its territory and the right to travel without restriction; b. full information on the place where persons deprived of their liberty are being held; c. unlimited access to any place where persons are deprived of their liberty, including the right to move inside such places without restriction; d. other information available to the Party which is necessary for the Committee to carry out its task. In seeking such information, the Committee shall have regard to applicable rules of national law and professional ethics.
3. The Committee may interview in private persons deprived of their liberty.
4. The Committee may communicate freely with any person whom it believes can supply relevant information.
5. If necessary, the Committee may immediately communicate observations to the competent authorities of the Party concerned.

Article 9

1. In exceptional circumstances, the competent authorities of the Party concerned may make representations to the Committee against a visit at the time or to the particular place proposed by the Committee. Such representations may only be made on grounds of national defence, public safety, serious disorder in places where persons are deprived of their liberty, the medical condition of a person or that an urgent interrogation relating to a serious crime is in progress.
2. Following such representations, the Committee and the Party shall immediately enter into consultations in order to clarify the situation and seek agreement on arrangements to enable the Committee to exercise its functions expeditiously. Such arrangements may include the transfer to another place of any person whom the Committee proposed to visit. Until the visit takes place, the Party shall provide information to the Committee about any person concerned.

Article 10

1. After each visit, the Committee shall draw a report on the facts found during the visit, taking account of any observations which may have been submitted by the Party concerned. It shall transmit to the latter its report containing any recommendations it considers necessary. The Committee may consult with the Party with a view to suggesting, if necessary, improvements in the protection of persons deprived of their liberty.
2. If the Party fails to co-operate or refuses to improve the situation in the light of the Committee's recommendations, the Committee may decide, after the Party has had an opportunity to make known its views, by a majority of two-thirds of its members to make a public statement on the matter.

Article 11

1. The information gathered by the Committee in relation to a visit, its report and its consultations with the Party concerned shall be confidential.
2. The Committee shall publish its report, together with any comments of the Party concerned, whenever requested to do so by that Party.
3. However, no personal data shall be published without the express consent of the person concerned.

Article 12

Subject to the rules of confidentiality in Article 11, the Committee shall every year submit to the Committee of Ministers a general report on its activities which shall be transmitted to the Consultative Assembly and made public.

Article 13

The members of the Committee, experts and other persons assisting the Committee are required, during and after their terms of office, to maintain the confidentiality of the facts or information of which they have become aware during the discharge of their functions.

Article 14

1. The names of persons assisting the Committee shall be specified in the notification under Article 8, paragraph 1.
2. Experts shall act on the instructions and under the authority of the Committee. They shall have particular knowledge and experience in the areas covered by this Convention and shall be bound by the same duties and independence, impartiality and availability as the members of the Committee.
3. A Party may exceptionally declare that an expert or other person assisting the Committee may not be allowed to take part in a visit to a place within its jurisdiction.

Article 17

1. This Convention shall not prejudice the provisions of domestic law or any international agreement which provide greater protection for persons deprived of their liberty.
2. Nothing in this Convention shall be construed as limiting or derogating from the competence of the organs of the European Convention on Human Rights or from the obligations assumed by the Parties under that Convention.
3. The Committee shall not visit places which representatives or delegates of Protecting Powers or the International Committee of the Red Cross effectively visit on a regular basis by virtue of the Geneva Conventions of 12 August 1949 and the Additional Protocols of 8 June 1977 thereto.

III.4   1969 American Convention on Human Rights

Article 1 Obligation to Respect Rights

1. The States Parties to this Convention undertake to respect the rights and freedoms recognized herein and to ensure to all persons subject to their jurisdiction the free and full exercise of those rights and freedoms, without any discrimination for reasons of race, color, sex, language, religion, political or other opinion, national or social origin, economic status, birth, or any other social condition.
2. For the purposes of this Convention, "person" means every human being.

Article 5 Right to Humane Treatment

1. Every person has the right to have his physical, mental, and moral integrity respected.
2. No one shall be subjected to torture or to cruel, inhuman, or degrading punishment or treatment. All persons deprived of their liberty shall be treated with respect for the inherent dignity of the human person.
3. Punishment shall not be extended to any person other than the criminal.
4. Accused persons shall, save in exceptional circumstances, be segregated from convicted persons, and shall be subject to separate treatment appropriate to their status as unconvicted persons.
5. Minors while subject to criminal proceedings shall be separated from adults and brought before specialized tribunals, as speedily as possible, so that they may be treated in accordance with their status as minors.
6. Punishments consisting of deprivation of liberty shall have as an essential aim the reform and social readaptation of the prisoners.

Article 7 Right to Personal Liberty

1. Every person has the right to personal liberty and security.
2. No one shall be deprived of his physical liberty except for the reasons and under the conditions established beforehand by the constitution of the State Party concerned or by a law established pursuant thereto.
3. No one shall be subject to arbitrary arrest or imprisonment.
4. Anyone who is detained shall be informed of the reasons for his detention and shall be promptly notified of the charge or charges against him.
5. Any person detained shall be brought promptly before a judge or other officer authorized by law to exercise judicial power and shall be entitled to trial within a reasonable time or to be released without prejudice to the continuation of the

proceedings. His release may be subject to guarantees to assure his appearance for trial.

6. Anyone who is deprived of his liberty shall be entitled to recourse to a competent court, in order that the court may decide without delay on the lawfulness of his arrest or detention and order his release if the arrest or detention is unlawful. In States Parties whose laws provide that anyone who believes himself to be threatened with deprivation of his liberty is entitled to recourse to a competent court in order that it may decide on the lawfulness of such threat, this remedy may not be restricted or abolished. The interested party or another person on his behalf is entitled to seek these remedies.

7. No one shall be detained for debt. This principle shall not limit the orders of a competent judicial authority issued for nonfulfilment of duties of support.

III.5 1981 African Charter on Human and People's Rights

Article 1

The Member States of the Organization of African Unity parties to the present Charter shall recognize the rights, duties and freedoms enshrined in this Charter and shall undertake to adopt legislative or other measures to give effect to them.

Article 2

Every individual shall be entitled to the enjoyment of the rights and freedoms recognized and guaranteed in the present Charter without distinction of any kind such as race, ethnic group, colour, sex, language, religion, political or any other opinion, national and social origin, fortune, birth or other status.

Article 3

1. Every individual shall be equal before the law.
2. Every individual shall be entitled to equal protection of the law.

Article 4

Human beings are inviolable. Every human being shall be entitled to respect for his life and the integrity of his person. No one may be arbitrarily deprived of this right.

Article 5

Every individual shall have the right to the respect of the dignity inherent in a human being and to the recognition of his legal status. All forms of exploitation and degradation of man particularly slavery, slave trade, torture, cruel, inhuman or degrading punishment and treatment shall be prohibited.

Article 6

Every individual shall have the right to liberty and to the security of his person. No one may be deprived of his freedom except for reasons and conditions previously laid down by law. In particular, no one may be arbitrarily arrested or detained.

Article 7

1. Every individual shall have the right to have his cause heard. This comprises: a) The right to an appeal to competent national organs against acts of violating his fundamental rights as recognized and guaranteed by conventions, laws, regulations and customs in force; b) the right to be presumed innocent until proved guilty by a competent court or tribunal; c) the right to defence, including the right to be defended by counsel of his choice; d) the right to be tried within a reasonable time by an impartial court or tribunal.

2. No one may be condemned for an act or omission which did not constitute a legally punishable offence at the time it was committed. No penalty may be inflicted for an offence for which no provision was made at the time it was committed. Punishment is personal and can be imposed only on the offender.

Appendix IV General Comments by the UN Human Rights Committee

IV.1 General Comment 7, Article 7 (Sixteenth Session, 1982)*

1. In examining the reports of States parties, members of the Committee have often asked for further information under article 7 which prohibits, in the first place, torture or cruel, inhuman or degrading treatment or punishment. The Committee recalls that even in situations of public emergency such as are envisaged by article 4(1) this provision is non-derogable under article 4(2).

Its purpose is to protect the integrity and dignity of the individual. The Committee notes that it is not sufficient for the implementation of this article to prohibit such treatment or punishment or to make it a crime. Most States have penal provisions which are applicable to cases of torture or similar practices. Because such cases nevertheless occur, it follows from article 7, read together with article 2 of the Covenant, that States must ensure an effective protection through some machinery of control.

2. As appears from the terms of this article, the scope of protection required goes far beyond torture as normally understood. It may not be necessary to draw sharp distinctions between the various prohibited forms of treatment or punishment. These distinctions depend on the kind, purpose and severity of the particular treatment. In the view of the Committee the prohibition must extend to corporal punishment, including excessive chastisement as an educational or disciplinary measure. Even such a measure as solitary confinement may, according to the circumstances, and especially when the person is kept incommunicado, be contrary to this article. Moreover, the article clearly protects not only persons arrested or imprisoned, but also pupils and patients in educational and medical institutions. Finally, it is also the duty of public authorities to ensure protection by the law against such treatment even when committed by persons acting outside or without any official authority. For all persons deprived of their liberty, the prohibition of treatment contrary to article 7 is supplemented by the positive requirement of article 10 (1) of the Covenant that they shall be treated with humanity and with respect for the inherent dignity of the human person.

3. In particular, the prohibition extends to medical or scientific experimentation without the free consent of the person concerned (art. 7, second sentence). The Committee notes that the reports of States parties have generally given little or no information on this point. It takes the view that at least in countries where science and medicine are highly developed, and even for peoples and areas outside their borders if affected by their experiments, more attention should be given to the possible need and means to ensure the observance of this provision. Special protection in regard to such experiments is necessary in the case of persons not capable of giving their consent.

[* General Comment 7 was replaced by General Comment 20 (Forty-fourth session, 1992). Complaints about ill-treatment must be investigated effectively by competent authorities. Those found guilty must be held responsible, and the alleged victims must themselves have effective remedies at their disposal, including the right to obtain compensation. Among the safeguards which may make control effective are provisions against detention incommunicado, granting, without prejudice to the investigation, persons such as doctors, lawyers and family members access to the detainees; provisions requiring that detainees should be held in places that are publicly recognized and that their names and places of detention should be entered in a central register available to persons concerned, such as relatives; provisions making confessions or other evidence obtained through torture or other treatment contrary to article 7 inadmissible in court; and measures of training and instruction of law enforcement officials not to apply such treatment.]

APPENDIX IV   GENERAL COMMENTS BY THE UN HUMAN RIGHTS COMMITTEE

IV.2 General Comment 8, Article 9 (Sixteenth Session, 1982)

1. Article 9 which deals with the right to liberty and security of persons has often been somewhat narrowly understood in reports by States parties, and they have therefore given incomplete information. The Committee points out that paragraph 1 is applicable to all deprivations of liberty, whether in criminal cases or in other cases such as, for example, mental illness, vagrancy, drug addiction, educational purposes, immigration control, etc. It is true that some of the provisions of article 9 (part of para. 2 and the whole of para. 3) are only applicable to persons against whom criminal charges are brought. But the rest, and in particular the important guarantee laid down in paragraph 4, i.e. the right to control by a court of the legality of the detention, applies to all persons deprived of their liberty by arrest or detention. Furthermore, States parties have in accordance with article 2(3) also to ensure that an effective remedy is provided in other cases in which an individual claims to be deprived of his liberty in violation of the Covenant.

2. Paragraph 3 of article 9 requires that in criminal cases any person arrested or detained has to be brought "promptly" before a judge or other officer authorized by law to exercise judicial power. More precise time-limits are fixed by law in most States parties and, in the view of the Committee, delays must not exceed a few days. Many States have given insufficient information about the actual practices in this respect.

3. Another matter is the total length of detention pending trial. In certain categories of criminal cases in some countries this matter has caused some concern within the Committee, and members have questioned whether their practices have been in conformity with the entitlement "to trial within a reasonable time or to release" under paragraph 3. Pre-trial detention should be an exception and as short as possible. The Committee would welcome information concerning mechanisms existing and measures taken with a view to reducing the duration of such detention.

4. Also if so-called preventive detention is used, for reasons of public security, it must be controlled by these same provisions, i.e. it must not be arbitrary, and must be based on grounds and procedures established by law (para. 1), information of the reasons must be given (para. 2) and court control of the detention must be available (para. 4) as well as compensation in the case of a breach (para. 5). And if, in addition, criminal charges are brought in such cases, the full protection of article 9(2) and (3), as well as article 14, must also be granted.

IV.3 General Comment 15 (Twenty-seventh Session, 1986)

The position of aliens under the Covenant

1. Reports from States parties have often failed to take into account that each State party must ensure the rights in the Covenant to "all individuals within its territory and subject to its jurisdiction" (art. 2, para. 1). In general, the rights set forth in the Covenant apply to everyone, irrespective of reciprocity, and irrespective of his or her nationality or statelessness.

2. Thus, the general rule is that each one of the rights of the Covenant must be guaranteed without discrimination between citizens and aliens. Aliens receive the benefit of the general requirement of non-discrimination in respect of the rights guaranteed in the Covenant, as provided for in article 2 thereof. This guarantee applies to aliens and citizens alike. Exceptionally, some of the rights recognized in the Covenant are expressly applicable only to citizens (art. 25), while article 13 applies only to aliens. However, the Committee's experience in examining reports shows that in a number of countries other rights that aliens should enjoy under the Covenant are denied to them or are subject to limitations that cannot always be justified under the Covenant.

3. A few constitutions provide for equality of aliens with citizens. Some constitutions adopted more recently carefully distinguish fundamental rights that apply to all and those granted to citizens only, and deal with each in detail. In many States, however, the constitutions are drafted in terms of citizens only when granting relevant rights. Legislation and case law may also play an important part in providing for the rights of aliens. The Committee has been informed that in some States fundamental rights, though not guaranteed to aliens by the Constitution or other legislation, will also be extended to them as required by the Covenant. In certain cases, however, there has clearly been a failure to implement Covenant rights without discrimination in respect of aliens.

4. The Committee considers that in their reports States parties should give attention to the position of aliens, both under their law and in actual practice. The Covenant gives aliens all the protection regarding rights guaranteed therein, and its requirements should be observed by States parties in their legislation and in practice as appropriate. The position of aliens would thus be considerably improved. States parties should ensure that the provisions of the Covenant and the rights under it are made known to aliens within their jurisdiction.

5. The Covenant does not recognize the right of aliens to enter or reside in the territory of a State party. It is in principle a matter for the State to decide who it will admit to its territory. However, in certain circumstances an alien may enjoy the protection of the Covenant even in relation to entry or residence, for example, when considerations of non-discrimination, prohibition of inhuman treatment and respect for family life arise.

6. Consent for entry may be given subject to conditions relating, for example, to movement, residence and employment. A State may also impose general conditions upon an alien who is in transit. However, once aliens are allowed to enter the territory of a State party they are entitled to the rights set out in the Covenant.

7. Aliens thus have an inherent right to life, protected by law, and may not be arbitrarily deprived of life. They must not be subjected to torture or to cruel, inhuman or degrading treatment or punishment; nor may they be held in slavery or servitude.

Aliens have the full right to liberty and security of the person. If lawfully deprived of their liberty, they shall be treated with humanity and with respect for the inherent dignity of their person. Aliens may not be imprisoned for failure to fulfil a contractual obligation. They have the right to liberty of movement and free choice of residence; they shall be free to leave the country.

Aliens shall be equal before the courts and tribunals, and shall be entitled to a fair and public hearing by a competent, independent and impartial tribunal established by law in the determination of any criminal charge or of rights and obligations in a suit at law. Aliens shall not be subjected to retrospective penal legislation, and are entitled to recognition before the law. They may not be subjected to arbitrary or unlawful interference with their privacy, family, home or correspondence. They have the right to freedom of thought, conscience and religion, and the right to hold opinions and to express them. Aliens receive the benefit of the right of peaceful assembly and of freedom of association. They may marry when at marriageable age. Their children are entitled to those measures of protection required by their status as minors. In those cases where aliens constitute a minority within the meaning of article 27, they shall not be denied the right, in community with other members of their group, to enjoy their own culture, to profess and practise their own religion and to use their own language. Aliens are entitled to equal protection by the law. There shall be no discrimination between aliens and citizens in the application of these rights. These rights of aliens may be qualified only by such limitations as may be lawfully imposed under the Covenant.

8. Once an alien is lawfully within a territory, his freedom of movement within the territory and his right to leave that territory may only be restricted in accordance

with article 12, paragraph 3. Differences in treatment in this regard between aliens and nationals, or between different categories of aliens, need to be justified under article 12, paragraph 3. Since such restrictions must, inter alia, be consistent with the other rights recognized in the Covenant, a State party cannot, by restraining an alien or deporting him to a third country, arbitrarily prevent his return to his own country (art. 12, para. 4).

9. Many reports have given insufficient information on matters relevant to article 13. That article is applicable to all procedures aimed at the obligatory departure of an alien, whether described in national law as expulsion or otherwise. If such procedures entail arrest, the safeguards of the Covenant relating to deprivation of liberty (arts. 9 and 10) may also be applicable. If the arrest is for the particular purpose of extradition, other provisions of national and international law may apply. Normally an alien who is expelled must be allowed to leave for any country that agrees to take him. The particular rights of article 13 only protect those aliens who are lawfully in the territory of a State party. This means that national law concerning the requirements for entry and stay must be taken into account in determining the scope of that protection, and that illegal entrants and aliens who have stayed longer than the law or their permits allow, in particular, are not covered by its provisions. However, if the legality of an alien's entry or stay is in dispute, any decision on this point leading to his expulsion or deportation ought to be taken in accordance with article 13. It is for the competent authorities of the State party, in good faith and in the exercise of their powers, to apply and interpret the domestic law, observing, however, such requirements under the Covenant as equality before the law (art. 26).

10 Article 13 directly regulates only the procedure and not the substantive grounds for expulsion. However, by allowing only those carried out "in pursuance of a decision reached in accordance with law", its purpose is clearly to prevent arbitrary expulsions. On the other hand, it entitles each alien to a decision in his own case and, hence, article 13 would not be satisfied with laws or decisions providing for collective or mass expulsions. This understanding, in the opinion of the Committee, is confirmed by further provisions concerning the right to submit reasons against expulsion and to have the decision reviewed by and to be represented before the competent authority or someone designated by it. An alien must be given full facilities for pursuing his remedy against expulsion so that this right will in all the circumstances of his case be an effective one. The principles of article 13 relating to appeal against expulsion and the entitlement to review by a competent authority may only be departed from when "compelling reasons of national security" so require. Discrimination may not be made between different categories of aliens in the application of article 13.

APPENDIX IV   GENERAL COMMENTS BY THE UN HUMAN RIGHTS COMMITTEE

IV.4   General Comment 21, Article 10 (Forty-fourth Session, 1992)

1. This general comment replaces general comment 9 (Sixteenth session, 1982) reflecting and further developing it.

2. Article 10, paragraph 1, of the International Covenant on Civil and Political Rights applies to anyone deprived of liberty under the laws and authority of the State who is held in prisons, hospitals – particularly psychiatric hospitals – detention camps or correctional institutions or elsewhere. States parties should ensure that the principle stipulated therein is observed in all institutions and establishments within their jurisdiction where persons are being held.

3. Article 10, paragraph 1, imposes on States parties a positive obligation towards persons who are particularly vulnerable because of their status as persons deprived of liberty, and complements for them the ban on torture or other cruel, inhuman or degrading treatment or punishment contained in article 7 of the Covenant. Thus, not only may persons deprived of their liberty not be subjected to treatment that is contrary to article 7, including medical or scientific experimentation, but neither may they be subjected to any hardship or constraint other than that resulting from the deprivation of liberty; respect for the dignity of such persons must be guaranteed under the same conditions as for that of free persons. Persons deprived of their liberty enjoy all the rights set forth in the Covenant, subject to the restrictions that are unavoidable in a closed environment.

4. Treating all persons deprived of their liberty with humanity and with respect for their dignity is a fundamental and universally applicable rule. Consequently, the application of this rule, as a minimum, cannot be dependent on the material resources available in the State party. This rule must be applied without distinction of any kind, such as race, colour, sex, language, religion, political or other opinion, national or social origin, property, birth or other status.

5. States parties are invited to indicate in their reports to what extent they are applying the relevant United Nations standards applicable to the treatment of prisoners: the Standard Minimum Rules for the Treatment of Prisoners (1957), the Body of Principles for the Protection of All Persons under Any Form of Detention or Imprisonment (1988), the Code of Conduct for Law Enforcement Officials (1978) and the Principles of Medical Ethics relevant to the Role of Health Personnel, particularly Physicians, in the Protection of Prisoners and Detainees against Torture and Other Cruel, Inhuman or Degrading Treatment or Punishment (1982).

6. The Committee recalls that reports should provide detailed information on national legislative and administrative provisions that have a bearing on the right provided for in article 10, paragraph 1. The Committee also considers that it is necessary for reports to specify what concrete measures have been taken by the competent authorities to monitor the effective application of the rules regarding the treatment of persons deprived of their liberty. States parties should include in their reports information concerning the system for supervising penitentiary establishments, the specific measures to prevent torture and cruel, inhuman or degrading treatment, and how impartial supervision is ensured.

7. Furthermore, the Committee recalls that reports should indicate whether the various applicable provisions form an integral part of the instruction and training of the personnel who have authority over persons deprived of their liberty and whether they are strictly adhered to by such personnel in the discharge of their duties. It would also be appropriate to specify whether arrested or detained persons have access to such information and have effective legal means enabling them to ensure that those rules are respected, to complain if the rules are ignored and to obtain adequate compensation in the event of a violation.

8. The Committee recalls that the principle set forth in article 10, paragraph 1, constitutes the basis for the more specific obligations of States parties in respect of criminal justice, which are set forth in article 10, paragraphs 2 and 3.

9. Article 10, paragraph 2 (a), provides for the segregation, save in exceptional circumstances, of accused persons from convicted ones. Such segregation is required in order to emphasize their status as unconvicted persons who at the same time enjoy the right to be presumed innocent as stated in article 14, paragraph 2. The reports of States parties should indicate how the separation of accused persons from convicted persons is effected and explain how the treatment of accused persons differs from that of convicted persons.

10. As to article 10, paragraph 3, which concerns convicted persons, the Committee wishes to have detailed information on the operation of the penitentiary system of the State party. No penitentiary system should be only retributory; it should essentially seek the reformation and social rehabilitation of the prisoner. States parties are invited to specify whether they have a system to provide assistance after release and to give information as to its success.

11. In a number of cases, the information furnished by the State party contains no specific reference either to legislative or administrative provisions or to practical measures to ensure the re-education of convicted persons. The Committee requests

specific information concerning the measures taken to provide teaching, education and re-education, vocational guidance and training and also concerning work programmes for prisoners inside the penitentiary establishment as well as outside.

12. In order to determine whether the principle set forth in article 10, paragraph 3, is being fully respected, the Committee also requests information on the specific measures applied during detention, e.g., how convicted persons are dealt with individually and how they are categorized, the disciplinary system, solitary confinement and high-security detention and the conditions under which contacts are ensured with the outside world (family, lawyer, social and medical services, non-governmental organizations).

13. Moreover, the Committee notes that in the reports of some States parties no information has been provided concerning the treatment accorded to accused juvenile persons and juvenile offenders. Article 10, paragraph 2 (b), provides that accused juvenile persons shall be separated from adults. The information given in reports shows that some States parties are not paying the necessary attention to the fact that this is a mandatory provision of the Covenant. The text also provides that cases involving juveniles must be considered as speedily as possible. Reports should specify the measures taken by States parties to give effect to that provision. Lastly, under article 10, paragraph 3, juvenile offenders shall be segregated from adults and be accorded treatment appropriate to their age and legal status in so far as conditions of detention are concerned, such as shorter working hours and contact with relatives, with the aim of furthering their reformation and rehabilitation. Article 10 does not indicate any limits of juvenile age. While this is to be determined by each State party in the light of relevant social, cultural and other conditions, the Committee is of the opinion that article 6, paragraph 5, suggests that all persons under the age of 18 should be treated as juveniles, at least in matters relating to criminal justice. States should give relevant information about the age groups of persons treated as juveniles. In that regard, States parties are invited to indicate whether they are applying the United Nations Standard Minimum Rules for the Administration of Juvenile Justice, known as the Beijing Rules (1987).

Appendix V UNHCR Executive Committee Conclusions

V.1 Conclusion No. 22 (XXXII) – 1981 – Protection of Asylum Seekers in Situations of Large-Scale Influx

The Executive Committee,

Noting with appreciation the report of the Group of Experts on temporary refuge in situations of large-scale influx, which met in Geneva from 21–24 April 1981, adopted the following conclusions in regard to the protection of asylum seekers in situations of large-scale influx:

I General

1. The refugee problem has become particularly acute due to the increasing number of large-scale influx situations in different areas of the world and especially in developing countries. The asylum seekers forming part of these large-scale influxes include persons who are refugees within the meaning of the 1951 United Nations Convention and the 1967 Protocol relating to the Status of Refugees or who, owing to external aggression, occupation, foreign domination or events seriously disturbing public order in either part of, or the whole of their country of origin or nationality are compelled to seek refuge outside that country.

2. Asylum seekers forming part of such large-scale influx situations are often confronted with difficulties in finding durable solutions by way of voluntary repatriation, local settlement or resettlement in a third country. Large-scale influxes frequently create serious problems for States, with the result that certain States, although committed to obtaining durable solutions, have only found it possible to admit asylum seekers without undertaking at the time of admission to provide permanent settlement of such persons within their borders.

3. It is therefore imperative to ensure that asylum seekers are fully protected in large-scale influx situations, to reaffirm the basic minimum standards for their treatment pending arrangements for a durable solution, and to establish effective arrangements in the context of international solidarity and burden-sharing for assisting countries which receive large numbers of asylum seekers.

II Measures of protection

A. Admission and non-refoulement

1. In situations of large-scale influx, asylum seekers should be admitted to the State in which they first seek refuge and if that State is unable to admit them on a durable basis, it should always admit them at least on a temporary basis and provide them with protection according to the principles set out below. They should be admitted without any discrimination as to race, religion, political opinion, nationality, country of origin or physical incapacity.
2. In all cases the fundamental principle of non-refoulement including non-rejection at the frontier must be scrupulously observed.

B. Treatment of asylum seekers who have been temporarily admitted to country pending arrangements for a durable solution

1. Article 31 of the 1951 United Nations Convention relating to the Status of Refugees contains provisions regarding the treatment of refugees who have entered a country without authorization and whose situation in that country has not yet been regularized. The standards defined in this Article do not, however, cover all aspects of the treatment of asylum seekers in large-scale influx situations.
2. It is therefore essential that asylum seekers who have been temporarily admitted pending arrangements for a durable solution should be treated in accordance with the following minimum basic human standards:
(a) they should not be penalized or exposed to any unfavourable treatment solely on the ground that their presence in the country is considered unlawful, they should not be subjected to restrictions on their movements other than those which are necessary in the interest of public health and public order;
(b) they should enjoy the fundamental civil rights internationally recognized, in particular those set out in the Universal Declaration of Human Rights;
(c) they should receive all necessary assistance and be provided with the basic necessities of life including food, shelter and basic sanitary and health facilities; in this respect the international community should conform with the principles of international solidarity and burden-sharing;
(d) they should be treated as persons whose tragic plight requires special understanding and sympathy. They should not be subjected to cruel, inhuman or degrading treatment;
(e) there should be no discrimination on the grounds of race, religion, political opinion, nationality, country of origin or physical incapacity;
(f) they are to be considered as persons before the law, enjoying free access to courts of law and other competent administrative authorities;

(g) the location of asylum seekers should be determined by their safety and well-being as well as by the security needs of the receiving State. Asylum seekers should, as far as possible, be located at a reasonable distance from the frontier of their country of origin. They should not become involved in subversive activities against their country of origin or any other State;
(h) family unity should be respected;
(i) all possible assistance should be given for the tracing of relatives;
(j) adequate provision should be made for the protection of minors and unaccompanied children;
(k) the sending and receiving of mail should be allowed;
(l) material assistance from friends or relatives should be permitted;
(m) appropriate arrangements should be made, where possible, for the registration of births, deaths and marriages;
(n) they should be granted all the necessary facilities to enable them to obtain a satisfactory durable solution;
(o) they should be permitted to transfer assets which they have brought into a territory to the country where the durable solution is obtained; and
(p) all steps should be taken to facilitate voluntary repatriation.

III Co-operation with the Office of the United Nations High Commissioner for Refugees

Asylum seekers shall be entitled to contact the Office of UNHCR. UNHCR shall be given access to asylum seekers. UNHCR shall also be given the possibility of exercising its function of international protection and shall be allowed to supervise the well-being of persons entering reception or other refugee centres.

IV International solidarity, burden-sharing and duties of States

(1) A mass influx may place unduly heavy burdens on certain countries; a satisfactory solution of a problem, international in scope and nature, cannot be achieved without international co-operation. States shall, within the framework of international solidarity and burden-sharing, take all necessary measures to assist, at their request, States which have admitted asylum seekers in large-scale influx situations.

(2) Such action should be taken bilaterally or multilaterally at the regional or at the universal levels and in co-operation with UNHCR, as appropriate. Primary consideration should be given to the possibility of finding suitable solutions within the regional context.

(3) Action with a view to burden-sharing should be directed towards facilitating voluntary repatriation, promoting local settlement in the receiving country, providing resettlement possibilities in third countries, as appropriate.

(4) The measures to be taken within the context of such burden-sharing arrangements should be adapted to the particular situation. They should include, as necessary, emergency, financial and technical assistance, assistance in kind and advance pledging of further financial or other assistance beyond the emergency phase until durable solutions are found, and where voluntary repatriation or local settlement cannot be envisaged, the provision for asylum seekers of resettlement possibilities in a cultural environment appropriate for their well-being.

(5) Consideration should be given to the strengthening of existing mechanisms and, if appropriate, the setting up of new arrangements, if possible on a permanent basis, to ensure that the necessary funds and other material and technical assistance are immediately made available.

(6) In a spirit of international solidarity, Governments should also seek to ensure that the causes leading to large-scale influxes of asylum seekers are as far as possible removed and, where such influxes have occurred, that conditions favourable to voluntary repatriation are established.

V.2 Conclusion No. 44 (XXXVII) – 1986 – Detention of Refugees and Asylum Seekers

The Executive Committee,

Recalling Article 31 of the 1951 Convention relating to the Status of Refugees;

Recalling further its Conclusion No. 22 (XXXII) on the treatment of asylum seekers in situations of large-scale influx, as well as Conclusion No. 7 (XXVIII), paragraph (e), on the question of custody or detention in relation to the expulsion of refugees lawfully in a country, and Conclusion No. 8 (XXVIII), paragraph (e), on the determination of refugee status;

Noting that the term "refugee" in the present Conclusions has the same meaning as that in the 1951 Convention and the 1967 Protocol relating to the Status of Refugees, and is without prejudice to wider definitions applicable in different regions;

(a) Noted with deep concern that large numbers of refugees and asylum seekers in different areas of the world are currently the subject of detention or similar restrictive measures by reason of their illegal entry or presence in search of asylum, pending resolution of their situation;

(b) Expressed the opinion that in view of the hardship which it involves, detention should normally be avoided. If necessary, detention may be resorted to only on grounds prescribed by law to verify identity; to determine the elements on which the claim to refugee status or asylum is based; to deal with cases where refugees or asylum seekers have destroyed their travel and/or identity documents or have used fraudulent documents in order to mislead the authorities of the State in which they intend to claim asylum; or to protect national security or public order;

(c) Recognized the importance of fair and expeditious procedures for determining refugee status or granting asylum in protecting refugees and asylum seekers from unjustified or unduly prolonged detention;

(d) Stressed the importance for national legislation and/or administrative practice to make the necessary distinction between the situation of refugees and asylum seekers, and that of other aliens;

(e) Recommended that detention measures taken in respect of refugees and asylum seekers should be subject to judicial or administrative review;

(f) Stressed that conditions of detention of refugees and asylum seekers must be humane. In particular, refugees and asylum seekers shall, whenever possible, not be accommodated with persons detained as common criminals, and shall not be located in areas where their physical safety is endangered;

(g) Recommended that refugees and asylum seekers who are detained be provided with the opportunity to contact the Office of the United Nations High Commissioner for Refugees or, in the absence of such office, available national refugee assistance agencies;

(h) Reaffirmed that refugees and asylum seekers have duties to the country in which they find themselves, which require in particular that they conform to its laws and regulations as well as to measures taken for the maintenance of public order;

(i) Reaffirmed the fundamental importance of the observance of the principle of non-refoulement and in this context recalled the relevance of Conclusion No. 6 (XXVIII).

V.3 Conclusion No. 58 (XL) – 1989 – Problem of Refugees and Asylum Seekers Who Move in an Irregular Manner from a Country in Which They Had Already Found Protection

a) The phenomenon of refugees, whether they have been formally identified as such or not (asylum seekers), who move in an irregular manner from countries in which they have already found protection, in order to seek asylum or permanent resettlement elsewhere, is a matter of growing concern. This concern results from the destabilizing effect which irregular movements of this kind have on structured international efforts to provide appropriate solutions for refugees. Such irregular movements involve entry into the territory of another country, without the prior consent of the national authorities or without an entry visa, or with no or insufficient documentation normally required for travel purposes, or with false or fraudulent documentation. Of similar concern is the growing phenomenon of refugees and asylum seekers who wilfully destroy or dispose of their documentation in order to mislead the authorities of the country of arrival;

b) Irregular movements of refugees and asylum seekers who have already found protection in a country are, to a large extent, composed of persons who feel impelled to leave, due to the absence of educational and employment possibilities and the non-availability of long-term durable solutions by way of voluntary repatriation, local integration and resettlement;

c) The phenomenon of such irregular movements can only be effectively met through concerted action by governments, in consultation with UNHCR, aimed at:
i) identifying the causes and scope of irregular movements in any given refugee situation,
ii) removing or mitigating the causes of such irregular movements through the granting and maintenance of asylum and the provision of necessary durable solutions or other appropriate assistance measures,
iii) encouraging the establishment of appropriate arrangements for the identification of refugees in the countries concerned, and
iv) ensuring humane treatment for refugees and asylum seekers who, because of the uncertain situation in which they find themselves, feel impelled to move from one country to another in an irregular manner;

d) Within this framework, governments, in close co-operation with UNHCR, should:
i) seek to promote the establishment of appropriate measures for the care and support of refugees and asylum seekers in countries where they have found protection pending the identification of a durable solution and

ii) promote appropriate durable solutions with particular emphasis firstly on voluntary repatriation and, when this is not possible, local integration and the provision of adequate resettlement opportunities;

e) Refugees and asylum seekers, who have found protection in a particular country, should normally not move from that country in an irregular manner in order to find durable solutions elsewhere but should take advantage of durable solutions available in that country through action taken by governments and UNHCR as recommended in paragraphs (c) and (d) above;

f) Where refugees and asylum seekers nevertheless move in an irregular manner from a country where they have already found protection, they may be returned to that country if:
i) they are protected there against refoulement and
ii) they are permitted to remain there and to be treated in accordance with recognized basic human standards until a durable solution is found for them. Where such return is envisaged, UNHCR may be requested to assist in arrangements for the re-admission and reception of the persons concerned;

g) It is recognized that there may be exceptional cases in which a refugee or asylum seeker may justifiably claim that he has reason to fear persecution or that his physical safety or freedom are endangered in a country where he previously found protection. Such cases should be given favourable consideration by the authorities of the State where he requests asylum;

h) The problem of irregular movements is compounded by the use, by a growing number of refugees and asylum seekers, of fraudulent documentation and their practice of wilfully destroying or disposing of travel and/or other documents in order to mislead the authorities of their country of arrival. These practices complicate the personal identification of the person concerned and the determination of the country where he stayed prior to arrival, and the nature and duration of his stay in such a country. Practices of this kind are fraudulent and may weaken the case of the person concerned;

i) It is recognized that circumstances may compel a refugee or asylum seeker to have recourse to fraudulent documentation when leaving a country in which his physical safety or freedom are endangered. Where no such compelling circumstances exist, the use of fraudulent documentation is unjustified;

j) The wilful destruction or disposal of travel or other documents by refugees and asylum seekers upon arrival in their country of destination, in order to mislead the national authorities as to their previous stay in another country where they have protection, is unacceptable. Appropriate arrangements should be made by States, either individually or in co-operation with other States, to deal with this growing phenomenon.

Appendix VI UNHCR Guidelines

VI.1 1995 UNHCR Guidelines on Detention

1. The use of detention against asylum seekers is, in the view of UNHCR, inherently undesirable. This is even more so in the case of vulnerable groups such as single women, children, unaccompanied minors and those with special medical or psychological needs.

2. Of key significance to the issue of detention is Article 31 of the 1951 Convention. Article 31 exempts refugees coming directly from a country of persecution from being punished on account of their illegal entry or presence, provided they present themselves without delay to the authorities and show good cause for their illegal entry or presence. The Article also provides that Contracting States shall not apply to the movements of such refugees restrictions other than those which are necessary and that any restrictions shall only be applied until their status is regularized or they obtain admission into another country.

3. It follows from this Article that detention should only be resorted to in cases of necessity. The detention of asylum seekers who come "directly" in an irregular manner should, therefore, not be automatic, nor should it be unduly prolonged. The reason for this is that once their claims have been examined they may prove to be refugees entitled to benefit from Article 31. Conclusion No. 44 (XXXVII) of the Executive Committee on the Detention of Refugees and Asylum Seekers sets the standard in more concrete terms of what is meant by the term "necessary". It also provides guidelines to States on the use of detention, and recommendations as to certain procedural guarantees to which detainees should be entitled.

4. The term "coming directly" covers the situation of a person who enters the country in which asylum is sought directly from the country of origin, or from another country where his protection could not be assured. It is clear from the travaux préparatoires, however, that the term also covers a person who transits an intermediate country for a short time without having applied for or received asylum there. The drafters of the Convention introduced the term "coming directly" not to exclude those who had transited another country, but rather to exclude those who "had settled temporarily" in one country, from freely entering another (travaux préparatoires A/CONF.2/SR 14 p. lO). No strict time limit can be applied to the concept "coming directly", and each case will have to be judged on its merits. The

issue of "coming directly" is also related to the problem of identifying the country responsible for examining an asylum request and granting adequate and effective protection.

5. Given the special situation of a refugee, in particular the frequent fear of authorities, language problems, lack of information and general insecurity, and the fact that these and other circumstances may vary enormously from one refugee to another, there is no time limit which can be mechanically applied associated with the term "without delay" [a condition foreseen in Article 31(1)]. Along with the term "good cause" [another condition foreseen in Article 31(1)], it must take into account all of the circumstances under which the asylum seeker fled (e.g. having no time for immigration formalities).

6. The term "asylum seeker" throughout the survey and these guidelines also includes individuals who have been rejected from the refugee status determination procedure on purely formal grounds (for example pursuant to the application of the safe third country concept) or on substantive grounds with which UNHCR would not concur (such as in case of persecution by non-State agents). In the absence of an examination of the merits of the case in a fair and efficient asylum procedure or when the rejection after substantive examination of the claim is not in conformity with UNHCR doctrine, such rejected asylum seekers continue to be of concern to UNHCR. These guidelines do not, however, relate to "rejected asylum seekers stricto sensu", that is, persons who, after due consideration of their claims to asylum in fair procedures (satisfactory procedural safeguards as well as an interpretation of the refugee definition in conformity with UNHCR standards), are found not to qualify for refugee status on the basis of the criteria laid down in the 1951 Convention, nor to be in need of international protection on other grounds, and who are not authorized to stay in the country concerned for other compelling humanitarian reasons.

Guideline 1   Scope of the Guidelines

These Guidelines apply to all asylum seekers who are in detention or in detention-like situations. They apply to all persons who are confined within a narrowly bounded or restricted location, including prisons, closed camps, detention facilities or airport transit zones, where the only opportunity to leave this limited area is to leave the territory.[1]

---

1   This definition is based on the Note of the Sub-Committee of the Whole on International Protection of 1986 (37th Sesssion EC/SCP/44 Paragraph 25) which defined detention to mean "confinement in prison, closed camp or other restricted area, on the assumption

Persons who are subject to limitations on domicile and residency are not generally considered to be in detention.

When considering whether an asylum seeker is in detention, the cumulative impact of the restrictions as well as the degree and intensity of each one should also be assessed.

Guideline 2   General rule

The right to liberty is a fundamental right, recognised in all the major human rights instruments, both at global and regional levels. The right to seek asylum is, equally, recognised as a basic human right. The act of seeking asylum can therefore not be considered an offence or a crime. Consideration should be given to the fact that asylum seekers may already have suffered some form of persecution or other hardship in their country of origin and should be protected against any form of harsh treatment.

As a general rule, asylum seekers should not be detained.

The position of asylum seekers differs fundamentally from that of the ordinary alien and this element should be taken into account in determining any measures of punishment or detention based on illegal presence or entry. Reference is made to the provisions of Article 14 of the Universal Declaration of Human Rights, which grants all individuals the right to seek and enjoy asylum, and Article 31 of the 1951 Convention which exempts refugees from penalties for illegal presence or entry when "coming directly" from a territory where their life or freedom was threatened. There is consensus that Article 31 should not be applied restrictively.[2]

---

that there is a qualitative difference between detention and other restrictions on freedom of movement".
Although the concept of "detention" is not defined in ExCom Conclusion No. 44, it is stated in the 1988 Note on International Protection (39th Session A/AC.96/713) that the Conclusion is of direct relevance to situations other than detention in prisons.

[2] Article 31 of the 1951 Convention; for further reference and interpretation see above introductory notes to the UNHCR Guidelines.
EXCOM Conclusion No. 22 (XXXII) Paragraph II B 2(a)
EXCOM Conclusion No. 44 (XXXVII) Paragraph (d)
Note on International Protection 1987 Paragraph 16
Sub-Committee of the Whole on International Protection EC/SCP 44 1986 Paragraph 31

Guideline 3 Exceptional grounds of detention

Detention of asylum seekers may exceptionally be resorted to, if it is clearly prescribed by a national law which is in conformity with general norms and principles of international human rights law.[3]

The permissible exceptions to the general rule that detention should normally be avoided must be prescribed by law. In such cases, detention of asylum seekers may only be resorted to, if necessary, in order:
(i) to verify identity;
(ii) to determine the elements on which the claim for refugee status or asylum is based,
(iii) to deal with cases where refugees or asylum seekers have destroyed their travel and/or identity documents or have used fraudulent documents in order to mislead the authorities of the State in which they intend to claim asylum,[4] or
(iv) to protect national security or public order.

Where detention of asylum seekers is considered necessary it should only be imposed where it is reasonable to do so and without discrimination. It should be proportional to the ends to be achieved (i.e. to ensure one of the above purposes) and for a minimal period.[5]

---

3   Article 9(1) International Covenant on Civil and Political Rights (ICCPR)
    Article 37(b) UN Convention on the Rights of the Child (CRC)
    Article 5(1)(f) European Convention for the Protection of Human Rights (ECHR)
    Article 7(3) American Convention on Human Rights 1969 (American Convention)
    Article 6 African Charter on Human and People's Rights (African Charter)
    ExCoM Conclusion No. 44 (XXXVII)
4   ExCom Conclusion No. 44 (XXXVII)
    Detention for the purposes of a preliminary interview to determine the elements of the refugee status or asylum claim is not the same as detention of a person for the entire duration of a prolonged asylum procedure, which the Conclusion does not endorse. As regards asylum seekers using fraudulent documents or travelling with no documents at all, the Conclusion recognizes that detention is only permissible when there was an intention to mislead the authorities. Thus, asylum seekers who arrive without documentation because they were unable to obtain any in their country of origin, should not be detained solely for that reason (see Note on International Protection, A/AC.96/713 para. 19, 15 August 1988).
5   Article 9(1) ICCPR
    Article 37(b) CRC
    Article 5(I)(f) ECHR
    Article 7(3) American Convention
    Article 6 African Charter
    EXCOM Conclusion No. 44 (XXXVII)

APPENDIX VI   UNHCR GUIDELINES

Where there are monitoring mechanisms which can be employed as viable alternatives to detention (such as reporting obligations or guarantor requirements), these should be applied first unless there is evidence to suggest that such an alternative will not be effective.

Detention of asylum seekers which is applied for any other purpose, for example, as part of a policy to deter future asylum seekers, is contrary to the principles of international protection.[6]

Under no circumstances should detention be used as a punitive or disciplinary measure for failure to comply with administrative requirements or breach of reception centre, refugee camp or other institutional restrictions.

Escape from detention should not lead to automatic discontinuance of the asylum procedure, nor to return to the country of origin, having regard to the principle of non-refoulement.[7]

Guideline 4   Procedural safeguards[8]

Upon detention, asylum seekers should be entitled to the following minimum procedural guarantees:
(i) the right to be informed of the reasons for detention and of the rights in connection thereto, in a language and in terms which they understand;
(ii) the right to challenge the lawfulness of the deprivation of liberty promptly before a competent, independent and impartial authority, where the individual may present his arguments either personally or through a representative. Such a right should extend to all aspects of the legality of the case and not simply to the lawful exercise by the executive of the discretion to detain. To this end, he should receive legal assistance. Moreover, there should be a possibility of a periodic review.

---

[6] Sub-Committee of the Whole on International Protection Note EC/ECP/44 Paragraph 51(c)
[7] Sub-Committee of the Whole on International Protection Note EC/SCP/44 Paragraph 41
[8] Article 9(2) and (4) ICCPR
Article 37(d) CRC
Article 5(2) and (4) ECHR
Article 7(1) African Charter
Article 7(4) and (5) American Convention
EXCOM Conclusion No. 44 (XXXVII)
UN Standard Minimum Rules for the Treatment of Prisoners 1955
UN Body of Principles for the Protection of All Persons under Any Form of Detention or Imprisonment 1990

(iii) the right to contact the local UNHCR office, available national refugee or other agencies and a lawyer. The means to make such contact should be made available.

Guideline 5   Detention of persons under the age of 18[9]

In accordance with the General Rule stated at Guideline 2 and the UNHCR Guidelines on Refugee Children, minors who are asylum seekers should not be detained.

However if States do detain children, this should, in accordance with Article 37 of the Convention on the Rights of the Child, be as a measure of last resort, for the shortest appropriate period of time and in accordance with the exceptions stated at Guideline 3.

Particular reference is made to:
* Article 3 of the Convention on the Rights of the Child, which provides that in any action taken by States Parties concerning minors, the best interests of the child shall be a primary consideration;
* Article 9 which grants children the right not to be separated from their parents against their will; and
* Article 22 according to which States Parties are obliged to provide special measures of protection to refugee children and asylum seekers who are minors, whether accompanied or not.

If children who are asylum seekers are detained in airports, immigration holding centres or prisons, they must not be held under prison-like conditions. All efforts must be made to have them released from detention and placed in other accommodation. If this proves impossible, special arrangements must be made for living quarters which are suitable for children and their families.

During detention, children have the right to education which should optimally take place outside the detention premises in order to facilitate the continuance of their education upon release. Under the UN Rules for Juveniles Deprived of their Liberty, States are required to provide special education programmes to children of foreign origin with particular cultural or ethnic needs.

---

9   CRC Articles 3, 9, 20, 22 and 37
     UN Rules for Juveniles Deprived of their Liberty
     UNHCR Guidelines on Refugee Children 1994

Children who are detained benefit from the same minimum procedural guarantees (listed at Guideline 4) as adults. In addition, unaccompanied minors should be appointed a legal guardian.

Guideline 6 Conditions of detention[10]

Conditions of detention for asylum seekers should be humane with respect for the inherent dignity of the person. They should be prescribed by law.

Reference is made to the applicable norms and principles of international law and standards on the treatment of such persons. Of particular relevance are the UN Standard Minimum Rules for the Treatment of Prisoners of 195S, the UN Body of Principles for the Protection of All Persons under any form of Detention or Imprisonment of 1990, the UN Rules for the Protection of Juveniles Deprived of their Liberty and the European Prison Rules.

The following points in particular should be emphasized:
(i) the segregation within facilities of men and women, and children from adults (unless these adults are relatives); and asylum seekers from convicted criminals;
(ii) the possibility regularly to contact and receive visits from friends, relatives and legal counsel;
(iii) the possibility to receive appropriate medical treatment and to conduct some form of physical exercise; and
(iv) the possibility to continue further education or vocational training.

It is also recommended that certain vulnerable categories such as pregnant women, nursing mothers, children, the aged, the sick and handicapped should benefit from special measures which take into account their particular needs whilst in detention.

---

10 Article 10(l) ICCPR
UN Standard Minimum Rules for the Treatment of Prisoners 1955
UN Body of Principles for the Protection of All Persons under Any Form of Detention or Imprisonment 1990
UN Rules for Juveniles Deprived of their Liberty 1990
European Prison Rules 1987

VI.2 1994 UNHCR Guidelines on Refugee Children

Chapter 7: Personal Liberty and Security

IV Detention

It is UNHCR's policy that refugee children should not be detained. Unfortunately, refugee children are sometimes detained or threatened with detention because of their own, or their parents', illegal entry into a country of asylum. Because detention can be very harmful to refugee children, it must be "used only as a measure of last resort and for the shortest appropriate period of time" (CRC art. 37(b)).

Alternate accommodation: If refugee children are detained in airports, immigration holding centres or prisons, they must not be held under prison-like conditions. Special arrangements must be made for living quarters which are suitable for children and their families. Strong efforts must be made to have them released from detention and placed in other accommodation. Families must be kept together at all times, which includes their stay in detention as well as being released together.

International standards: Protection and assistance should make sure international standards are complied with whenever children are in detention.

Lawfulness: Detention must be in conformity with the State's law (CRC art. 37(b)). A distinction must be made between refugees/asylum seekers and other aliens.

Proper justification: Detention must only be used as a last resort and must always have a proper justification. For example, when identity documents have been destroyed or forged, a State might choose to detain an asylum seeker while identity is being established, but detention must be for the shortest period of time possible (CRC art. 37(b)). Executive Committee Conclusion No. 44 (1986) discusses the limited circumstances when asylum seekers can be detained, and sets out basic standards for their treatment. Detention must never be used to punish asylum seekers or to deter or scare off other potential asylum seekers.

Humane conditions: The conditions must be humane, which means that the needs of refugee children must be met (CRC art. 37(c)). These needs are defined throughout these Guidelines, and include protection from physical abuse, keeping the family together, access to education, and play. Asylum seekers and refugees should never be placed with common criminals.

Detailed standards: The UN General Assembly has adopted detailed standards that apply whenever juveniles are deprived of their liberty. See the UN Rules for the Protection of Juveniles Deprived of their Liberty (1990) (UN General Assembly Resolution 45/113, 14 December 1990).

Juvenile delinquency: Refugee children must comply with the laws of the country of asylum, in the same way as adults. When children are deprived of their liberty because of violations of criminal or delinquency laws, the standards of CRC arts. 37 and 40 should be applied. In addition to the UN Rules referred to above, the General Assembly has adopted detailed standards especially for situations where minors are accused of violating the law. See the UN Standard Minimum Rules for the Administration of Juvenile Justice (1985), commonly referred to as "The Beijing Rules" (UN General Assembly Resolution 40/33, 29 November 1985).

Appendix VII   NGO Recommendations

VII.1   1996 ECRE Position Paper on Detention

<u>ECRE Summary of key recommendations on the detention of asylum seekers</u>

1. The European Council on Refugees and Exiles (ECRE) supports the well established position of the UN High Commissioner for Refugees and other human rights organisations that, as a general rule, asylum seekers should not be detained. Detention may only be used in exceptional cases, and should carry full procedural safeguards.

2. The grounds for detention prescribed by national law should, inter alia, reflect the fact that illegal entry to the territory of a European State is in itself unacceptable as grounds for the detention of an asylum seeker.

3. Alternative, non-custodial measures such as reporting requirements should always be considered before resorting to detention.

4. The detaining authorities must assess a compelling need to detain that is based on the personal history of each asylum seeker.

5. An absolute maximum duration for any such detention should be specified in national law.

6. Any review body should be independent from the detaining authorities.

7. Unaccompanied minors should never be detained.

8. Detainees should be given a clear understanding of the grounds for their detention and their rights while in detention.

9. Detainees should have unrestricted access to independent, qualified and free legal advice.

10. Specialised NGOs, UNHCR and legal representatives should have access to all places of detention, including transit zones at international ports and airports.

11. Conditions in detention should reflect the non-criminal status of the detainees and be consistent with all international standards.

12. All staff should receive training related to the special situation and needs of asylum seekers in detention.

13. National authorities should provide detailed information on relevant policy, practice, and statistics in order to ensure transparency.

14. Any forthcoming efforts to harmonise the practice of European states in the area of detention of asylum seekers should reflect the standards which ECRE here advocates.

Position paper on the detention of asylum seekers by the European Council on Refugees and Exiles[1]

General remarks

1. ECRE believes that, as a general rule, asylum seekers[2] should not be detained. The right to liberty and security of the person is a fundamental principle of international human rights law.

2. ECRE urges European States to consider the full range of alternative, non-custodial measures available to them, which are both more humane and more effective.[3]

3. Deprivation of liberty obstructs and undermines the operation of a fair and efficient procedure for the determination of refugee status. For example, detention can physically interfere with the provision of legal advice to an asylum seeker and creates an intimidating atmosphere for persons undergoing the interview process.

4. Asylum seekers may have already suffered imprisonment and torture in the country from which they have fled. Therefore, the consequences of detention may be particularly serious, causing severe emotional and psychological stress and may amount to inhuman and degrading treatment.

5. Detention of asylum seekers should never be used as a deterrent, either indirectly to deter possible future arrivals or directly to deter the detainee from pursuing his or her asylum claim.

6. Systematic use of detention as a part of reception or determination procedures in any European state is strongly condemned by ECRE.

7. ECRE notes with particular concern the connection between the detention of asylum seekers which is increasing in nearly all European states and the introduction of the "safe third country" practice. The fact that in many cases asylum seekers have

---

1   In general, the provisions in international law which form the basis of many of ECRE's recommendations have not been cited. Readers are referred to the Summary of International Legal Standards and the footnotes attached to Guidelines in UNHCR's recent publication: Detention of Asylum Seekers in Europe (1995).
2   "Asylum seekers" is here used as a term of convenience, and includes many de facto refugees. Please see the attached Annex for a full explanation of this paper's scope.
3   See below ("Exceptional Grounds for Detention" para. 10), and also a forthcoming paper by ECRE elaborating upon the issue of alternatives [ed.: reproduced in Appendix VI.4].

been repeatedly detained during chain deportations on "safe third country" grounds provides a further powerful argument against that deportation practice.[4]

8. ECRE welcomes the recent UNHCR Guidelines on Detention as a very useful contribution to international standard setting. However, these Guidelines elaborate upon the UNHCR ExCom Conclusion No. 44 (XXXVII)–1986 which ECRE feels is now an insufficient statement, given the serious erosion of refugee protection through the use of detention in the 1990s.

9. It should therefore be noted that ECRE's position extends the position of UNHCR in a number of important ways:

- ECRE does not accept as adequate the grounds for detention as set out in point (b) of ExCom Conclusion No. 44 and in the recent "Guideline 3", feeling that they are too general and can therefore be interpreted by States as providing the basis for detaining large numbers of asylum seekers;
- ECRE's position contains greater detail regarding the conditions of detention and statements concerning the psychological effects of detention upon asylum seekers;
- ECRE emphasises the vital role of NGOs and suggests practical ways to improve the current situation of those in detention (eg. para 29);
- ECRE calls for greater transparency with regard to this practice at both the national and international level;
- ECRE does not find it advantageous to emphasise the refugee/migrant distinction when advocating the reform of detention conditions (see Annex).

Exceptional grounds for detention[5]

10. Asylum seekers should only be detained, as a last resort, in exceptional cases and where non-custodial measures have been proven on individual grounds not to achieve the stated, lawful and legitimate purpose.
Alternative, non-custodial measures include:

- supervision systems;
- a regime of reporting requirements;
- bail or guarantee systems (However, consideration must be given to the very limited financial assets of most asylum seekers. Such systems would only be

---

[4] For further information, please see the ECRE report: *Safe Third Countries – Myths and Realities*, London, February 1995.
[5] See ECRE policy paper: *A European Refugee Policy in the Light of Established Principles*, Recommendation (i) paras. 48 and 49.

reasonable if the amounts were regulated to not exceed a relatively low level and if there were organisations or community groups willing and able to help offer these securities on behalf of asylum seekers);
- the promotion of voluntary return through intensive and personalised counselling work prior to and during detention for all rejected asylum seekers.

11. Detention must not be imposed arbitrarily and never purely for the convenience of the authorities. It must be lawful (in accordance with a procedure and based on grounds prescribed by law), reasonably predictable (asylum seekers should be clearly told if detention is a consequence of failing to comply with alternative restrictions, for example), necessary, and applied without discrimination.[6]

12. ECRE accepts that detention may be resorted to on the following grounds:

- if the asylum seeker is liable for prosecution for a serious non-political offence, other than an offence under national aliens or immigration law;
- as a measure of last resort if there is a repeated and unjustified failure to comply with reporting requirements imposed by the authorities;
- if, following a fair and efficient refugee determination procedure, there is a failure by a rejected asylum seeker to comply with an order to leave the territory. This is also on condition that there has been a possibility to appeal against the order to leave the territory and that there are no humanitarian grounds to grant a permit to stay.

13. A demonstrable threat to "national security" or "public order", as those terms have been defined by the jurisprudence of the European Court and Commission of Human Rights, may be grounds for detention of an asylum seeker. It is preferable if the provision for detention on such grounds is located within the general law applying to all nationals and aliens, rather than specifically within the asylum law.

Unacceptable grounds for detention

14. Asylum seekers may have unwittingly or out of necessity infringed immigration laws in their effort to reach safety, but detention is not an appropriate response to such an infringement. Nor is verification of identity and/or travel route sufficient grounds for the detention of an asylum seeker. What must be

---

[6] With regard to non-discrimination: asylum seekers should not be detained on medical grounds, unless a national of the host state would be similarly confined under a mental health code or similarly held as part of the treatment of a communicable disease.

demonstrated is that there has been an unjustifiable failure to co-operate with the process of verification.

Asylum seekers are often forced to resort to illegal channels and false documentation in order to flee and gain access to the territory in which they seek international protection. For reasons which ECRE has often highlighted, it may be impossible for an asylum seeker to approach the authorities in his or her country of origin in order to obtain the necessary travel documents. Measures such as carrier sanctions and visa restrictions increasingly force genuine asylum seekers to enter illegally. The powers to detain illegal immigrants therefore must take account of the special situation of asylum seekers.

15. Rejected asylum seekers should not be detained for prolonged periods as a result of states failing to cooperate in the deportation process (for example, refusals by embassies or consulates to issue the necessary travel documents) or for any other reasons beyond the detainee's own control.

Persons who are unable to return to their countries of origin due to the situation in these countries and/or the risk of being "subjected to torture or to inhuman or degrading treatment or punishment" (ECHR Article 3) should not be detained while the host state waits for a change of situation which would allow return.

16. Expression by the asylum seeker of a particular political opinion or his/her unwillingness to co-operate with deportation to another country should not form part of the grounds for detention but rather may be central elements in the asylum claim itself.[7]

17. ECRE emphasises that the grounds for detaining asylum seekers should be narrowly defined, as above, in order to discourage the growth of xenophobic attitudes which cast all asylum seekers as fraudulent and as presenting a threat to their host society.

18. If states continue to detain asylum seekers on grounds other than those listed above – for example, to verify identity or because the individual is deemed "likely to abscond" – the recommendations of this paper also apply, particularly the standards of evidence described in paragraph 19.

---

[7] In the United States, there have been cases in which asylum seekers' political activities in their countries of origin, as a result of which they claimed to have suffered persecution, was produced as justication for their detention by the US authorities. ECRE wishes to guard against the spread of such practice to Europe.

The initial decision to detain

19. The initial decision to detain should always be based on the individual circumstances and personal history of each asylum seeker. They should always contain clear reasons why other non-custodial measures would be inadequate for the purpose and, in the light of existing alternative measures, there should be clear proportionality between the detention and the end to be achieved. There should be a presumption in favour of release.

Information on the decision to detain

20. The asylum seeker should be informed promptly and in a language s/he understands of the grounds for his or her detention, his/her rights and how to exercise them. This information should be provided in writing both to the asylum seeker and to his/her legal representative. In addition, the written statement should always be explained verbally to the asylum seeker in a language s/he understands.

Adequate possibilities for review[8]

21. All initial decisions to detain should be automatically and promptly referred for review to a judicial or other competent body independent of the detaining authorities and prescribed by law. The detention should thereafter be reviewed periodically in order to ascertain whether the detention still serves the stated purpose and is proportional. Reviews should consider not only the legality of the decision to detain but also the substantive grounds for the detention, with the authorities required to prove the compelling need to prolong detention. The periodic reviews should take place regardless of whether the asylum seeker has exercised their right to appeal. Detainees and their legal representatives should have the right to attend any review hearings and to present their case. The reviews should include an opportunity for the detainee to rebut any assertions made by the detaining authorities. Interpretation, if required, should be available at such hearings.

Appeal rights

22. Detained asylum seekers should have the right to appeal against the first instance and the review decisions and should be provided with the means, through legal assistance, to exercise this right. Again, detainees should have the right to attend any appeal hearings and to present their case. If the periodic review rights

---

[8] See *A European Refugee Policy in the Light of Established Principles*, **Recommendation** (ii) paras. 48 and 49.

described in paragraph 21 are not fully provided, the right to appeal must at least be guaranteed.

Duration of detention

23. Detention of asylum seekers should be for the minimum period necessary. An absolute maximum duration for any such detention should be specified in national law.

The right of access to legal counsel

24. Detained asylum seekers should be given the unrestricted assistance of a qualified, impartial legal counsel of his/her own choice.[9]

25. Legal counsel should be assigned by the competent authority if the detainee does not have a legal advisor of his/her own choice or does not have the means to obtain legal advice.

26. The detainee should be informed, immediately upon detention, of his/her right to legal advice, including a full written and oral explanation of this right and how to exercise it, in a language which s/he understands.

27. A qualified and impartial interpreter should be available for all visits between the detainee and his/her legal advisor, and during all contact between the asylum seeker and the national authorities.

Other rights in detention

28. Detained asylum seekers should also benefit from the following rights, including a full written and oral statement of these rights and how to exercise them, in a language which s/he understands:

- the right to contact UNHCR and/or NGOs;
- the right to communicate freely and in privacy with family, friends, members of a trained and recognised visitors group, and a social or religious counsellor. (Supervised visits are acceptable practice only in cases involving criminal grounds or a threat to national security and where there is concrete evidence to suggest that the right to privacy would be abused).

---

[9] See *A European Refugee Policy in the Light of Established Principles*, Recommendation (iii) paras. 48 and 49.

As a general principle, the rights of detained asylum seekers should never be fewer than or inferior to those enjoyed by nationals of the state detained on criminal charges.

29. ECRE recommends that the following measures be taken in order to ensure asylum seekers can effectively exercise the above rights (paras. 24–28):

- access to telephones in places of detention at times which allow detainees to contact and be contacted by the persons and agencies listed in paragraphs 24–28;
- access to free telephones for the purpose of contacting a legal representative and/or UNHCR in all international ports and airports;
- exchange of correspondence, unopened and without interference from the detaining authorities, between legal representatives and detainees;
- prompt notification of legal representatives when their client is to be transferred between places of detention;
- places of detention not to be geographically isolated but instead should be easily accessible for visitors;
- access to independent and qualified interpreters in order to avoid the use of other detainees for this purpose.

Access to detained asylum seekers[10]

30. UNHCR, designated NGOs and legal representatives should be granted access to places where asylum seekers are detained, including transit zones at international ports and airports.

31. UNHCR, a legal representative or a designated NGO should be automatically contacted by the authorities if an asylum claim is withdrawn during the claimant's detention. The detainee should receive counselling from UNHCR or the designated NGO and be allowed to reconsider their decision.

Children

32. Children (under the age of eighteen) who are unaccompanied should never be detained.[11]

---

[10] See *A European Refugee Policy in the Light of Established Principles*, Recommendation (v) paras. 48 and 49.

[11] Guardianship arrangements and other orders of the authorities to care for child asylum seekers are not to be confused with measures depriving the child of his/her liberty.

33. Children and their "primary care-givers" should not be detained unless the government authorities can prove that this is the only means of maintaining family unity. Such detention should occur only in the most exceptional cases. Nursing mothers and women in the later stages of pregnancy should not be detained.

34. Asylum seekers should be given the benefit of the doubt when their age is uncertain or disputed. Medical certificates should only be issued if the age can not be established through the information of family members or if genuine documents can not be obtained.

Conditions in detention[12]

35. ECRE recognises that within Europe there is significant regional variance regarding the capacity of state authorities and other agencies to provide social assistance to asylum seekers and to improve the conditions of detained asylum seekers. The following recommendations should be read in this context as normative statements towards which states should strive in accordance with the concept of "progressive implementation". ECRE, however, asserts that all current EU member states are capable of taking immediate action to implement the following recommendations, and that no state should undertake to detain unless capable of ensuring conditions in detention which respect the inherent dignity of the person.

36. ECRE emphasises that even when physical conditions are acceptable, detention often inflicts unnecessary psychological suffering on asylum seekers who in many European states remain uncertain as to either the grounds for, or the likely duration of, their detention. Asylum seekers may have undergone traumatic experiences in their country of origin, such as torture during arbitrary detention, and therefore detention in the country of reception is a particularly disproportionate response to, for example, arrival at a border without a visa.

37. As a general principle, the place and conditions of detention for asylum seekers should reflect their status as unconvicted persons and certainly should not be inferior to the conditions provided for nationals of that state detained on criminal charges.

38. Neither asylum seekers nor rejected asylum seekers should be detained together with other prisoners detained on criminal charges.

---

12 See ECRE's *Working Paper on Airport Procedures in Europe*, February 1993 – III, Recommendation 3.

40. Separate facilities should be made available for men and women. On the other hand, husbands and wives and other family members in detention should be permitted to live together.

41. Medical and health screening should be introduced at the beginning of detention to detect, where possible, persons who may already be suffering from trauma due to experiences in the country they have fled, and/or to detect suicidal risk. Where such cases can be identified, release should be strongly recommended by the examining doctor and should be granted.

The overall health and mental health of every detainee should subsequently be monitored. Monitoring for suicidal risk should not become punitive in that it should not involve isolation or transfer of the detainee to a prison wing.

42. Detainees should have access to 24 hour emergency medical services and regular access to general medical treatment. Doctors should be independent and where possible there should be a choice of doctor, including a choice between a male and female doctor. All medical staff should receive special training on the situation of asylum seekers in detention and should have the use of interpreters when meeting the detainees. Detainees should, where necessary, be referred for specialist treatment.

Detainees and, with patient permission, their legal advisers should have access to medical records.

43. Places of detention should have natural light and sufficient space.

44. Detainees should have the opportunity for physical exercise and should never be placed in isolation.

45. In those rare cases where children have to be detained in order to maintain family unity, they should never be held in prison-like conditions and they should benefit from appropriate recreational and educational facilities. Special provision should be made for their particular cultural and linguistic needs.

46. During prolonged detention, adult education and training should be provided and it should attend to cultural and linguistic needs. Such activities should help to prepare detainees both for the process of integration in host societies and for the process of reintegration in their countries of origin.

It is crucial for the mental health of detainees that they are not deprived of access to constructive activities during a prolonged period of detention.

APPENDIX VII   NGO RECOMMENDATIONS

47. Detainees have the right to freedom of religion which implies not only the right to be visited by a representative of their denomination but also, for example, the right to wear religious clothing or follow a religious diet. Detainees should be given the space to celebrate, to grieve or to otherwise express their cultural identity.

48. Asylum seekers should not be transferred to prisons as a punitive measure unless they have been convicted of a criminal offence.

49. There should be a mechanism allowing detainees to submit complaints regarding the conditions of their detention, including complaints about abuse inflicted by other detainees.

Detaining authorities and their staff

50. ECRE notes with concern the practice in several European states of contracting private security companies to administer places in which asylum seekers are detained. Such companies must be regulated in such a way as to be held accountable for actions taken on behalf of the state.

51. All staff should receive proper training on basic matters relating to the right of asylum, on the causes of refugee movements relevant to the main countries of origin, on relevant cultural factors, and on methods of recognizing and responding appropriately to the symptoms of stress-related illness which asylum seekers in detention may exhibit. Authorities should seek assistance from UNHCR and specialised NGOs in order to provide such training.

52. There should be a channel for any complaints by detainees concerning misconduct by staff. All complaints should be thoroughly investigated and appropriate action taken. Serious allegations involving racist or physical abuse should be investigated by an impartial body.

53. Where a detainee dies in custody, legal aid should be made available to the family or friends of the deceased so that they can be represented at an inquest. Relevant records, reports and statements should be made available.

Transparency[13]

54. ECRE urges national governments to make publicly available information regarding asylum seekers held in detention. Such information should be published periodically and not only as a result of parliamentary questions. It should include:

- the total number of asylum seekers in detention, including those held at international ports and airports
- the total number of rejected asylum seekers[14] in detention, including those held at international ports and airports
- the range of lengths of detention

April 1996

Annex   Definitional issues

Throughout this paper, the term "asylum seeker" has been used for the sake of convenience. ECRE considers its recommendations on detention to be applicable to all the following persons:

a) Refugees as defined by the 1951 Convention and 1967 Protocol relating to the Status of Refugees
b) Those persons, often termed de facto refugees in the European context, who are in need of international protection but fall outside of the 1951 Convention definition
c) Refugees protected by Temporary Protection arrangements
d) Asylum seekers who may be refugees in the sense of (a), (b) or (c)
e) Asylum seekers who have been rejected by a refugee status determination procedure on purely formal grounds without an examination of the substance of their claim, particularly asylum seekers awaiting removal on "safe third country" grounds[15]
f) Asylum seekers who have received an initial rejection but are still in the process of appealing the negative decision or of appealing against their removal.

---

13 See also: Conclusion 8 adopted by ECRE in 1982 at a seminar on detention which rightly connects the issue of transparency of official information with the issue of access by NGOs and UNHCR to asylum seekers in detention.
14 See Annex. The government authorities should accompany any statistics with a note as to whether "rejected" applies strictly to those who have received a final rejection after a full and substantive examination of their claim.
15 See Safe Third Countries – Myths and Realities, February 1995.

APPENDIX VII   NGO RECOMMENDATIONS

Naturally, ECRE has additional concern for the detention of rejected asylum seekers who have not benefitted from an examination of their claim under fair and efficient procedures, as defined elsewhere by ECRE,[16] and also for rejected asylum seekers in cases where the 1951 Convention has been interpreted in a restrictive manner with which ECRE and UNHCR would not concur. The exclusion of persons persecuted by non-governmental agents would be an example of such restrictive interpretation.[17] Many of this position paper's recommendations are therefore also applicable to these persons.

It should be noted that although ECRE seeks to advocate specifically on the detention of refugees and asylum seekers, not all of ECRE's recommendations are dependent upon acceptance of ECRE's definitional terms. Thus, although the acceptable grounds for detention should be much more limited where an asylum claim is involved, many of the recommended rights and conditions apply equally to all migrants who are detained. Rejected asylum seekers therefore deserve to be treated in accordance with human dignity during pre-deportation detention even if they have been rejected on substantive grounds by a fair procedure.

ECRE recognises a qualitative difference between detention and other restrictions on an asylum seeker's freedom of movement. ECRE endorses UNHCR's recent comments on what constitutes detention, particularly the inclusion of transit zones at international ports on the list of detention locations, and believes that definitions of the deprivation of liberty developed under wider human rights law are applicable.

The present recommendations are concerned with detention and not with any other restrictions on freedom of movement. However, ECRE recognises the very real problems arising from reception centres that are located too far from towns or transport, and from residence restrictions that may present obstacles to asylum seekers enjoying their right to family unity.

ECRE realizes that camps may have to be used in some mass influx situations, however such camps should be "open" rather than "closed". Closed camps are clearly places of detention, and therefore all camps should be open unless a threat to national security is involved, such as an armed group using the camp as a base for cross-border attacks.

---

16   See ECRE's report: *Fair and Efficient Procedures for Determining Refugee Status*, October 1990.
17   See ECRE's *Note on the Harmonisation of the Interpretation of Article 1 of the 1951 Geneva Convention*, June 1995.

VII.2 ECRE Research Paper on Alternatives to Detention – Practical alternatives to the administrative detention of asylum seekers and rejected asylum seekers

A   Introduction

In its 1996 Position Paper on the Detention of Asylum Seekers, the European Council on Refugees and Exiles (ECRE) sets out the extremely exceptional grounds on which it is reasonable for governments to detain an asylum seeker (see paras. 12 and 13). The present paper attempts to describe various measures which, though not necessarily ideal in themselves, are at least preferable alternatives to the detention of asylum seekers who are detained on other than exceptional grounds (including rejected asylum seekers who are in the process of appeal).

Non-governmental organisations believe that, in the majority of cases, the alternative to detention should simply be liberty. The various alternatives set out below should therefore not be seen as recommendations, but as preferable solutions in cases where detention is at present considered the only option – i.e. as a substitute for detention where the authorities believe that some form of supervision or control is required. If these substitutes were widely implemented as a matter of general policy, it would bring European practice more closely into line with UNHCR's 1986 Executive Committee Conclusion No. 44 and UNHCR's 1995 Guidelines on the Detention of Asylum Seekers.

As its starting point, the paper takes government statements of the reasons for detaining asylum seekers at face value: European governments say that they increasingly resort to detention because they need to reduce the number of asylum seekers who abscond during the asylum procedure or who fail to comply with deportation orders. The most common ground for detention is thus "likelihood of absconding", a likelihood which is assessed broadly, with reference to nationality or to the fact that the person perhaps entered the country with false documents.

ECRE has therefore conducted research into systems which are, or could be, used to keep track of asylum seekers and ensure their compliance with national asylum procedures and other regulations governing aliens, but which stop short of detention in the strict sense of the term. Experts from the field of criminal justice have been consulted in order to identify what systems of pre-trial monitoring exist, what bail support schemes are used, and whether any of these systems could by analogy be applied to secure the release of asylum seekers and other immigration detainees.

Leaving aside for one moment the overwhelming human rights arguments against detention of asylum seekers, it can also be argued that the financial costs of detention are so high that governments have an incentive for this reason alone to seek alternatives. According to the German Federal Ministry of the Interior,

APPENDIX VII   NGO RECOMMENDATIONS

detention costs DM 116 per asylum seeker per day, which would amount to an annual total of over DM 50 million. In the United Kingdom, the Home Office reports that the average weekly cost of detaining an asylum seeker in an immigration detention centre is GBP 600. The cost of detention in police or prison cells in the UK ranges from GBP 298 to GBP 874 per night. Amnesty International has estimated the annual cost at GBP 20 million. One prison visitors board stated in its Annual Report for 1994 that holding asylum seekers in prisons "constitutes an improper use of Prison Service resources and the taxpayer's money".

Furthermore, the identification of those asylum seekers not genuinely requiring the constant form of control which detention represents is, for the authorities, a question of efficiency. This is the case particularly where space in detention facilities is limited. In the United States, for example, there are approximately 100,000 persons in removal proceedings at any one time, and 10,000 places for immigration detainees. As these 10,000 places are usually filled at any one time, it is in the interests of the authorities to ensure that they are filled by the "right" 10,000 people – in other words, those who really have a record of absconding and no other incentives to stay in the system. Asylum seekers whose cases are still pending do, generally speaking, have an incentive not to disappear and can stay in contact with the authorities by other means.

In Section B of this paper, various categories of alternative are listed, with reference to countries in which they are used, if not nationwide, then at least in certain areas where NGOs have taken initiatives. These country examples are then described in greater detail in Section C. A number of the examples of specific NGO initiatives have been collected from outside Europe (the United States, Canada and Australia) so that the possibility of introducing them in Europe can be considered. Section D outlines international standards governing non-custodial measures which should be applied to all alternative models.

B   Categories of alternative measures

B.1   Supervised release of children and young adults to local social services[1]

If a detainee's age is in dispute, the children's section of the local social services may be asked to visit them and, if appropriate, these social services may volunteer to find the person a placement with supervision. If a specific alternative place of accommodation is known to be available and the local social services are prepared to take responsibility for that person's whereabouts, it is more likely that the authorities will agree to release.

Country example: United Kingdom

---

1   See also the ECRE's 1996 *Position Paper on Refugee Children*.

B.2 Supervised release to an NGO

Certain groups of asylum seekers may be defined as eligible for release into the hands of an NGO which holds a contract with the authorities stating that they will supervise such individuals if provided with financial support from the State. Such release can be structured around a combination of incentives and penalties, along the lines of a probation service. The incentives can include additional assistance with their cases and with preparing for appointments, and the penalties can include reports to the immigration authorities or the certainty of being re-detained if they fail to cooperate.

All asylum seekers who are detained on grounds other than those which ECRE would recognise as reasonable could be eligible for such release. This should include in particular:

1. persons whose claims enter the full (non-accelerated) asylum procedure, especially where the person has a very well documented claim;
2. persons arriving without documents but with "manifestly" credible stories;
3. persons who are awaiting return under the terms of the Dublin Convention or return to a "safe third country";
4. families in which the identity of at least one member has been verified;
5. persons who are unlikely to be removed even if their claim for refugee status is rejected, due to the human rights situation in their country of origin;
6. persons who are unlikely to be removed even if their claim for refugee status is rejected, due to the general non-cooperation of their national authorities (unwillingness to provide replacement passports etc.);
7. persons who clearly have sufficient means to sustain themselves and their family in the host country without any assistance from the State;
8. persons with substantive appeal cases.

Particular efforts could be put into securing the release of those who, in the United States, are called "affirmative asylum seekers". These are asylum seekers who have come forward either upon entry, or after entry through a legal immigration channel, to make their claim, as opposed to persons who apply after they have received a deportation order or after they have been arrested for illegal residence, so-called "defensive asylum seekers". However, it should be noted that this prioritisation of affirmative cases should not imply that defensive cases are lacking in credibility – restrictive asylum and entry laws in Europe currently encourage asylum seekers to be "defensive".

Country example: United States.

APPENDIX VII   NGO RECOMMENDATIONS

B.3   Supervised release to an individual citizen – release on "bail"

Individual citizens could offer to act as guarantors and take responsibility for the appearance of an asylum seeker at hearings and all official appointments. This could be guaranteed in terms of penalty payments imposed on the guarantor if the asylum seeker fails to appear. This system could function well during the initial stages of an asylum claim but may be less suitable for guaranteeing compliance with deportation orders.

A system could be established whereby any interested citizens could apply, and gradually a set register of citizens (or groups, such a church volunteer groups) willing to give such guarantees could be built up. It would obviously be most suitable for those cases where an asylum seeker already has a relative or friend who is a citizen or is permanently resident in the host country.

In some countries, it is currently possible for the asylum seeker facing detention to apply to the authorities for release in return for payment of "bail".[2] Eligibility for bail is assessed on a case by case basis but one drawback in practice is that this assessment is not automatic. The asylum seeker has, in the first place, to be made aware of his or her right to apply and he or she (or the legal representative) must initiate an application. It is not a very effective legal remedy in most cases because the asylum seeker does not possess sufficient funds. Thus one idea for an alternative is to explore systems of raising the bail, either from donations, or from a bail support scheme similar to those provided for young criminal offenders.

"Bail hostels" often accompany the payment of bail for asylum seekers, providing a fixed address where there is a supervisor or rota of supervisors at the hostel making it easier for the authorities to contact the residents.

Country examples: Canada, the United Kingdom.

B.4   General restrictions on freedom of movement or place of residence

Under this system, asylum seekers are instructed by the authorities to reside in a certain locality or at a certain address, and if they fail to report regularly to the local police then they may be penalised by the withdrawal of social assistance. This may be preferable to detention or compulsory residence in a large collective centre, but is nevertheless a limitation upon the individual's human right to free movement within the country.

---

[2] The term "bail" is used to denote a financial deposit placed with the authorities in order to guarantee the asylum seeker's future attendance for interviews during the processing of his case. This means that the sum of money is returned if the asylum seeker appears as required or otherwise is forfeited.

In certain European countries, this system is used not only as a substitute for detention, but also as a way of distributing the "burden" of asylum seekers. After immediate reception, they are settled in different locations throughout the country on the basis of local population size. The system has however been criticised because important factors such as family ties, availability of support from an ethnic community, job opportunities or an individual's special needs are all too rarely taken into account.

Country examples: Germany, Austria, Switzerland and Sweden.

B.5   Reporting requirements

Asylum seekers can be asked to surrender their passports and other travel documents, and to report to the State authorities at regular intervals – e.g. twice a week. This is closely related to the above system of internal distribution, in that people are usually registered at a nearby reception centre even if they are living independently in the community, and are thus restricted to the areas near the assigned centre.

Official reporting points could be established all over a country, so that an asylum seeker is not restricted in his or her freedom of movement, but can report into a centralised computer system at a wide variety of locations. Provision of social assistance could then be made conditional upon sustained reporting. Collection of this assistance could be limited to a certain locality where there is a fixed address, as it is for nationals, so that the asylum seeker would always be free to travel away from this specified locality and collect the accumulated assistance upon their return. In practice, of course, it should be noted that factors other than the collection of social assistance will limit the freedom of movement of asylum seekers: the need to stay in touch with their lawyer, the need to collect mail or renew their papers, or lack of money.

Country examples: several European countries, including Denmark and France.

B.6   Open centres

Compulsory collective accommodation is far from being the ideal form of accommodation: assistance with finding accommodation in the community is greatly preferable. Non-governmental organisations, social workers and medical practitioners across Europe have all reported problems, such as depression and loss of independence, arising from residence in such centres/camps after a period of some months.

Open centres can provide an alternative in cases where asylum seekers might otherwise be held in detention, as such centres can control the whereabouts of the residents to varying degrees. In some open centres, the authorities operate a curfew at night but allow the residents to leave during the day. In others, residents are asked to register whenever they leave and re-enter the centre, stating where they intend to go during each excursion. In many cases, however, these centres are situated in inconveniently remote locations (as indeed are most detention centres), and this in itself serves as a form of control on the residents' movements.[3]

Other than release, it is difficult to suggest alternatives to very short-term detention in airports or in attached airport buildings/hotels. However, long-term detention in airports (lasting for many months) certainly requires an alternative – open centres could be built near to international airports if necessary, for example.

Country examples: in Germany, Switzerland and the Netherlands, residence in a collective centre is compulsory for part or all of the asylum procedure. In Belgium, Norway, Denmark, Slovakia, Poland and the Czech Republic, eligibility for financial assistance from the State is conditional upon residence in such a centre.

C   Country examples

C.1 Australia

In Australia, unauthorised or "spontaneous" refugee arrivals are usually detained throughout the determination procedure.

The Australian Refugee Council and an independent rapporteur have recently developed an Alternative Detention Model which has been submitted to the government. This proposal is based on the argument that individual cases can be reviewed on a regular basis in order to choose the level of control demonstrably required for each person. There are three levels:

Level 1: Closed detention (which all asylum seekers experience initially upon arrival at a port);
Level 2: Open detention (which equates to open centres of compulsory collective accommodation in Europe). Open detention would involve accommodation in a hostel with a curfew from 7 p.m. to 7 a.m., and asylum seekers would be eligible to work or to receive financial assistance;
Level 3: Community release, which involves residence at a designated address and reporting requirements. There are three forms of control here:
   a) Family release. It is proposed that this form of release would be at a designated address, with a nominated close family member, and that the asylum seeker must report to the authorities at regular intervals, the

---

[3] For further details on standards and conditions within such centres, see ECRE's *1997 Position on the Reception of Asylum Seekers*.

frequency of which is to be decided by the case officer after an individual assessment. The family member would be required either to pay a bond in advance or to sign a recognisance with the authorities. If called upon at any time, the asylum seeker must report to the authorities within 24 hours;
b) Community organisation release;
c) Release upon own recognisance.

Applicants can be moved flexibly up or down these levels of control as their circumstances change. The level is stated upon their visa, and a new visa must therefore be issued every time that the level is adjusted. Anyone who is not released must be provided with a statement of the reasons for his or her detention

The Alternative Detention Model proposes that priority be given to securing and sustaining the community release of children, close relatives of children, elderly persons, single women, persons with special health needs or persons with previous experience of torture or the symptoms of trauma.

The penalty for an unjustified failure to cooperate with any of the non-custodial levels of control is return to detention, with a brief period in which it is impossible to apply for re-release.

C.2 Belgium

Since 17 January 1997, all asylum seekers in Belgium who are not detained have been systematically assigned to open centres of collective accommodation.[4] The only exceptions are for the few asylum seekers who do not need to receive any assistance, or if there are no available places in these centres. A coordination unit keeps an inventory of available places and will take humanitarian considerations into account when deciding where to assign each person. Two more such centres were being built in the spring of 1997.

C.3 Canada

In Canada, asylum claimants are not re-distributed throughout the country and usually tend to live in the provinces where they first arrive. The individual is nevertheless free to move to another province (as it is a violation of the Canadian Charter of Rights and Liberties to restrict internal freedom of movement in any

---

[4] In summary, asylum seekers in Belgium tend to be detained: at the border, if they lack the required documents, if they have left a previously designated place of residence, if they have applied after a legal residence permit has expired, or if they are appealing against a negative decision.

way), but the authorities may refuse to change the venue of the hearings so that the person must travel back to attend. Immigration detainees are quite often released on bond (bail) either by cash deposit or by someone with proven means signing for their release. Reporting requirements may be imposed in addition.

An initiative has been taken in Toronto called the Toronto Bail Program, which is an adaptation of a scheme originally designed to help people in the criminal justice system who cannot afford bail. A rigorous screening of asylum seekers in detention takes place in order to find suitable candidates (those who are unlikely to abscond but who do not have friends and relatives able to post bail). When the asylum seeker is then released he or she is carefully supervised in the community. It should be noted that a number of NGOs have criticised the Toronto Bail Program because, by its mere existence, it encourages the immigration services to opt for supervised, as opposed to unconditional, release.

C.4   Denmark and Finland

Asylum seekers in Denmark are asked to surrender their passports and to stay at a Red Cross reception centre. In practice, only asylum seekers who are unidentified or whose travel route is unknown are subject to detention. According to police guidelines, however, some categories are exempt from detention, e.g. women asylum seekers with minor children, and may be asked to report to the police at fixed times instead. Only if the asylum seeker fails to comply with these restrictions will detention be imposed. A similar system operates in Finland, where reporting to the police can be required every day for the duration of a relatively short asylum procedure.

C.5   France

The main control mechanism in France is the need to renew the *autorisation de séjour* every three months, and to collect financial support every month, which requires a fixed address. The Schengen Convocation stamp also needs to be renewed every 15 days, and this acts as a form of additional reporting requirement in Schengen cases.

C.6   Germany

Asylum seekers' right to free movement within Germany is restricted by the government authorities. Though this policy is mainly motivated by a belief in internal "burden sharing" between Federal States, it is also notable that asylum seekers awaiting a first decision on their claim are not normally detained (with notable exceptions such as the detention of asylum seekers in the special "airport procedure" at Frankfurt Airport). Thus alternative control measures are deemed sufficiently effective, despite the large number of registered asylum seekers in the country and a large underground economy of illegal workers.

Each residence permit states the asylum seeker's enforced place of residence (in a collective accommodation centre for the first three months – containing a minimum of 300 persons – and then in the community) and a compelling reason is needed to leave the designated address and surrounding zone. Population size is the only criterion used in the distribution of asylum seekers, though minors are able to live in the same place as family members and unaccompanied minors can choose the district in which they want to stay. The main problem which NGOs have witnessed with this system is the fact that families are separated too fast – often asylum seekers spend a lot of energy trying to get to the same district as their friends and family. They then go to the local reception centre to apply for asylum, only to be told that they will be sent to the other side of the country within a few days. This can be very traumatic, and if the distribution system was slightly slower it would be more humane. Another problem is the fact that asylum seekers are sent to rural areas where they have trouble getting access to all the necessary services – lawyers, interpreters, community support – and where jobs may be particularly scarce. On the positive side, however, it means that citizens and local authorities in every part of the country have to think about how to accommodate and integrate refugees, thus dispelling prejudices arising from a lack of experience.

C.7 Norway

A system of compulsory collective accommodation operates, with all asylum seekers sent to one of 20 centres. The centres are open, but any movement outside the centre must be registered and of limited duration. Asylum seekers must stay at the centres if they wish to receive financial assistance.

C.8 Sweden

There is an internal distribution system in Sweden (as in Germany). This distribution takes place in proportion to the municipality's population, but also in proportion to the number of lawyers and interpreters in each place. Since 1994, asylum seekers no longer have to live in camps to receive State assistance but are free to live in private accommodation. They are, however, registered at a nearby camp and there is a social worker there who is responsible for them. This extent of monitoring has been found beneficial both to the individual asylum seekers and to the authorities. It has been found that asylum seekers under the new system have been more willing to comply with the asylum decision, even if it ends in a deportation order.

APPENDIX VII   NGO RECOMMENDATIONS

C.9 United States

In New York City, the Vera Institute of Justice has signed an agreement with the immigration authorities to run a three year "demonstration project" called the Appearance Assistance Program (AAP). The aim of the AAP is to provide an effective, credible system of pre-hearing supervised release, which takes those who do not need to be detained out of detention, and at the same time results in increased appearance rates at interviews and increased compliance with deportation orders.

The Vera Institute is an independent organisation, which has a history of working on joint projects with government agencies involved in the justice system. It was responsible for the pioneering development of pre-trial release systems for offenders in the 1960s and the current project is based on the expertise acquired from this experiment. The Immigration Service is funding the project.

Screening of possible participants in the project takes place at Kennedy and Newark airports, as well as at a number of detention centres where staff make recommendations for release. One or two members of staff from the Vera Institute work at each location. At the airport, they aim to interview people within 24 hours, but not until the new arrivals have had an opportunity to rest. They interview asylum seekers who are still eligible to apply for a legal remedy but whom the Immigration Authorities indicate are to be detained. Suitability for supervised release is determined according to the following criteria:

1. there is some substance to the asylum claim;[5]
2. they are not a risk to public safety;
3. they are "amenable to supervision", which implies that:
   a) they have a verified private address (not a shelter) where they could live;
   b) they have an individual (this may be a relative, friend or employer who is a citizen or a permanent resident and over 18 years of age) or a recognised community group willing to act as their "community sponsor". This person or group is not legally or financially responsible, however – it is a sponsorship involving time and effort rather than cash;
   c) they do not have a previous record of non-appearance at official appointments etc.

The staff making these assessments have three weeks of specific training, including some basic training in refugee law and the psychological effects of torture.

---

5   Interestingly, the key to the assessment is not whether the asylum seeker has a good case, but rather whether the asylum seeker *thinks* he or she has a good case, on the basis that as long as the asylum seeker *believes* the claim to be a deserving one then he or she will go to appointments and is unlikely to abscond.

Some, but not all, have legal backgrounds. The staff involved in the AAP are, as a whole, ethnically diverse, possess a wide range of language skills and have experience of working with New York's ethnic communities.

After an asylum seeker is accepted into the AAP, the Vera Institute acts as a kind of probation service. Asylum seekers must report twice a month to a Reporting Assistance Center. Incentives to ensure that they do come in are a resource library with materials that might help their cases (human rights reports, recent maps, etc) and a referral service for social assistance and legal advice. The asylum seekers are sent extra reminders from the Vera Institute about what official appointments they have to attend and what deadlines they have to meet. If they are rejected in the procedure but are willing to cooperate with deportation proceedings, they also receive additional return assistance in the form of information and administrative assistance.

Every participant in the AAP has a certain officer responsible for them and also a field officer who will come and visit them to verify, both by appointment and through spot-checks, where they are living.

The only real penalty for people who abuse the AAP and abscond is that they will be detained without doubt if and when they are apprehended again. The Vera Institute may also write a report to the immigration authorities informing them of the person's behaviour. This possibility is usually a sufficient incentive in itself to ensure compliance with the requirements.

This demonstration project will be evaluated after three years in operation by both the NGOs and the authorities to see if it has indeed met both sets of needs and demands.

Another project to provide an alternative to detention in the US is Gay Hartner's Refugee Immigration Ministry in Boston. It is similar to the above in so far as it is a place to which people can be released on bail, located near to a detention centre, but is based on religious charity and supported by a congregation. Vermont Refugee Assistance (VRA) is a similar local operation, started in 1987, whereby volunteers organise "host homes" for asylum seekers so that they can be released to an individual citizen's responsibility. The People of the Golden Vision (an NGO set up in Pennsylvania to help the Chinese who landed on the Golden Venture boat in 1993) have also recently purchased a "halfway house" to accommodate asylum seekers whom the authorities would otherwise insist on detaining.

Finally, the Florence Project in the US takes voluntary return seriously as an alternative in certain cases and therefore produces a video which asylum seekers can watch when they are first detained, explaining their rights but also presenting the legal system and definition which will be applied to them so that non-refugees can "self-identify" and opt for voluntary return at an early stage.

APPENDIX VII   NGO RECOMMENDATIONS

D   Safeguards and standards attached to non-custodial alternatives

ECRE would suggest that any alternatives implemented by European States should, as a minimum, conform to the United Nations Standard Minimum Rules for Non-Custodial Measures (the "Tokyo Rules").

The Tokyo Rules are the most comprehensive statement of principles relating to non-custodial sentencing in the criminal justice field. While emphasising that very few of the asylum seekers held in detention in Europe have committed offences other than illegal entry to the national territory, it is nevertheless enlightening to analyse how these standards of criminal justice could relate to any alternatives to detention of asylum seekers.

The Tokyo Rules are the result of global discussion and exchange of experience, pursuant to Section XI of the Economic and Social Council Resolution 1986/10. They demonstrate an evolving understanding of the negative effects of imprisonment, which, in the case of an asylum seeker, may be compounded by the possibility of previous arbitrary detention and/or torture in the country of origin.

The majority of penal sanctions which may be imposed on convicted offenders around the world are therefore, in the 1990s, non-custodial. The guiding principle is that of a balance between the human rights of the detainee and the overall concerns of society. It should be noted that immigration offences are "victimless crimes" and therefore the interests of a victim do not need to be assessed. It is also noted under the Tokyo Rules' commentary on "fundamental aims" that community involvement in non-custodial models has the added advantage of improving public understanding. Such public understanding certainly needs to be fostered with regard to asylum.

Rule 3.6 states that the [asylum seeker][6] should be entitled to make a complaint or request regarding the non-custodial measure imposed. Rule 3.9 relates to ensuring respect for the person's dignity, 3.11 to respect for privacy, and 3.12 to respect for confidentiality.

> "Taken together, [Rules 3.9–3.12] require that supervision shall not be carried out in a way that would harass the [asylum seekers], jeopardise their dignity or intrude on their privacy or that of their families. Methods of supervision that treat [asylum seekers] solely as objects of control should not be employed. Surveillance techniques should not be used without the [asylum seekers'] knowledge. Third parties other than properly accredited volunteers should not be employed for the surveillance of [asylum seekers]."[7]

---

[6]   The term "asylum seeker" is inserted to replace reference to criminal offenders in the various Rules.

[7]   Commentary on the Tokyo Rules, p. 13.

Rule 7 relates to "social inquiry reports" which are compiled for individual criminal offenders, relating to their past and present circumstances. This is similar to the Australian model, described above, which calls for more individual assessment in the treatment of asylum seekers. Those who are unlikely to abscond, for example, when the expected outcome of their cases begins to look positive, are promptly identified, and those who should be released for other humanitarian reasons are also identified. At the moment it is extremely rare for individually-related evidence of the "likelihood of absconding" to be produced by any national authorities.

Rule 10.3 states that not only detention, but also "supervision ... should be periodically reviewed and adjusted as necessary". The commentary on this Rule then adds that "the important element is the personal relationship between the supervisor and the [asylum seeker]". It describes supervision as a "highly skilled task", combining a control function with a welfare function. "Parts of the supervisory task may be delegated or contracted out to the community groups or volunteers" while statutory power remains with the State authorities.

Rule 12.3 relates to the quality of information provided to the person who is the subject of the non-custodial measure. It notes that well explained obligations are more likely to be met.

Rule 14.3 states that "[T]he failure of a non-custodial measure should not automatically lead to the imposition of a custodial measure." It comments that minor transgression can be handled by a good supervisor and that factors to consider include whether the non-compliance takes place at an early stage or after a period of time during which there was full compliance. Factors beyond the person's control should also be taken into account.

Rule 15.1 includes the statement that "policy regarding staff recruitment should take into consideration national policies of affirmative action and reflect the diversity of the [asylum seekers] to be supervised".

Rule 17 encourages public participation and notes that "ethnic organisations" can be a resource. Rule 19 similarly describes the role of volunteers, seeing them as doing a favour for the State and for society, which requires training, recognition and reimbursement of costs incurred.

Rule 18.1 implies that the government should look favourably on funding NGO schemes to secure release of detainees. Rule 20 encourages research and experimental projects in this field, and Rule 21 stresses the importance of evaluation. All these considerations apply equally, if not more so, to the search for alternatives to detention of asylum seekers.

E   Conclusion

It is simply unsustainable for European countries to continue to detain non-criminals asylum seekers at the present rate. A cost-benefit analysis should be commissioned

APPENDIX VII   NGO RECOMMENDATIONS

by each government into its current system of immigration-related detention as compared to other systems of reporting requirements, open centres etc. Such an analysis would prove that it is in the interests of States, as well as being their clear humanitarian obligation, to seek other means of supervising asylum seekers and rejected asylum seekers awaiting the outcome of appeals.

The above examples have categorised some of the ways in which detention can be avoided when there is a political will to do so. Joint initiatives with non-governmental organisations and building relationships of trust with local community groups are clearly central to the success of a number of these non-custodial alternatives. European NGOs should take the lead from their north American counterparts who are establishing release schemes, with governmental permission and funding, in several local situations. European governments should also learn from one another how to implement non-custodial alternatives, in a spirit of regional cooperation.[8]

This paper was researched and written by Ophelia Field (Policy Officer, ECRE), with the assistance of Elsa Seguin.

London, September 1997

---

[8] See, as a basis for such cooperation, Recommendation 1327 (1997) of the Parliamentary Assembly of the Council of Europe, in which member states are urged "to give priority to non-custodial measures such as supervision systems, the requirement to report regularly to the authorities, bail or other guarantee systems" (vii g).

VII.3 The Australian Alternative Detention Model

The Challenge

The detention of asylum seekers has aroused intense community debate since the arrival of the first boats from Cambodia in 1989. The issue attracted further controversy with the opening of the Port Hedland immigration detention centre in north western Australia in 1991. The isolation of the centre, reports of poor facilities for detainees and the slow processing of their applications, generated adverse media attention and some deep seated community divisions.

Community concerns have been raised by numerous groups throughout Australia, including major Church and non-governmental organisations and the Human Rights and Equal Opportunity Commission.[1]

Australian detention practice has also attracted adverse comment from international organisations including the US Department of State[2] and the International Secretariat of Amnesty International.[3]

In 1994 a number of peak organisations in Australia endorsed a Charter of Minimum Requirements for Legislation Relating to the Detention of Asylum Seekers. This Charter, a copy of which is attached, is an important statement of agreed norms relating to the detention of asylum seekers.

While detention remains the norm for unauthorised boat arrivals, there have been a number of positive developments over the past three years, not least of these being:

* significant improvements in the conditions in the detention centres;
* priority processing of detainees at both primary and review levels;
* case management of detainees in some facilities;
* more rigorous and expert determination of claims;
* provision for release from detention for certain designated groups of asylum seekers.

Despite these sigificant improvements, serious concerns continue to be voiced by eminent community leaders.[4]

---

[1] See, for example, the submissions to the Joint Standing Committee on Migration for its report, *Asylum, Border Control and Detention*, in February 1994

[2] Department of State's Country Reports on Human Rights Practices for 1994; see also 1995 Report

[3] *Amnesty International Urges the Australian Govenment to Change its Policy of Automatic Dentention of Asylum Seekers*, Media release, 16 June 1994

[4] See, for example, comments by Dr Peter Carnley, Anglican Archbishop of Perth (*Boat people plight shameful*, The West Australian (20 April 1992); Most Reverend Ian George, Anglican Archbishop of Adelaide (*Racist policies threat to Asian ties: cleric*, The

APPENDIX VII   NGO RECOMMENDATIONS

The main criticisms focus on:

- the human rights implications of the detention of asylum seekers;
- the suffering imposed on the detainees; and
- the significant costs of the detention of asylum seekers.

The rationale for keeping asylum seekers who enter the country without immigration clearance is immigration control. An additional reason sometimes given is deterrence.

This submission recognises the place of detention as an instrument of immigration control. Detention is, however, costly – politically, socially and economically – as well as in human terms. It is therefore desirable to modify the present regime so as achieve a better balance between immigration objectives on the one hand and, the costs of detention on the other.

The Alternative Detention Model.

The alternative model, set out below, envisages a number of modifications to the present detention regime. Under this model restrictions of the current type on the liberty of protection visa applicants should be kept to a minimum, usually to less than 90 days. After the initial period in closed detention, most applicants would pass on to a more liberal regime; one that is most appropriate to the individual's circumstances. Regular review of each applicant's detention status is recommended so as to improve the ability to relate the applicant's circumstances more equitably to the restrictions imposed on his/her liberty. Finally, a review process is recommended to establish an ongoing process leading to a higher level of equity in the case management of each applicant.

The alternative model proposes a simple three stage regime. The stages represent a linear progression ranging from severe restrictions on personal liberty to increasingly liberal provisions.

Australian 25/5/93); Justice Murray Wilcox, Federal Court Judge *(Detention harsh and costly, says judge*, Sydney Morning Herald 24/6/93); Justice Marcus Einfeld, Federal Court Judge (*Australia and the International Refugee Crisis*, address to the Migration Institute of Australia, 16/3/95); Justice Alastair Nicholson, Chief justice of the Family Court (*Judge damns refugee camps*, The Australian 20/7/95); Malcolm Fraser, former Prime Minister (*Fraser backs refugees*, Sydney Morning Herald 24/7/95), Sir Ronald Wilson, former High Court Judge and President of the Human Rights and Equal Opportunity Commission (*Boat People: The Limits of Tolerance and Refuge*, address to the Centre for Research in Culture and Communication, Murdoch University 14/10/95).

The three stages of detention are:

i) Closed detention:
represents the most severe form of detention. All applicants who have not been immigration cleared would be initially held in closed detention. During this initial period, the applicant's identity and circumstances would be established to the point where a decision can be made about the form of detention that is most appropriate. It is envisaged that most applicants would be moved to one of the two more liberal detention regimes within 90 days of arrival in Australia. Closed detention would be under DIEA control; the regime would be as at the Port Hedland facility.

ii) Open detention:
represents an intermediate regime. It would facilitate those applicants who were considered to be unsuitable for community release, either because this was judged not to be in the interests of the community or not to be in the best interests of the applicant. Freedom of movement would be restricted by curfew requirements. Residential facilities would be maintained and regulated by DIEA.

iii) Community release:
represents the most liberal regime within the detention model. DIEA would not be responsible for the accommodation and welfare of the applicants. Under some forms of community release, family members or community organisations should undertake some responsibilities for the applicant. Restriction on personal liberty would be limited to residing at a designated address and reporting requirements.

Community release would take one of three forms:
* Family release;
* Community organisation release;
* Release upon own recognisance.

The alternative model would enable the responsible authorities to move applicants over the range of detention stages to best suit changing circumstances as well as in response to past behaviour.

Advantages:

The alternative detention model offers a range of advantages by providing:

* A more humane regime, which reduces individual suffering and hardship by providing for alternative detention mechanisms which can be responsively linked to individual circumstances.

* Greater flexibility, by being able to move applicants from one detention stage to another as their circumstances change.
* Enhanced equity, by reducing the present disparities in treatment between those applicants who are immigration cleared and those who are not (under the current provisions its usually only the non immigration cleared asylum seekers who are subject to detention.)
* Reduced Costs:
  - Financial savings can be achieved by the significantly reduced use of closed detention which is the most costly regime. Furthermore, the alternative model does not require additional capital works.
  - Political costs would be reduced. The alternative model addresses community concerns such as those put forward by the Charter of Minimum Requirements thus rendering detention a less divisive issue.
* Closer harmony with international guidelines, as the model would bring detention practice in Australia into consistency with instruments such as the 1951 Convention and the 1967 Protocol Relating to the Status of Refugees, the International Covenant on Civil and Political Rights, the Convention on the Rights of the Child, the Convention on the Elimination of All Forms of Discrimination Against Women, and the various guidelines published by the United Nations High Commissioner for Refugees (UNHCR), including the Guidelines on the Detention of Asylum Seekers (1995) and the Executive Committee of UNHCR's Conclusion No. 44, Detention of Refugees and Asylum Seekers (1986). Closer harmonisation with international norms would render Australia less open to international criticism for its immigration detention practice.
* Ease of implementation, as the alternative model requires few administrative adjustments to the existing visa, assistance (ASA) and review framework.

The Alternative Detention Model

Stage 1   Arrival, reception and consideration for release

A. Presumption for release within three months

There is a presumption that all applicants for a protection visa ("applicants") will be released from detention within three months of arrival, unless the case officer is satisfied that any one of the following grounds for detention exists with respect to the individual applicant.

B. Grounds for detention

1. Identity: the identity of the applicant cannot be verified as far as practicable.
2. Claim: a valid application for a protection visa – which includes the elements on which the applicant's claim for asylum is based – has not been lodged with DIEA.
3. National security: the applicant is a threat to the national security or public order.
4. Likelihood of absonding: there is a demonstrable likelihood that the individual applicant is likely to abscond.
5. Health check: the applicant has failed to complete a health check, or undertake to complete a health check, when required to do so by the case officer.

C. Special circumstances requiring priority processing:

The case officer shall give priority to the processing for release from detention of an applicant where any of the following special circumstances exist:

1. Children and close relatives of children: the applicant is less than 18 years of age, or is a close relative of another applicant who is less than 18 years of age.
2. Aged persons: the applicant is aged above 75 years.
3. Unaccompanied minors: the applicant is an unaccompanied minor.
4. Single women: the applicant is a single woman.
5. Health: the applicant has a special need based on health in respect of which a medical specialist (and/or an appropriately qualified medical practitioner) has certified that the applicant cannot properly be cared for in a detention environment.
6. Torture/trauma: the applicant has a special need based on previous experience of torture or trauma in respect of which a medical specialist (and/or an appropriately qualified medical practitioner) has certified that the applicant cannot properly be cared for in a detention environment.

Stage 2   Release from detention

A. Criteria for release from detention

An applicant who complies with all of the requirements as set out in Stage 1, paragraphs B(1)–(5) must, within three months of arrival in Australia, be released from detention.

APPENDIX VII   NGO RECOMMENDATIONS

B. Forms of release from detention

Applicants who qualify for release from detention shall be granted a bridging visa which matches the appropriate form of release. The type of bridging visa which is granted is to be determined by the case officer.

C. Forms of bridging visa

The following bridging visa shall be available for applicants who are to be released from detention:

    1. Open detention bridging visa
    2. Community release bridging visa:
(a) Family release
(b) Community organization release
(c) Release upon own recognisance.

D. Statement of reasons

An applicant who is not released must be provided with a statement of the reasons for his or her detention.

E. Priority processing of asylum claims for persons held in detention

An applicant who is not released shall be given priority in processing of his or her application for a protection visa.

1. Open detention bridging visa

The elements of this bridging visa are as follows:
(i)   Accommodation and daily requirements provided by DIEA.
(ii)   The holder can leave the centre between the hours of 7.00 a.m. and 7.00 p.m.
(iii)   The holder must sign out of the hostel every morning and in to the hostel every evening.
(iv)   Eligibility for Permission to Work will be available in the terms contained in Bridging Visa E. If the holder obtains employment, a fee for accommodation shall be payable by the holder.
(v)   Eligibility for Asylum Seekers' Assistance shall be in the terms currently available to other asylum seekers. If ASA is granted, a fee for accommodation shall be deducted prior to payment to the holder.

2. Community release bridging visa

(a) Family release

The elements of this bridging visa are as follows:
(i) The holder must reside at a designated address with a nominated close family member. Any change of address must be notified to DIEA within 48 hours.
(ii) The holder must report at regular intervals to DIEA, to be specified by the case officer.
(iii) The holder or the nominated close family member may be required to pay a bond to DIEA or sign a recognisance with DIEA.
(iv) If called upon to do so, the holder shall within 24 hours present to an officer of DIEA.
(v) The holder will be required to sign an undertaking in writing that he or she shall comply with the conditions of the visa and, in the event that a condition of this visa is breached, may be returned to detention.
(vi) Eligibility for permission to work will be available in the terms contained in Bridging Visa E.
(vii) Eligibility for Asylum Seekers' Assistance shall be in the terms currently available to other asylum seekers.

(b) Community organization release

The elements of this bridging visa are as follows:
(i) The holder must reside at a designated address nominated by a recognised community organisation. Any change of address must be notified to DIEA within 48 hours.
(ii) The holder must report at regular intervals to DIEA, to be specified by the case officer.
(iii) If called upon to do so, the holder shall within 24 hours present to an officer of DIEA.
(iv) The holder will be required to sign an undertaking in writing that he or she shall comply with the conditions of the visa and, in the event that a condition of this visa is breached, may be returned to detention.
(v) Eligibility for permission to work will be available in the terms contained in Bridging Visa E.
(vi) Eligibility for Asylum Seekers' Assistance shall be in the terms currently available to other asylum seekers.

APPENDIX VII NGO RECOMMENDATIONS

(c) Release upon own recognisance

The elements of this bridging visa are as follows:
(i) The holder must reside at a designated address. Any change of address must be notified to DIEA within 48 hours.
(ii) The holder must report at regular intervals to DIEA, to be specified by the case officer.
(iii) If called upon to do so, the holder shall within 24 hours present to an officer of DIEA.
(iv) The holder will be required to sign an undertaking in writing that he or she shall comply with the conditions of the visa and, in the event that a condition of this visa is breached, may be returned detention.
(v) Eligibility for Permission to Work will be available in the terms contained in Bridging Visa E.
(vi) Eligibility for Asylum Seekers' Assistance shall be in the terms currently available to other asylum seekers.

Stage 3   Return to detention

A. Breach of conditions

If the applicant breaches any one of the conditions set for his or her release, and fails to show good reason for such breach to the case officer, he or she may be returned into detention and shall not be eligible to re-apply for release until a period of 90 days from the time of return to detention.

B. Change in circumstances

If any of the circumstances set out in Stage 1, paragraphs B(l)–(5) occur, the applicant may be returned to detention.

Stage 4   Review

A. By case officer

(i) Where the applicant remains in detention, the case officer must review that person's detention at the end of every 90 days.
(ii) The case officer has a non-enforceable discretion to review the detention and/or release status of an applicant at any time should there be a change in the circumstances of the applicant.

(iii) The case officer must review the detention and/or release status of the applicant upon request by the applicant, save that the case officer is not required to consider any such application more than once every 90 days.
(iv) In determining whether there should be a change in the detention and/or release status of the applicant, the case officer must take into account any change in circumstances since such status was last set.
(v) If the detention status of the applicant is to be changed, the case officer must provide a statement of reasons for the decision.

B. By the Immigration Review Tribunal (IRT)

(i) Upon request by the applicant, the IRT may review a decision of a case officer with respect to:
* the detention status of an applicant;
* the conditions of release imposed on the applicant;
* any alleged breach of any condition of release imposed on the applicant.
(ii) The IRT is not required to consider any such application more than once every 90 days.
(iii) If no decision is made by the case officer as to the detention status of an applicant within 90 days of the applicant's arrival in Australia, the IRT must review the detention status of that applicant.
(iv) Any review by the IRT under this provision is a review *de novo* on the merits of the application. The IRT may at its discretion impose any of the available bridging visas upon the applicant, regardless of the status of the applicant at the time of application or of the type of bridging visa originally sought by the applicant.

C. By the Federal Court of Australia

The Federal Court of Australia has the power to review decisions relating to detention status as with all IRT reviewable decisions.

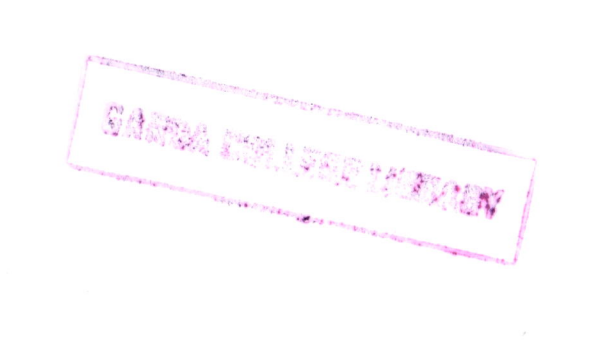